This is the first collection of modern critical essays on the work of John Clare, a writer who, despite a long history of marginalisation and neglect, is coming to be seen as one of the most important English poets of the nineteenth century. Taken together, these new essays constitute a reassessment of a great writer of rural England who has as yet found no place within the existing Romantic and Victorian canon. By contextualising his work in relation to poetic tradition, Romantic literature, criticism, politics, natural history and contemporary science, they show the ways in which his charged vernacular poetry radically contests dominant notions of culture, poetry and knowledge. Contributors include distinguished Clare scholars Mark Storey and Kelsey Thornton, the literary critic John Lucas, the historian of madness Roy Porter, and the Irish poet Seamus Heaney who, in an important essay, looks at Clare from the perspective of post-colonial poetry today. In the wake of his bi-centenary this volume represents a landmark in the history of Clare's reception and a valuable resource for all students of his poetry.

JOHN CLARE IN CONTEXT

JOHN CLARE IN CONTEXT

EDITED BY

HUGH HAUGHTON

University of York

ADAM PHILLIPS

Charing Cross Hospital

GEOFFREY SUMMERFIELD

New York University

CAMBRIDGE
UNIVERSITY PRESS

Published by the Press Syndicate of the University of Cambridge
The Pitt Building, Trumpington Street, Cambridge CB2 1RP
40 West 20th Street, New York, NY 10011–4211, USA
10 Stamford Road, Oakleigh, Melbourne 3166, Australia

© Cambridge University Press 1994

First published 1994

Printed in Great Britain at the University Press, Cambridge

A catalogue record for this book is available from the British Library

Library of Congress cataloguing in publication data

John Clare in context: bi-centenary essays in memory of Geoffrey
Summerfield / edited by Hugh Haughton, Adam Phillips,
Geoffrey Summerfield.
p. cm.
Includes bibliographical references and index.
ISBN 0 521 44547 7 hardback
1. Clare, John, 1793–1864–Criticism and interpretation.
I. Summerfield, Geoffrey. II. Haughton, Hugh, 1948– .
III. Phillips, Adam.
PR4453.C6Z74 1994
821'.7–dc20 93–24231 CIP

ISBN 0 521 44547 7 hardback

In memory of Geoffrey Summerfield

Contents

Preface

This volume was originally planned by the distinguished Clare scholar Geoffrey Summerfield as a bi-centenary celebration of the relatively neglected English Romantic poet John Clare.

Modern Clare scholarship might be said to date from 1961 when Geoffrey Summerfield first began transcribing the Clare manuscripts at Northampton Library and invited Eric Robinson to join him on the principle that, as he said, 'the undertaking did indeed require two pairs of eyes'. This resulted in their joint editions of *Later Poems of John Clare* (Manchester University Press, 1964), *John Clare: The Shepherd's Calendar* (Oxford University Press, 1964) and *Clare: Selected Poems and Prose* (Oxford University Press, 1966). After completing his superbly accessible and idiosyncratic *John Clare, Selected Poetry* (Penguin, 1990), Geoffrey envisaged this bi-centenary collection of new essays on Clare as something of a companion volume, an attempt to open up Clare to a wider and not wholly academic audience. Having commissioned the essays in the present volume, Geoffrey sadly and unexpectedly died in February 1991 before he could bring the volume to completion. At the suggestion of his widow, Judith Summerfield, we took over the final co-ordinating and editing of the book. We hope it is substantially the book he had planned and it is now dedicated to his memory.

Hugh Haughton, Adam Phillips

Notes on contributors

NICHOLAS BIRNS is currently Visiting Assistant Professor at
Western Connecticut University. He received his Ph.D. from
New York University, where he completed a dissertation on
Christianity and modernity in recent American literature. He
has articles published or forthcoming in *Exemplaria*, *Studies in
Romanticism* and *Arizona Quarterly*.

DOUGLAS CHAMBERS is Professor in the Department of English at
the University of Toronto. He is also author of a history of the
late seventeenth- and early eighteenth-century landscape
garden, to be published by Yale University Press, advisory
editor of *Journal of Garden History*, and editor of the poems of
Traherne.

MARILYN GAULL is Professor of English at Temple University
and Adjunct Professor at New York University and is the author
of *English Romanticism: The Human Context* (1987), and editor of
The Wordsworth Circle.

JOHN GOODRIDGE is a Lecturer in the Department of English
and Media Studies at the Nottingham Trent University and
author of a study of Allan Ramsey's manuscripts in the *Index of
English Manuscripts*. He is currently working on *Rural Life in
Eighteenth-Century English Poetry* and an edition of John Dyer, *The
Fleece*. He is also editor of the *John Clare Society Journal*.

HUGH HAUGHTON is Senior Lecturer in English and Related
Literature at the University of York. He is the editor of Gustav
Janouch, *Conversations with Kafka* (1986), Rudyard Kipling, *Wee
Willie Winkie* (1988), *The Chatto Book of Nonsense Poetry* (1988)
and Lewis Carroll, *Alice in Wonderland* and *Through the Looking-*

Glass (1994). He is currently completing a book on modern poetry.

SEAMUS HEANEY is Boylston Professor of Rhetoric and Oratory at Harvard University, and Professor of Poetry at Oxford. He is the author of eight volumes of poetry, the most recent of which is *Seeing Things* (1992). His *New Selected Poems 1966–1987* was published in 1990. He is also the author of two volumes of critical prose, *Preoccupations: Selected Prose 1968–78* (1980) and *The Government of the Tongue* (1988).

JOHN LUCAS is Professor of English at the University of Loughborough. He is also the author of numerous critical studies including *Romantic to Modern Literature* (1982), *Modern English Poetry from Hardy to Hughes* (1986) and *England and Englishness: Ideas of Nationhood in English Poetry 1688–1900* (1990).

JAMES McKUSICK is Associate Professor of English at the University of Maryland, Baltimore County. He is author of *Coleridge's Philosophy of Language* (1986) and a number of essays on Clare. He is currently completing a book on ideologies of language in Romantic poetry.

ADAM PHILLIPS is Principal Child Psychotherapist at Charing Cross Hospital. He is the author of *Winnicott* (1988) and *On Kissing, Tickling and Being Bored: Psychoanalytic Essays on the Unexamined Life* (1993). He is also the editor of Edmund Burke, *A Philosophical Enquiry* (1990), Charles Lamb, *Selected Prose* (1985), and Walter Pater, *The Renaissance* (1986).

ROY PORTER is Senior Lecturer at the Wellcome Institute for the History of Medicine and author of *English Society in the Eighteenth Century* (1982), *Mind-Forg'd Manacles* (1987), and *The Social History of Madness* (1987). He is editor of *Patients and Practitioners* (1985), *The Faber Book of Madness*, and co-editor of *Dictionary of the History of Science* and *The Anatomy of Madness*.

MARK STOREY is Professor of English Literature at the University of Birmingham and author of *The Poetry of John Clare: A Critical Introduction* (1974), *Poetry and Humour from Cowper to Clough* (1979) and *Byron and the Eye of Appetite* (1986). He is the editor of *Clare: The Critical Heritage* (1973) and *The Letters of John Clare* (1985) and is currently working on a life of Robert Southey.

KELSEY THORNTON is Professor of English at the University of Birmingham and author of *The Decadent Dilemma* (1983). He has edited two volumes of Clare's poetry, *The Rural Muse* (1982) and *The Midsummer Cushion* (1979, 1990). He is also editor of *Poetry of the 'Nineties* (1971), Nicholas Hilliard, *The Arte of Limning* (1981), Ivor Gurney, *War Letters* (1983), *Severn and Somme and War's Embers* (1987) and *Collected Letters* (1991).

CHAPTER I

Introduction: relocating John Clare

Hugh Haughton and Adam Phillips

1

> So here I am homeless at home and half-gratified to feel that I
> , can be happy any where.[1]

Clare wrote these words in 1841 towards the close of the *Journey out of Essex*, after his escape from Dr Allen's asylum on his return home to Northborough. They reflect Clare's lifelong preoccupation with locating himself in many senses, and in defiance of other people's attempts to place him.

Two hundred years after Clare's birth, Clare still speaks to us with something of the exemplary perplexity of the displaced person, of an exile within his own country. Returned 'home', he is still driven by a sense of estrangement and marginality that renders him 'homeless' within his familiar world. If the poets of the Romantic period can be distinguished according to their respective nostalgias, John Clare is the poet of a nostalgia peculiarly difficult to define but which is bound up with a thwarted project of identification with place – or rather a place – a geographical place of course, but as urgently a place in language, literary tradition and culture in the widest sense. As one of Clare's finest recent critics Tom Paulin has said in a book devoted to the historical politics of literary language:

Clare emerges for readers in this society as a displaced, marginalized poet whose reputation is gradually being rehabilitated – as Mandelstam's is in the Soviet Union. It may be many years, though, before his name is given the kind of official recognition which is accorded to Wordsworth and Keats, and only when social readings of poetic texts have been generally accepted is it likely that his work will be widely read and studied. But it could be that Clare – shy, feral, intensely gifted – will never be redeemed from all the neglect and mutilation he has suffered.[2]

Clare's work, both during his own lifetime and now, foregrounds what we could call a politics (as well as a poetics) of recognition. The occasion of the bi-centenary of his birth in 1993 has prompted the present collection of essays. It offers an opportunity if not to 'rehabilitate' Clare then to resituate him and address the problem of his continued marginalisation within Romantic literature and English poetry. The essays in this volume might make us ask what Romanticism and indeed the history of English poetry in the nineteenth century would look like if Clare, rather than Wordsworth or Keats, were taken as a central and representative figure in the period.

2

John Clare was born on 13 July 1793, in Helpston, a place he described in *Sketches in the Life of John Clare*, written in 1821, as 'a gloomy village in Northamptonshire, on the brink of the Lincolnshire fens' (*Sketches* p. 1).[3] As he tells us in one of these autobiographical fragments, he was the son of Parker Clare, 'one of fate's chance-lings who drop into the world without the honour of matrimony' (p. 2), 'a thresher and a laboring rustic' (p. 118). His father Parker Clare was a barely literate casual farm worker and his mother, Ann Stimson, was illiterate, though 'as she said she expirenced enough in her own case to avoid bringing up her childern in ignorance' and did what she could to make their son John 'a good scholar' (p. 2). Clare was the eldest of four children, two of whom, including his twin sister, died in infancy, and his childhood and early life were spent in the tough and often near-destitute conditions of the rural poor.

By the age of ten, Clare was working with his father for 'the scanty rewards of industry' (p. 3), threshing in winter, tending, birdscaring and weeding in spring and summer. Up to the age of eleven or twelve he had, by his own account, three months or more of schooling a year, first with a woman in Helpston, then with John Seaton of Glinton. At the age of twelve, Clare befriended Mary Joyce, a local farmer's daughter, at school in Glinton, and though their relationship ended around 1816, her memory was to haunt him for the rest of his life and he was later to imagine she was his 'first wife'.

His adolescent years, by his own later accounts, were passed eking out a living doing a combination of precarious, temporary labouring jobs, from lime-burning to hedging and ditching during the enclosure of local land. Between 1810 and 1816, he worked at a variety of casual jobs in the Helpston area including brief spells as militia recruit, gang labourer, harvester and assistant in the kitchen garden at Burghley House near Stamford. Despite living and working during this period as a casual agricultural hand like others of his class and place, he simultaneously pursued, from an early age, a highly unusual obsession with reading and writing poetry. After encountering Thomson's *The Seasons* at the age of thirteen, he bought his own copy and, as he tells us, 'got into a strain of descriptive ryhming on my journey home' which resulted in 'The Morning Walk', 'the first thing [he] commited to paper' (p. 10). As he recounts in the *Sketches*, from then on 'poetry was a troublsomely pleasant companion anoying and cheering me at my toils' (p. 64). Anxious to conceal his 'scribbling', Clare was 'with all secresy possible' (p. 11) taking off from work whatever time he could find to write verse on whatever scraps of paper he could get hold of. As a gardener in the village, he says 'I coud not stop my thoughts and often faild to keep them till night so when I fancyd I had hit upon a good image or natural description I usd to steal into a corner of the garden and clap it down but the appearance of my employers often put my fancys to flight' (pp. 64–5). He found working in the fields easier in this respect: 'I usd to drop down behind a hedge bush or dyke and write down my things upon the crown of my hat' (p. 65). The bulk of his writing, however, seems on his own evidence, to have been accomplished on Sundays when he foresook the 'church going bell' to pursue instead 'the religion of the fields' and the 'restless revels of ryhme' (p. 65).

At first, the only audience he found for his experiments in poetry was his parents. Pretending, by a strategy of inverse plagiarism, that what he was reading had been written by other people, he records that he 'scribbld on unceasing for 2 or 3 years, reciting them every night as I wrote them when my father returnd home from labour and we was all seated by the fire side' (p. 12). His almost illiterate parents were his first critics, and he claims to have found their criticism 'useful' because 'I thought if they coud not understand me my taste shoud be wrong founded and not agreeable to nature' (p. 12). In time he built up a body of work and cautiously approached people outside the family, and in 1817 his proposal for publishing a volume of his poems by subscription caught the attention of Edward Drury, a Stamford bookseller who was the cousin of the London publisher John Taylor. Clare consequently met Taylor in 1819, who published his first volume of poems, *Poems Descriptive of Rural Life and Scenery* in 1820, the title page of which described the author as a 'Northampton-shire Peasant'. Within a year Clare's first book had sold over 3,000 copies and by 1821 it had gone into four editions – a phenomenal success for a first volume of poems by a completely unknown poet (Keats's *Lamia, Isabella and The Eve of St Agnes* published by Taylor in the same year, 1820, by contrast sold only 500 copies). 1820 was a momentous year for Clare in other respects, too. He married Martha Patty Turner and made his first journey to London, where he met, among others, his future patron, Eliza Emmerson, and his friend, the painter Edward Rippingille. At this time, the labourer from Helpston must have seemed on the verge of a successful literary career.

Following the sensational success of *Poems Descriptive*, Clare published a second volume, *The Village Minstrel and Other Poems*, in 1821. Though the second book was nothing like as successful as the first, the following years were ones of increasing literary fame on the one hand and debilitating depression and financial and literary anxiety on the other. In 1821, he drafted *Sketches in the Life of John Clare*, an unfinished and unpublished autobiography on which he continued to work intermittently later in the decade and in which he tried to make narrative sense of his early life and his struggles to become a writer. A classic Romantic autobiography, it is also a memorable first-hand record of village labour and the slippery interface between illiterate and literate culture. In the mid-decade, he wrote but did not publish *The Parish*, one of his most ambitious literary projects, a vitriolic and energetic satire on the corruptions and pretentions of village society. It reveals the intensity of Clare's political and moral critique of rural culture in the wake of the enclosure movement. Other unpublished projects of the time show Clare's more positive sense of his local culture. Clare's father had 'a tolerable good voice' and was an accomplished ballad-singer and during the 1820s the poet, who could play the fiddle, set about collecting and recording popular traditional songs and tunes, many derived from his father, making him, as George Deacon has claimed, 'the earliest collector of the songs people actually sang in Southern England'.[4] He also set about recording local flora and fauna and began the never-completed *A Natural History of Helpstone* written in the form of letters on the model of Gilbert White's *Natural History of Selbourne*.[5]

During these years, Clare made a number of visits to London and made the acquaintance of Keats, Lamb, Hazlitt, De Quincey, Reynolds, Cary and other literary figures, leaving astute and ironic portraits of them in his fragmentary autobiographical writings and correspondence. As the decade went on, Clare continued to write poetry at a frantic rate but his relationship with his publisher, John Taylor, became increasingly fraught as both the market for poetry underwent a drastic change and Clare gained in confidence about his own work. Clare's third book, *The Shepherd's Calendar; with Village Stories and Other Poems*, was a latter-day English book of hours and robust illuminated diary of the agricultural year written from the standpoint of a village labourer. It was published by Taylor in 1827 but sold only 400 copies, and the decade ended with Clare's literary, psychological and economic fortunes in decline. From 1828 to 1831, in a state of chronic disappointment and desperation, he returned to working in the fields. The copious letters Clare fired off to friends, publishers and patrons during this decade dramatise his literary and economic frustrations, his struggle for poetic and financial 'independence' (a recurring keyword in his vocabulary at this time), and the psychological crises he underwent as he found it impossible to support himself and his family, either by manual work on the land or by his pen. They reveal an intensely self-conscious literary talent taking on the established social and cultural power-structures of his day and foundering among the appalling and unresolvable contradictions of his position as pauperised 'Northamptonshire Peasant' on the one hand and productive Poet on the other. As Clare wrote feelingly elsewhere about the poor man in general, he was 'a combatant with difficulty and a steeple climber all his life'.[6]

In 1832, the year of the Reform Act, Clare left his native village and moved to nearby Northborough, a village three miles away where he and his family settled as tenants in a newly built cottage on the Fitzwilliam estate, provided by Earl Fitzwilliam. To supplement his pension from patrons and his meagre income from publications, Clare intended 'to commence cottage farmer' in what he described in his letters as 'a home that I have long wished for' (*Letters*, pp. 574–6).[7] The new cottage had a few acres of land with it and Clare saw the move as potentially bringing him the 'independence' he so desperately sought at this time. He declared:

All my anxiety dwells upon that independance of mind that I hope to arrive at by using the means that are my own & freeing myself of obligations that

burthen & oppress me ... my whole ambition is to arrive at that climax when
I can say I owe no man a shilling & feel that I can pay my way (*Letters*, p. 567)A

His literary independence mattered to him too, and he spent much of
1832 drumming up subscriptions for a new volume of poetry – to be
called *The Midsummer Cushion* – of which he wrote: 'I wished to be
judged of by the book itself without any appeals to want of education
lowness of origin or any other foil that officiousness chuses to
encumber my path with' (*Letters*, p. 594).

Yet this new start did not turn out as Clare hoped. Though the new
house was much bigger than the family cottage in Helpston and came
with a smallholding, Clare had neither the capital nor experience to
make a success of life as a 'cottage farmer' and he found it increasingly
difficult to support himself and his now 'large family' (*Letters*, p.
592). His literary projects proved equally intractable. The fourth
book Clare had been planning for some time and desperately needed
to publish was continually delayed, involving the poet in drawn-out
mutually soul-destroying negotiations with his publisher, John
Taylor, throughout the early years of the decade. It eventually
appeared under the title of *The Rural Muse* in 1835, a pruned and
boiled-down version of *The Midsummer Cushion* volume that he had
originally planned, edited by John Taylor and Eliza Emmerson.
Unhappily for Clare, *The Rural Muse* was to prove the last book he
published during his lifetime. It sold poorly and made little
impression. As far as his public reputation went, Clare's brief star had
definitely set. The briefly feted country boy prodigy of *Poems
Descriptive* lionised by literary London in the early 1820s disappeared
into obscurity and neglect. He came to be remembered, if at all, only
as an 'uneducated' labourer poet or literary peasant, a glamorous
but doomed literary and sociological freak brought into the spotlight
of literary fashion by the Romantic primitivism of the period – like
the unspoiled minstrel, Edwin, of James Beattie's immensely popular
The Minstrel (1771–4) and like the poets Stephen Duck, Robert Burns
and Robert Bloomfield before him.

In retrospect, the period during which he wrote *The Shepherd's
Calendar* and *The Midsummer Cushion*, the decade 1825–35, before and
after the move to Northborough, was probably the most productive
and important of his writing life, as recorded in the modern editions
of those works by Eric Robinson and Geoffrey Summerfield, and
Anne Tibble. At the time, however, and apart from the support of a

few friends, it saw Clare's increasing marginalisation and neglect. The tide of literary fashion had moved on, leaving Clare stranded in his anomalous position in his Northamptonshire backwater. The combination of financial insecurity and literary failure had profound psychological consequences for the poet. Clare's move to Northborough also took its toll, and some of his most powerful verse of the period, like 'The Flitting' and 'Remembrances', shows that his uprooting from Helpston helped precipitate an inner crisis in Clare's life, comparable to that caused by enclosure in his early life and mourned in his earliest verse.

Throughout these years Clare suffered periodically from bouts of acute depression and anxiety, but after 1836 his state of health gave increasing cause for concern. In his brief letters of the time he continually complains of being ill and unable to write. He began to suffer from memory loss and delusions and when in November 1836 John Taylor visited him at home with his wife and seven children in Northborough, he found him 'sadly enfeebled':

He is constantly speaking to himself and when I listened I heard such words as these, pronounced a great many times over and with great rapidity – 'God bless them all', 'Keep them from evil', 'Doctors'. But who it was of whom he spoke I could not tell – whether his children, or doctors, or everybody. But I think the latter.[8]

In 1837, Taylor arranged secretly for Clare to be taken to a private asylum at High Beech near Epping Forest, run by Dr Matthew Allen. Without warning, a man presented himself at Clare's house bearing a note from Taylor to the effect that 'The bearer will bring you up to town and take all care of you on the way.' Clare spent the next four years (1837–41) as a patient at High Beech Asylum and the rest of his life was indeed to be overshadowed by 'Doctors'.

Dr Allen, the author of *Cases of Insanity* (1831) and *Essay on the Classification of the Insane* (1837), was an advocate of enlightened 'judicious moral and medical management' of the insane. Writing in 1840, he described Clare's state of mind on his arrival at High Beech three years earlier:

He was then exceedingly miserable, every instant bemoaning his poverty, and his mind did not appear so much lost and deranged as suspended in its movements by the oppressive and permanent state of anxiety, and fear, and vexation, produced by the excitement of excessive flattery at one time, and neglect at another, his extreme poverty and over exertion of body and mind, and no wonder that his feeble bodily frame, with his wonderful native powers of mind, was overcome.[9]

Allen thought a 'small pension' would be enough to cure Clare and probably enable him to remain 'well for life' and in 1841 he helped launch an unsuccessful public campaign to secure an annuity for the poet. Clare's health seems initially to have improved in the sheltered atmosphere of the asylum. He was encouraged to walk freely in the woods round about – '"the country is the finest I have ever seen" he told his wife' (*Letters*, p. 642) – and also, more importantly, to write freely. Among the numerous productions of the asylum are his two Byronic sequences, the elegiac masterpiece of deracination, *Child Harold or Prison Amusements*, and the fragmentary and virulently satirical *Don Juan*. When he visited Clare in 1841 Cyrus Redding described him as 'busily engaged with a hoe, and smoking', talking in a 'communicative' way about the 'quality of the ground' he was hoeing, the 'aspect of the country' compared to his native fens, his 'loneliness away from his wife', his need for books and his 'great desire to go home'.[10] Redding also records Clare's obsession with prize-fighters and there is evidence in his letters and elsewhere that Clare developed a complicated series of multiple identities at this time – among them Lord Byron and prize-fighters such as Jack Randall – while also living out a fantasy that he had two wives, his adolescent sweetheart Mary Joyce and his legal wife Patty. In a letter to Mary Joyce, in 1841, he wrote 'No one knows how sick I am of this confinement possessing two wives that ought to be my own & cannot see either' (*Letters*, p. 646) and in another of the same year he speaks of 'this Hell of a Madhouse' (*Letters*, p. 647). Desperately homesick, Clare escaped from the asylum that July and, in a state of increasing destitution and exhaustion, walked the eight miles home from Essex to Northborough.

Soon after getting home, he wrote the *Journey out of Essex*, a meticulous record of his traumatic trek up the Great York Road to Northborough. As he noted there and in a letter scribbled at the time, he almost immediately felt 'homeless at home', and the five months Clare spent with his wife and family from July to December 1841 were miserably troubled. So much so that on 28 December, doctors intervened once more. Dr Page and Dr Skrimshire certified that Clare was 'in a state of Lunacy', and on the 29th he was removed to the newly built Northamptonshire General Lunatic Asylum where he was entered as a farmer 'addicted to Poetical prossing', to be paid for by Lord Fitzwilliam at the pauper's rate of eleven shillings a week.[11] So began the final chapter of Clare's life. His last twenty-two years, from December 1841 to his death aged seventy in May 1864, were passed in the Northamptonshire General Lunatic Asylum. He never returned home again.

The Northampton hospital was, like High Beech, run in a relatively benign and open way, and during the stewardship of Dr Pritchard, until 1845, and of William Knight, up to 1850, Clare was encouraged to write and move freely around the asylum grounds and outside them, in Northampton or the neighbouring countryside. The bulk of the 1,000 pages of *The Later Poetry of John Clare: 1837–1864* (eds. Eric Robinson and David Powell) were composed at Northampton. A large proportion of these, filling some 800 pages, survive in transcripts made by Clare's doctor, William Knight, who both supported Clare in his poetic vocation and made moves (albeit unsuccessful) to have his asylum verse published in book form. During these years, some poems leaked out into magazines and newspapers; others accumulated in notebooks, to be edited and published posthumously. Clare's image during this time shifts from 'Peasant Poet' to 'Mad Poet'. In neither role, however, could he exercise full authorial control over his texts.

Apart from the poetry itself – a miscellaneous archive of song and ballad and descriptive notations, more traditional and folkloric in form than the work of his middle years – there is scant evidence of Clare's life during his last two decades spent in the asylum. The reports made by his psychiatrists and visitors, though indicating that he was subject to 'delusions' of multiple identity, are largely benign, and suggest that as a 'harmless' lunatic he could roam and read quite freely for much of the time – though possibly less so after 1854, when Dr Wing took over responsibility for him. One of his visitors, Spencer Hall, thought that 'Taken for all in all, Clare's treatment at Northampton Asylum was the most genial he had ever for any long period together received'.[12] There are relatively few surviving letters from these years however – only 30 of the almost 700 pages of the *Letters* contain letters from Northampton – and they give a much starker view of Clare's state of mind. The moving family letters to his son Charles and wife Patty constantly harp on his longing for 'home' and his horror of the 'Madhouse' which, in a letter apparently written by a river in a green meadow, he terms 'the purgatoriall hell

& French Bastile of English liberty' (*Letters*, p. 657). Elsewhere, he refers to it as a 'Prison', 'Hell', 'Captivity among the Babylonians', 'the English Bastile a government Prison where harmless people are trapped & tortured till they die', and 'the land of Sodom where all the people's brains are turned the wrong way'.

Accounts of Clare in these years do not suggest a man with his 'brains... turned the wrong way', but Dr Wing's case-books tell us that 'laterly his intellect had become sadly clouded', that he suffered from 'delusions about his identity' and was 'haunted by phantoms of his own creation'.[13] Doctors and visitors alike record his unusual sense of multiple identity. One visitor to the asylum describes Clare as saying 'I'm John Clare now. I was Byron and Shakespeare formerly. At different times you know I'm different people – that is the same person with different names'.[14] After his stay at High Beech, where he had written 'Jack Randall's Challenge to All the World', Clare seems to have taken on the identities of prize-fighters as well as prize poets, and when asked in Northampton whether he was more proud of his fame as a poet or of his 'prowess as a prize-fighter', he replied 'Oh, poetry, ah, I know, I once had something to do with poetry, a long while ago: but it is no good. I wish, though, they could get a man with courage enough to fight me'.[15] An incongruous role for such a quiet man, yet both roles, poet and prize-fighter, offered him the possibility of becoming an active agent in his own destiny and achieving public recognition. Both roles also offered someone in his socially marginal and disempowered position, first as labourer then as lunatic, ways of challenging 'All the World'. There must have been times when that challenge seemed to have ended in total failure and in 1860 he told a visitor that 'Literature has destroyed my head and brought me here'. He offered her a final terrible image for his sense of alienation and linguistic dispossession:

they have cut off my head, and picked out all the letters of the alphabet – all the vowels and consonants – and brought them out through my ears; and then they want me to write poetry! I can't do it.[16]

He died in the asylum on 20 May 1864, aged seventy, and was buried in the churchyard of his native village of Helpston.

3

The question of reception is everywhere central in Clare's work. Clare's problematic relationship to poetic tradition and social categorisation reproduces itself in the problems Clare has posed for his subsequent readers and editors. In reading Clare now we are inevitably involved in a revealing history of concealments and marginalisations, of attempted rescues and recuperations alongside a history of persistent neglect. Looking back, it is remarkable that none of the poets and critics we now classify as modernist had anything to say about Clare at all. If we turn to Pound or Yeats or Auden for illumination or information on Clare, we draw a complete blank. This neglect is not simply part and parcel of the modernist rejection of Romanticism associated with the criticism of T. S. Eliot and Ezra Pound. In the era of high modernism, Clare was simply beyond the pale and out of earshot. Clare's reputation was kept alive during the twentieth century by an alternative line of marginalised but very much 'native' English poets, writing outside the modernist canon – Arthur Symons, Edward Thomas, Edmund Blunden, Geoffrey Grigson and Robert Graves. Thanks to their advocacy, Clare's voice continued to be heard. Unfortunately it was mainly heard as part of a contentedly nostalgic and ruralist tradition of minor English nature poetry. Even for these advocates, Clare remained something of a backwater poet, not part of the mainstream of English poetry. Edward Thomas, for example, a sympathetic reader who wrote of Clare that 'it is hard to imagine a combination with more possibilities for wretchedness than that of poet and agricultural labourer' called him 'a real poet, however small'. There is too often that touch of condescension, of affectionate patronage, in critical estimates of Clare. As Edmund Blunden wrote in 1964, 'he is still too little known, and perhaps is one of the English writers most difficult to estimate'.[17]

It is in large part thanks to the pioneering editorial work of Geoffrey Summerfield, Eric Robinson, David Powell, Margaret Grainger, Mark Storey and others that, from the 1960s onwards, Clare has been made available in a new way. At last, thanks to the work of editorial scholarship, Clare's texts have become accessible in something like their original form, and readers can approach this most approachable of poets through his own words and, as it were, through his own voice, effectively for the first time. This editorial reclamation of the Clare manuscripts has opened up the poet's actual writing, irrevocably changing our sense of the scale, development and vocal timbre of his poetry. Despite this, Clare remains a marginal figure in most accounts of Romanticism and most histories of nineteenth-century poetry. If he is now finally readable, there is a lot of evidence to suggest he has not actually been read. He is certainly not prominently part of the current historical canon, even the canon of Romanticism recently redefined by such influential critics as M. H. Abrams, Harold Bloom, Geoffrey Hartman, Paul De Man, Marilyn Butler and Jerome McGann. If we scan their essays and overviews on Romantic poetry, Clare's name figures fleetingly at best – in the occasional footnote or as passing evidence of some cultural or social trend. Harold Bloom is something of an exception in this respect. His influential map of Romantic poetry, *The Visionary Company*, includes a short chapter on 'John Clare: the Wordsworthian shadow'.[18] Yet, while Bloom sees it as the fate of all poets to operate in the anxious shadows of earlier stronger poets, his title, like his essay, has the effect of confirming Clare's overshadowment by other writers of the period.

In other large-scale accounts of the period, Clare occupies an equally shadowy and peripheral place in relation to the established Romantic and Victorian canon. Stuart Curran, for example, in his historically panoramic map of Romantic poetic genres in *Poetic Form and British Romanticism*, bypasses Clare altogether, even in his chapters on Pastoral and the sonnet – genres in which Clare was one of the period's great reshapers (he rates a single mention in the notes as part of 'Romantic Georgic poetry').[19] Similarly, neither M. H. Abrams's monumental *Natural Supernaturalism*, a modern apologia for Romanticism,[20] nor Jerome McGann's revisionary *Romantic Ideology*, a critique of Romanticism, finds a place for Clare at all. McGann's much-publicised and revisionary *The New Oxford Book of Romantic Period Verse* astonishingly represents Clare's work by only one poem, the brief lyric 'My Mary'.[21] Other contemporary anatomies of Romantic ideology reproduce the same blindspot. *Romanticism and Ideology*, edited by David Aers, John Cook and David Punter, alludes to Clare only once and that by way of reference to Wordsworth,[22] while *Beyond Romanticism*, edited by Stephen Copley and John Whale, only alludes to him by way of an acknowledgement to John Barrell's historical work in the period and the 'exclusions it "remedies" (the case of Clare, for example)'.[23] It seems that the case of Clare still remains in historical brackets.

That neither exponents nor critics of 'Romantic ideology' consider the 'case' of Clare at all suggests something about their shared critical assumptions as well as about received accounts of Romanticism. Even Marilyn Butler in her wide-ranging and groundbreaking historical account of the period, *Romantics, Rebels and Reactionaries*, while rehabilitating figures such as Southey and drawing attention to the politics of Romantic literary culture, passes over Clare in relative silence. She includes him in her sociological survey of 'more isolated country dwellers' who brought the 'external world into poetry with a new precision' in the late eighteenth and early nineteenth centuries, noting that 'the working men who succeeded in publishing poetry in this generation and the next were non-city-dwellers, rustics – Burns in Scotland, Langhorne, Bloomfield and Clare in England'.[24] In fact Clare remains almost entirely 'isolated' in most histories of the period, a passing instance of the poet as labourer or rustic. Kelvin Everest in his recent *English Romantic Poetry* mentions him only as 'still an underrated and relatively neglected figure'.[25] He is mainly famous for being neglected. J. R. de J. Jackson in his *Poetry of the Romantic Period* allots Clare two sympathetic paragraphs, yet though Clare is praised for his 'strength' of 'observation' and 'freshness' of 'expression', his work is represented as drastically restricted in intellectual scope. 'His weakness', we are told, 'at least in all the poetry he published before 1836...is that he has so very little to say, he is so ineffectually reflective'.[26]

What is clear from this brief survey of some of the influential surveys of the period is that modern literary historians and critics have very little to say about Clare. Perhaps in this respect they too have been ineffectually reflective.

Yet, if the critics have continued to neglect him in the main – with the honourable exceptions of Raymond Williams, John Barrell, John Lucas and Tom Paulin – modern poets have not, and Clare is a real presence in the work of many recent poets. He figures as an inspiration for numerous poets of our time who recognise in him a fostering precursor and example. Contemporary poets as diverse as John Ashbery, Seamus Heaney, Michael Longley, Ed Hirsch, Peter Levi, David Constantine and Tom Paulin have paid generous tribute to Clare. Curiously few of these are English. Despite the historically informative advocacy of critics such as John Barrell, Mark Storey and Raymond Williams, there is a sense in which Clare is indeed still homeless at home. Seamus Heaney in his essay on 'Englands of the mind' notices that many recent English poets share a 'defensive love of territory' previously characteristic of 'post-colonial poets' like Yeats, MacDiarmid or William Carlos Williams, a love that is intimately bound up with affiliations to regional and vernacular versions of the English language.[27] It may be that poets today, writing in recoil from the imperious colonial mapping and policing of the language associated with the British Empire, are in a position to respond to the emancipatory force of Clare's verse. For Heaney, 'it was the unique achievement of John Clare to make vocal the regional and the particular, to achieve a buoyant and authentic lyric utterance at the meeting-point between social realism and conventional romanticism'.[28] However, it is not only a question of the poetic vernacular championed by Seamus Heaney and Tom Paulin but of the mobile, casual-seeming and open attitude towards poetic form that characterises Clare's best work. Poets have proved more receptive to the open reach of Clare's art and the grain of his voice than almost any critics.

It is indeed remarkable that the critics who have redefined Romanticism – and who in various ways read Romanticism in terms of its epistemological preoccupations and its transvaluations of tradition – should find no place for Clare. He has been treated fleetingly at best, at worst condescendingly as a sociological case-history. History is repeating itself. Clare continues to resist institutional recognition. He still poses unresolved problems for criticism, even for the critics who are most attentive to the issues which Clare is negotiating in his verse – problems of canon-formation, of the relations between margin and centre, the politics of publishing, the relationship between culture and class, debates about regional and vernacular language as alternatives to dominant linguistic models, questions about ecology and the ruinous exploitation of the natural world, crises of identity and belonging. To some extent, all these issues are played out in the concrete details of Clare's individual poems as they attempt to articulate his sense of place – and his knowledge of displacement – his quest for linguistic identity in a world where language, like land, is owned, governed and legislated for by other people. When he was writing in the Northampton asylum, Clare took as a title and a model for his distraught autobiographical and elegiac quest sequence, the archetypal Romantic poem of displacement, Byron's *Childe Harold* (which Clare, with his unchivalric romance of childhood, spells as *Child Harold*).

Clare's tragic knowledge of estrangement is different from Byron's in part because of his different social position, but like the free-wheeling aristocrat who wrote *Childe Harold* Clare writes from an experience of exile – an experience comparable to that Nadezhda Mandelstam referred to, in a phrase adopted by Seamus Heaney, as 'internal exile'. This is painfully true, in particular of the late asylum verse but, as early as 'The Fate of Genius', the experience of misrecognition is integral to Clare's poetry of recognition. Clare's knowledge is a deeply territorial one, born of a thwarted Heideggerian sense of belonging to his place. It is also, in so many of the great poems like 'The Flitting' or 'The Lament of Swordy Well' or 'The Mores', an extra-territorial one, born of disenfranchisement and social disenchantment.

The essays in this book foreground the question of Clare's knowledge and the intimate relationship between *language* and knowledge. In reading Clare's poetry, you hear different ways of knowing at work. There is indeed something like an epistemological as well as political contest in play in Clare's struggle with received language – and received forms of knowledge such as botany, grammar, science, aesthetics and political economy. This is as evident in the poems about birds and natural history as in those about rural labour (*The Shepherd's Calendar* for example), place and his own history. His work, like that of all revolutionary poets, calls into question the prevailing economies of altitude, notions of 'high' and 'low', dignified and undignified, important and trivial, superior and inferior kinds of knowledge. One of the reasons Clare has never formed part of the agenda of Romantic studies is that he has not been taken to be engaged in the grand epistemological debates over the nature of imagination, subjectivity and self-consciousness we associate with Wordsworth, Coleridge, Blake, Byron, Shelley and Keats. It has looked as though Clare was the uneducated poetic consciousness, the peasant poet, working at a lesser degree of intellectual intensity and in relative obliviousness of the quasi-philosophical questioning associated with the now-dominant Romantic tradition. It is of course difficult to recognise the epistemologies which operate outside established philosophical traditions. Clare may be the only major contemporary figure who had not read Locke or heard of post-Kantian German philosophy. Yet, as all the contributors to this volume make plain, despite their very different accounts of the poetry, when we read any single poem by Clare just as when we confront his work as a whole, we are confronted with something comparable to the epistemological crises and debates about legitimacy around which the poetics and history of Romanticism have been written. This is a crisis over the ownership of language, of knowledge, of poetic legitimacy, as it is played out so self-consciously in poems such as 'The Progress of Ryhme'. For Clare, poetry was a form of knowledge – a place where his absolutely particular, but also historically and socially representative, knowledge of place might finally be acknowledged. The question was, how does such knowledge gain status, given the established hierarchy of forms and institutions of knowledge which disown and discredit it. If Clare's poems are different from most of the poems we read, this has something to do with the entry into poetry of disowned and disenfranchised ways of knowing. Reading any Clare poem, like reading those of William Carlos Williams, Robert Creeley or Frank O'Hara – there are no comparable English examples – we find ourselves confronting the question of what a poem is, and where to situate ourselves towards it. Some of the pleasure of reading Clare comes from the ways his poetry liberates us from institutionalised ways of knowing.

Clare addressed himself to the problem of knowledge in a prose fragment which bears on all this.

Knowledge gives a great number of lessons for nothing like Socrates she is not confined to Halls or colledges or forum[s] but like him accompanys us in our walks in the fields and attends on us at our homes.[29]

What is at stake is Clare's continuing negotiation with the authority that he meets as he writes out of his experience of the familiar world. This negotiation is continually being worked out within the absolutely distinct density and noise of his medium, language. Clare's poetry enacts a struggle for legitimacy outside 'Halls or colledges or forum', a struggle operating at many levels and on many fronts but which was inherent in what he claimed in 'The Progress of Ryhme' as his 'right to song'.[30]

Knowledge of Clare has, of course, depended on the availability and legitimacy of texts. Since the publication of *Poems Descriptive* in 1820, the relationship between what Clare wrote and what his editors have published has been fraught. Exasperated by the genteel interference ('False delicasy') of his first editor, John Taylor, in his first book, Clare declared 'I think I shall soon be qualified to be my own editor' (*Letters*, p. 83). In fact Clare had little choice in the matter and was never considered 'qualified' to be his own editor. None of the four volumes Clare published in his lifetime took the form he originally envisaged, and nothing he wrote while he was alive appeared verbatim in printed form. After confinement to High Beech Asylum in 1837 and thereafter during the long years in Northamptonshire Asylum, Clare effectively lost whatever control he had had over the fate of his poems and in fact no other volume appeared in his lifetime. Since his death, the text of the poetry has been largely determined by the choices of his editors. Their selections and textual preferences have governed readers' access to Clare's entire poetic universe. Though this is the posthumous history of all poetry, Clare's case uniquely reproduces the struggle for ownership of his own texts in which he engaged during his lifetime. Unlike contemporaries such as Wordsworth, Coleridge and Keats, Clare's work has never been monumentalised in the form of a canonical *Collected Poems*. It is as if he had never been accorded the status of an established poet in his own right, or acknowledged to have an *oeuvre* in the way that other Romantic and Victorian poets have. The posthumous history of John Clare's texts is haunted by the obstacles – social, linguistic, economic – which thwarted him during his life. When Robert Bloomfield, the author of the immensely popular *The Farmer's Boy* (1800), died in 1823, the publication of his *Remains* prompted Clare to reflect that:

neglect is the only touchstone by which true genius is proved   look at the every day scribblers I mean those nonsense ginglings called poems 'as plenteous as blackberrys' published every now & then by subscription & you shall find the list belarded as thickly with my Lord this & my Lady tother as if they were the choicest geniuses nature every gave birth too while the true poet is left to struggle with adversity & buffet along the stream of life with the old notorious companions of genius Dissapointment & poverty tho they leave a name behind them that posterity falls heir too & Works that shall give delight to miriads on this side eternity   well the world is as it is & we cannot help it (*Letters*, pp. 300–1)

Clare had a profound identification with Bloomfield, a poet who came from the same rural labouring class as himself, became a highly successful pastoral poet for a time but died in penury. It is important to recognise the precisely targeted social anger which fuels Clare's notion of a tradition of 'Dissapointment' in these comments. The ferocity of Clare's poetic conviction and social resentment has too often been assimilated as pathos or pathologised as madness. It has been difficult for this deep note of political anger – an anger provoked by, among other things, the difficulties he experienced in getting a hearing within his lifetime – to get a hearing after his death. We need to hear the hard ironic edge of Clare's voice in *The Parish* (where 'satires muse puts on a russet gown') as well as the throatily celebrant voice of *The Shepherd's Calendar*. The subsequent history of the poet's own 'Remains' confirms the truth of his suspicions. It is a bitter irony that 'posterity' has had until recently only limited access to those 'Works'.

Despite pioneering editions by the Tibbles and Geoffrey Grigson earlier in the century, it was not until the collaboration of Geoffrey Summerfield and Eric Robinson in the early 1960s that we were given texts of Clare's work that respected the literal forms of Clare's poems and the contexts of their production. J. W. Tibble's massive two-volume edition of *The Poems of John Clare* completed in the thirties included, in the editor's words, 'the bulk of the poems published during Clare's lifetime and after his death', but the editor acknowledged that 'the poems still left in manuscript still outnumber all those included'.[31] As far as the text itself went, Tibble followed Taylor's editions and the Knight transcripts for work published in the poet's lifetime, while declaring in his introduction that 'in the poems published after Clare's death and in all new poems, the manuscript versions have been faithfully followed save in the matter of punctuation and spelling'.[32] In other words, spelling and punctuation were regularised. It was against this practice that the new editors of Clare in the 1960s and after, led by Geoffrey Summerfield and Eric Robinson, reacted when they sought to reproduce Clare's manuscripts verbatim, as far as possible, in all their peculiarities of spelling and punctuation.

During the last quarter-century, Clare's buried work has been gradually emerging into the light of day. Eric Robinson and Geoffrey Summerfield opened the door with their editions of *The Later Poems* (1964), *The Shepherd's Calendar* (1964) and *The Selected Poems and Prose* (1966), and in their wake have come a series of important editions which include Anne Tibble and Kelsey Thornton, *The Midsummer Cushion* (1979), Margaret Grainger, *The Natural History Prose Writings of John Clare* (1983), Mark Storey, *The Letters of John Clare* (1985), Eric Robinson, *John Clare's Autobiographical Writings* (1983) and *The Parish* (1985), and the massive ongoing collected edition of the poems edited by Eric Robinson and David Powell, which to date includes

The Later Poetry of John Clare: 1837–64 (1984) and *The Early Poems of John Clare* (1989). In other words, it was not until a hundred years after his death that Clare's idiosyncratic vernacular art could be fully recognised. Unlike for his contemporaries, public recognition of Clare has depended on a belated reclamation of texts effectively buried in local libraries (though the belated publication of the early versions of many of Wordsworth's texts, such as the two-part *Prelude* of 1798–9, has also drastically transformed the way we read his *oeuvre*). In this respect, Clare's poetic afterlife has something in common with that of two other edged-out and linguistically way-out poets of the vernacular, Emily Dickinson and Gerard Manley Hopkins, whose influence was deferred due to their posthumous publication.

Even now, editorial problems remain. The guiding principle behind the massive Oxford edition of Clare currently in progress under the direction of Eric Robinson is fidelity to the literal transcription of Clare's manuscripts in all their idiosyncrasies of spelling, punctuation and syntax. As a result, modern editorial transcriptions of Clare's manuscripts editorially displace Taylor's published texts and Knight's transcripts. They give final authority to the poet's manuscript, in whatever state of draft or incompletion. Where, in the absence of any manuscript in Clare's hand, Robinson and Powell in their *The Later Poetry of John Clare* have to depend on Knight's transcripts, they even 'correct' Knight's conjectured 'corrections' of Clare's spelling and punctuation in order to bring the texts back to what they conjecture might have been Clare's original text. There is a huge pay-off for readers as a result of this new respect for Clare's actual writing, but it can be argued that there is a price to pay too. Reproducing uncorrected manuscript versions in print form, as Robinson and Powell do, goes contrary to normal publishing practice in Clare's time and today. There is not a shred of evidence to suggest that Clare, despite his distrust of grammar – 'grammar in learning is like Tyranny in government' (*Letters*, p. 231) – conventional spelling and genteel poetic culture, wanted his manuscripts published in the 'raw' form adopted by recent editors, a form that apotheosises his status as textual outsider. The Cornell Wordsworth, reprimanded by Jack Stillinger for what he calls 'textual primitivism', reproduces all the manuscript versions of Wordsworth's poems and the manuscripts in all their rawness and messiness, but it also produces 'reading texts' of the poems at various stages.[33] With Clare, the writing text displaces the 'reading text' in most cases. This has the virtue of bringing us back to an 'uncleaned up' authentically Clarean original text – such as the marvellous text of *The Shepherd's Calendar* edited by Geoffrey Summerfield and Eric Robinson, which emerged like a freshly restored painting once the editorial accretions and deletions of John Taylor were removed. However, it has the unfortunate side-effect of making Clare's writing, in all its freshness and idiomatic energy, less accessible to the general reader. Less *readable* in fact. Clare's poems in the new editions sometimes look dauntingly peculiar and difficult. On the page, they look more like experimental modernist works than the poems Clare is more likely to have imagined he was writing or would have expected to see in print.

This recent respect for the unique timbre of Clare's voice, his dialect and syntax and even the shifting idiosyncrasies of his scribbled manuscripts, has revealed him to be a very different poet to the one hitherto published, and it is impossible to regret the new Clare. The new editions have revealed a great and copious poet of an unprecedented kind. What is important, however, is to acknowledge that this too, for all its non-interventionist and primitivist methodology, represents an editorial intervention of a radical kind. In print in this form, Clare's poetry is not 'of' print. Whereas, in creating a readable text of poems by Keats, Byron or Wordsworth, modern editors have taken it upon themselves to respect print conventions as well as the authority of manuscripts, in the case of Clare modern editions leave his poems in an obstinately 'raw' state. There is everything to be gained by reproducing the exact vocabulary, syntax and dialect of Clare's poetry, but it is not clear what is to be gained by religiously referring to 'The Progress of Ryhme' rather than 'The Progress of Rhyme' – a mistake that any editor of a newspaper or book of poems, even in the wake of modernism, would normally normalise. In *The Parish*, after all, Clare damns Young Brag for producing 'illspelt trash' (line 763).[34] Current editorial practice certainly makes Clare a difficult poet to read for non-specialists who may be disorientated by the unusual spelling, lack of capitalisation and minimal unconventional punctuation of the modern texts. It may also paradoxically reduce his audience and make this wonderfully accessible vernacular poet less accessible and less vernacular, confirming his marginal status as poetic outsider and textual freak.

It was with some such reservations about the editorial revolution that he in part inaugurated, that Geoffrey Summerfield produced his *Selected Poetry* of Clare for Penguin in 1990 which, while respecting

Clare's dialect and grammar, modified some of the spelling, capitalisation and punctuation, 'where', as he writes in the introduction, 'the idiosyncracies of Clare's manuscripts distract the reader'.[35] Though this is inherently contentious and contestable, his edition reminds us that there is more than one way of editing Clare and that it is important that alternative editions should compete with each other and that even the monumental and scholarly Oxford edition now in progress should be contested too, as editions of Wordsworth, Shelley and Keats have to contest each other. It is important, for example, that the recent editions of *The Midsummer Cushion* and *The Rural Muse* should be available alongside the texts of the Oxford edition, giving us access to the book Clare originally conceived as well as the editorial selection that finally emerged in book form. These too, however, set out to reproduce manuscript peculiarities and irregularities verbatim, rather than create a 'print' text. Yet if manuscripts are to be our only authority, why not attempt to reproduce their materiality and complexity? In the case of *Child Harold*, for example, why not attempt to reconstruct in print its relation in the original manuscripts in the library at Northampton and the Bodleian Library to the chronologically and thematically related *Don Juan* and to the paraphrases of the psalms also undertaken at High Beech; or, on the model of the Cornell Wordsworth, to show the development of the sequence from the early draft in MS 8 to the later but uncompleted revision in MS 6; or, as John Lucas has argued, to include drawings and other related material scribbled in the notebooks alongside it?[36] Editing inevitably involves cleaning, selecting and interpreting, and Clare's problematic relation to textual production and editorial intervention remains unresolved.

That said, modern editions have made Clare available as never before, and in a way which reflects the linguistic specificity and formal originality of his vast *oeuvre*. As we have got used to reading Emily Dickinson without conventional punctuation, and to the punctuation styles of modern American poets such as William Carlos Williams, so, no doubt, readers will get used to Clare. The essays in this book bear witness to the deferred action, the delayed provocation, of Clare's work and his extremely belated appointment with the poets and the critics. Only now, perhaps, two centuries after his birth in late eighteenth-century Helpston, are we in a position to assess the politics of his neglect and the quality of his poetry.

Since the 1960s, our knowledge of Clare has been transformed by studies by John Barrell, Raymond Williams, Tim Chilcott, Johanne Clare and others.[37] However, it would be ironic if Clare's work were to remain the province of editors and experts. Celebrated as a poet of a specific locale, there is a risk that by the same token he might be relegated to the margins of the larger map of English poetry. As remarked earlier, the new availability of Clare's *oeuvre* has not noticeably impinged on dominant readings of Romanticism or the history of English poetry – with the notable exception of John Lucas in *England and Englishness* (1990) and Tom Paulin in *Minotaur* (1992).

In his scholarly work on Clare, as in his revolutionary anthologies of poetry for children, called *Voices*, Geoffrey Summerfield, to whose memory this present book is dedicated, was committed above all to the project of making poetry, in particular Clare's poetry, popularly available. Geoffrey Summerfield's interest in Clare was of a piece with his interest in oral culture and its transformation into print, the history of children's literature, the repressed social histories of England and an anti-mandarin approach to the teaching and reading of literature. Having completed John Clare, *Selected Poetry* for the Penguin Poetry Library in 1990 – a selection designed to respect the authority of Clare's manuscripts while providing an easily accessible text for the general reader – Geoffrey planned this volume of essays to celebrate the bi-centenary of the poet's birth in 1793, hoping that it would provoke new readings of Clare's work and help to open it up for a wider audience.

4

It was integral to Geoffrey Summerfield's conception of both this volume of essays and the rediscovery of John Clare in our time that Clare should not be recruited for a consensual reading. He wanted to make Clare available for a diversity of interpretations and approaches. The essays in this volume reflect this.

There is a marked variety of subject matter and approach. Mark Storey writes about the history of Clare's reception, John Lucas about his politics, Roy Porter about his experience of psychiatry, Douglas Chambers about his attitudes towards botany, Hugh Haughton about his related attitudes towards poetic and natural history, Seamus Heaney about his role as model or sponsor for poets writing in the era of post-colonialism.

Despite the range of perspectives Clare's poetry now seems to invite, certain central preoccupations emerge. The question of how we place Clare's work in relation to dominant cultural institutions recurs everywhere. Questions of centre and margin, dominance and subordination, ownership and trespass, return in different guises and in different contexts as the critics writing here explore the complex relationships between Clare's literary language and the dominant cultures of his and our time. Clare's art in all its fluidity and variousness, and with its apparently so unmisgiving attitude towards the natural world, brings into question, into jeopardy even, many of the reigning assumptions about the place of art itself in relation to other cultural institutions. Despite the powerful individuating strain of the local Northampton vernacular in Clare's work, and the legacy of oral and folk poetry, Clare's art is profoundly literary but in such a way as to foreground some of the hidden and repressed relationships between the 'literary' and the unliterary and even illiterate. The poetic in Clare is intimately bound up with ways of knowing and questions of knowledge, as we suggested earlier, and these studies show that in reading Clare we are inevitably involved in reading a larger social and intellectual history – of poetry, politics, class, and even science. Just as it records some of the hidden landscapes of rural England, his poetry exposes some of the hidden networks of power as they are refracted in language.

As John Goodridge and Kelsey Thornton show in their essay 'John Clare: the trespasser', Clare's poetic ambition developed in relationship to a profound sense of trespass. In that classic statement of twentieth-century feminism, *A Room of One's Own*, Virginia Woolf dramatises herself at the outset as a female trespasser in the privileged realm of male Oxbridge culture.[38] Goodridge and Thornton draw attention to Clare's comparably representative autobiographical account of trespassing in Burghley Park the day he bought Thomson's *The Seasons* and wrote his first poem. They imply that this might be seen as the primal scene in the poet's account of his vocation. As Clare's life was so largely shaped by exclusion from the spheres of property and culture, his poetic appropriations were experienced in some sense as transgressions, giving him a lifelong fascination with gypsies, trespassers and outsiders, but also giving a particular transgressive energy to his verse. The very ways that Clare inherited language and poetic tradition, as Nicholas Birns, Seamus Heaney and James McKusick show from their very different critical perspectives, inevitably engaged him in acts of illicit revision. McKusick aligns this with Bakhtin's account of heteroglossia. The exile has to found his own kind of colony, even a post-colonial one. Seamus Heaney in his bicentenary lecture on Clare sees Clare's poetic stance towards language as akin to such globally far-flung contemporary poets as the Australian Les A. Murray, the Scottish Liz Lochead, the English Tony Harrison, and the Caribbean Derek Walcott and Edward Kamau Brathwaite, for all of whom, in their various post-colonial contexts, poetic identity is stolen, forged in contest with the dominant culture. For Nicholas Birns in his 'The riddle nature could not prove' and Adam Phillips in his essay on 'The exposure of John Clare', Clare's poetic identity is altogether more opaque and problematic for reader and writer alike than is usually assumed. In the poet's peculiarly ambivalent psychic economy, his very receptiveness to the random intensities of the natural world endangers the identity – of poet and of poem – that he works to construct. Clare, Birns suggests in his panoptic historical view of the work, is terrified of the excess of meaning he cannot help but find in the natural world, while for Phillips he is inevitably committed to a process of continual self-relocation.

For obvious reasons that have to do with Clare's difficult social position and reliance on patronage and publication for a living, Clare could also never 'come out' in a straightforward way as a politically committed writer. In the 'Sketches in the Life of John Clare' he claimed: 'In politics I never dabbled to understand them thoroughly with the old dish that was served to my forefathers I am content' (p. 26). Yet his disavowal in his autobiography of all interest in 'revolution and reform', 'ranters' or 'radicalism', his conservative rejection of 'novelties' of all kinds and his various statements of devotion to king and country, do not tell us the whole story. John Lucas in his essay on 'Clare's politics' reflects on the ambiguities of Clare's commitments but identifies a disguised and explicit radicalism in his work, making a strong case for Clare as poet of political protest.

Clare's work, then, in all its contradictoriness and mobility, can be read, though with some special pleading perhaps, as a protest against the appropriation of land and language by those in power. As Mark Storey in his essay on Clare's reception at the hands of the critics, and Roy Porter in his discussion of Clare's treatment at the hands of the psychiatrists, tell us, Clare's appropriation by the experts of his day brought him costly and equivocal recognition. As both writers show, neither the critics nor doctors can be demonised, and Clare might even be described as having been well treated by both in terms of the currency of the day. At the same time, this was at a terrible cost, as the confusions of his life and poetry suggest, and as the collapse of his literary career and subsequent hospitalisation brutally dramatise. In the light of these formative confusions, however, and in ways few if any readers of his time could recognise, Clare was able to improvise, as James McKusick implies in 'Beyond the Visionary Company', his own distinctive poetics, drawing on an extraordinary range of voice and idiom, much of it lying beyond the reach of the conventionally poetic and, in McKusick's view, the canonic Romantic tradition.

Hugh Haughton attributes to Clare an unironically sophisticated poetic self-consciousness about his relationship to literary tradition and the Romantic poetry of his time, connecting Clare's work to the languages of contemporary natural history. He demonstrates how Clare's self-consciousness towards received poetic and scientific forms of language can be read in the intimate detailed shaping of individual texts which offer themselves as paradigms of a new form of knowing and recording the natural world. This testing of poetry against natural history and the claims of scientific knowledge provides the focus of the essays by Douglas Chambers and Marilyn Gaull on Clare's botany and contemporary science respectively. Marilyn Gaull reminds us of the 'dark system' of the contemporary scientific scene in Clare's time, while Douglas Chambers looks at Clare's verse from the standpoint of earlier botanical and horticultural writing, suggesting that Clare's revaluation of weeds and wild flowers represents an innovation of a piece with his attitudes towards demotic language. Read from these perspectives, the poet is involved in a more radical and concerted project than has been acknowledged in the past, involving him in a surprisingly confident revisionary stance towards poetry, language and 'scientific' natural history. It is part of Clare's daring to make out of what might have been disabling exclusions from the sphere of privileged culture the inspiration for an art that contests the authority of specialist forms of knowledge and the acknowledged owners and legislators of his world.

Two hundred years after the poet's death, this volume brings together a range of diverse new readings of John Clare which seek not to 'place' him or 'contextualise' him in any final sense but to locate him through his dislocations. In 1841, Clare wrote from the asylum:

Having been cooped up in this Hell of a Madhouse till I seem to be disowned by my friends & even forgot by my enemies for there is none to accept my challanges which I have from time to time given to the public I am almost mad in waiting for a better place & better company & all to no purpose (*Letters*, pp. 647–8)

Clare has always deserved a better place in English culture and has had a long wait. The challenge represented by his work has only recently begun to be taken up. It represents a lifelong struggle against the forces which displaced and immarginated him within his own country, history and language. It can be argued that Clare is a deeply anti-colonial poet, and that his beautiful repossession of the vernacular and local, across the length and breadth of his immense *oeuvre*, offers a liberatingly undomineering paradigm of poetic pleasure and of non-proprietorial respect for the natural world. His work also comes increasingly to represent not only the expression in print of a unique and moving voice from a largely repressed historical culture but an inviting and unrepressive model of how we might know the world.

NOTES

1 Eric Robinson (ed.), *John Clare's Autobiographical Writings* (Oxford, 1986), p. 160.
2 Tom Paulin, *Minotaur: Poetry and the Nation State* (London, 1992), p. 48.
3 'Sketches in the life of John Clare, written by himself', in Robinson, *Autobiographical Writings*, pp. 1–2. Unless otherwise specified all references for other biographical quotations are to this edition.
4 George Deacon, *John Clare and the Folk Tradition* (London, 1983), p. 18.
5 See Margaret Grainger (ed.), *The Natural History Prose Writings of John Clare* (Oxford, 1983).
6 Eric Robinson and David Powell (eds.), *John Clare, The Oxford Authors* (Oxford, 1984), pp. 450–1.
7 Mark Storey (ed.), *The Letters of John Clare* (Oxford, 1985), pp. 574–6.
8 John Taylor, quoted in J. W. and Anne Tibble, *John Clare: A Life* (London, 1932), p. 374.
9 Quoted in J. W. and A. Tibble, *A Life*, p. 384.
10 Cyrus Redding from *English Journal*, 20 and 22 (15 May and 29 May 1841), 305–9 and 340–3; reprinted in M. Storey (ed.), *John Clare: The Critical Heritage* (London, 1973) pp. 247–56.
11 J. W. and A. Tibble, *A Life*, p. 439.
12 Spencer T. Hall, 'Bloomfield and Clare' (dated 1866) in *Biographical Sketches of Remarkable People* (Burnley, 1873); reprinted in M. Storey, *Critical Heritage*, pp. 275–82.
13 Cited in J. W. and A. Tibble, *A Life*, p. 439.

14 Ibid. p. 418.
15 Hall in M. Storey, *Critical Heritage*, p. 280.
16 Agnes Strickland, quoted in J. W. and A. Tibble, *A Life*, p. 437.
17 Hall in M. Storey, *Critical Heritage*, p. 440.
18 Harold Bloom, *The Visionary Company* (Ithaca, London, 1961, revised edn, 1971).
19 Stuart Curran, *Poetic Form and British Romanticism* (New York, Oxford, 1986) p. 237.
20 M. H. Abrams, *Natural Supernaturalism* (New York, 1971).
21 Jerome McGann, *Romantic Ideology* (Chicago, London, 1981); *The New Oxford Book of Romantic Period Verse* (Oxford, 1993).
22 D. Aers, J. Cook and D. Punter (eds.), *Romanticism and Ideology* (London, 1981).
23 Stephen Copley and John Whale *Beyond Romanticism* (London, 1992), p. 2.
24 Marilyn Butler, *Romantics, Rebels and Reactionaries* (Oxford, 1981), p. 35.
25 Kelvin Everest, *English Romantic Poetry* (Milton Keynes, 1991), p. 2.
26 J. R. De J. Jackson, *Poetry of the Romantic Period* (London, Boston, Henley, 1980), p. 23.
27 S. Heaney, *Preoccupations: Selected Prose 1968–78* (London, 1980).
28 Ibid. p. 180.
29 Robinson and Powell, Oxford *Clare*, p. 482.
30 Ibid. p. 155.
31 J. W. Tibble (ed.), *The Poems of John Clare*, with an introduction by the editor, (2 vols., London, 1935), vol. I, p. vi.
32 Ibid. p. xv.
33 Jack Stillinger, 'Textual primitivism and the editing of Wordsworth', *Studies in Romanticism*, 28 (1989), 3–28.
34 Eric Robinson (ed.), *The Parish*, (Harmondsworth, 1985), p. 50.
35 Geoffrey Summerfield (ed.), John Clare, *Selected Poetry* (Harmondsworth, 1990), p. 24.
36 See John Lucas, 'Revising Clare', in Robert Brinkley and Keith Hanley (eds.), *Romantic Revisions*, (Cambridge, 1993), p. 253. We would like to acknowledge the influence, on this account of the problems of editing *Child Harold*, of conversations with Cathy Taylor, currently researching Clare's later writings at York University.
37 See bibliography for further details of these critical studies.
38 'What idea had sent me so audaciously trespassing I could not now remember', Virginia Woolf *A Room of One's Own* (London, 1977), pp. 7–8. She takes up the idea later: 'Literature is open to everybody. I refuse to allow you, Beadle though you are, to turn me off the grass. Lock up your libraries if you like; but there is no gate, no lock, no bolt that you can set upon the freedom of my mind.' (p. 72).

CHAPTER 2

Clare and the critics

Mark Storey

Just as in his own day Clare could seldom produce a poem without a sense of an actual or anticipated critical response, so, now, he still carries his critical baggage with him. Our whole sense of Clare as a poet – what kind of writer he is, what kind of claims we want to make for him – is deeply coloured by the various forms of reception given to his work ever since that now infamous introductory essay by Octavius Gilchrist in the *London Magazine* in January 1820, the very month of publication of *Poems Descriptive of Rural Life and Scenery*.[1] What I am interested in exploring in this essay is two strands of thought: firstly, the intimate, complex relationship between Clare and the critics of his own day (and this includes his friends and patrons and editors, who were in important respects the most influential critics of his early work), and, secondly, the extent to which we, as modern readers of Clare's poetry, now celebrating his bi-centenary, have to come to terms with the ramifications of that critical tradition. To put it another way, the 'and' of my title has a lot of work to do.

Perhaps not surprisingly, in view of his heightened consciousness of his origins and the soubriquet of the 'Northamptonshire Peasant Poet', Clare's attitude to critics and criticism was never straight-forward. Forever anxious, especially in the early years, to see what the reviewers had to say, he was none the less able, no doubt partly as a result of his own experiences, to develop a sustained scorn for the critics and their views. If he found himself caught between a desire to herald himself, or to be heralded, as the native genius of 'humble Helpstone' and a wish to curl up, like Wordsworth's Lucy, 'A violet by a mossy stone / Half hidden from the eye', so he expected praise ('Fair as a star, when only one / Is shining in the sky') from the very quarter he might have least welcomed it. If Sir Richard Phillips of the *Monthly Magazine* could only offer 'meek milk and water' criticism,[2]

28

then Clare could do without it. As so often, he was caught on the horns of an impossible dilemma. But, with his typical wit, he was eventually able to form some kind of critical theory about the state of the contemporary critical play of which he seemed increasingly to fall foul. When he awaited publication of his final volume, *The Rural Muse*, it was only his 'severe indisposition' that made him 'careless almost of either censure or praise'.[3] In any case, we should not underestimate the strength of that 'almost'. No writer can afford to be careless of his critical reception. Yet Clare had witnessed some rather extraordinary effects of the whirligig of time, criticism and fashion: against Byron's popularity could be set the fate of Keats.

The claims of posterity against passing fashion form the bulwark of Clare's *Essay on Popularity* (1825), one of the few pieces of prose published in his own lifetime:

Popularity is a busy talker she catches hold of topics & offers them to fame without giving herself time to reflect wether they are true or false & fashion is her favourite deciple who sanctions & believes them as eagerly & with the same faith as a young lady in the last century read a new novel & a tavern-haunter in this reads the News it is natural with such foundations to ask wether popularity is fame.[4]

Clare goes on to write, rather confusingly if not confusedly, about a number of aspects of common life that have had their portion of fame or popularity; but it could be argued that the confusion is part of the point. The dividing line between popularity and deserved fame is a fine one, and Byron offers himself, as Clare acknowledges, as a convenient exception that proves the rule. Shakespeare, on the other hand, according to Clare, enjoyed little popularity in his own time but is now not only known but ten times greater than Byron. Clare is tempted to have his cake and eat it, for Byron's appeal has been to the common people, rather than to the critics. However much Clare might go on to urge the claims of Wordsworth ('his lack of living praise is no proof of his lack of genius – the trumpeting clamour of public praise is not to be relied on as the creditor for the future'), he is clearly fascinated by the way Byron broke all the rules:

He looked upon critics as the countryman does on a magistrate he beheld them as a race of petty tyrents that stood in the way of genius they were in his eyes more of stumbling blocks than guides & he treated them accordingly he let them know there was another road to parnassus without taking theirs & being obliged to do them homage not stooping to the impediments of their

authorities like the paths of a besieged city encumbered with sentinels he
made a road for himself & like Napoleon crossing the Alps he let the world
see that even in the eye of a mortal their greatest obstacles were looked on
as 'the dust in a ballance' he gained the envied eminence of living
popularity by making a breach were it was thought impregnable were
others had laid siege for a lifetime & lost their hopes & their labour at last
he gained the parnassus of popularity by a single stride & looked down as a
freebooter on the world below scorning the applause that his labour had
gained him & scarcely returning a compliment for the laurels which fashion
so eagerly bound round his brows – while he saw the alarm of his leaden-
footed enemies & withered them to nothings with his sneer he was an Oliver
Cromwell with the critics he broke up their long-standing Parliament &
placed his own will in the speaker's chair & his will they humbly accepted.

This is a crucial passage; not only is Clare evidently enjoying Byron's
stinging rebuke to the critics, he relishes the political implications of
what Byron has done. He might describe himself, in another context,
as a 'King & Country' man,[5] but in terms of the politics of criticism,
he is definitely a republican. We should not be surprised at Clare's
moving account of Byron's funeral on his third visit to London, when
the cortege passes, and a young girl sighs and utters 'poor Lord
Byron', and Clare says 'I coud almost feel in love with her for the sigh
she had uttered for the poet   it was worth all the News paper puffs
and Magazine Mournings that ever was paraded after the death of a
poet since flattery and hypoc[ris]y was babtizd as the name of truth
and sincerity.'[6] Once again a brief quotation underplays the
significance of this episode for Clare's view of himself; his relation, on
the one hand, to poetic tradition, and, on the other, to the 'common
people' who 'are the best feelings of a prophecy of futurity... they are
the veins and arterys that feed and quiken the heart of living fame
the breathings of eternity and the soul of time are indicated in that
prophecy'. This wonderful biographical moment brings us back full
circle to the apparent contradiction in the *Essay on Popularity*. Byron
is indeed the exception that proves the rule.

   Keats is less fortunate, but no less important as a yardstick. Clare
scoffs at the claims of Campbell and Rogers when set alongside
Keats: they

must be fine very fine   Because they are the critics own childern nursd in
the critics garden & prund by the fine polishing knifes of the critics – they
must be good no soul dare say otherwise – it woud be out of the fashion –
dont ye think a critic like a gardener uses his pruning knife very often to keep

it in action & find as he calls it a job – an old proverb is among us – 'a gardener woud cut his fathers head off were he a tree' so woud the other if his father was a book – to keep his hand in –[7]

Keats does not belong in such an ordered garden, he is 'a child of nature warm & wild'. It is worth remembering that Clare's full-blown anger at the 'cursd critics' has grown out of their obsession with 'their rule & compass' when it comes to the sonnet. Anticipating Byron in this respect, in his blithe irreverence, Keats 'la[u]nches on the sea without compass – & mounts pegassus without saddle or bridle as usual'. Significantly, only a week later, Clare is praising Wordsworth as a sonneteer for his wildness, his 'lunatic Enthuseism of nature', defying 'all art', as against Milton, who is only too conscious of the rules.[8] Rather like the sacred caverns in Xanadu, the wildness represented by Keats and Byron and Wordsworth is a direct challenge to the stately pleasure dome of the formal garden beloved of the critics: it is Milton who sits 'down to write according to the rul[es of] art in the construction of the Sonnet just as a architect sets about abuilding'. If it is possible (as it surely is) to see a political dimension to 'Kubla Khan', then Clare makes a political point with reference to Keats that anticipates what he was to say about Byron. In lamenting the neglect into which Keats's work has fallen so soon after his tragic death, he cries out indignantly:

is the cold hearted butchers of annonymous Critics to cut up everything that escapes their bribery or thinks contrary to them is polotics to rule genius – if it is – honesty & worth may turn swindlers & liberty be thrown to the dogs & worried out of existance – & that she has been long ago –[9]

The tyranny of fashion is such a recurrent theme in Clare's writings that it cannot lightly be dismissed; he chews at it in his poems and his letters. His sense of integrity will not allow him to agree even with his friend Allan Cunningham's review of his work: 'his observation that Poets should conform their thoughts or style to the taste of the country by which he means fashion – is humbug & shows that he has no foundation of judgment for a critic that might be relyed on his lights lead astray'.[10] A rather similar battle had been fought by Wordsworth and Coleridge in the preface of 1800 to *Lyrical Ballads*, where the radical claims of the imagination were urged with rather greater force than someone like Robert Southey was usually prepared to echo. It is worth reminding ourselves that behind *Lyrical Ballads* lay a debate on the possible democratisation of poetry, and that this was not a matter of the 'taste of the country' but, on the contrary, a political and literary radicalism.

Clare knows that 'Fashion is a fine dog'; but he knows too that it is 'a very false one it barks at shadows & lets monsters of every description pass by to its ladys library without a growl'.[11] He can be comic here, but there is no room for laughter when he contemplates the death of Hazlitt in 1830. He recognises the man's originality and genius, all the more so because so few others do: 'when will the cant & hypocrasy of trifling be put aside & the sterling merit of superior minds be so valued as to be considerd worthy of universal reward & the humbug of party cavils & party interest be done away with'[12] Clare's answer to his own question has all the bleakness of a truth felt upon the pulses: 'I doubt never'. At the beginning of the same year, he had had cause to consider some of the wilder excesses of fashion. As the country struggled with the consequences of recession – a severe depression in agriculture and industry leading on a personal level to what Clare tersely calls 'sales & bankrupts' – John Nash's rather extreme solution to the problem of reconstructing Buckingham House (knocking down the wings of the forecourt to create Buckingham Palace), prompted Clare to resort to a concept of taste that would certainly have had Wordsworth cheering in 1800 (though not in 1830): 'taste now has nothing to do with such things where fashion is every thing & royal fashions too they must be excellent or it woud evidently be considered radicalism to think otherwise'.[13]

In a similar vein, Clare writes to his good friend, the translator H. F. Cary. Clare has been reading Erasmus Darwin's poetry, and cannot understand his neglect:

I am no Critic & my judgment goes no further then being pleased in itself not having the confidence to feel what is likely to please others – I think many Poets only want to be more known to be more esteemed & admired & that the neglect is only owing to the Publics finding no path that leads to their beautys – it is something like the case of the 'Sleeping Beauty' that had remained so long unkown in her pallace of Solitude that the paths which led to it were all choaked up & over grown with trees & brushwood that took the knight errant even a number of years to cut them down ere he could get at his prize & break the spell of solitude that bound her beauty in its almost impenetrable veil – I think it is so with once popular poets they only want to be known agen to be esteemd dont you think so[14]

Once again, Clare hits on a beautifully apt image for the hidden beauties of long-lost or unknown poets and, once again, as he had, in an earlier letter, linked himself with George Darley in a turn back to a previous age where they both might find their spiritual ancestors, so here he effectively allies himself not only with Darwin but also with his correspondent, the rather shy translator of Dante, himself not one to curry fashion's favour.

Whilst Clare is looking back here, as so often, he is also looking ahead, forward to a time when the path will be beaten to his door, and he too will be kissed into life by some 'knight errant'. He had, after all, just endured one of the most galling entries into a blankly hostile critical world. The delays to *The Shepherd's Calendar* meant that it appeared at a time when Taylor felt that 'the time [had] passed away in which Poetry will answer'; Taylor even went so far as to say that he thought the public no longer knew what poetry was.[15] Clare's response had been realistic:

I feel very dissapointed at the bad sale of the new Poems but I cannot help it if the public will not read ryhmes   to tell them what they ought to think of poetry would be as vain as telling the blind to see   the age of Taste is in dotage & grown old in its youth[16]

Small wonder that one of Clare's most carefully worked and deeply felt poems is called 'Shadows of Taste'. Small wonder, too, that in the following January, in response to what he sees as an unseemly flood of praise from James Montgomery, he protests that 'all I aspire to is that I may win a nitch among the minor bards in the memory of my country & I shall be content to live a flower under the shelter of the laurels & Bays of my more high & deserving Brothers in Song'.[17]

It is, indeed, this 'small nitch' that he has occupied for much of the long time since he first appeared before the public in 1820; to some extent he has fulfilled his own prophecy. Yet posterity, as he hoped, has also come to his aid, and we are now prepared to make claims he himself would have demurred at in those years when he felt that his best critic was his publisher, John Taylor. When he is asked by Taylor to write some essays on the sublime and the beautiful he replies: 'I so seldom see other peoples judgments who are considered not only men of taste but men of unerring critisism coinciding with mine that I feel I am only an individual indulging in an erroneous fancy'.[18] Characteristically, he sees the modern age as one that has perverted taste for the sake of fashion, leaving all notions of the natural far behind, and his only consolation is that eventually 'nature will be herself again & nature will out live them all'.

What is true of fashion and criticism is true of his own poetry and that of those he considers his peers. When he defends Bloomfield in 1824 against Byron's attack in *English Bards and Scotch Reviewers* he does so partly in his favourite terms, those of posterity and nature: 'his poems will meet posterity as green & growing on the bosom of English nature & the muses as those of the Peer';[19] but he defends him also because Bloomfield belongs to the same group as himself, Cunningham and James Hogg, all of them 'looked upon as intruders & stray cattle in the fields of the Muses'. They are all outside the accepted canon, but 'never mind, we will do our best'. Like Wordsworth's Idiot Boy, Clare knows that doing one's best can be quite sufficient, that it can, in fact, constitute a kind of glory. However, it is the kind of knowledge that is hard won and difficult to hold onto; that is Clare's problem, and the major reason for his continuous debate, throughout his publishing life, with critics and about the nature of criticism.

In the prospectus he published in 1818, to drum up subscribers for his first book, Clare did his best to forestall what he called 'the iron hand of *Criticism*' by blatantly appealing to the public's necessary awareness of his circumstances. Referring to those early poems, he wrote: 'It is hoped that the humble situation which distinguishes their author will be some excuse in their favour, and serve to make an atonement for the many inaccuracies and imperfections that will be found in them.'[20] Not until the preface to *The Shepherd's Calendar* in 1827 did he feel sufficiently confident to press his claims on other grounds. For nearly ten years, any discussion of the relative merits of Clare's poetry had to address the issue of his origins; and much later, when his work came to be re-read at the end of the nineteenth and the beginning of the twentieth centuries, the same considerations regularly dominated the debate. The close connection between the man, the work and social class has been a recurrent theme, scarcely surprising when criticism has been as unsure about its footing as Clare himself.

John Taylor's introduction to *Poems Descriptive of Rural Life and Scenery* might seem, initially, to be hedging its bets rather cunningly, with an opening sentence of veiled ambiguity: 'The following Poems will probably attract some notice by their intrinsic merit; but they are also entitled to attention from the circumstances under which they were written.'[21] In fact, he presents a persuasive case

for his poet, making something of a virtue out of that potentially awkward, if necessary, connection between life and work. For a
start, his biographical account is free of the uneasy playfulness that
had marred Gilchrist's attempt;[22] and Taylor can see that Clare
turns what he thought of as a deficiency – the frustrations of
someone with an inadequate vocabulary and style – to his own
advantage. Taylor is in fact one of the very few early writers to talk
directly about Clare's language, a topic that has only recently
begun to be fully explored. He recognises that Clare is forced into
linguistic and grammatical innovation of a kind that links him with
all the best poets of the English tradition. Furthermore, Taylor is
prepared to defend Clare's provincialisms, as they take us back to
what he calls 'the unwritten language of England'. In other words,
there are more traditions than just the literary one, and in extolling
the virtues of an oral, non-literary tradition, to which Clare is so
deeply attached, Taylor anticipates the drift of recent critics who
have accepted that the word 'peasant' can be more than a
sociological put-down (whether self-inflicted or not) – that it can in
fact represent an oral culture and a local culture every bit as valuable as the established, literate and literary one. To this extent, it
is as though Taylor sees the connection between Clare and
Wordsworth.

One of Wordsworth's aims in the *Lyrical Ballads* had been to appeal
to that wider constituency, bred on the sustenance of a ballad
tradition; twenty years later, here is Clare emerging as a representative figure of that very constituency. By a nice kind of poetic
justice, Taylor is able, in praising Clare's novelty and originality, to
quote Wordsworth: 'the Poetry of the period intervening between
the publication of the Paradise Lost, and the Seasons, does not
contain a single new image of external nature'. It is not that Clare
sees himself in competition with others who have tackled this
problem, but rather that he cannot help himself. 'He is most
thoroughly the poet as well as the child of nature', declares Taylor,
thereby rebuking Mrs Emmerson's repeated insistence that Clare is
primarily 'nature's child':

and, according to his opportunities, no poet has more completely devoted
himself to her service, studied her more closely, or exhibited so many
sketches of her under new and interesting appearances...He loves the fields,
the flowers, 'the common air, the sun, the skies;' and, therefore, he writes
about them.[23]

There is something wonderfully accepting about that 'therefore'. There is no need to suppose that to talk of 'love' is to sentimentalise Clare. It would be fair to say that Taylor presents the best possible case for Clare, on the basis of a volume that is one of promise rather than fulfilment.

Not all the reviews of *Poems Descriptive* were ready to accept Taylor's terms for the debate. It is instructive to see how the *New Monthly Magazine* can move from apparent praise for Clare's 'true and minute delineations of external nature, drawn from *actual observation*' to the more damningly restrictive qualification, 'Clare is strictly a descriptive poet'.[24] This is a move that is to be repeated countless times, right up to the present day. It allows cold water to be poured on the grammatical 'inaccuracies' and provincialisms which Taylor had seen as part and parcel of Clare's vision. Rather more helpfully, the *Monthly Review* decided that the reader should not be distracted by the biographical details, since these were, so far as aesthetic judgement went, irrelevant:

> though it is very honourable to him that he has surmounted [his disadvantages], they can neither add to nor detract from their poetic excellence. If they were, indeed, totally devoid of this quality, Clare might be applauded, and rewarded for exertions so singular in his sphere of life, but the sooner his writings were forgotten the better. This, however, is not the case; since, though his pieces are very defective in expression, and frequently in grammar, they manifest the spirit and truth of poetry.[25]

Whereas Taylor had been anxious to balance the biographical with the critical comments, the *Monthly Review* takes a more radically aesthetic line which, interestingly, does not mean that Clare's poetry gets consigned to oblivion. Of course, the 'spirit and truth of poetry' remain out of the reach of ready definition, but it is to the *Monthly Review*'s credit that it makes the crucial distinction between Clare's detailed minuteness, and those poets 'who have generalised the beauties of nature'. As it points out, Clare 'frequently introduces images which, according to our preconceived notions, can scarcely be called poetical'; but these notions derive from the generalising tradition which Clare is challenging. Once again, we might hear echoes of the Advertisement to *Lyrical Ballads*; and just as Hazlitt praised, in his ambiguous way, Wordsworth's 'levelling Muse', the *Monthly Review* says that 'with [Clare] there is no *aristocracy of beauty*, but the stag and the hog, the weed and the flower, find an equal place in his verse'. It seems preferable to dwell on this insight, rather than on the faintly dismissive comparison with the apparently superior Burns; the latter is common, and seldom made to Clare's advantage, whilst it is rarer for a critic to see the virtues of a 'levelling Muse'. Timothy Brownlow's recent persuasive account of Clare's use of a 'molehill for Parnassus' belongs to this same tradition of acknowledging Clare's essentially democratic opening of the poetic realm.[26]

John Scott's review in the *London Magazine* extended this argument in an important direction by putting the emphasis on place.[27] True, there were predictable comments on the detail of the poetry, its charm, 'true' 'sentiment', the 'unchangeable faith in [Providence's] goodness' – the latter a source of comfort to more than just Lord Radstock and Mrs Emmerson. Yet, these comments, though representative, are less significant than what Scott has to say about Clare's 'ardent attachment to places'. For Scott, 'Helpstone' provides an example of what he calls this 'amiable tendency'. Perhaps it is only later, with poems such as 'Decay', 'Remembrances' and 'The Flitting', that we can see how close Scott is to a recognition of the centrality of place in Clare's poetry. It was not until 1972, when a critical book on Clare was deemed allowable, that John Barrell was able to explore fully the ramifications of this 'sense of place', in a way that has seldom been surpassed.[28]

It was left to the *Eclectic Review* (and most probably the poet Josiah Conder) to redefine the terms of the debate. Whilst recognising the significance for Clare's development, and for his critical reception, of the biographical details, the *Eclectic* was prepared to put these to one side in favour of a critical view that placed Clare firmly along the axis of Blake, Wordsworth and Coleridge. It is not surprising, in what we loosely call the Romantic period, to find the term 'genius' frequently bandied about in discussions of Clare; but it is refreshing to find someone sufficiently confident of the critical ground to refer directly to Coleridge for sanction of Clare's distinctiveness. He ceases to be another 'peasant poet', and becomes an archetypal Romantic poet, as readily linked to the vision of Blake as to that of Wordsworth and Coleridge, to that of *Songs of Innocence and of Experience* as that of *Lyrical Ballads*.

If it be the characteristic privilege of genius, as distinguishable from mere talent, 'to carry on the feelings of childhood into the powers of the man,' – to combine the child's sense of wonder and novelty with the every day appearances of nature,
    With sun and moon and stars throughout the year,

With man and woman, –
and if there be any truth in the assertion, that, 'so to represent familiar
objects as to awaken the minds of others to a like healthy freshness of
sensation concerning them, is its most unequivocal mode of manifestation,'
[Coleridge] – there can be no hesitation in classing the Author of these
poems, to whatsoever rank in society he should prove to belong, among the
most genuine possessors of this dangerous gift.[29]

With our advantage of hindsight, with the asylum poems in mind, we
can see how prophetic this comment is.

References to genius were not always helpful. Gilchrist had another
try at Clare when he reviewed *Poems Descriptive* for the *Quarterly
Review*,[30] and he was conscious of the dangers of comparisons with
Burns and Bloomfield. The *Anti Jacobin* was to proclaim Clare a
'second Burns',[31] the *British Critic* was to advise him to avoid Burns as
a model;[32] Gilchrist saw that the differences in their lives made for
differences in their poetry. He could not grant to Clare the wit or
pathos of Burns, but saw in him 'a vivacity, and a delicacy in
describing rural scenery, which the mountain bard has not often
surpassed'. Gilchrist had already diagnosed Clare as a 'creature of
feeling rather than fancy', and this enabled him to distinguish
between Clare and Bloomfield:

Clare writes frequently from the same suggestions; but his subject is always
enlivened by picturesque and minute description of the landscape around
him, and deepened, as we have said, with a powerful reference to emotions
within. The one is descriptive, the other contemplative.

This is a distinction that has not always been made, but any critics
anxious to further Clare's claims have sooner or later had to
acknowledge its truth. J. G. Lockhart in *Blackwood's Edinburgh
Magazine* was happy to echo the *Guardian*'s denial of genius;[33] if Burns
was to be brought into the argument, it should be as a warning. 'Let
them [his patrons] pause and think of the fate of the far more highly-
gifted Burns, and beware alike of the foolish zeal and the sinful
neglect of *his* countrymen.'

On the publication of *The Village Minstrel* in 1821, the *Monthly
Magazine* attacked the whole concept of genius, the whole fashion for
the 'uneducated' and the 'obscure' to come forth with their poetical
wares.

Ploughmen, milkmaids, and other similar prodigies have thus acquired an
ephemeral celebrity; and the error of these writers appears to us far more

excusable than that of their professed admirers, in mistaking the very common disease of a love for rhyming, for that rare poetic genius which, in all ages, has been accorded only to a favoured few.[34]

Comparisons with Burns, Bloomfield, even Beattie, were of no use to such as Clare. Just as the *Literary Gazette*,[35] whilst acknowledging an apparent improvement in Clare's second volume, complained that Clare remained too irredeemably provincial (and dangerously radical in his use of vulgar language), too intent on setting his sights on the lowly, humdrum scenes around him, so the *Monthly Magazine* could not bring itself to more than faint praise: 'But we fear, when every allowance is made, that sober judges will hardly be disposed to assign these poems at the utmost, a place above mediocrity'. This was a harsh put-down (and the *Monthly Magazine* was not alone in resorting to the Horatian dismissal of mediocrities), but it was partly prompted by the claims that Taylor had made in his introduction to *The Village Minstrel*. This introduction, and Taylor's later essay, prompted by a visit to Clare at Helpston, deserve fuller consideration.

After providing, in his introduction, further biographical details, Taylor was reluctant to say too much about particular poems.[36] He was all too conscious of what he called the 'illiberal spirit of criticism' to go in for any of the special pleading he had been tempted into a year before. The fate of Keats at the hands of the reviewers was much in his mind, so much so that, in spite of his natural caution, he made a direct comparison between Keats and Clare. Clare was embarrassed by the comparison, and Taylor made the reference more oblique by removing Keats's name; none the less, the claim for Clare was a considerable one. It is one thing to be, for better or worse, another Bloomfield or Burns; this is something rather different.

Clare has created more of these never-dying forms, in the personification of things inanimate and abstract, – he has scattered them more profusely about our paths, than perhaps any poet of the age except one; – and having contributed so much to our gratification, what ought we to render him in return? – He deserves our favour…our thanks…our sympathy…and our regard and admiration…

No one had been prepared to make this leap, and this is an important historical moment in the development of Clare criticism; it is all the more important in that Taylor relates this generosity and fecundity of Clare's imagination to its apparent obverse, his sense of loss. Taylor

clearly does not understand the full force of the letter he quotes, and
therefore of the centrality of loss to Clare's vision; but by quoting
Clare's letter he allows his voice to ring out, placing him in a line from
Cowper to Hopkins. Once we have heard that voice, the old category
of 'descriptive' poet ceases to have much force:

My two favourite elm trees at the back of the hut are condemned to die –
it shocks me to relate it, but 'tis true. The savage who owns them thinks they
have done their best, and now he wants to make use of the benefits he can
get from selling them. O was this country Egypt, and was I but a caliph, the
owner should lose his ears for his arrogant presumption; and the first wretch
that buried his axe in their roots should hang on their branches as a terror
to the rest. I have been several mornings to bid them farewel

   Taylor returned to this collocation of celebration of what is seen,
and mourning for its loss, in his account of 'A Visit to John Clare',
published in the *London Magazine* in November 1821.[37] Several people
had spoken of Clare's ability to write about the ordinary, the
Wordsworthian 'common' things of life. Taylor had cause to think
precisely of Wordsworth when he heard Clare's account of the origin
of the poem 'The Last of March', prompted by a chance encounter
at Lolham Brigs:

I question whether Wordsworth's pedlar could have spoken more to the
purpose... to me, the triumph of true genius seemed never more conspicuous,
than in the construction of so interesting a poem out of such common-place
materials. With your own eyes you see nothing but a dull line of ponds, or
rather one continued marsh, over which a succession of arches carries the
narrow highway: look again, with the poem in your mind, and the wand of
a necromancer seems to have been employed in conjuring up a host of
beautiful accompaniments, making the whole waste populous with life, and
shedding all around the rich lustre of a grand and appropriate sentiment.
Imagination has, in my opinion, done wonders here, and especially in the
concluding verse, which contains as lovely a groupe as ever was called into
life by the best 'makers' of any age or country.

That most astute of twentieth-century readers of John Clare, the poet
and critic Geoffrey Grigson, was wise, in his introduction to *The
Selected Poems of John Clare* (1950),[38] to seek Taylor's authority, in this
passage, for his own view of Clare as a poet whose imagination could,
in the Wordsworthian sense, transform the commonplace. Taylor
was wise also to turn for such celebratory vision to that darker sense
of loss and decay that imbued Clare's poem on Langley Bush. He

hears the 'melancholy cadence' in a poem whose end foreshadows so much of Clare's later verse:

> My last doubts murmur on the zephyr's swell.
> My last look lingers on thy boughs with pain;
> To thy declining age I bid farewel,
> Like old companions, ne'er to meet again.

Taylor is also readier than his contemporaries to praise Clare's provincial language, its energy and appropriateness: 'Clare is highly commendable for not *affecting* a language, and it is a proof of the originality of his genius'. We can see how Clare and Taylor had much in common against the fashion of the times, against the rules of the critics in wolf's clothing. Anxious to establish Clare's originality, Taylor sees it precisely in his language:

In poetry, especially, you may estimate the originality of the thoughts by that of the language; but this is a canon to which our approved critics will not subscribe: they allow of no phrase which has not received the sanction of authority, no expression for which, in the sense used, you cannot plead a precedent. They would fetter the English poet as much as they circumscribe the maker of Latin verses, and yet they complain that our modern poets want originality!

Clare's originality is a challenge to the age, 'for we abound with machinery'.

Josiah Conder must have read Taylor's essay, for in an unsigned review in the *Eclectic Review* the following January he pursues the image with almost Carlylean fervour.

This is the age of mechanism. Mechanism of all kinds has been carried to its utmost perfection; and poetry, that exquisite species of mechanism, has, like every thing else, been wrought up to a steam-engine nicety. The same increased facility of production, too, which has overstocked with cottons our foreign markets, has produced a glut of literary commodities, especially in the article of verse, at home... In other words, there is no want of good poetry: that is, lively, sparkling, elegant, classical, clever composition, – composition as superior to these poems of our Northamptonshire Peasant, as a Dutch tulip is to a hedge-row violet.[39]

The distinction between the mechanical and the material helps Conder to see something of Clare's value, even if it draws him into one of the first of many comparisons with pictorial artists, in this case Morland's 'inimitable drawings'. When he turns to *The Village Minstrel*, and its particular form of social verisimilitude, the pictorial analogy is again brought into play: 'It is not Westall, but Wilkie, that could alone transfer the portrait to canvass.'

References to the visual arts are always tempting; different critics resort to them in different ways, apparently able to damn or praise a poet according to which artist is pulled out of the hat. Conder uses the parallel with Morland again when he reviews *The Shepherd's Calendar* in 1827, again to Clare's advantage.[40] However, Hazlitt had learnt that to liken Crabbe to the Dutch painters was a neat form of critical attack.[41] This underlines the critical problem: how was the originality, the genius, of 'description' to be accounted for? Many critics were content, as was the Reverend W. Allen, in his series of lengthy critical essays addressed to Lord Radstock in 1823, to harp on the theme of simplicity, and to account for the success of the descriptive element by talk of Clare's being, again and still, a 'child of nature'.[42] The pictorial analogy was an attempt to counter such rhetoric, but it became as rhetorical in effect as talk of inspiration and genius. Once again, it seems that it was John Taylor who was most conscious of the problem. With the growth and publication of *The Shepherd's Calendar*, he begins to feel uneasy about what he sees as the sameness of what Clare has been writing. A glance at the heated debate over *The Shepherd's Calendar* will show something of the critical problem as Taylor sees it from his rather different angle.

Quite contrary to what he had said even five years earlier, Taylor told Clare on 4 March 1826:

I have often remarked that your Poetry is much the best when you are not describing common Things, and if you would raise your views generally & Speak of the Appearances of Nature each Month more philosophically (if I may say so) or with more Excitement, you would greatly improve these little poems; some parts of the November are extremely good – others are too prosaic – they have too much of the language of common every Day Description; – faithful I grant they are, but that is not all... You wish to make it a complete Record of Country affairs. I would have you only make a Selection of the Circumstances that will best tell in Poetry.[43]

Hessey had said something similar two years earlier: 'The great fault of the whole of them is that they abound too much in mere description & are deficient in Sentiment and Feeling and human Interest.'[44] The problem was partly one of repetition. Clare had written about all these things before, and the public now expected something more; Clare could not remain a 'descriptive poet'; the incidents of common life 'must be subordinate to higher objects'.

This kind of criticism had been lurking from the very beginning, in one form or another. Relatively few had been prepared to accept Taylor's embrace of Clare's commonplaceness; the call had been for greater reflection. Hessey's suggestion for *The Shepherd's Calendar*, as early as October 1823, had been for 'a human interest – a Story or a more particular delineation of character',[45] and this led Clare to produce a number of Crabbe-like narrative poems which at times he was inclined to think preferable to the 'Descriptive Pieces'. Taylor was not much happier with what Clare busied himself with after *The Shepherd's Calendar*: 'Summer Images', for example, which drew rhapsodic praise from Mrs Emmerson, was 'too long, too little select – you have gathered into it many Images which you have given before in Language sometimes more happy, – & it rambles too much'.[46]

In the reviews, not only was Clare charged with repetitiveness, he was accused of lack of a sense of form. The virtues that Taylor and others had seen in Clare's early work had ceased to be virtues; the old terms had apparently outlived their usefulness. Even Josiah Conder, so long a supporter of Clare, and still able to applaud his detailed observation, his narrative strain, and his determination to 'stand on his own bottom', would have liked a higher, religious strain.[47] The *London Weekly Review* could barely conceal its hilarity: 'Wretched taste, poverty of thought, and unintelligible phraseology'.[48] There was comfort to be had from the *Literary Chronicle*, but again it was the recycling of the old bogeymen, Burns and genius.[49] The author meant well, and Clare was pleased, especially as 'The Dream' was commended for its Byronic strength. In view of his later Byronic persona, this has some prophetic significance, more so, perhaps, than Thomas Clarke's resort to the old coinage of simplicity and pictorial detail in the *Druids' Monthly* (in response to *The Rural Muse* in 1835),[50] or the *Athenaeum*'s approval of the same volume (again, Bloomfield and genius are the touchstones).[51] John Wilson's long retrospective account of Clare, in *Blackwood's Edinburgh Magazine*,[52] was one of the first attempts to see Clare whole. Yet, sadly, he did not see Clare freshly, and was still prepared to place Clare below Bloomfield.

By the time E. P. Hood wrote his account of Clare in *The Literature of Labour* (1851),[53] Clare was, as he said, 'confined in an asylum in the neighbourhood of Northampton'. Hood's task was ambitious: he aimed at an account of Clare's achievement, ranging over the whole of the available *oeuvre*. There is a streak of religious sentimentality

that vitiates Hood's view of Clare, but he recognises some truths that
had been allowed to slip out of sight as Clare had become the
battleground for others' wars. Hood recognises the value for Clare of
the natural world in all its raw surface detail, in all its abundance, in
its quirky individuality and strange equality in which 'every object in
Nature [is] a beloved object, because the whole is beloved'. But he
also sees, as Taylor and Hessey and others had been unwilling to do,
that Clare reaches out towards 'Fancy, Feeling, and Philosophy or
Reflection'; poems such as 'The Eternity of Nature' are an acknowledgement of the fact that 'to the simplest things in Nature, to his
eye, there is entwined a spirit sublime and lasting'. As Hood rather
nicely puts it:

Eternal youth and eternal mystery, the unfading beauty and the unfading
sublimity of Nature – these are everywhere seen; seen as remarkably in the
most insignificant as in the most majestic. The fancies and the freaks of
Nature are a sort of pledge of unfailing truthfulness.

In the claims that he was prepared to make for Clare, Hood was
anticipating the debate that would ensue upon Clare's death. J. L.
Cherry's *Life and Remains of John Clare* of 1873[54] was also an attempt
to look at Clare whole, and to address in particular the critical
implications of the asylum verse. Ever since then, the debate as to
Clare's stature has had to confront the complicating and desolating
fact of his years in the asylum. The initial response was scarcely wildly
enthusiastic. The pathos and the tragedy were readily acknowledged,
but the *Manchester Guardian*[55] was not speaking merely for itself when
it dismissed Clare's claims to be considered above 'the Kirke White,
Ebenezer Elliott, David Gray, and Bloomfield class of poets – a small
but rare band, whose noble rage, in spite of the poet's words, chill
penury did not repress, and the genial current of whose soul was not
frozen by their poverty'. Richard Heath's comments on Clare dated
originally from 1873, but they were collected in book form, in *The
English Peasant*, in 1893.[56] Clare's first centenary, then, saw him being
celebrated as 'the poet of English peasant life... Clare lived it, felt its
joys, and endured all its woes'. The poetry has got lost somewhere in
the sociological comment. As the century dribbled away, Clare's star
was hardly in the ascendant.

As so often with Clare, it has been the editors who have effected
changes in the way his work has been viewed. Arthur Symons's
selection of 1908 was as important as any in this respect.[57] It could be

argued that he was consciously shaping Clare for the twentieth century. Symons at least felt confident in placing Clare above Bloomfield and shifting the whole nature of the 'peasant poet' debate. Far from being a peasant in the accepted sense, Clare was a poet who happened to have been born into an environment where he did not really belong; he was a restless wanderer who could not bear change. 'He was torn up by the roots, and the flower of his mind withered.' Symons is persuaded that this deracination 'exalted him as a poetic consciousness, and that the verse written in the asylum is of a rarer and finer quality than any of the verse written while he was at liberty and at home'. This can be related to Symons's emphasis on the childlike vision, another of those themes running throughout so much of Clare criticism; he realises that what gives a poem like *The Shepherd's Calendar* its force is the recollection of that childhood vision, the recollection of things as they were in all their clarity and precision; and what is true of *The Shepherd's Calendar* is so much truer of the asylum verse.

Symons's volume prompted others to make their own claims and counterclaims for Clare. Edward Thomas, by calling Clare's asylum poems 'songs of innocence',[58] makes the increasingly frequent connection with Blake; it was perhaps this that led Hugh Walker to feel confident in applying the word 'great' to Clare's work.[59] Alan Porter,[60] having worked with Edmund Blunden on *Poems Chiefly from Manuscript* (London, 1920), declared the poet's greatness with a stridency that led J. C. Squire to insist that

we must keep our sense of proportion. We have enough of Clare's work to be certain that we shall never think him a great poet. Even a 'final' edition of him must be a selection. Clare was not a Keats or a Shelley that his feeblest fragments must be scoured for and perpetuated; an edition of him in ten volumes would be a monument not to his genius but to an admirer's folly.[61]

This is coat-trailing with a vengeance; and seventy years later it is fair to say that such an edition, now in progress, is viewed rather differently. Hugh Massingham was quite clear in 1921 that it was no longer sufficient to think of Clare as a minor poet;[62] this was because of Clare's uniqueness of voice and vision, his ability to lose himself in 'the inner life of nature' in an almost Keatsian way. Massingham also saw, perhaps more clearly than anyone before him, the relation between the pre-asylum and asylum verse. Although Clare was uprooted, the paradoxical effect was for 'him to become more imaginative, and at the same time more closely drawn into the truth behind the forms of nature...what he lost in the acute sense of a particular locality, he gained in a wider interpretation'. This is to anticipate the arguments of more recent critics such as John Barrell and Thomas Frosch, although they both see the shift in rather different ways.[63]

In contrast to Massingham and Porter, John Middleton Murry found himself in something of a cleft stick, deeply admiring much of Clare's work, but certain that Clare was not a great poet and determined not to succumb to the dangers of over-enthusiasm.[64] In spite of his hesitations, Murry displays a rare sympathy for Clare's achievement. He almost finds himself placing Clare above Wordsworth: 'one is tempted for a moment to believe that while Wordsworth was engaged in putting the poetry of nature wrong by linking it to a doubtful metaphysic, John Clare was engaged in putting it right.' However, the qualifications he makes are reminiscent of some of the earlier comments about Clare's lack of form; for Murry, Clare 'had nothing of the principle of inward growth' of a Wordsworth, and none of Keats's gift for loading every rift with ore. In turning to 'Song's Eternity' as 'Clare's most perfect poem', Murry unfortunately emphasises the artlessness of Clare's verse, and we are back with the untutored child's vision: 'as with Shelley's skylark, his art was unpremeditated and his strains profuse'. Before long, the corollary of this is confronted: 'he did not know when to stop'. It is not that Murry cannot see Clare's virtues; what he says about Clare's relationship with the natural world, about his observation and impulsiveness as a poet, had not been better put before. He recognises the occasional quirkiness of the vision, its 'absurdity' even, but what he refuses to acknowledge is the art. 'The emotion is hardly mediated at all.' We might ask how this can be, and of course at the same time realise just how much of a hostage Murry is offering to fortune. He says in a later piece that Clare's most enthralling quality is 'the beauty of his seeing';[65] but he does not fully recognise the double-edged nature of 'seeing things', so wonderfully captured, in 1991, by Seamus Heaney's volume of that title.[66]

Edmund Gosse[67] was quick to challenge some of the assumptions lying behind Murry's essays: to some extent these two represent the two extremes of Clare criticism in the early and mid-twentieth century: on the one hand the visionary, naive poet who is almost 'too perfect' (whatever that means), on the other the purely descriptive poet, a De Wint not a Velasquez, with no organic sensibility and no powers of reflection. As far as Gosse is concerned Clare is little better than a camera. Whereas the *Times Literary Supplement* could say in 1935 that Clare's 'place is secure among the poets',[68] without any recourse to the peasant poet label, John Speirs was carping at his limitations, at the lack of development and the dangers of over-praising the asylum verse.[69] It was left to Geoffrey Grigson, in his two seminal volumes, *Poems of John Clare's Madness* (London, 1949) and *Selected Poems of John Clare* (1950), to give an account of Clare that was true to the man and the poet, and which did not hide behind the skirts of critical caution. As he went on to say in an unsigned review in the *Times Literary Supplement* in 1956, Clare was an intruder into the canon in the same way that Hopkins was:[70] part of his value, dangerous as it was, lay precisely in the fact that he challenged most preconceptions, 'since he strips away certain current pretensions about verse-reading..., and since he demands discernment, in a situation not already mapped out and signposted'.

The nature of the literary canon has become a central issue in literary studies in recent years. In the context of this debate, Clare has been seen to have a unique value, since he was so conscious himself of being an outsider, of not belonging to the literary establishment. Attempts (such as Harold Bloom's)[71] to claim for him a place in the canon only as some kind of descendant of Blake or Wordsworth or Coleridge, can be misleading. Some of the most useful work on Clare has been built on the premise that, whatever his literary debts and allegiances, Clare is a poet *sui generis*, and that to demonstrate this it is necessary to look at Clare's work with the kind of detailed, intense gaze that he himself proffered to the world in which he lived. This is not the place to gauge the respective merits of the criticism of the past twenty years; but the roll-call is an honourable one, including such names as John Barrell, Greg Crossan, Timothy Brownlow, Janet Todd, Johanne Clare, Tim Chilcott, Barbara Strang, Kelsey Thornton, Lynne Pearce, Edward Strickland. Each critic has in different ways picked up on aspects of the critical debate that emerged in Clare's lifetime, but which were seldom pushed to their limit; each critic has been bolstered by the belief that Clare is a major poet, without need of apology, a belief first expressed by the much-maligned but invaluable Tibbles.

Finally, it has to be said that none of this recent critical activity would have been likely, let alone possible, without the editorial labours of many people, starting with the Tibbles, but then above all of Eric Robinson and Geoffrey Summerfield. Ever since 1964, the centenary of Clare's death, they have produced (helped by others, notably Margaret Grainger and David Powell), the necessary texts which could form the foundation of critical debate, but which were themselves built on this fundamental belief in Clare's stature as a poet. For this reason, as for many others, we and posterity must be eternally grateful that in 1961 Geoffrey Summerfield began to transcribe Clare's poems from the manuscripts in Northampton Public Library. He realised, in looking at a poet with a distinctive vision, that he too was 'seeing things'.

NOTES

1 Octavius Gilchrist, 'Some account of John Clare, an agricultural labourer and poet', *London Magazine*, 1 (January 1820), 7–11 (reprinted in Mark Storey (ed.), *John Clare: The Critical Heritage* (London, 1973), pp. 35–42). For the sake of convenience, all reviews and comments on Clare are taken from the *Critical Heritage* volume.
2 M. Storey (ed.), *The Letters of John Clare* (Oxford, 1985), p. 217.
3 Ibid. p. 618.
4 J. W. and Anne Tibble (eds.) *The Prose of John Clare* (London, 1951), pp. 206–10.
5 M. Storey, *Letters*, p. 110.
6 Eric Robinson (ed.), *John Clare's Autobiographical Writings* (Oxford, 1983), p. 147.
7 M. Storey, *Letters*, pp. 80–1.
8 Ibid. p. 87.
9 Ibid. pp. 188–9.
10 Quoted in ibid. p. 207.
11 Ibid. p. 463.
12 Ibid. p. 517.
13 Ibid. p. 495.
14 Ibid. p. 403.
15 Quoted in ibid. p. 394.
16 Ibid. p. 394.
17 Ibid. p. 412.
18 Ibid. p. 539.
19 Ibid. pp. 302–3.
20 M. Storey, *Critical Heritage*, p. 30.
21 Ibid. pp. 43–54.
22 See n. 1 above.
23 M. Storey, *Critical Heritage*, p. 66.
24 Ibid. pp. 68–73.

25 Ibid. pp. 73–6.
26 See Timothy Brownlow, *John Clare and Picturesque Landscape* (Oxford, 1983).
27 M. Storey, *Critical Heritage*, pp. 78–80.
28 John Barrell, *The Idea of Landscape and the Sense of Place: 1730–1840: An Approach to the Poetry of John Clare*, (Cambridge, 1972).
29 M. Storey, *Critical Heritage*, pp. 88–92.
30 Ibid. pp. 94–100.
31 Ibid. pp. 105–6.
32 Ibid. pp. 103–4.
33 Ibid. pp. 102–3; for the *Guardian*, ibid. pp. 100–1.
34 Ibid. pp. 150–6.
35 Ibid. pp. 141–5.
36 Ibid. pp. 136–40.
37 Ibid. pp. 157–65.
38 Ibid. p. 404.
39 Ibid. pp. 168–71.
40 Ibid. pp. 202–6.
41 See Walter E. Broman, 'Factors in Crabbe's eminence in the early nineteenth century', *Modern Philology*, 51 (August 1953), 42–9.
42 M. Storey, *Critical Heritage*, pp. 176–82.
43 Ibid. pp. 197–8.
44 Ibid. p. 194.
45 Ibid.
46 Ibid. p. 212.
47 Ibid. pp. 202–6.
48 Ibid. pp. 206–7.
49 Ibid. pp. 208–10.
50 Ibid. pp. 240–4.
51 Ibid. pp. 221–2.
52 Ibid. pp. 225–38.
53 Ibid. pp. 257–66.
54 Ibid. pp. 287–8.
55 Ibid. pp. 290–1.
56 Ibid. pp. 292–7.
57 Ibid. pp. 301–8.
58 Ibid. pp. 311–19.
59 Ibid. pp. 310–11.
60 Ibid. pp. 320–1.
61 Ibid. pp. 323–4.
62 Ibid. pp. 325–8.
63 Barrell, *The Idea of Landscape*; Thomas R. Frosch, 'The descriptive style of John Clare', *Studies in Romanticism*, 10 (1971), 137–49.
64 M. Storey, *Critical Heritage*, pp. 329–39.
65 Ibid. pp. 359–64.

66 Seamus Heaney, *Seeing Things* (London and Boston, 1991).
67 M. Storey, *Critical Heritage*, pp. 343–6.
68 Ibid. pp. 382–4.
69 Ibid. pp. 384–6.
70 Ibid. pp. 416–21; Geoffrey Grigson confirmed that he was the author of this review.
71 Harold Bloom, 'Beddoes, Darley, Clare and others', in *The Visionary Company: A reading of Romantic poetry* (New York, 1961), pp. 428–50; M. Storey, *Critical Heritage*, pp. 428–39.

CHAPTER 3

Progress and Rhyme: 'The Nightingale's Nest' and Romantic poetry

Hugh Haughton

1

The question of John Clare's poetic status remains puzzlingly unresolved. Despite the advocacy of powerful poets, critics and editors, his work still has a curiously marginal, one-off status. It is not seen as part of the major English Romantic literary canon but as a kind of special case. If he is no longer exclusively seen as John Clare 'Northamptonshire Peasant', he is not yet fully recognised as 'John Clare, Poet'.

In 1832, Clare wrote to Eliza Emmerson:

all I wish now is to stand upon my own bottom as a poet without any apology as to want of education or anything else & I say it not in the feeling of either ambition or vanity but in the spirit of common sense[1]

Clare was exasperated by what he took to be the failure of critics and readers to appreciate his poetry on its own terms – or to recognise that he stood, as a poet, on his own 'bottom'.

What was true of Clare's own contemporaries is by and large true today. Criticism has not been able to appropriate John Clare's poetry for its canons – or its institutional languages. It may be that this reflects a failure in Clare, but it might equally reflect a failure of criticism.

One of the most problematic features of Clare's case is that he does not seem 'problematic' at all. Why should it be difficult to understand a poet who isn't a 'difficult' poet? 'I found my poems in the fields' he once claimed, 'and only wrote them down'.[2] Critics have written Clare down because he does not seem, in their terms, to have adequately problematised his own poems when he 'only wrote them down'. As a poet, Clare moves easily, all too easily perhaps, between the available forms of poetry – from ballad and sonnet to reflective and loco-descriptive genres, satire to song – but he might not seem to modern eyes to have confronted the *problem* of form itself at all, in the way that Wordsworth, Coleridge, Blake or Keats so evidently did. His poems do not represent anything aesthetically comparable to the kind of 'organic unity' associated with Coleridge, the psychological complexity of Wordsworth, the playful generic self-consciousness of Byron or the 'well-wrought' closure of the narratives and odes of Keats. As a result, they neither lend themselves to the aesthetic discipline of close reading or the athletic exercise of deconstruction. They sprawl, they ramble, they spill over. Moreover, they are too often, as is said, 'merely descriptive'. If we are open to the idea of 'open form', as we sometimes say we are, we are still evidently uneasy with poetry that is open as Clare's is. For Clare, poetry itself is an open field and akin to the open-field landscape he knew in his childhood. In a world of, in Schiller's terms, inescapably sentimental poetics, Clare's appears fatally naive.[3] If he has not inspired a sophisticated criticism this is because he has not been perceived as a sophisticated poet – and this is largely as true for those who admire his poetry as for those who marginalise it or patronise it.

My argument is that this is a fateful misperception, and that Clare is an intimately sophisticated and self-conscious writer, not only aware of his place in the world (and the world of his place, a comparable thing), but of his place in poetry – the poetry of his time.[4]

There are a number of ways we might try to break out of the critical impasse, to expose the limits of conventional criticism and celebrate the liberating openness of Clare's centrifugal poetics. There are also a number of ways I could attempt to substantiate my claim for his poetic self-consciousness, even as a poet of 'description' who 'found' his poems in the field. One way, despite his dependence on received forms such as the ballad and sonnet, would be to formulate retrospectively an 'open field' poetics for Clare comparable to that of modern American poets such as William Carlos Williams. Another would be to outline an aesthetics of 'description' comparable to that proposed by Svetlana Alpers in *The Art of Describing* in relation to Dutch painting of the seventeenth century.[5] Another would be to test Clare's work against and within the canonical terms and tropes of Romantic poetry – as Harold Bloom suggested might be possible. Another would be to test the scale of his recorded statements about poetics and the natural world and treat him as a reflective poet like Wordsworth or Coleridge, a poet evolving a philosophy of poetry and of nature such as theirs. Another, on the lines laid down by John Barrell and more recently Johanne Clare, would be to situate his work more precisely historically within the society and culture of his time, and to read out their contradictions within Clare's verse.[6]

There is something in all these strategies, but they all depend on explicit programmatism of a potentially reductive kind. However self-conscious and supple Clare might be as a poet, he does not seem to be explicitly engaged in an epistemological or political programme comparable to that of earlier Romantics such as Blake, Coleridge and Wordsworth, or even contemporaries such as Shelley and Keats. His poetic action is elsewhere, and both more and less explicit. His verse is appealingly and absurdly open and available – but it is also curiously secretive and enigmatic. This strange doubleness is hard to take on board but it is inherent in all the best things he wrote. Clare, at least in his pre-asylum period, is not a poet of generalisations but of specificities – Carlos Williams's 'no ideas but in things' is a motto he might have understood – and in his mature work he evolves a poetics based on local knowledge, local detail, the thrill of individuation in the world beyond the individual. As a result I have chosen to demonstrate my claims about Clare's poetry – and poetics – by talking through the particularities of a particular poem. As I hope to show, the fact that his verse is not ambitiously symbolic does not mean that it is naively literal. If it is not figurative, it might be described as *configurative*. Clare's configurative poetry dwells within a profoundly local world, but in such a way as to imply much larger configurations that involve wider social and cultural issues that take us beyond Helpston or Northborough and the individual 'life of things'.

Romantic poetry is fascinated by the poetry of 'vision', Clare's by *seeing* – something very different. The poetry of Wordsworth, Coleridge, and Keats is of course one of the contexts of Clare's work (as is that of eighteenth-century reflective rural poets such as Thomson and Goldsmith), but so also is the pictorial art of Bewick, Cotman, Constable and Turner – the great lookers and recorders of English weather and landscape, the great particularists of the age. Visual particularists seem to be easier to accommodate than their poetic analogues such as Clare, Hardy, William Carlos Williams and Elizabeth Bishop. Such poets often enjoy a popular reputation but not an academic one. Clare wrote various poems to visual artists, such as De Wint and Bewick, and they suggest the poet's eager sense of affinity with visual artists. Indeed if you turn from a Bewick print or a Cotman watercolour to a Clare sonnet, your eyes open to the analogy between their entranced dedication to the ordinary and Clare's. Seeing is not, of course, believing, but in the case of Clare the belief in seeing was fundamental and the intimate conspiracy between seeing and saying is the motor force of his finest writing.

2

The poem I have chosen in order to approach the question of Clare's poetic self-consciousness is 'The Nightingale's Nest' (*Selected Poetry*, p. 108), which first appeared in *Friendship's Offering* in 1833 and was then included in *The Rural Muse* of 1835.[7] It was originally intended for publication in *The Midsummer Cushion* in 1832 and is to be found in the reconstruction of that volume by Anne Tibble and R. K. R. Thornton, first published in the 1970s.[8] It is not an avowedly programmatic or polemical poem, nor an explicitly social or critical one. It is one of the popular and highly approachable series of poems he consecrated to birds' nests – like 'The Fern Owl's Nest', 'The Yellowhammer's Nest', 'The Moorhens Nest', 'The Pettichaps Nest' and so on. The very approachability of such poems makes them both apt and suspect for my purposes. Clare the poet of birds and birds' nests joins Clare the English naturalist as part of the modern, cosily nostalgic, 'National Trust' mythology of the English countryside. The naturalist's Clare and the ornithologist's Clare are kin to the local historian's Clare, the social historian's Clare and the political ideologist's Clare – all attempts to 'redeem' Clare as a descriptive catalogist by appropriating him to other descriptive categories. Though these are germane to Clare's achievement my interest is in his integrally *poetic* project – a project that indeed integrates these other dimensions but has its own inherent integrity, its 'own bottom' as he wrote in the letter. In the poem I have chosen to discuss, Clare's self-conscious engagement with natural history is absolutely central, as I hope to show, but its very subject, the nightingale's nest, is inevitably and palpably an index of his self-consciousness about poetry. In the later 'To the Nightingale', Clare refers to the bird as 'the Poet of the Woods' and in another poem he speaks of 'the song of the bird that gives poets delight', confirming that in poetry nightingales are almost synonymous with poets and poetry – not least in the Romantic period in the wake of Coleridge's intensely self-conscious 'The Nightingale: A Conversation' published in one of the definitive expressions of the spirit of the age, the *Lyrical Ballads*.[9]

In a poem devoted to the 'Autumn Robin', Clare talks of 'The far famed nightingale that heirs / Cold public praise from every tongue', suggesting that 'The popular voice of music heirs / & injures much [the robin's] undersong'.[10] Clare's poem was written within a decade or so of what is now the most publicly praised of all poems about nightingales and poetry, Keats's 'Ode to a Nightingale'; and at one point in the poem Clare seems to draw attention to the fact, as we will see later. In writing of nightingales, Clare was inescapably writing of poetry – 'The Nightingale's Nest' was originally conceived as forming part of the same book as 'The Autumn Robin', with its reference to the 'far-famed nightingale' as 'the popular voice of music'. Yet he was also, of course, writing of nightingales. If Clare was a contemporary of Keats, he was also a contemporary of Bewick and at one time thought of producing an entire collection of poems entitled 'Birds Nesting', a poetic equivalent of Bewick's marvellously illustrated *History of British Birds*, first published in two volumes in 1797 and 1804. Keats's Odes and Bewick's *Birds* compose two axes of Clare's poem. It continually tests itself against both poetry and natural history.

In his unfinished and unpublished 'Natural History Letters', written between 1824 and 1826 on the model of Gilbert White's *Natural History of Selborne*, Clare repeatedly sets poetry and natural history side by side.[11] In fact nightingales' nests figure prominently in a couple of letters and one of them is largely devoted to the competing natural and poetic histories of the nightingale.[12] Even in his attempts at natural historical prose the poetic nightingale compels his recognition. It also compels him to confront the traditional poetic *misrecognition* of the real bird. If the cult of the nightingale causes people to slight the 'undersong' of such an underbird as the robin, its own fame conceals its nature. One of the letters begins with an account of a spectacular piece of metropolitan misprision about real nightingales:

I forgot to say in my last that the Nightingale sung as common by day as night & as often tho its a fact that is not generaly known your Londoners are very fond of talking about this bird & I believe fancy every bird they hear after sunset a Nightingale I remember when I was there last [while] walking with a friend in the fields of Shacklwell we saw a gentleman & lady listning

very attentive by the side of a shrubbery and when we came up we heard
them lavishing praises on the beautiful song of the nightingale which
happend to be a thrush ... such is the ignorance of nature in large Citys that
are nothing less then over grown prisons that shut out the world & all its
beautys[13]

'Your Londoners are very fond of talking about this bird' – Clare's
comment is a mischievous commentary on nature-loving, pastoral-
seeking townies but also on the poetic tradition they reproduce and
represent. The natural history letter was directed to Taylor and
Hessey as his London editors but Taylor was also editor of *The London
Magazine*, so that Clare's reference to 'your Londoners' is particularly
loaded. Clare is cocking a snook at the pretensions of the metropolitan
amateurs of nature in general, such as the readers of Taylor's
magazine, but 'Londoners' could also be construed as referring more
specifically to the writers maliciously labelled 'The Cockney School'
– not only writers like Hazlitt (who wrote regularly for *The London
Magazine*) but also 'Cockney' poets such as Reynolds and Keats (also
published by Taylor and Hessey). In his correspondence with Taylor,
Clare often invokes Keats's poetry with enthusiasm, especially
Endymion, but in a later letter to Herbert Marsh of 1830 he
accompanied a gift of Keats's early romance with some criticism
which aligned its dead author with the ignorant Londoners of the
letter quoted above:

Keats keeps up a constant alusion or illusion to the Grecian Mythol[og]y &
there I cannot follow but as far [as] I can judge his descriptions of senery are
often very fine but as it is the case with other inhabitants of great citys he
often described nature as she ... appeared to his fancys & not as he would
have described her if he had witnessed the things he describes – thus it is he
has often undergone the Blackwoods stigma of Cockneyism & what appears
as beautys in the eyes of a pent up citizen are looked upon as consiets by
those who live in the country[14]

'Your Londoners' are all 'pent up citizens', of course, but the
similarity of the two passages suggests Keats may be one of the targets
of the earlier criticism. The relation between describing and
witnessing is an important one for Clare and there is clearly a link
between the absurdly misconstrued nightingale spotted by the young
couple from London and Keats's description of 'nature as she ...
appeared to his fancys'. 'Alusion' and 'illusion' are next of kin. In
writing 'The Nightingale's Nest', an unusually allusive poem in

Clare's *oeuvre*, Clare is keenly alive to the poetic tradition represented by Keats's poem. The final line of 'The Nightingale's Nest' refers to 'the old woodlands legacy of song', but it is as aware of the particularly *poetic* legacy of the bird as much as that of the local woodland. Among other things, 'the Nightingale's Nest' is a response to the 'immortal bird' of Keats's ode – and the 'pent up' poetics it represents.

The eleventh 'Natural History Letter' opens with a walk towards a particular wood and shimmers with particularities:

> I went to take my walk to day & heard the Nightingale for the first time this season in Royce wood just at the town end we may now be assured that the summer is nigh at hand you asked me a long while back to procure you a Nightingales nest & eggs & I have try'd every season since to find if the birdnesting boys have ever taken one out but I have not been able to procure one – when I was a boy I used to be very curious to watch the nightingale to find her nest & to observe her color & size for I had heard many odd tales about her & I often observed her habits & found her nest so I shall be able to give you a pretty faithful history – she is a plain bird somthing like the hedge sparrow in shape & the female Firetail or Redstart in color but more slender then the former & of a redder brown or scorchd color then the latter… they generally seek the same solitudes which they haunted last season & these are the black thorn clumps & thickets… & sing their varied songs with short intervals both in the night & day time & sing in one as common as the other I have watchd them often at their song their mouths is open very wide & their feathers are ruffled up their wings trembling as if in extacy the superstition of laying their throats on a sharp thorn is a foolish absurdity but it is not the only one ascribed to the nightingale[15]

Clare is scrupulous not only about exact details of the bird's colour and habitat but his own qualifications for describing them: 'I usd to be very curious to watch… to find… to observe'. The letter commemorates the continuity between the young Clare's curiosity (caught in that wonderfully poised trinity of active verbs) and the adult writer's.

The letter is in part a response to Taylor's request for the bird's nest and eggs. If Clare is not able to procure an actual nightingale's nest, he succeeds in capturing a description of one in this luminously detailed prose and in the poem 'The Nightingale's Nest'.[16] Clare has a lot in common with the 'birdnesting boys' he appeals to in the letter. One of the triumphs of 'The Nightingale's Nest' is to bring us on a bird-nesting expedition into the 'same solitudes', bring us close to the bird's threatened private nesting space and leave it still intact.

The abortive natural history letters also show the *limits* of Clare's toleration of natural history. Poetry without a real grounding in the natural world he distrusts, but he also distrusts natural history which loses touch with the same ground. If there is a continuity between Clare's kind of observation and the scientific observer's, there is also a real difference. Asked about the cuckoo, he says that his friend 'Artis has one in his collection of stuffd birds' but confesses to not having 'sufficient [scientific] curiosity about me to go & take the exact description' or make measurements from it.[17] He then goes on to justify his reluctance in the name of 'poetic feeling':

these old bookish descriptions you may find in any natural history if they are of any gratification for my part I love to look on nature with a poetic feeling which magnifys the pleasure I love to see the nightingale in its hazel retreat & the cuckoo hiding in its solitudes of oaken foliage & not to examine their carcasses in glass cases yet naturalists & botanists seem to have no taste for this poetical feeling they merely make collections of dryd specimens classing them after Leanius into tribes & familys & there they delight to show them as a sort of ambitious fame with them 'a bird in the hand is worth two in the bush' well every one to his hobby I have none of this curiosity about me tho I feel as happy as they can in finding a new spieces of field flower or butter flye[18]

If there is a contrast here between 'poetic feeling' and the 'ambitious fame' of the 'naturalists & botanists', there are two other equally important factors. The first is his sense of the bird in its natural habitat, in its 'hazel retreat' rather than as an exhibit or one of a series of 'carcasses in glass'. He prefers two birds in the bush to any number in the hand. The second is his unscientific devotion to the pleasure principle – 'I love to look on nature with a poetic feeling which magnifies the pleasure', he writes, and later in the same letter: 'to look on nature with a poetic eye magnifys the pleasure she herself being the very essence & soul of Poesy'.[19] As a poetic naturalist, he is not interested in magnifying glasses but magnifying feelings. He rejects the botanical and ornithological classifications of the privileged collector and naturalist in favour of another kind of 'gratification' altogether. In 1818 *Blackwood's Magazine* published an article called 'Proofs of the increasing taste for Natural History' which, it said, had 'now become a general study' for 'the man of business as well as the philosopher' and Margaret Grainger reminds us that 'Clare lived through [the] period of natural history's greatest popularity'.[20] Clare's desire to write a *Natural History of Helpstone* and the 'Natural History Letters' are proofs of Clare's response to that 'increasing taste'. On the other hand, the ironic toleration he expresses in this letter for the gentleman scientists is positively lordly: 'well every one to his hobby'.

However, if Clare distances himself from the naturalists, he casts a wary eye on the poets too. In a postscript to the letter, Clare pooh-poohs the ignorance of one of Taylor's friends who questioned whether nightingales really sang by day and asked 'whether their notes be grave or gay':

> if the man does but go into any village solitude a few miles from London next may their varied music will soon put away his doubts of its singing by day – nay he may get rid of them now by asking any country clown the question for its such a common fact that all know of it ... the poets indulgd in fancys but they did not wish that those matter of fact men and the Naturalists shoud take them for facts upon their credit[21]

Clare's position is a complex one, a balancing act between 'those matter of fact men the Naturalists' and those matter of fancy men the Poets. He wants to be true to a certain kind of knowledge, that of alert and attentive observation of flora and fauna in their native habitat, but also to the mobile 'poetic eye' of the observer. The poem in the same breath offers a critique of natural history and of poetry.

3

In 'The Nightingale's Nest', Clare steers a path between such matters of fact and matters of poetic feeling. No doubt aware of his audience of 'Londoners' and others, he offers us something different to a dried specimen or a stuffed bird in a case. He offers us an experience of participant observation. The same can be said of many of the 'Birds Nesting' series of course, but this particular nest arouses inherently 'poetic' feelings – feelings about poetry itself. The poem introduces us to a particular world and place – but also to a new mode of poetic particularity. The path the poem takes might be taken as a kind of paradigm of the way a poem can 'magnify the pleasure' we take in the natural world. Clare's Nightingale is unlike its literary forebears and the poem's ability to mark that is a mark of its own originality – and Clare's self-consciousness.

The poet accomplishes this delicate balancing act by an unusual technical trick. He relates the poem in the present tense – an intimate narrative present – and then quite literally steers his reader up a path.[22] The opening takes the reader by the arm and leads us 'pent up citizens' into Clare's 'village solitude':

> Up this green woodland ride let's softly rove
> And list' the nightingale – she dwelleth here
> Hush, let the wood-gate softly clap – for fear
> The noise might drive her from her home of love

The technique is familiar to us now from TV documentaries and nature programmes, an attempt to transport us vicariously to the bird's habitat in the company of an expert local guide. It is rare, though, in the poetic traditions Clare is working within. For all its hushed immediacy, the opening is not without its conspicuous poeticisms – 'list' and 'dwelleth' sound a definitely archaic note. This is probably perfectly conscious – Clare was steeped in Elizabethan poetry and the nightingale is steeped in poetic diction. Anyway, the note changes with the breathtaking illusionism of the third line – 'Hush let the wood-gate softly clap' – which, with its repeated 'softly' and consciousness of noise, makes believe we are actually there with the speaker. 'Home' is one of Clare's most resonant terms and 'home of love' insists on the nightingale's rights of habitation, the rhyme balancing our freedom to 'rove' with the bird's fostering local 'love'. Clare goes on to confirm that our access to this world is only made possible by the fact of his being on home territory too:

> For here I've heard her many a merry year
> At morn and eve nay all the live-long day
> As though she lived on song – this very spot
> Just where the old man's beard all wildly trails
> Rude arbours o'er the road and stops the way
> And where that child its blue bell flowers hath got
> Laughing and creeping through the mossy rails
> There have I hunted like a very boy
> Creeping on hands and knees through matted thorns
> To find her nest

The ostensive gesture towards 'Here' sharpens in focus to 'this very spot' and then to 'just where the plant trails and 'that child' creeps with his blue bell flowers. The apparently incidental details increase our sense of verisimilitude and immediacy, giving a sense too of the poem's potential openness to everything within the field of vision – the sense you get in, say, William Carlos Williams's 'The Right of Way', the poet's licence (or right of way indeed) to pick out the ordinary sights that come his way without thematic justification.[23] By now too we are aware of the easy irregularity of the poet's attitude towards rhyme – every line rhymes with another somewhere in its vicinity but on no fixed rhyme scheme, occasionally in couplets but more usually taking the form of 'wild trails' which loosely bind the fluid pulse of the verse into a wavering assonantal pattern. The somewhat formulaic 'many a merry year' and 'all the live-long day' may seem flat, but like the clichés of Ashbery or O'Hara, they relax the air of the poem, while at the same time counteracting the brand of metropolitan ignorance about the habits of nightingales exposed in the letters to Taylor. They remind us that, unlike their literary stereotype, real nightingales sing by day and can be merry. Coleridge took issue with the 'most musical, most melancholy bird' of Milton's *Il Pensoroso* on the latter point, of course, in his 'The Nightingale: A Conversation', but he still represented it as a nocturnal if not a 'most melancholy bird'.[24] The creeping child reminds Clare of creeping 'like a very boy' himself – a sign of Clare's marvellous freedom from poetic starchiness, his never standing on his dignity. I am reminded of Seamus Heaney's 'Personal Helicon' in which the poet compares his childhood fascination with staring into wells with his adult Muse: 'Now, to pry into roots, to finger slime, / To stare big-eyed Narcissus, into some spring / Is beneath all adult dignity. I rhyme / To see myself, to set the darkness echoing'.[25] Heaney has subsequently expressed some embarrassment about his anxieties for his 'adult dignity' in 'Personal Helicon', but Clare is impressively free of such worries here.

It is precisely at this point, when the poet remembers creeping on hands and knees through matted thorns, that the question of the bird's poetic 'renown' first comes into play:

> And vainly did I many hours employ
> All seemed as hidden as a thought unborn
> And where these crimping fern-leaves ramp among
> The hazel's underboughs I've nestled down
> And watched her while she sung and her renown
> Hath made me marvel that so famed a bird
> Should have no better dress than russet brown
> Her wings would tremble in her extacy

> And feathers stand on end as 'twere with joy
> And mouth wide open to release her heart
> Of its out-sobbing songs – the happiest part
> Of summer's fame she shared – for so to me
> Did happy fancies shapen her employ

The thought of 'a thought unborn' is unusually introspective for Clare in poems like this one and it suggests the link between the bird's song and the poetic process, the 'hidden' dimension of both. Keats in his 'Ode' says he 'cannot see what flowers are at [his] feet' and presents himself as a spellbound eavesdropper ('Darkling I listen') in an 'embalmed darkness' that leaves the bird itself embalmed in mysterious invisibility, a pure source of song, all music.[26] Clare *watches* while his bird sings, and, as in the letter, notices such things as its wide open mouth, trembling wings and ruffled feathers. There is nothing embalmed about *his* singer. At the same time, nestled as he is, the poet is awake to the 'renown' of 'so famed a bird' and the way it shares 'summer's fame', the way that it is a kind of literary as well as proverbial symbol of summer. At the close of Keats's poem, the poet complains ruefully that 'the fancy cannot cheat so well / As she is famed to do'; Clare allows his 'fancys' to 'shapen her employ' too but without cheating, consciously shaping it in an archaic Spenserian idiom. His lines have an easy Elizabethan grandeur about them and, out of context, I suspect it would be hard to identify historically the author of the following cadences:

> her renown
> Hath made me marvel that so famed a bird
> Should have no better dress than russet brown

Part of the pleasure of this depends on Clare's enjoyable identification with the bird's plain 'russet brown'.[27] This nightingale is no courtier from some golden version of pastoral, and nor is she a 'light-winged Dryad of the trees' or classical Philomel 'far from home'. She is an ordinary English country dweller like the 'rude boys' evoked later in the poem. Or Clare himself. Fame and social obscurity go together here, and it is of course precisely Clare's agricultural and labouring origins that give him his privileged knowledge of the bird – and perhaps his affinity with it too. If the bird's song can expressively 'release her heart', the thought of it releases the poet's dreamy identification with its combination of lowliness and 'renown', an identification that the poem itself wonderfully realises in the breath of its spacious sentences and its luxuriant appropriation of poetic tradition.

It is when the poem evokes the effect of the song itself that Clare seems most conscious of the ghost of Keats. In *Adonais*, Shelley's classical elegy for the Romantic poet of the 'Ode to a Nightingale', Shelley had written:

> He is made one with Nature; there is heard
> His voice in all her music, from the moan
> Of thunder, to the song of night's sweet bird.[28]

It is hard not to hear Keats's voice in the following lines written by Clare (who had also of course written an elegy, in sonnet form, for Keats):

> The timid bird had left the hazel bush
> And at a distance hid to sing again
> Lost in a wilderness of listening leaves
> Rich extacy would pour its luscious strain

In his 'Ode', Keats is half in love with easeful Death as he hears the bird 'pouring forth [its] soul abroad in such an ecstasy' and, though there is no explicit 'alusion or illusion' to Keats's poem in Clare, his presence flickers through the uncharacteristically 'luscious strain' of these lines. Keats disclaims 'envy' of the bird's 'happy lot' and interestingly Clare's bird spurs another bird to poetic envy:

> Till envy spurred the emulating thrush
> To start less wild and scarce inferior songs
> For cares with him for half the year remain
> To damp the ardour of his speckled breast
> While nightingales to summer's life belongs
> And naked trees and winter's nipping wrongs
> Are strangers to her music and her rest
> Her joys are evergreen her world is wide

As in the letter about the deluded nature-loving Londoners who mistake a thrush for a nightingale, Clare appeals once more to the competition between nightingales and thrushes, significantly just after his most nearly audible 'alusion or illusion' to the song of Keats's 'Ode'. What he calls 'the emulating thrush' is this time 'spurred' by 'envy' of the nightingale 'to start less wild and scarce inferior songs'. Is it too Bloomian a fancy to see in this a recreation of the traditional singing contest of Theocritan pastoral in which Clare's summer bird competes enviously with Keats's 'immortal bird', even as Coleridge contested Milton's 'melancholy bird' in *The Nightingale*?[29]

Keats's seasonal sense is consummated in 'To Autumn', but Clare's work is always saturated in the seasonal, is indeed a thoroughly seasoned music – more like the thrush's than the nightingale's. Witness the many wonderful season songs entitled 'Spring' or 'Summer' or 'Autumn' or 'Winter', and the dense celebratory seasonal inventories of *The Shepherd's Calendar*. 'Her joys are evergreen her world is wide' might just, I suppose, apply to the nightingale rather than the thrush, but must in the first place refer to the latter as a bird for all seasons. John Jones in his *John Keats's Dream of Truth* speaks of the 'end-stopped' excitements of the Keatsian sensibility, Keats's interest in 'havens' of intensity. Clare too is interested in secret, havened places like the site of the nightingale's nest, but he is also interested in locating them in a larger landscape inhabited by other creatures. His world is wide. Poems like 'The Nightingale's Nest' depend on this sense of wideness as well as of privileged access to the special enclosure he names the bird's 'home of love'.

Though we have heard the song and seen the russet singer, we have not at this stage of the poem reached the nest itself. Clare is unusual among poets in his nesting instinct. Songs are related to nests, and if songs are in a manner public, nests are inherently private, hidden. After we and the bird have been 'lost in a wilderness of listening leaves', the poet returns us to the immediate place and the quest for the nest with a comfortably demotic 'shush':

> – Hark, there she is as usual let's be hush
> For in this blackthorn clump if rightly guest
> Her curious house is hidden – part aside
> These hazel branches in a gentle way
> And stoop right cautious 'neath the rustling boughs
> For we will have another search to day

If the nightingale is a figure for poetry, it is also territorial, a figure for habitation, the architect of its own place. Keats's 'immortal bird' is international, fabulous, archaic: it has been heard 'in ancient days by emperor and clown', by the biblical Ruth in alien corn, and by others in 'faery lands forlorn'. It is also as unanchored, as lyrically isolated as its author. Clare's bird on the other hand is a dweller rather than a traveller, and ordinary rather than fabulous – 'there she is as usual' is poetically unusual in placing the bird at the heart of her own 'usual' world. She is not a mobile symbol only but a creature surviving in a threatened but protective habitat, and the author of a nest ('her curious house'). Keats travels effortlessly to his tryst with the bird on the 'viewless wings of Poesy' – 'Already with thee! tender is the night'. Clare's poem by contrast is the antithesis of 'viewless' and moves cautiously, and with difficulty, across a dense prickly terrain. More pedestrian than Keats, Clare is happy to keep his feet firmly on the ground.

> We'll wade right through. It is a likely nook
> In such like spots and often on the ground
> They'll build where rude boys never think to look
> Aye as I live her secret nest is here
> Upon this whitethorn stulp

With Clare, we 'stoop', we 'hunt', we 'wade' through thick grass and 'trample' brambles before stumbling upon the 'secret nest'. The moment of discovery ('Aye as I live her secret nest is here') has the exclamatory immediacy of a 'Eureka' in the face of that downright palpable and demotic 'stulp'.

We get 'near' here – but not too near. As usual, Clare is acutely aware of the bird's sense of threat at human intrusion and fears to violate its space:

> – How subtle is the bird she started out
> And raised a plaintive note of danger nigh
> Ere we were past the brambles and now near
> Her nest she sudden stops – as choaking fear
> That might betray her home – so even now
> We'll leave it as we found it – safety's guard
> Of pathless solitude shall keep it still

'We'll leave it as we found it' – the phrase is like a motto for Clare's poems which prefer recognitions to appropriations. The poem has taken us on a route towards the nest of its title but respects the fact that the bird is protected because its 'home' is 'pathless'.

In poem after poem, Clare is interested in walks, wanderings, tracks, traces. 'I love roads', wrote Edward Thomas, but Clare, like the Wordsworth of the *Prelude*, prefers walking in 'pathless' places, ideally in the unenclosed landscape of his childhood. It is this which gives the social and autobiographical protest against enclosure in

'The Mores' its real impetus. Clare is an accessible poet, but more importantly, he is a poet of accessibility – who is interested in exploring a natural world available to all, though actually explored by few. 'The Mores' is a model of and apologia for such accessibility, a defiant celebration of the mobility of what it calls the 'following eye', thriving on the inexplicit analogy between the unenclosed landscape of Clare's early life and the openness of the poem – what I have called Clare's 'open field poetics'.

'The Nightingale's Nest' is another instance of the 'following eye'; it gives us temporary access to the nightingale's world in all its privileged solitude – but leaves it intact. Its song after all depends on it:

> See there she's sitting on the old oak bough
> Mute in her fears – our presence doth retard
> Her joys and doubt turns every rapture chill

'The nightingale', Clare had written in one of the 'Natural History Letters', 'is a shoy bird if any one approaches too near her secret haunts its song ceases till they pass' – quoting some lines of Chaucer in support of this piece of natural history ('The new abashed nightingale / That stinteth first when she beginneth sing').[30] The nightingale's shyness in the poem offers some analogy with Clare's own problems as a writer. Clare's letters exhibit a complex sense of his difficulties with his audience – with publishers, readers, critical interlocutors, social superiors and intellectual inferiors – and give expression to comparable 'doubt' and 'chill'. The problematic relationship between his own place and his alien audience is worked over in letter after letter: Clare had an exacerbated sense of what retarded not only his joys but his poetic song. The poem's moving recognition that its own quest for knowledge threatens the bird and renders her 'mute in her fears', is characteristic – Clare fears being invaded by others but he also fears his own invasiveness. At the heart of a poem about song and the archetypal song-bird, Clare sets a moment of terrible muteness.

In this slowed-down, step by step journey towards the poem's goal, we only gain access to the nest itself towards the end of the final paragraph. Up to this point the bird has been described in the third person, but now, faced with its fearful muteness, the poet, as he celebrates its 'dower', addresses it with something of the high music of Keats's 'Thou wast not born for death, immortal bird'. When he reaches the goal of his quest, Clare in fact evokes two distinct spaces associated with the bird, and in two quite different voices. First comes the 'spot of happiness' shaped by its song, which the poet captures in his stateliest Romantic Elizabethan cadences:

> Sing on sweet bird may no worse hap befall
> Thy visions then the fear that now decieves
> We will not plunder music of its dower
> Nor turn this spot of happiness to thrall
> For melody seems hid in every flower
> That blossoms near thy home – these harebells all
> Seem bowing with the beautiful in song
> And gaping cuckoo with its spotted leaves
> Seems blushing of the singing it has heard[31]

Then, abruptly, the poem's high music shifts register and Clare launches into an account of the bird's homely nest and eggs in his plainest manner:

> How curious is the nest no other bird
> Uses such loose materials or weaves
> Their dwellings in such spots – dead oaken leaves
> Are placed without and velvet moss within
> And little scraps of grass – and scant and spare
> Of what seems scarce materials, down and hair
> For from man's haunts she seemeth nought to win
> Yet nature is the builder and contrives
> Homes for her childern's comfort even here
> Where solitude's deciples spend their lives
> Unseen save when a wanderer passes near
> That loves such pleasant places – Deep adown
> The nest is made an hermit's mossy cell
> Snug lie her curious eggs in number five
> Of deadened green or rather olive brown
> And the old prickly thorn bush guards them well

The pastoral conceits of the bowing harebells and blushing cuckoo flower show Clare confident enough to plunder the Tudor lyric of its 'dower' and it is a mark of Clare's daring that he can use a plant with a bird's name to capture the Orphic influence of the ornithological song on the local flora.[32] The subsequent description of the 'curious nest' and its eggs is 'scant and spare' by contrast, closer to the language of those 'matter of fact men the Naturalists'. Poets don't usually dwell on nightingale's eggs as Clare does here. A rare exception is Tennyson who in *Aylmer's Field* describes a passion lying hidden 'as the music of the moon / Sleeps in the plain eggs of the nightingale' – so making a characteristically rich Tennysonian music out of those plain eggs.[33] If Clare is impressed by the poetic 'dower' of song, and attentive in his language to the poetic tradition he shares with Keats, he is also intrigued by the 'loose materials' out of which the bird weaves its nest and reports back on those 'plain eggs' in plain un-Tennysonian terms which are very close to those of the 'Natural History' I quoted from earlier:

> they make a large nest of the old eak leaves that strew the ground in woods & green moss & line it with hair & somtimes a little fine witherd grass or whool it is a very deep nest & is generally placed on the root or stulp of a black or white thorn somtimes a little height up the bush & often on the ground they lay 5 eggs about the size of the woodlarks or larger and of a deep olive brown without spot or tinge of any other color[34]

Clare has worked hard to get all the details right in the poem too. If he is happy to conceive of the nest poetically as a 'hermit's mossy cell', he is also keen to be accurate about its 'peculiar' construction and the number and colour of the eggs just as he is in the letter and in his several jottings on nightingales' nests in his journals. 'Nature is the builder' is a comfortable commonplace but acquires more vividness with the poem's high fidelity to the lowly details of the nest's actual contrivance.

Having finally arrived at the nest and its eggs guarded by the 'prickly thorn bush', the poem abruptly breaks off:

> And here we'll leave them still unknown to wrong
>   As the old woodland's legacy of song

The closing couplet's appeal to 'The old woodland's legacy of song' opens out the wonderfully close-up focus of the poem onto the wider world. It reminds us that the nightingale's song is part of one particular old woodland known to the poet but also of the legacy of Britain's old woodlands in general. Beyond both of these, beyond the poet's world and the natural one, 'the old woodland's legacy of song' suggests poetic tradition itself. I think of Keats in 'On Sitting Down to Read *King Lear* Once Again' addressing Shakespeare and the clouds of Albion as 'Begetters of our deep eternal theme' and praying:

> When through the old oak forest I am gone,
>   Let me not wander in a barren dream,
> But when I am consumed in the fire,
> Give me new Phoenix wings to fly at my desire[35]

Clare's 'woodland's legacy' is almost as far-reaching as Keats's 'old oak forest'. It characteristically naturalises the poetic tradition as birdsong but also recognises the long lyric tradition in which the nightingale plays its privileged part.[36] The rhyme of 'wrong' and 'song' suggests the threat of potential violation even while refusing it, while 'still unknown to wrong' reverberates with something of the ominous precariousness of Keats's 'still unravished bride of quietness'. The poem brings us closer to knowing a bird that is not only 'still unknown to wrong' but paradoxically 'still unknown', and tries, by its technical and visual intimacies, to get closer to knowing it poetically without wronging it in other ways.[37]

The couplet leaves the intent, rambling poem with a sudden and surprisingly abrupt sense of closure. Yet at the close, we are also left with a vivid sense that the individuality of Clare's art depends on its recognition of individuation at large, attentiveness to other things outside itself. In this respect it is a beautiful instance of a view of poetry conjured up on one of Keats's letters to Reynolds:

Poetry should be great & unobtrusive, a thing which enters into one's soul and does not startle it or amaze it with itself but with its subject, – how beautiful are the retired flowers! how would they lose their beauty were they to throng into a highway crying out 'admire me I am a violet! dote upon me I am a primrose!' Modern poets differ from the Elizabethans in this[38]

Clare's 'The Nightingale's Nest' represents a world and an eye and an art which are profoundly different from those represented by the hushed aesthetic closure of 'Ode to a Nightingale', but it is surely 'great & unobtrusive' in the way Keats speaks of in the letter. The loose and 'unobtrusive' weave of Clare's art is integral to his way of seeing and being in the world:

> How curious is the nest no other bird
> Uses such loose materials or weaves
> Their dwellings in such spots

The same might be said of Clare's formal imagination.

4

Clare planned his 'Birds Nesting' poems to be in various stanza forms, and it may be that his interest in nests, the relation of nest architecture to bird cries and songs, has an affinity with his sense of art. In 'The Moorhen's Nest' (*Selected Poetry*, p. 155), a poem in easy-

going couplets about a bird which is more of an architect than a
singer, this becomes very plain: the bird's 'Rich architecture' goes
with its choice of 'homes' to create 'picturesque dwellings' which
make them cognate with 'the wild romances of a poet's mind'. In
'The Yellow Hammer's Nest' (*Selected Poetry*, p. 104), a poem like
'The Nightingale's Nest' built up out of beautifully straggling
rhymes, the bird's architecture is more apparently primitive yet
equally poetic:

> – Aye here it is, stuck close beside the bank
> Beneath the bunch of grass that spindles rank
> Its husk-seeds tall and high – 'tis rudely planned
> Of bleached stubbles and the withered fare
> That last year's harvest left upon the land
> Lined thinly with the horse's sable hair
> – Five eggs pen-scribbled over lilac shells
> Resembling writing, scrawls which fancy reads
> As nature's poesy and pastoral spells
> They are the yellowhammer's and she dwells
> A poet like – where brooks and flowery weeds
> As sweet as Castaly to fancy seems
> And that old molehill like as Parnass hill

Clare enjoys turning Parnassus into a molehill and *vice versa*, and here
he spells out his creative analogy between nests and 'nature's poesy'
more explicitly than anywhere else.[39] The yellowhammer is 'poet
like' and her eggs, like Clare's poems, are 'pen-scribbled'. The
'rudely planned' nest made up of unpromising left-overs from last
year's harvest is Clare's equivalent to Seamus Heaney's 'Personal
Helicon', an emblem as well as instance of the place of writing.[40]
Many of the nest poems, like 'The Fern Owl's Nest' (*Selected Poetry*,
p. 100), are in fact sonnets – but sonnets constructed in uniquely
asymmetrical, Clare-like ways, intricately various and woven out of
all sorts of 'loose materials' and earthy idiom. In such poems, Clare
maps the world of other creatures and other habitats but also suggests
the profound analogy between art and habitat that was the origin of
his own finest work. In exploring his interest in the place and
architecture of the nightingale's nest, Clare tells us a lot about his
sense of the connection between his own 'poetic feeling' and his sense
of place.

As the letter quoted earlier (p. 57) tells us, the nightingale's nest is
associated for Clare with Royce Wood in particular. In 'The Flitting'

(*Selected Poetry*, p. 198), the great poem he wrote after leaving Helpston for Northborough in 1832, Clare elegiacally explores the relationship between his rural muse and his 'own home or homes' in Helpston. The crisis of poetic feeling represented there first crystallises around the association of the bird and the word:

> I sit me in my corner chair
> That seems to feel itself from home
> And hear bird-music here and there
> From awthorn hedge and orchard come
> I hear, but all is strange and new
> – I sat on my old bench in June
> The sailing puddock's shrill 'peelew'
> Oer Royce Wood seemed a sweeter tune
>
> I walk adown the narrow lane
> The nightingale is singing now
> But like to me she seems at loss
> O'er Royce Wood and its shielding bough
>
> (*Selected Poetry*, p. 199)

Probably early in 1832, Clare seems to have written a note prefiguring his feelings about leaving his home territory, and planning return trips to particularly important places:

There are some things that I shall regret leaving & some journeys that I shall make yearly – to see the flood at Lolham Briggs – to gather primroses in hilly wood & hunt the nightingales nest in royce wood[41]

In fact Clare had as many or more opportunities to hear nightingales in Northborough as he had in Helpston – 'I never had greater oppertunitys of observing the Nightingale then I had this summer – because she was constantly as it were at my very door', he wrote in the summer of 1832 after the move.[42] Nevertheless, because of 'The Flitting' and its crisis of displacement, we recognise that the association of song and a particular place is integral to Clare's vision. The same claim is implicit in the marvellous, varied poems of the 'Birds Nesting' series, and, in particular, the poem about the nightingale's nest in Royce Wood.

In his *Poetics of Space*, an essay on what its author calls 'the material imagination', Gaston Bachelard devotes a chapter to the phenomenology of the nest.[43] Bachelard makes no mention of Clare in his study, but his terms of reference cast light on what I have called Clare's nesting instinct. In the phenomenology of what he terms the

'living nest', he says the nest 'becomes for a moment the center – the
term is no exaggeration – of an entire universe' and it tends to serve
as an analogy with our dream house, a place where we feel or felt at
home.[44] Analysing the imaginative paradox at the heart of our nest
fantasies, he calls it a 'precarious thing' which 'sets us daydreaming
of security'; 'when we examine a nest', he suggests, 'we place
ourselves at the origin of confidence in the world'.[45]

Bachelard sees the nest as lying at the source of the 'oneiric dream
house' and is mainly considering the way we imagine houses as nests,
not nests as houses. Clare is more interested in the latter and more
acutely aware of the precariousness of the nest. His interest is no
doubt intimately related to his instinct for confidence, his desire to
belong to a place, but, beyond that I am suggesting that he is drawn
to the nest as an image of the material imagination itself, a model of
poetic form, an instance of how form itself is a model for being in the
world. Surely this is one of the reasons why birds' nests and their eggs
in all their literalness are so arresting for him. With poignant
appositeness, Clare's fragmentary last poem, written in the winter of
1863 to 1864, was called 'Birds Nests'. An earlier sonnet with the
same title (*Selected Poetry*, p. 99) celebrates a moping hedge-sparrow
that 'weaves of homely stuff / Dead grass and mosses green, an
hermitage / For secrecy and shelter rightly made'.[46] 'Homely stuff'
and 'hermitage', 'secrecy and shelter': the nest, like the poem, is a
place of both self-enclosed meditation and secure habitation. It
represents the alliance between song – poetic utterance – and habitation, the almost Heideggerian dream of poetic dwelling in a
particular place and the place of the poem.

5

At the start I mentioned Constable, Bewick and Cotman and I have
often been struck by the analogies between these great idiosyncratic,
non-genteel artists and Clare. In particular, Constable's art and
ideas on art, as recorded in Leslie's memoir, have resonances for
anyone thinking of Clare. Constable continually emphasised the
priority of open-air study over mere connoisseurship. 'The art of
seeing nature is a thing almost as much to be acquired as the art of
reading the Egyptian hieroglyphics', he said, suggesting that *seeing*
was as difficult an art as historical scholarship.[47] He also continually
emphasised the dependence of his own and other painters' art on the

local, the familiar, the native. 'The Dutch painters', he said, 'were a
stay-at-home people, – hence their originality'.[48] Like that other intensely local artist, Clare, Constable was a deep-dyed particularist
and celebrated art as a profoundly particularising process – like
'creation' itself:

The world is wide; no two days are alike, nor even two hours; neither were
there ever two leaves of a tree alike since the creation of the world; and the
genuine productions of art, like those of nature, are all distinct from each
other.[49]

Commenting on Constable's sketch-books, Constable's friend and
first biographer, Leslie, wrote:

The name of nearly every spot sketched is added, and in looking through
these books one thing is striking, which may be equally noticed of his
pictures, that the subjects of his works form a history of his affections.[50]

The history of Clare's affections might be contained within an even
more restricted circle than Constable's, and his art is equally *local* in
its 'quest of subjects' and obliviousness to the conventionally sublime
or picturesque. Leslie ends his *Memoirs* with an account of a visit to
Constable's birthplace which offers a vivid parallel between the
painter's and the poet's art:

We found that the scenery of eight or ten of our late friend's most important
subjects might be enclosed by a circle of a few hundred yards at Flatford,
very near Bergholt…Travelling is now the order of the day, and it may
prove sometimes beneficial, – but to Constable's art there can be little doubt
that the confinement of his studies within the narrowest bounds in which,
perhaps, the studies of an artist ever were confined, was in the highest degree
favourable.[51]

If we substitute Helpston for Bergholt, the same might surely be said
of the author of 'The Flitting' and 'The Nightingale's Nest'.

'The Nightingale's Nest' is a genuinely natural historical poem.
Clare might not perhaps share Constable's view of his own profession
as '*scientific* as well as *poetic*' or the claim that 'imagination alone
never did, and never can, produce works that are to stand by a
comparison with *realities*', but he certainly showed in such poems a
subtle, supple and enduring conviction that poetry should be
grounded in such '*realities*'.[52] 'The Nightingale's Nest' can stand
beside Constable's sketches of cloud and water, Cotman's gate,
Bewick's birds and vignette landscapes – all of which are reminders
that much of the greatest art of the Romantic period was a record of

looking at the hitherto overlooked familiar world. Clare's sonnet 'To Dewint', originally published in the same volume, is a tribute to another such artist:

> Yet in thy landscapes I can well descry
> The breathing hues as natures counterpart
> No painted freaks – no wild romantic sky
> No rocks nor mountains as the rich sublime
> Hath maded thee famous but the sunny truth
> Of nature that doth mark thee for all time
> Found on our level pastures spots forsooth
> Where common skill sees nothing deemed divine
> Yet here a worshipper was found in thee
> Where thy young pencil workd such rich surprise
> That rushy flats befringed with willow tree
> Rival'd the beauties of italian skies[53]

De Wint had designed the frontispiece for Clare's previous book, *The Shepherd's Calendar*, and Clare's sonnet portrays De Wint's art as a 'counterpart' not only of nature but of his own very consciously innovative pastoral poetry.[54]

Turning back to the 'Natural History Letters', we find Clare imagining an essay that would be a kind of manifesto for his new way of writing and seeing:

I think an able Essay on objects in nature that woud beautifye descriptive poetry might be entertaining & useful to form a right taste in pastoral poems that are full of nothing but the old thread bare epithets of 'sweet singing cuckoo' 'love lorn nightingale' 'fond turtles' 'sparkling brooks' 'green meadows' 'leafy woods' &c &c these make up the creation of Pastoral & descriptive poesy & every thing else is reckond low & vulgar in fact they are too rustic for the fashionable or prevailing system of ryhme till some bold and innovative genius rises with a real love for nature & then they will no doubt be considerd as great beautys which they really are[55]

Leslie reports Constable once exclaiming 'I never saw an ugly thing in my life' and quotes a letter saying he held 'the genuine pastoral feeling of landscape to be very rare and difficult of attainment'.[56] Clare's vision is similar and 'The Nightingale's Nest' embodies a kind of 'descriptive poetry' which exposes those 'threadbare epithets' of 'lovelorn nightingale' and the like, to reveal the 'rustic' and 'vulgar' as the 'great beautys which they really are'. In representing the nightingale as dressed in rustic 'russet brown' like his fellow villagers, Clare resituates the 'poetic' itself. I would suggest that, like

Constable in painting, Clare is just the self-consciously 'bold and innovative genius' he invokes in the letter to oppose 'the prevailing system of rhyme'.

6

In the list of birds in his notebooks, Clare described the skylark as 'of much use in poetry as the Nightingale' and the skylark is the other famous poetic bird of the Romantic period.[57] Shelley's 'To a Skylark' has always been read as a self-conscious model for lyric poetry, a miniature embodiment of the poetics of *The Defence of Poetry* and a figure of a poet very consciously opposing 'the prevailing system'. A comparison of Clare's 'The Sky Lark' (*Selected Poetry*, p. 103) with Shelley's 'To a Skylark' on the lines of our running comparison between the nightingale poems of Clare and Keats suggests how antithetical were their respective modes of opposition – and their poetics. Clare's 'The Sky Lark' is written in the laid-back mobile couplet form he often favoured, and shifts in focus from its opening shot of rolls and harrows and a battered road to a view of an open field where hares hide and hedge boys crop early blossoms, before it rises with the frightened skylark high into the air:

> And from their hurry up the skylark flies
> And o'er her half-formed nest with happy wings
> Winnows the air – till in the clouds she sings
> Then hangs a dust spot in the sunny skies

Where Shelley from the outset hails his skylark as a 'spirit', congratulating it on transcending mere bird status ('bird thou never wert'), Clare's bird remains conscious of her 'half-formed nest'; her winnowing wings and 'dust spot' appearance relate her more closely to the agricultural landscape she soars above than to Shelley's intellectual empyrean. This offers a parallel to the Northamptonshire poet's invocation to his muse in 'The Flitting':

> Give me no highflown fangled things
> No haughty pomp in marching chime
> Where muses play on golden strings
> And splendours passes for sublime...

> I love the verse that mild and bland
> Breaths of green fields and open sky
> I love the muse that in her hand
> Bears wreaths of native poesy (*Selected Poetry*, p. 203)

Wary of such 'highflown fangled things', Clare's skylark sings in the clouds but nests firmly on the ground – unheeded by the daffy boys with their Shelleyan fantasies of would-be transcendence:

> Then hangs a dust spot in the sunny skies
> And drops and drops till in her nest she lies
> Where boys unheeding passed, ne'er dreaming then
> That birds which flew so high would drop again
> To nests upon the ground where any thing
> May come at to destroy. Had they the wing
> Like such a bird, themselves would be too proud
> And build on nothing but a passing cloud
> As free from danger as the heavens are free
> From pain and toil – there would they build and be
> And sail about the world to scenes unheard
> Of and unseen – O were they but a bird –
> So think they while they listen to its song
> And smile and fancy and so pass along
> While its low nest moist with the dews of morn
> Lye safely with the leveret in the corn

The poem veers between sky and ground, bringing the skylark redemptively down to earth, while satirising the boys' 'highfangled' cloud-cuckoo dreams of nesting in the clouds without danger or sailing about the world. Shelley's Skylark, like Keats's Nightingale, is a familiar incarnation of Romantic poetry. Clare's Skylark and Nightingale have lesser fame but are paradigms of a different poetic, able to soar and sing, sensitive to high diction and the 'legacy' of the past, but nesting 'upon the ground where any thing / May come at to destroy'. In its precarious but specific home ground, accessible to anyone who looks, but hidden too, Clare's skylark catches something of the enigmatic obviousness of Clare's earth-bound, nest-bound poetry.

> While its low nest moist with the dews of morn
> Lye safely with the leveret in the corn[58]

There is a precedent for reading these poems as paradigms of poetry. In fact one of the first readers of Clare's 'The Nightingale's Nest', his friend Eliza Emmerson, recognised that it could be read as a figure of the poet and his art. Unfortunately, her poem 'On reading the Nightingales Nest of John Clare', dated December 1832, is not only a gesture of recognition but a map of misrecognition, a misreading of Clare's careful natural historical map. She not only slips back into the conventional poetic misrecognition of the bird that Clare was contesting in the poem but superimposes a sentimentally Romantic reading of both bird and poet:

> 'Up the green woodland' – did he say,
> He heard her chanting forth her lay?
> Oh! no – 'tis in the *Poet's brest*
> The nightingale hath made her 'nest' –
> And given her soul of melody
> Unto the bard! – cannot we
> Hear in his love-inspired note,
> The very warblings of her throat –
> The jug-jug-jug! the plaintive moan –
> The self-same spirit in each tone?
> 'Clare' and the 'Nightingale' are one![59]

Eliza Emmerson is absolutely right to see the poem as being somehow as much about the poet as about local ornithology, and to identify at its heart questions of poetic voice and feeling. Her own poem, though, hopelessly confuses poet and bird in a way which travesties Clare's intricately self-conscious but robustly outward-looking configurative poem. A reader who hears in 'The Nightingale's Nest' only a bard's 'plaintive moan' seems to have missed its 'self-same spirit'. In fact, she inverts what happens. Clare is not at all like the 'poor wretch' Coleridge rebukes in his 'The Nightingale: A Conversation' who 'filled all things with himself / And made all gentle sounds tell back the tale / Of his own sorrow'.[60] 'The Nightingale's Nest' is paradigmatic of Clare's naturalistic poetics because, though it thrives on the analogy between poetry and the bird's nest (and song) it is constructed around the poet's interest in seeing the bird's world as genuinely distinct from his own – a world not only beyond this particular poem but beyond poetry.[61]

7

In conclusion, I want to invoke two very different representations in Clare's work of the nightingale's *song*. One occurs in a private natural history jotting and the other at the heart of one of his most self-consciously public poems about his art and its history, 'The Progress of Ryhme'.

A note written soon after his arrival in Northborough records Clare's informal appreciation of the formal unpredictability and variety of the nightingale's song. It also registers a vivid sense of the gap between human language and the bird's:

I can sit at my window here & hear the nightingale singing in the orchard & I attempted to take down her notes but they are so varied that every time she starts again after the pauses seems to be somthing different to what she utterd before & many of her notes are sounds that cannot be written the alphabet having no letters than can syllable the sounds[62]

By good fortune Clare's attempt to 'take down her notes' also survives and it represents the one genuine attempt in the period to reproduce the song of the nightingale, as it were, verbatim.

Chee chew chee chew chee
chew chew chew chew chee
– up cheer up cheer up
tweet tweet tweet jug jug jug

wew wew wew – chur chur
woo it woo it tweet tweet
tweet jug jug jug

tee rew tee rew tee rew – gur
gur – chew rit chew rit – chur-chur chur
chur will-will will-will tweet-em
tweet em jug jug jug jug

grig grig grig chew chew[63]

The poetic dialect Clare deciphers here is a far cry from the Romantic lyric as we normally conceive it yet his attempt to 'syllable the sounds' is surely, among other things, 'native poesy'.

Clare embodies a comparable phonetic transcription of nightingale song at the heart of one of his most lyrically powerful long poems, the rambling open-air *ars poetica* he called 'The Progress of Ryhme', a poem about the origins of lyric power and what might be meant by 'native poesy' in the fullest sense.

The work is very different from the eighteenth-century 'Progress of Poetry' genre which the title suggests – poems which genealogically trace the history of the poetic art and of classical culture from ancient Greece to the present. Clare's 'Progress' is a Romantic document of the writer's sense of vocation, a literary equivalent of *The Pilgrim's Progress*, improvised in shimmering and relaxed tetrameter couplets.

Like his unfinished autobiography, 'Sketches in the Life of John Clare', which it closely parallels, it is a record of Clare's struggle to legitimate his access to literate – and literary – culture, his 'right to song' (line 80):[64]

> And so it cheered me while I lay
> Among their beautiful array
> To think that I in humble dress
> Might have a right to happiness
> And sing as well as greater men   (lines 105–9)[65]

Poetry here begins less as an authoritative bardic voice of 'civilisation' than a therapeutic family romance – a celebratory and compensatory art which performs the roles of 'friend' (line 29), 'parent' (line 30), and 'love' (line 31) for the young Clare. Without it, he claims, he would have remained 'an idle rustic boy' (line 45). Yet, as the poem develops, the adolescent poet's solitary pleasure in art involves him in making claims for himself which go beyond art. In laying claim both to the 'right to song' and the 'right to happiness', the writer inevitably makes the poetic and the political claims equivalent. For all its apotheosis of the 'natural' poetics of birdsong, it is shot through with an acutely class-conscious understanding of poetic culture. Though written in a disarming vein of candid Romantic retrospect and bardic self-mythologising, it is also very much alive to the iconography of literary tradition and incorporates almost subliminal references to the classical and biblical prototypes of the poet so integral to the 'Progress' poem – 'to show I knew the goddess there' (line 54) remembers classical visions of Aphrodite as Goddess of Love and 'the harp imagination strung' (line 43) remembers not only the recent pseudo-archaic bards of Gray, Beattie and Moore, among others, but also the David of the Psalms, the archetypal shepherd poet. If, in this working-class autodidact's buoyant manifesto, 'the rights of bards' seem at first out of reach of the Northamptonshire boy's work-soiled hands, it is just such rights which the poem progressively claims for Clare as it develops – and through him those hitherto debarred from claiming such a 'title'.

Clare's 'Progress' is a quasi-pastoral portrait of the artist as young man but it challenges the whole poetic tradition of 'minstrelsy' it invokes. For even as he lays claim to poetic status, the poet insists on his minimal social status as one of the agricultural labouring class outside the pale of literary (and of course political) culture. At first he has no audience except himself, then his parents, but the poem is not content with reproducing a conventional poetic solitude. The search for an audience is inherent in the 'moment' of inspiration. We are reminded of 'burghley park', the great house and its aristocratic estate by Stamford where Clare had worked as a gardener in his youth. Beside it he sets his vivid self-portrait of the artist 'with ragged coat and downy chin / A clownish silent haynish boy / Who even felt ashamed of joy / So dirty and so low' (lines 307–8). That shame is shaming. The 'right to song' he claims as a social and a political right. It is as if one of Andrew Marvell's mowers or gardeners were to become a real pastoral poet, not just a poetic figure out of pastoral.

At the heart of this miniature *Prelude* is birdsong once more, birdsong notated within a precisely registered social history. Clare remembers his boyish attempts 'To mock the birds with artless skill' (line 216) by playing with blades of grass and retrospectively enjoys his naive self-satisfaction with his DIY birdsong ('No music in the world beside / Seemed half so sweet – till mine was tried'). Pondering his success with eliciting responses from blackbirds, he harks back to the music of the archetypal poetic songbird:

> And nightingales O I have stood
> Beside the pingle and the wood
> And oer the old oak railing hung
> To listen every note they sung   (lines 228–32)

There follows a wonderfully undignified phonetic riff for nearly twenty lines of transcribed nightingale song just as in the jotted fragment quoted earlier – of 'chew-chew', 'cheer-cheer', 'wew-we', 'Woo-it woo-it', 'chur chur chur', 'Tee-rew tee-rew', 'grig-grig-grig-grig', 'tweet tweet tweet' and finally the conventional 'jug jug jug'. Clare becomes the Messiaen of Helpston. Unembarrassedly naive and down-to-earth as this homespun onomatopoeic knock-about is, it is again the result of the kind of painstaking observation recorded in the natural history jottings collected by Margaret Grainger. The poet is doing the textual equivalent of the boy blowing with the blade of grass. If this does not seem like the expected agenda of a poem about the progress of Rhyme, its relevance soon becomes clear:

> Words were not left to hum the spell
> Could they be birds that sung so well
> I thought – and may be more then I

That musics self had left the sky
To cheer me with its magic strain
And then I hummed the words again
Till fancy pictured standing bye
My heart's companion poesy   (lines 258–64)

'Musics self', 'my heart's companion poesy' – Fancy situates Clare among Keatsian terms and high Romantic figures. The nightingale is classical figure and local fact. In all its naive and vernacular immediacy, it epitomises – epiphanises, one might even say – his sense of the poetic and its 'spell'. It bridges the gap between the lyric tradition of classical pastoral and Clare's life as English country labourer. Furthermore, it legitimises his ambition to write in the absence of any fostering social context other than his parents. 'No not a friend on earth had I', he notes, 'But my own kin and poesy'. Some of the barely acknowledged drama of this unembarrassedly descriptive poem concerns the way it makes poesy and poetic tradition his 'kin'.

It is the nightingale which crystallises the poet's relationship with poetry, the scruffy country boy's engagement with the Muse. The nightingale's privacy and vernacular virtuosity serve as a model within his native place for the art to which he aspired, both as liberation and compensation. Only it and his phantom lover, Mary, body forth in this poem about the social obstacles to and embarrassments of art, the thrill of liberated utterance.[66] 'The Progress of Ryhme' tunes in to Clare's deepest preoccupations with poetry and his attempts to establish his 'right to song'. The auditory encounter with nightingale song at its heart displaces the sublime tropes and topoi that encumbered the conventional Progress poem of the time just as it exuberantly dissolves the starchy routine iconography surrounding nightingales, and even Keats's lusciously embalmed 'immortal bird'. With a seemingly casual self-elaboration and cocking-a-snook cheek, Clare once again, as in 'The Nightingale's Nest', remakes the nightingale as a figure of 'Ryhme' and in such a way as to make 'poesy' his 'kin'.

With an intricately self-delighting but always potentially tragic self-consciousness, and in poems as different from each other as 'The Nightingale's Nest' and 'The Progress of Ryhme', Clare in his best work gives voice to vernacular energies and forms of local knowledge hitherto masked by neo-classical and Romantic accounts of the progress of poetry. By doing so, he began to redraw the historical map of English poetry in ways that we are only now beginning to recognise.

NOTES

1 Letter of 13 November 1832, Mark Storey (ed.), *The Letters of John Clare* (Oxford, 1985), p. 604.

2 Eric Robinson and David Powell (eds.), *The Later Poetry of John Clare* (Oxford, 1984), pp. 19–20, lines 15–16.

3 For a fuller discussion and a different view, see Juliet Sychrava, *Schiller to Derrida* (Cambridge, 1989).

4 Clare disclaims any such awareness it is true, and in a letter to Taylor of 1826, in which he turns down the idea of writing a critical essay on other poets, writes: 'I fear I am not able to do any thing with the Poets either of the last age or the present for I know little or nothing about what they have written & [th]e very names of half of them are utter strangers to me' (M. Storey, *Letters*, p. 354). Despite this disclaimer, Clare's letters, journal and library suggest that he was much more aware of other writers than this suggests – even if he was unwilling to write in public as a critic of them.

5 Svetlana Alpers, *The Art of Describing: Dutch Art in the Seventeenth Century* (Chicago, 1983).

6 See John Barrell, *The Idea of Landscape and the Sense of Place 1730–1840: An Approach to the Poetry of John Clare* (Cambridge, 1972); Johanne Clare, *John Clare and The Bounds of Circumstance* (Montreal, 1987).

7 All quotations from Clare's poems in this essay refer to Geoffrey Summerfield (ed.), *John Clare, Selected Poetry* (London, 1990), unless otherwise specified. R. K. R. Thornton (ed.), *The Rural Muse* (Northumberland, 1982), a second edition of Clare's volume of 1835.

8 Anne Tibble (ed.), *John Clare: The Midsummer Cushion*, associate editor, R. K. R. Thornton (Northumberland, 1979).

9 'To the Nightingale', in Robinson and Powell, *Later Poetry*, vol. 1, pp. 16–17. The following quotation comes from an unpublished passage from 'A Walk in the Fields' quoted in Margaret Grainger (ed.), *The Natural History Prose Writings of John Clare* (Oxford, 1983), p. 67. Grainger's meticulously edited book, a comprehensive compilation of all the natural history scraps and jottings Clare wrote, is an indispensable companion to his poetry.

10 A. Tibble, *Midsummer Cushion*, p. 124.

11 Grainger, *Natural History*. Evidence of dating of the 'Natural History Letters' is provided in Margaret Grainger's textual introduction, p. lxviii.

12 Letter II and Letter XI, ibid. pp. 36ff. and pp. 66ff. There are numerous other references to nightingales and their nests in the journal and natural history notes, which bear out Clare's continuing interest in the bird.

13 Ibid. pp. 36–7.

14 M. Storey, *Letters*, p. 519.

15 Grainger, *Natural History* pp. 66–8.

16 Compare, in the same letter, Clare talking about specimens of butterflies and flowers: 'I have no specimens to send you so be as it may you must be content with my descriptions & observations'; ibid. p. 39. A journal entry of 1825 confirms Clare's searches for the nest: 'Wrote another portion of my Life & took a Walk to seek a nightingale's nest'; ibid. p. 238. As the eleventh 'Natural History' letter tells us, 'their nests are very difficult to find indeed it is a hopeless task to hunt for them as they are seldom found but by accident', ibid. p. 68.

17 Ibid. p. 38.

18 Ibid.

19 Ibid. p. 41.

20 Ibid. p. xlii.

21 Ibid. p. 42.

22 He uses the same device in 'The Holiday Walk', an account of a walk with children through a busy agricultural landscape in summer, in A. Tibble, *Midsummer Cushion*, pp. 168–74.

23 William Carlos Williams, *The Collected Earlier Poems* (New York, 1966), pp. 258–9.

24 S. T. Coleridge, *Poetical Works*, ed. E. H. Coleridge (Oxford, 1969), pp. 264–7. Grainger quotes a manuscript variation on this by Clare which bears closely on the search for truth in his 'Nightingale's Nest':

> Some sing her leaning on a thorn
> & give her music pain
> Some make her wretched & forlorn
> & make her pleasure vain
> Some vow she sings at night alone
> So darkness has its day
> While she is called the verse to own
> & patronise the lay
> Poor idle tales for idle minds
> Who never seek for truth (*Natural History*, p. 68).

25 Seamus Heaney, *Death of a Naturalist* (London, 1966), p. 57.

26 All quotations from 'Ode to a Nightingale' from John Keats, *The Complete Poems*, ed. John Barnard, 2nd edn (London, 1977), pp. 346–8.

27 Compare the manuscript of 'A Walk in the Fields': ''Tis as plain as a sparrow in plumage & make / Yet that is the nightingale sister of may', quoted Grainger *Natural History*, p. 67. The sociological significance of the 'russet brown' is confirmed by *The Shepherd's Calendar* where Clare harks back to an earlier age and regrets 'the old freedom that was living then / When masters made him merry with their men / Whose coat was like his neighbours russet brown / And whose rude speech was vulgar as his clown' ('June', lines 157–60). Clare's archetypal songbird is dressed like a farm-labourer – or John Clare.

28 Donald H. Reiman and Sharon B. Powers (eds.) *Shelley's Poetry and Prose* (New York and London, 1977), p. 402.

29 Clare in 1825 described Bloomfield as 'the English Theocritus & the first of rural Bards in this country' (M. Storey, *Letters*, p. 322), as well as 'the most original poet of the age & the greatest Pastoral Poet England ever gave birth too', (ibid. p. 300). Clare presumably had impressive social as well as personal reasons to make these claims for Bloomfield as the representative of the true pastoral tradition, but it is not with Bloomfield that the poetic contest I am intimating would take place.

30 Grainger, *Natural History* p. 37. The Chaucer quotation is from *Troilus and Criseyde*, Book III.

31 Compare '*The Journal*': 'I never take up Johnsons Lives but I regret his beginning at the wrong end first & leaving out those beautiful minstrels of Elizabeth – had he forgot there were such poets as Spencer Drayton Suckling etc.', 4 October 1824, Grainger, *Natural History*, p. 189.

32 'The Joys of Childhood' mentions 'Cuckoos with spotted leaves from woods beguiled' and the first 'Natural History Letter' makes much of this particular flower:

> what the common people call 'cuckoo' with us is one which is a species of the 'Orchis' as Henderson tells me: there is a vast many varietys of them with us such as the 'bee Orchis' the 'pigeon Orchis' the 'flye Orchis' & 'butterfly Orchis' etc. etc. namd so from the supposd resemblance the flowers bear to those things these is my cuckoos & the one that is found in Spring with the blue bells is the 'pouch lipd cuckoo bud' I have so often mentioned its flowers are purple and freckld with paler spots inside & its leaves are spotted with jet like the arum they come & go with the cuckoo & in my opinion are the only cuckoo flowers of England let the commentators of Shakespeare say what they will nay shakspear himself has no authority for me in this particular the vulgar wereever I have been know them by this name only & the vulgar are always the best glossary to such things (ibid. pp. 15–16)

This triumph of the 'vulgar' is in some measure replicated in Clare's use of the 'cuckoo' to pay homage to the nightingale in the poem.

33 Tennyson, *Poems*, ed. Christopher Ricks (London, 1969), p. 1163.

34 Grainger, *Natural History*, p. 68.

35 Keats, *Complete Poems*, p. 220.

36 In his article on 'Keats, Reynolds and the "Old Poets"', John Barnard draws attention to Keats's 'greenwood mode' in the 'Robin Hood' poems and notes the parallel with Hunt's *Foliage* of 1818, which was divided into two parts called 'Greenwoods, or Original Poems' and 'Evergreens; or Translations from Poets of Antiquity', modelled on Ben Jonson's division of his poems into 'The Forest' and 'The Under-wood', *Proceedings of the British Academy*, 75 (1989). The poetic legacy of woodlands was evidently a current issue for some of Clare's contemporaries, including Keats who shared Clare's interest in the 'Old Poets'.

37 There is a later poem on the nightingale – a sonnet written during

Clare's incarceration in Northamptonshire Asylum – which also closes with the rhyme of 'wrong' and 'song'. Neither the rhyme nor the sonnet offers anything comparable to the precarious sense of recognition caught in the earlier poem – the poet's sense of both song and wrong is much fainter. 'This is the month, the Nightingale, clod-brown, / Is heard among the woodland shady boughs', it begins, but despite the eye-openingly down-to-earth initial epithet ('clod-brown'), the poem gives a largely conventional account of the bird's 'sweet melodious song' and its setting is comfortable English pastoral. 'SONNET: The Nightingale', in Robinson and Powell, *Later Poetry*, vol. I, p. 372.

38 Hyder E. Rollins (ed.) *Letters of John Keats*, vol. I (Cambridge, Mass., 1958), p. 221.

39 Compare the letter to Edward Villiers Rippingille of 1826 in which Clare describes himself 'not in a Pallace on Parnassus but in a Hut two storys high'. In the same letter he describes the countryside around Helpston with defensive mock-pastoral irony, touching briefly on the nightingale of pastoral tradition and the 'woodlands legacy of song': 'we have a many woods on one hand & many nightingales but no Chloes or Phillises worth the mention we have brooks & wild bowers for Poets but no piping shepherds', M. Storey *Letters*, p. 379.

40 Seamus Heaney, 'Personal Helicon' in *Death of a Naturalist* p. 57.

41 Grainger, *Natural History* p. 318.

42 Ibid. p. 313.

43 Gaston Bachelard, *The Poetics of Space*, translated from the French by Maria Jolas (Boston, Mass., 1969), pp. 90–104.

44 Ibid. p. 99.

45 Ibid. p. 103.

46 'Birds Nests', like 'The Nightingale's Nest', was originally to have been part of *The Midsummer Cushion* (p. 489). Clare's 'nesting instinct' may have been most in evidence during the time before and after he moved from Helpston to Northborough, around 1832. Interestingly, Clare noted that the nightingale, though a bird of passage, was a 'bad flyer' and as 'timid on the wing as a young bird', so that he found himself doubting 'wether its a bird of any passage at all', Grainger *Natural History* p. 108. Clare himself was an even more reluctant bird of passage of course.

47 C. R. Leslie, *Memoirs of the Life of John Constable Composed Chiefly of his Letters* (London, 1951), p. 327.

48 Ibid. p. 319.

49 Ibid. p. 273.

50 Ibid. p. 288.

51 Ibid. p. 285.

52 Ibid. p. 303.

53 *The Midsummer Cushion*, p. 404. It was published in *The Rural Muse* with 'The Nightingale's Nest' in 1835; Thornton, *Rural Muse*, p. 119.

54 In a letter of October 1827, Clare thanks De Wint for the frontispiece and praises the engraving as a 'beautiful thing', while noting that 'the bottle in the reaper's hand is too big for the company in fact it appears too big for a bottle at all in my eye but thats perhaps its own fault and not the bottles', M. Storey, *Letters*, pp. 399–440. Some of De Wint's sketches and paintings of Lincolnshire are in the Lincoln Museum.

55 Grainger, *Natural History*, p. 51.

56 Leslie, *Memoirs*, p. 280 and p. 132.

57 Grainger, *Natural History*, p. 139.

58 In his journal Clare recorded: 'it is often reported that the Sky lark never sings but on the Wing this report is worth little truth like a many others I saw one this morning sing on the ground', ibid. p. 239. Clare's skylark is happily earthbound. 'The Sky Lark' is preceded in *The Rural Muse* (1835) by 'To a Poet', an address to an unrecognised 'Poet of mighty power'. It is a highly generalised and formulaic tribute to poetry as an evergreen laurel, but its proximity to the bird poem is certainly suggestive.

59 Mark Storey (ed.), *John Clare: The Critical Heritage* (London, 1973), pp. 218–19. Storey also notes that 'we have...to avoid the rash equation made by the enthusiastic Mrs Emmerson, whereby Clare and bird become one', in M. Storey (ed.) *The Poetry of John Clare* (London and Basingstoke, 1974), p. 122. On the other hand, Eliza Emmerson's 'enthusiastic' misreading has the great advantage of drawing attention to the profound identifications within the poem between the poet and the nightingale's world. She recognises that what are at stake here are Clare's claims about his poetry.

60 E. H. Coleridge (ed.), *The Poems of Samuel Taylor Coleridge* (Oxford, 1912).

61 Compare William Carlos Williams, *Paterson*, Book 2; 'Outside / outside myself / there is a world, / he rumbled, subject to my incursions / – a world / [to me] at rest, / which I approach / concretely'.

62 Grainger, *Natural History*, pp. 311–12.

63 Ibid. p. 312.

64 In *John Clare's Autobiographical Writings*, ed. Eric Robinson, (Oxford, 1986).

65 Quotations from 'The Progress of Ryhme', in Eric Robinson and David Powell (eds.), *John Clare*, The Oxford Authors (Oxford, 1984), pp. 153–61.

66 In the closing stanza of *Child Harold*, Clare dubs 'the song of birds' 'nature's song of freedom', invoking 'The Thrush and Nightingale and timid dove' as examples of this libertarian lyricism.

CHAPTER 4

John Clare : the trespasser

John Goodridge and Kelsey Thornton

CLIMBING THE WALL

John Clare was about thirteen when he first saw Thomson's *The Seasons*. Within days he had bought his own copy of the poem and in order to read it unobserved, climbed over a wall into a private estate, Burghley Park. Afterwards he composed a poem of his own and for the first time wrote it down. Here is his own account of this sequence of events (omitting a digression on religious fanaticism):

this summer I met with a fragment of Thompsons Seasons   a young man, by trade a weaver, much older then myself, then in the village, show'd it me
     I knew nothing of blank verse nor ryhme either otherwise than by the trash of Ballad Singers, but I still remember my sensations in reading the opening of Spring   I cant say the reason, but the following lines made my heart twitter with joy:

  Come gentle Spring ethereal mildness come
  And from the bosom of yon dropping cloud
  While music wakes around, veild in a shower
  Of shadowing roses, on our plains desend.

I greedily read over all I coud before I returnd it and resolvd to posses one my self, the price of it being only 1s/6d... On the next Sunday I started to stamford to buy Thompson, for I teazd my father out of the 1s/6d and woud not let him have any peace till he consented to give it me, but when I got there I was told by a young shop boy in the street who had a book in his hand which I found to be 'Collins Odes and poems' that the booksellers woud not open the shop on a Sunday   this was a dissapointment most strongly felt and I returnd home in very low spirits, but haveing to tend horses the next week in company with other boys I plannd a scheme in secret to obtain my wishes by stelth, giving one of the boys a penny to keep my horses in my absence, with an additional penny to keep the Secret   I started off and as we was generally soon with getteing out our horses that they might fill themselves before the flyes was out I got to Stamford I dare say before a door had been opend   I loiterd about the town for hours ere I coud obtain my wishes   I at length got it with an agreeable dissapointment in return for my first, buying it for 6d less then I had propos'd and never was I more pleasd with a bargain then I was with this shilling purchase   On my return the Sun got up and it was a beautiful morning and as I did not like to let any body see me reading on the road of a working day I clumb over the wall into Burghly Park and nestled in a lawn at the wall side   the Scenery around me was uncommonly beautiful at that time of the year and what with reading the book and beholding the beautys of artful nature in the park I got into a strain of descriptive ryhming on my journey home   this was 'the morning walk' the first thing I commited to paper[1]

The central excitement here is that Clare's initiation into literature involves a literal and metaphorical trespass. The appropriate act for climbing into the world of literature is climbing into the private land of the aristocracy. This is a key moment for Clare, one which emblematises and focusses a number of fundamental issues in his life and writings. By climbing the wall into Burghley Park, Clare is ostensibly avoiding the detection of his transgressions; but he is also (whether consciously or not) turning the event into a complete act of subversion, a three-fold trespass on the time, culture and land of his social superiors. It is one small step for John Clare the truant farmboy, but a giant leap for John Clare the poet; for once he has crossed the wall and can wander freely within the pastoral landscape of Burghley Park and the pastoral poetry of Thomson's *The Seasons*, Clare feels sufficiently released from the bonds of social class and economic necessity to write down a poem – something he has never dared do before. It is as though he has moved into a different lifestyle, a world apart from that of the working man. He has bought his first book and written down his first poem, and the trespass into Burghley stands as a rite of passage, marking his entry into the brave new world of literature.[2]

It may of course be seen as merely an instinctive or expedient act for Clare to climb the wall in order to read, but the context in which he sets the scene suggests that it is part of a series of ideas and images of trespass that are closely associated in his mind. In the opening pages of his autobiography, in which this unusual adventure is set, Clare graphically describes the cultural environment in which he grew up: a 'gloomy village in Northamptonshire', where a love of books is 'a sure indication of laziness', book-reading fit only for 'quallyfiing an idiot for a workhouse'; parents who were 'illiterate to the last degree'; a mother for whom higher learning was 'the blackest arts of witchcraft'; and a father who made him a child-sized threshing flail and taught him early that his legacy was to be 'the hardship which adam and Eve inflicted on their childern by their inexperienced misdeeds'. Clare exaggerates some of the detail, such as his parent's illiteracy (his father certainly could and did read, and his mother had always hoped her son might be a scholar), but the general sense of cultural deprivation is clear enough. He is a sickly child, 'of a waukly constitution'; and he defines himself by his early attempts to acquire learning and culture, wandering off on his own, tracing the strange hieroglyphics of geometry on barn walls, and muttering to himself. His fellow villagers, though they have not perhaps read Gray's *Elegy*, are quick to recognise these strange moves as the telltale 'symtoms of lunacy', and the poet is marked for an outsider.

The one cultural area in which the young Clare does not feel alienated is that of popular literature, the 'supersti[ti]ous tales that are hawked about a sheet for a penny', the hundred ballads his father can sing, the 'Jiants, Hobbgoblins, and faireys' in the tales whose recounting makes working with the old women a pleasure, and the 'Sixpenny Romances of "Cinderella", "Little Red Riding Hood", "Jack and the bean Stalk", "Zig Zag", "Prince Cherry", etc', of which Clare 'firmly believed every page I read and considerd I possesd in these the chief learning and literature of the country'.

Thus it is especially striking that when he discovers literary culture, in the passage under consideration, Clare uncharacteristically rounds on the 'trash of Ballad Singers', seemingly angry at having been led to believe that popular literature was all there was. Having glimpsed something beyond the boundaries of this culture, he dismisses popular literature, and sets off as soon as he can to consolidate his engagement with the new, literary culture. In doing so, he discovers very quickly that the boundaries of culture are imposed, not only from within, but also from without; for the shop is closed on a Sunday, the one day on which a farmboy might visit it, and the conclusion that bookshops are not for working people seems inescapable.[3] This is, as he says, 'a dissapointment most strongly felt'; but Clare hardly pauses, and in the same sentence is describing his plan to 'obtain my wishes by stelth'. The syntactical continuity signals the fact that there can be no hesitancy, no turning back for Clare, no matter how strongly fenced off from him literary culture might be. Further transgressions follow thick and fast. We see Clare stealing time from his employer; Clare bribing his workmate; Clare sneaking off to Stamford; Clare 'loiter[ing] about the town'; and Clare getting a bargain.

All these unusual, morally dubious activities prepare us well for the moment when Clare climbs over the wall into Burghley Park. That action is immediately prompted by guilt. It has been a sub-text throughout, and Clare's ambiguous language signals its presence: 'loiterd about the town' suggests both the pleasure and the guilt of idleness; 'an agreeable dissapointment' actually means a pleasant surprise, but ambiguous feelings seem to inform the phrase as much as does the fact that English has no word for the opposite of 'disappointment'. Having stolen his employer's time, and obtained a precious piece of the culture which all his training has taught him is not for the likes of him, he must guiltily hide his crime. 'I did not like to let any body see me reading on the road of a working day', he admits; for if bookshops are not for labourers, neither is reading, and the fact that it is a working day makes this the more strongly felt. His 'trespass' against a culture which seems tacitly forbidden to him threatens to compound his 'trespass' against his employer's time. There is only one thing he can do, and that is to go even further along the primrose path, by making a literal, land trespass.

Clare's trespass into Burghley, then, like Wordsworth's boat-stealing episode in the first book of the *Prelude*, is 'an act of stealth / And troubled pleasure'.[4] Yet it is also a symbolic act which signals that to be what Clare became that day, a poet, he must trespass, he must transgress. In order to 'trespass upon parnuss plain' (as he later puts it),[5] he would have to cross social and economic, literary and land boundaries. One might say that his whole life would become a sort of trespass.

Thus trespass imagery, considered in the broad sense of boundaries, and those who break or challenge them, pervades the whole of John Clare's writings. The theme is taken up in major Clarean subjects such as enclosure and (especially in the asylum period) imprisonment. It informs his lifelong interest in Scotland and in gypsy culture. It may be discerned in the way he deals with such diverse subjects as love, identity, the role of the poet, and in his attitude to grammar and punctuation. Clare writes repeatedly of his own confrontations with physical and metaphysical boundaries, and he deploys in his writings a large and motley army of boundary-breakers, trespassers, and other free spirits. They include ants, birds, cattle, discharged soldiers,

drinkers, drovers, flies, ghosts, gypsies, herdboys, horses, mole-
catchers, moles, outcasts, poachers, packmen, schoolchildren, Scots,
sheep, shepherds, tramps, traders, weeds, the wind; and the poet
himself, in numerous guises.[6]

It would not be possible to examine here all the many kinds of
trespass experience in Clare's writings; nor can we consider more
than a few of Clare's battalions of trespassers. We shall therefore
concentrate in what follows on a few representative areas of the
subject. Firstly, we shall look a little further at Burghley Park, the
important site for a kind of trespass Clare used to help define and
create himself as a poet. We shall then look at some of the poet's
responses to boundaries, to trespassers and, finally, to land enclosure.
Clare will be seen to have a complex of responses to the idea of
trespass. He can be awed, afraid, angry at both his trespass and the
boundaries which compel him to trespass, yet also willing to
announce his trespass and deal with it (as in this first example) in a
way that uses poetry to transform guilt, through aestheticising his
experiences.

BURGHLEY

Burghley Park was an appropriate place for Clare to begin his new
life as a poet. It represented a topographical equivalent to the
pictorial landscapes described in his new treasure, *The Seasons*.[7] Its
ordered variety ('artful nature') inspired him to poetry (we must
think of Clare in terms of eighteenth-century poetic traditions at this
stage in his career), contrasting as it did with the flat landscape
outside the walls, which Clare often found oppressive and *un*inspiring.
It was a kind of Paradise for him, representing pastoral poetry,
inspiration, nature, and the pleasurable (but always fearful and
guilty) excitement of being where he knew he should not be.

An early topographical poem, 'Narrative verses Written after an
Excursion from Helpston to Burghley Park' provides an interesting
gloss on this, encapsulating his feelings towards this special place, and
confirming its significance to his development as a poet. From
Helpston to Burghley Park is not too complex as a physical journey,
but as a symbolic journey it is momentous, from the lowest in the land
to almost the highest. Margaret Grainger notes that the journey from
Helpston to Burghley is 'Clare's physical journey. But another
journey, of mind and spirit, is also taking place in the poem... To

enlarge his prospects, literally and metaphorically, he had been forced to venture away from home'.[8]

Grainger has noted echoes of Collins and Bloomfield in the poem. Another important presence is Keats, whose poem 'I stood tip-toe upon a little hill' begins with similar language and a similar atmosphere to Clare's opening lines:

> I stood tip-toe upon a little hill
> The air was cooling, and so very still,   (Keats)

> The faint sun tipt the rising Ground
> No Blustry wind – the air was still   (Clare)[9]

There are other similarities: both poets describe hills, bees, and other natural objects and pastoral images. More importantly, there is a similar sense of a poet using natural description to conjure a greater poetic purpose. 'I stood tip-toe' has been described as 'an attempt to explore the issues more fully realised in *Sleep and Poetry*', while in its companion poem 'Sleep and Poetry' Keats makes his 'first serious effort to outline his major concerns'.[10] Clare's poem gives a similar sense of a poet creating himself, working out his role as a poet through his relationship with landscape.

As with the wall-climbing episode, Clare's first task is to escape from familiar restrictions. He is 'from labour free' (line 5), and is careful to set off via a route well-hidden from 'the public view' (while protesting rather too much that a poet's natural love of thickets is the only reason for this):

> 2
> O! Joyful morn: – on pleasure bent
>   Down thy green slopes and fields I flew
> And thro' the thickest covert went
>   Which hid me from the public view
> Nor was it shame nor was it fear
>   No no it was my own dear choise
> I love the Brierey thicket where
>   Echo keeps her mocking voice[11]

Clare is very conscious of the fact that this is a special journey, and in the third stanza presents it in Bunyanesque terms:

> I left my own fields far behind
> And pilgrim-like trod foreign ground

Thus the landscape itself takes on a kind of enhanced reality: 'every wood and field me thought / A greener brighter prospect wore' (stanza 3); and although he notes the absence of conventionally poetic and sublime scenery ('no hughe rock... Nor lofty mountain', stanza 4), he is able to pursue the 'poetic' activities of wandering and musing. Preparing himself for Burghley, he muses on the legacy of ancient history (stanza 6), on memories of reading poetry (stanza 7) and on memories of places he passes on the journey (stanzas 8–10). The first allusion to Burghley, in stanza 11, is as both memory and desire (and, in the phrase 'ere the oak tree tops appeared', as something glimpsed in the distance). Like Bunyan's heavenly city, Burghley gleams; and as in eighteenth-century poetry, the poet's aesthetic pleasure in it is based on its happy mingling of opposites, its *concordia discors*:

> 11
> But O! that spot so long endear'd
> Gleaming rapterous on my sight
> Fill'd – ere the oak tree tops appeard
> My Breast with wonder and delight
> There art and nature friendly join'd
> Intermingling charm'd the eye
> And as their varying forms combin'd
> Each gave each a nobler dye[12]

The power of his 'fancy' provides him with memories of Burghley, and enables him to admire its inspiring contrasts:

> Enough thy power – the spacious park
> The towering chasenuts hughe and high
> The arching groves and walks so dark
> And all appear in mem'rys eye   (stanza 12)

Now, however, the mood of the poem changes, and in a typically Clarean way, doubts and fears begin to surface. He has reached Burghley in his mind: to reach it in reality will be more difficult. Will he be seen? Will he have enough time? And will he be caught trespassing? Again, he has to avoid people; and again this is presented as an aesthetic matter, the need to be what a modern critic calls 'a lonely poet surrounded by "nature"'[13] (though as Clare later admits, it also has much to do with fear of capture, punishment and ostracism):

> 13
> With deep regret I view'd the spire
> Which told the busy vil so nigh
> For lonley shades are my desire

Far from the reach of human eye
The foot pad turning to the town
No longer provd alone to me
Loud noisy murmurs filld the air
And spoild my deep sollemnity

The second familiar fear, of not having enough time, serves to spur him on, and forces an immediate trespass. He quits the pathways and, once again, finds himself climbing over a wall:

14
The passing hours jog'd on apace
    And in their progress seem'd to say
'Haste, and gain that destined place
    'Or soon thou'lt loose the flitting day'
I instantly obey'd their call
    Nor went to where the foot-pad lay
But clamberd oer an old rough wall
    And stole across the nearest way

This time, however, Clare is highly alert to his trespass. This is not Burghley Park, but an unspecified, perhaps more dangerous (because open) place to trespass. His fearful consciousness of danger restricts his ability to read the aesthetics of the landscape:

15
No spire I caught nor woody swell
    My Eye confind to lower bounds
Yet not to mark the flowrets bell
    But watch the owners of the grounds
Their presence was my only fear
    No boughs to shield me if they came
And soon amid my rash career
    I deem'd such trespasing to blame

16
For troubl'd thoughts began to rise
    Of ills almost beyond relief
Which might from this one cause arise
    And leave me there to whant reprief
So arguing with my self how vain
    An afterthought 'Still to keep free'
Made me to seek the road again
    And own the force of Liberty

As these stanzas show, Clare was immensely sensitive to implications, not only those of his own words, but also of the possible meanings that could be imputed to his actions. It is perhaps this quality that gave rise to his great shyness and his fear of the dark: he was always capable of being 'spooked' by unknown places and experiences. Here he is 'spooked' by his own trespass, and returns to the road to save himself from possible capture by the landowner. There are hints of self-reproach in this confession: he has abandoned his ritual and aesthetic responsibilities as a poet, in favour of naked self-preservation; and the words 'free' and 'Liberty' are ironically paradoxical (staying free by admitting he is not free) as well as confessionally honest.[14] Yet the final word of the stanza, 'Liberty', retains its rhetorical power, and enables Clare to rescue the memory (and his dignity) from what seems at face value to be an ignominious retreat. He continues:

> 17
> For O! its unabated power
> Did then my breast with raptures fill
> And sure it was a happy hour
> That led me up to Barnack hill
> There uncontrould I knew no bounds
> But lookt oer Villages a crowd
> And cots and spires to farthest rounds
> While far trees seem'd a misty cloud

One half-expected a Keatsian repetition of the word 'Liberty' at the start of the new stanza (as in 'faery lands forlorn. // Forlorn! the very word is like a bell'), and this kind of re-affirmative construction is implicitly present in Clare's exclamation, and through the pronoun 'its' (liberty remains the subject of the new sentence). Clare is able to rescue the situation, too, through his new position on Barnack Hill, overlooking Burghley from the only commanding height in the area, whose symbolic significance is enhanced by its position at the point where Ermine Street enters Burghley Park (as Margaret Grainger has noted).[15] He has in fact reached his destination, and can now perform the ritual for which he has come to Burghley: to make a wish, inspired by the scenery, aided and abetted by his Muse, for success as a pastoral poet:

> 18
> While tir'd with such farstretching views
> I left the green hills sideling slope
> But O! so tempting was the muse
> She made me wish she made me hope
> I wish'd and hop'd that future days

(For scenes prophetic fill'd my breast)
Whould grant to me a Crown of bays
By singing maids and shepherds drest

In the final stanzas (19–21) Clare ventures further into Burghley
Park, his interior vision (memory, fancy) responding to the exterior
visions in the Park: awe-inspiring groves, walks and views and the
'massy grated gate' of the Park (suggesting again themes of trespass
and entry). The combination of themes in the poem is interesting:
literature, poetic ambition and composition, the aristocratic house
and park, trespass and freedom, roads and hidden routes. His
engagement with the landscape is closely connected with his poetic
ambitions. At this stage in his career we can appropriately use
eighteenth-century terms to describe these connections: 'prospects'
(what he can see, and what his own 'prospects' are); 'decorum'
(where one should or should not venture, on the land or in poetry);
and 'the sublime', a term of particular relevance to the closing
stanzas, in which Clare's fear of being caught trespassing, and his
overawed response to the sense of aristocratic control implied by the
structures of Burghley Park, are easily translated into a poetic *frisson*
of sublime fear.

Burghley Park here becomes a touchstone for Clare, and the act of
trespassing in it – so casual and informal in the *Seasons* episode – is
here formalised into a solemn and dangerous ritual act, intimately
tied up with becoming a poet. The park encapsulates his greatest
hopes and fears as regards both landscape and poetry. It is a place of
inspiration, and has to be approached with the zeal of Bunyan's
Christian, yet with the guile of an intruder. In a later poem, 'The
Progress of Ryhme', it is remembered as a spiritually inspiring place,
the site of a visionary experience which left the young Clare 'itching
after ryhme':

> Both insects & the breath of flowers
> To sing their makers mighty powers
> Ive thought so as I used to rove
> Through burghley park that darksome grove
> Of Limes where twilight lingered grey
> Like evening in the midst of day
> & felt without a single skill
> That instinct that would not be still
> To think of song sublime beneath
> That heaved my bosom like my breath

That burned & chilled & went & came
Without or uttering or a name
Untill the vision waked with time
& left me itching after ryhme[16]

One could obviously find other locations which have something of this kind of resonance for Clare. 'Round Oak Waters', 'Swordy Well', 'Emmonsales Heath' and 'Langley Bush', to name four, have become familiar-seeming places to many poetry readers as a result of Clare's intense poetic engagements with them. However, Burghley is especially interesting because it is associated for Clare with momentous experiences in his development as a poet; and it would accordingly continue to hold a significant place in his poetry.[17] On the one hand, Burghley meant pleasure: enjoyment of its ordered, pastoral landscape; poetic ecstasy in the visionary experiences Clare felt there. On the other hand, there is a strong sense of limitation and anxiety about what he could and could not do there. The question of how far he could go within the literary culture he had discovered is metaphorically suggested by the issue of how far he could go within areas of the physical landscape which were forbidden to him.

The idea of trespass is of course central to both issues. Because this is so, the significance of Clare's anxieties about trespassing should not be underestimated. Several passages in his writings suggest not merely anxiety, but a real terror of being caught trespassing. For example, he records in his 'Journal' for Saturday 16 April 1825:

Took a walk in the field a birds nesting & botanizing & had like to have been taken up as a poacher in Hillywood by a meddlesome consieted keeper belonging to Sir John Trollop he swore that he had seen me in act more then once of shooting game when I never shot even so much as a sparrow in my life – what terryfying rascals these wood keepers & gamekeepers are they make a prison of the forrests & are its joalers[18]

Clare had good reason to live in terror of the keepers and the Trespass and Game Laws. The Hammonds (who remain the most eloquent chroniclers of the subject) record that 'a sort of civil war was going on between the labourers and the gamekeepers' in the period, a view which is put even more strongly by Harry Hopkins in his book *The Long Affray* (1985). The effects of poverty, exacerbated by wartime and post-war conditions, the agricultural slump of 1815, and the increasingly Draconian Game Laws (the Hammonds describe those of 1770, 1800, 1803, 1816 and 1831: there were many others), led to greatly increased levels of violence and brutality in this 'war'. Murderous spring guns which could kill or maim were, say the Hammonds, 'evidently common by 1817' (mantraps had long been familiar). And in the years between 1827 and 1831 'one in seven of all criminal convictions in the country were convictions under the Game Code'.[19]

The sources of Clare's fear are not hard to find in the Hammonds' account. Had the gamekeeper who accused him of poaching been believed, Clare could have been sentenced to imprisonment, with the possibility of a public whipping and/or hard labour, or (after 1816) seven years' transportation. To give an extreme (and admittedly somewhat unlikely) example, had the keeper attempted to arrest Clare, and been violently resisted, the poet could have been hung, under Lord Ellenborough's law of 1803. Should he so much as have broken the branch of a tree while trespassing, Clare could have been sent to the House of Correction under the Malicious Trespass Act of 1820. Of course the statutory penalties do not necessary indicate what actually happened in the countryside (though Harry Hopkins's trawl through the sources nets more than enough legally sanctioned brutality for the strongest stomach): there was indeed a strong, resistant sense in the countryside that the Game Laws were a perversion of natural law. No matter what the penalties, they would continue to be resisted by many. Yet we can see how intimidated by these Draconian measures Clare would be; and that his lifelong hatred of prisons clearly stems from real, well-founded fears.

Even Burghley Park itself, Clare's sacred grove, could be turned from an exclusive Eden into an enclosing prison, as it apparently was when Clare worked there as an under-gardener:

I learnt irregular habbits at this place which I had been stranger too had I kept at home   tho we was far from a town yet confinement sweetens liberty and we stole every oppertunity to get over to Stamford on summer evenings...we usd to get out of the window and climb over the high wall of the extensive gardens for we slept in the garden house and was locked in every night to keep us from robbing the fruit I expect – Our place of rendevouse was a public house calld 'the Hole in the wall'[20]

The ironically appropriate name of the escapees' meeting place, 'the Hole in the wall', humorously dramatises Clare's plight: in order to move freely, rules have to be broken, walls breached, risks taken. As with the *Seasons* episode, Clare has to engage in various kinds of subversion and subterfuge. Whether he is escaping (as he is here), or breaking in (as in the earlier texts quoted), the landscape, and the power structures it embodies, exercise a double psychological control over the poet: the sinister accompaniment to Clare's visionary ecstasy is a darker mood of fear, risk, and circumscription.

LAND BOUNDARIES AND THE VECTORS OF TRESPASS

The predominance of pleasurable imagery in Clare's descriptive poetry makes it hard for us to conceive of his environment, 'the countryside' which is the major site of his poetry, in terms of fear. Clare himself, for whom poetry is often a haven of optimism and an idealised alternative to the harsh realities of his life, characteristically discourages such a reading. Yet there are, as we have seen, clear suggestions of hostility and threat in Clare's environment. The sonnet which the Tibbles entitle 'Trespass' expresses a kind of horror of breaking the Trespass Laws, which is only partly alleviated by the poem's naive appeals to beauty and to the poet's unpropertied innocence:

> I dreaded walking where there was no path
> & prest with cautious tread the meadow swath
> & always turned to look with wary eye
> & always feared the owner coming bye
> Yet everything about where I had gone
> Appeared so beautiful I ventured on
> & when I gained the road where all are free
> I fancied every stranger frowned at me
> & every kinder look appeared to say
> Youve been on trespass in your walk to day
> Ive often thought the day appeared so fine
> How beautiful if such a place were mine
> But having naught I never feel alone
> & cannot use anothers as my own[21]

In his poem 'To John Clare', Neil Philip notes the 'happiest sanity' of Clare's ability to 'start so many poems with the words "I love"'.[22] This is well observed, and it is curious how unlike Clare the first line of the sonnet, 'I dreaded walking where there was no path', seems. We think of him always walking trackless ways; yet we have to realise how much that was a deliberate, often difficult and dangerous thing to do.

One of the results of this is that Clare's writings are permeated with the imagery of land boundaries, and of the two functions of boundaries, to enclose, and to exclude. We find them in the earliest part of his life, as when the young Clare grapples with the matter of the square on the hypotenuse:

> I Saw a Tree with Cheries Red,
> Whose Height was 40 Foot,
> A Moat against it hinder'd me
> That I could not get to't,
> The Moat was 30 Feet all Wet
> The Question now must be
> How Long a Ladder I must Set
> To reach the Top o' the Tree.[23]

We find them again in his middle years, as when he attempts, in increasing confusion and anger, to sort out his 'enclosed' money, in a letter to his publisher John Taylor:

To mend the fences of safety that guard my domestic benefits without bringing ⟨every⟩ the other matters to a conclusion – would be a vain attempt – it would be only repairing fences where destroying matters had crept in – & hedging them in to destroy more so the best way is to get them out before I begin to mend the outward fence[24]

And of course we find then, intensely re-literalised, in the writings of Clare's asylum period:

I love to clamber over these bridge walls & when I get off the banks on the road I instinctively look both ways to see if any passengers are going or coming or carts or waggons passing – now here is a stile partitioning off sombodys portion of the bank but the middle rail is off so I stoop under to get through instead of climbing over it[25]

These three very different examples of boundary images (one could obviously cite many others) show how pervasively this imagery is in Clare's thought and language. They also show the distinctive way in which Clare's thoughts about boundaries habitually move in the direction of getting past them. In the first example, fairy-tale like, and with cherries offered as a reward, we know (and so presumably does Clare) that there is a solution to the riddle, a particular formula for crossing the boundary. In the middle example, a deeply frustrating situation, in which his money is locked away from him by his trustees, and yet seems to him to be threatened with being trespassed against by others, is so problematic as to become almost incommunicable, and his extended metaphor of land boundaries collapses into a semantic muddle of hedge-breaking and hedge-building (this is, it must be said, an abandoned draft).

The third quotation, by contrast, is a classic example of Clare successfully negotiating land boundaries, and taking pleasure from doing so. He sizes up the boundary (a wall, then a stile), finding the weak spot (the missing middle rail) as instinctively as a mountain climber reaching for a handhold, and slips through it. He describes what he finds beyond the barrier as follows:

there is a pair of harrows painted red standing on end against the thorn hedge & in another ground an old plough stands on its beam ends against a dotterel tree sometimes we see a roll lying in on one corner & broken trays & an old gate off the hooks waiting to be repaired till repairs are useless – even these rustic implements & appendages of husbandry blend with nature & look pleasing in the fields[26]

At a time when enormous efforts were being put into farming efficiency and productivity Clare takes pleasure here in symbols of farming *un*-productivity: the stationary harrow, the old plough, the abandoned roller and, especially, the broken gate, symbol of freedom. In this kind of writing Clare uses trespass and the flouting of boundaries as a way of insisting on a rural aesthetic in which productivity and labour, and the orderly landscapes they require, are put aside. Even that favourite Clarean theme, the coming of spring, can be symbolised by a broken fence and a decayed haystack, in the poem 'Young Lambs':

> The spring is coming by a many signs;
>   The trays are up, the hedges broken down,
> That fenced the haystack, and the remnant shines
>   Like some old antique fragment weathered brown.
>
> (lines 1–4)[27]

To find this aesthetic in autumn is perhaps less surprising:

then the Autumn patches of painted wood-nooks with an old gate or broken stile or rails underneath[28]

In these sorts of image there is something of the mainstream pastoral and picturesque tradition in which labour is artistically beguiled – made to seem irrelevant, or pleasurable, or something to be carried out by someone else. However, Clare's focus on boundaries, with its particular emphasis on ways through them, and the aesthetic pleasure taken in broken gates, holes in hedges and the like, are his own. It brings together a number of his ideas and feelings. In the poem 'Evening Schoolboys', for example, Clare writes:

Where the retiring sun that rests the while
Streams through the broken hedge – How happy seem
Those schoolboy friendships leaning oer the stile[29]

There are several overlapping areas of interest here. First, Clare is
concerned with the way in which the setting sun naturally comes
through the break in the hedge (if the break is not exactly a natural
phenomenon it is to some extent restored to this status as compared
to an unbroken hedge, through which the sun would *not* shine). His
pleasure in the broken hedge has an aesthetic significance. Does it
also gain from the fact that the poet has ideological reasons for liking
flaws in hedges? The break is seen as a desirable thing, but any
sociological meaning Clare invests in it is channelled into its
aesthetics. The stile, the second vector mentioned, is given significance as a meeting place, associated with the pleasures of childhood
friendship. Yet the very fact that it is a stile, a way through a
boundary, deepens its significance. It is implicitly a route, not only to
the memory of childhood friendship, but also to whatever landscape
lies behind it. It does not much matter *what* that landscape is, in this
instance: a stile is by definition a way of getting through a barrier,
which for Clare is an inherently interesting thing to do.

If we cannot easily separate the various impulses feeding into
Clare's interest in the vectors of trespass, we can at least see what they
are. Clare's hatred of enclosure in general, and the enclosure of
Helpston in particular, is reiterated in poem after poem. Thus the
poet draws attention, again and again, to a political question whose
presence in the real world is indicated by fences, hedges, walls and
ditches. Given the centrality of this in his work, any mention of a
broken hedge will immediately draw the reader's attention to the
issue of enclosure, and to Clare's political as well as his aesthetic
dislike of a bounded landscape. The poet may overtly be admiring
the sun as it shines through a broken hedge, or the way broken gates
and stiles 'blend with nature', or even innocently celebrating the
heroic escape of a fox 'through the hedge':

> And when he rested to his dogs supprise
> The old fox started from his dead disguise
> And while the dog lay panting in the sedge
> He up and snapt and bolted through the hedge[30]

Yet he is also, in these and in many other such moments in his
writings, exploring questions of enclosure and trespass, probing the

weaknesses and limits of a parcelled-up landscape, developing fantasies of penetration and escape, and recreating in poetry a world without the 'hated sign' that says 'no road here'.[31] This does not of course remove anything from the overt significance of what he is doing in these texts. It ought, however, to warn us against the common critical tradition that Clare is a transparently descriptive poet, not in any deep sense metaphorical or aware of wider implications.[32] The theme of trespass does not simply reflect a personal, nostalgic reaction against the enclosure of Helpston, but is also a way for Clare to explore, in a broader sense, the politics of landscape, and the ideology and psychology of human boundedness and freedom. He examines these subjects through his own experiences, of course, but wider implications are never hard to find when we follow a theme like trespass through Clare's writings.

SOME CLAREAN TRESPASSERS

Clare's explorations of trespass and trespass-related subjects are sometimes overt and sometimes presented as sub-texts. Literal and metaphorical, social and psychological trespasses are closely intertwined. Some of the most powerful writing on these themes is directly autobiographical, as it is in the Burghley Park texts we looked at. However, trespass for Clare is not always a personal matter, a solitary, fearful game of hide-and-seek with gamekeepers and farmers. Although he often saw himself as an isolated figure, Clare had a number of allies who, if they could not always share his literary concerns, could certainly share his love of roaming free. Here we shall look in particular at two examples of such Clarean trespassers: gypsies and Scottish drovers.

Among the many kinds of trespasser we listed at the beginning, gypsies are overwhelmingly the most important human trespassers in Clare's writing, apart from the poet himself. They were his natural allies (unlike the static, alien breed of Wordsworth's 'Gipsies'). For Clare they were companions during Sunday escapes, receivers and sharers of stolen peas, and fellow music-lovers.[33] They apparently taught him to play the fiddle.[34] They helped him escape from High Beach.[35] They were, so to speak, natural trespassers, their whole way of life based on a counter-cultural ignoring of private property-oriented land use. They were also, of course, regular users of common land, maintaining its status as a sanctuary, in an increasingly enclosed landscape (in the same way, perhaps, that modern ramblers keep footpaths open by walking them regularly):

> In such lone spots these wild wood roamers dwell
> On commons where no farmers claims appear
> Nor tyrant justice rides to interfere[36]

They were also 'outsiders', and Clare had from his earliest writings seen himself in an outsiderly role. The alienated poet of Gray's *Elegy* (a text constantly echoed in the early poems) provided him with one model. However, Clare could only go so far along the road of solitary mopings. In the company of equals he was a naturally sociable man, and the great attraction of the gypsy lifestyle, as Clare's descriptions of it make clear, is its sociability.[37] Here one could be an outsider without the tragic sense of isolation felt by Gray's lonely poet. This seemed a genuine 'alternative society', which Clare, with his particular priorities and sensibilities, could not but admire and engage in.

Thus if Clare travelled to Burghley to enlarge his 'prospects' in one way, he visited the gypsies to do so in another way, by consulting a gypsy fortune-teller:

> Oft on my hand her magic coins bin struck
> & hoping chink she talkd of morts of luck
> & still as boyish hopes did erst agree
> Mingld wi fears to drop the fortunes fee
> I never faild to gain the honours sought
> & Lord & Squire was purchasd wi a groat[38]

Clare is ironic about the way the gypsy fortune-teller offers him the chance to 'purchase' his way into the freedoms of the aristocracy 'wi a groat', but he is also intrigued; and indeed it is clear that he is fascinated by all aspects of gypsy culture. Like broken gates and gaps in hedges, gypsies are seen as inherently beautiful; they enhance the appearance of the landscape:

I thought the gipseys camp by the green wood side a picturesque and an adorning object to nature and I lovd the gipseys for the beautys which they added to the landscape[39]

Clare is perhaps aware that his is a minority view – he characterises gypsies elsewhere as 'poor ragd out casts of the land', and as 'A quiet, pilfering, unprotected race'.[40] However, against the prejudiced view of gypsies as intruders, he casts them as natural intimates of the landscape, in tune with its mysteries:

They know the woods and every fox's den
And get their living far away from men;
The shooters ask them where to find the game,
The rabbits know them and are almost tame.
The aged women, tawny with the smoke,
Go with the winds and crack the rotted oak.[41]

When village boys hunt rabbits, it is a gypsy boy who initiates them
into the arts of digging rabbits out and training dogs:

When any comes they skulk behind the tree.
The gipsy joins them in his rags and glee
And digs the holes out with a rotten stake
And thrusts his hand and never cares for snake.
The dog, that follows all that passes by,
He ties him to his hand and makes him lie.[42]

Gypsy girls, on the other hand, are admired in a different way:

The beautiful gipsey with brown swarthy cheek
And a bosom of snow melting under her gown[43]

Here Clare's feelings for the exotic 'otherness' of gypsies are
eroticised, via the conventions of the gypsy ballad. One could indeed
read a number of Clare's poetic responses to trespass and to land
boundaries in sexual terms. If such responses are usually either
conventionalised (as in the example quoted) or available only as a
rather covert sub-text, this may reflect the heavy moral censorship
that affected writers in this period (especially writers like Clare and
Keats, who were perceived as being 'lower-class').[44]

If gypsies are generally read by Clare as being what we have called
'natural trespassers', they also trespass in specific ways. In Clare's
poem to 'Langley Bush', for example, their search for firewood has a
second effect:

... thou art reverenced even the rude clan
Of lawless gipseys drove from stage to stage
Pilfering the hedges of the husband man
Leave thee as sacred in thy withering age
Both swains & gipseys seem to love thy name
Thy spots a favourite wi the smutty crew
& soon thou must depend on gipsey fame[45]

Behind the negative implication of words like 'lawless' and 'pilfering'
one glimpses a thinning hedge, increasingly be-gapped and therefore,

as we have seen, of considerable positive interest to the poet; and, in *The Shepherd's Calendar* and elsewhere, Clare also refers to 'gaps the gypsey pilfers thin'.[46]

It would be incautious for the poet to be too positive about gypsy firewood-stealing and boundary-breaking, however; and the only mitigation this passage can overtly offer for the behaviour of the 'smutty crew' is the gypsies' reverential skirting of Langley Bush as a site for gathering firewood. In the opening decades of the nineteenth century, 'pilfering' anything in the countryside was solidly discouraged by laws and heavy social pressures – fences of an ideological kind to reinforce the literal ones the gypsies liked to thin out.[47] Yet for a writer, genre can often find ways round such ideological barriers, and poetry itself can offer a transformed version of the real world. Clare feels no restriction, for example, where he can channel rural pilfering and boundary-breaking into the safety of a comic/sentimental eulogy on a favourite horse. Farm animals are not subject to moral censorship, even when they have learned their tricks from the gypsies, as has the horse 'Dobbin', in the poem 'Going to the Fair':

> When loose from geers he roved as freedoms mate
> Hed find all gaps & open every gate
> & if aught sweet beyond his pasture grew
> No fence so thick but he would blunder thro'
> His youth from gipseys did these tricks recieve
> With them he toiled & worked his wits to live
> Bare roads he traced all day with nought to bite
> Then stole with them to stacks to feed at night
> Tho now a better life was Dobbins lot
> Well fed & fat youths tricks he neer forgot
> Still gaps were broke & Dobbin bore the blame
> Still stacks were pulled & Dobbin felt no shame[48]

Here we have something like a condensed guide to Clarean trespass: three ways to get through a fence (find the gaps, open the gate, or simply blunder through); gypsies and animals together finding ways to freedom; an amusing suggestion of the theme of the grass being greener on the other side; an appropriate pun on 'stole'; subversive trickery and 'wits'; freedom from 'shame'; and a comic turning upside down of the orderly rural world of fences and haystacks.

Most importantly, 'Dobbin' allows Clare to celebrate gypsy freedoms without ideological hesitancy of the sort we can detect in the language of 'Langley Bush'. The evidence of Clare's own writings is that gypsies and other trespassers would be dangerous allies for him to embrace. Among the prose materials on gypsies collected together in the *Autobiographical Writings* (pp. 68–72), for example, Clare quotes a Justice of the Peace whose view is that 'This atrosious tribe of wandering vagabonds ought to be made outlaws in every civilizd kingdom and exterminated from the face of the earth' (p. 69). Though Clare roundly condemns this opinion, we can well understand that the power of such magistrates would represent a deep threat, given Clare's propensity towards wandering and associating with gypsies. His fear of being taken as a trespasser or poacher is ultimately a fear of the magistrate before whom he may be taken. Elsewhere Clare describes a rather sinister incident in which, as a celebrated 'peasant poet', he is taken out for the day by a magistrate, who attempts to involve him in catching a phantom 'poacher', dreamed up by the magistrate on the basis of some innocent proletarian whistling:

he took me with him to see Falkingham joal a good distance from Morton and everyone we met gentle or simple he woud stop to speak too and almost ask their business nay he woud question those that appeard his inferiors as if they were under going an examination in a court of justice – once when we were going to see Belvoir Castle while walking by a plantation a labourer happend to break out into a brisk loud whistle of a song tune and he instantly stopt to listen and swore they were poachers and bade me go on the other side to watch which way they started   I tryd to convince him that the whistle was a song tune but it was no use – and as soon as the fellow heard or perhaps saw that he was suspected tho hid from us I expect he felt fearful and stopt his whistle   this convinced the other that his opinion was right – so after watching awhile the fellow made his appearance and met us to know if we was waiting for him   He askd him his business there and he said he was putting down fencing which satisfied the magistrate – who I verily believe mistrusted every stranger for thieves and vagabonds[49]

Clearly the paranoia of the countryside at this time was not just a manifestation of Clare's sensitivity. Everything about the incident signals the magistrate's urge to exercise control over others. He has dragged Clare away from the harvest, shown him a gaol, and spent the rest of the day demonstrating his officious desire to make everyone explain themselves to him. The language ('joal', 'gentle or simple', 'his inferiors', 'poachers', 'thieves and vagabonds') shows that Clare is aware this man is powerful and dangerous. This does not of course prevent the poet from capturing the ironies of the situation through his fine observation of details: that the magistrate should want him of all people to be impressed by a gaol (Clare loathed prisons); that a 'song' should be construed as clear evidence of criminality (in 'The Progress of Ryhme', line 80, Clare famously wrote of his own 'right to song' as a lyric poet); and that the labourer's 'putting down fencing' – constructing a land barrier – should have 'satisfied' the magistrate.

Yet to befriend gypsies would be seriously to provoke such men. Not surprisingly, Clare's writings often err on the side of caution, rendering gypsies safe by figuring them within the acceptable literary conventions of the picturesque, the comic, the sentimental or the exotic; or else employing the kind of orthodox terminology we saw in 'Langley Bush'. This is not always the case, however. In the group of prose passages on gypsies in the *Autobiographical Writings*, and in the gypsy passage in the poem 'The Village Minstrel' (stanzas 113–17) there is a more honestly documentary approach to the subject. No overt emotional appeal is needed to mitigate the fact that gypsies trespass and steal firewood, when we learn that need drives them to eat diseased sheep carcasses, or 'any nauceaous thing their frowning fates provide' ('The Village Minstrel', stanza 114). In such texts Clare repeatedly brings together hardship and law-breaking in this kind of way. The reader is made to look afresh at gypsies, not merely as interesting exotics, but as fellow mortals driven by familiar needs and contingencies, and particularly vulnerable to the hardship of rural life.

Clare's Scottish drovers, on the other hand, appear in an almost entirely Romantic aspect. The poet's pervasive 'Scottishness' is striking, and has a number of possible sources. He had a Scottish grandfather, the itinerant schoolmaster John Donald Parker, who left his son (Clare's father) behind him as 'one of fates chance-lings who drop into the world without the honour of matrimony'.[50] Clare took a keen interest in the Scottish ballad tradition and in the writings of Burns, Cunningham, Fergusson, Hogg, Ramsay, Scott and Tannahill. That six of these seven writers were from proletarian or otherwise humble backgrounds may be significant.[51] These facts begin to explain the extraordinary facility with which Clare could turn out an authentic-sounding Scottish ballad whenever the mood took him (which was often); and the Romantic yearning he often expresses in his poems for a country which he would never see.

Part of the explanation may also lie in Clare's experience of Scottish drovers, and in the unboundedness he associated with them and their native land. Unlike gypsies, drovers are not a common presence in Clare's writings, but where they do appear, in *The Shepherd's Calendar* ('July', pp. 76–7), their presence is powerful:

> Along the roads in passing crowds
> Followd by dust like smoaking clouds
> Scotch droves of beast a little breed
> In swelterd weary mood proceed
> A patient race from scottish hills
> To fatten by our pasture rills
> Lean wi the wants of mountain soil
> But short and stout for travels toil
> Wi cockd up horns and curling crown
> And dewlap bosom hanging down
> Followd by slowly pacing swains
> Wild to our rushy flats and plains
> At whom the shepherds dog will rise
> And shake himself and in supprise
> Draw back and waffle in affright
> Barking the traveller out of sight
> And mowers oer their scythes will bear
> Upon their uncooth dress to stare
> And shepherds as they trample bye
> Leaves oer their hooks a wondering eye
> To witness men so oddly clad
> In petticoats of banded plad
> Wi blankets oer their shoulders slung
> To camp at night the fields among
> When they for rest on commons stop
> And blue cap like a stocking top
> Cockt oer their faces summer brown
> Wi scarlet tazzeles on the crown
> Rude patterns of the thistle flower
> Untrickd and open to the shower
> And honest faces fresh and free
> That breath[e] of mountain liberty

Clare moves on, in the next line of the poem, to the activities of the 'pindar', the person who rounds up stray sheep and cattle, and in doing so he implicitly contrasts the territorial orderliness of his own bounded landscape with the free-ranging nature of the Scottish men, their beasts, and their native land.

For the drovers are, like the gypsies, exotic strangers who wander freely, and have a night-time camp-fire culture (there is ample evidence in Clare's writings that being abroad at night is in itself a kind of trespass).[52] Their clothing catches his eye, with the strange freedoms suggested by their 'petticoats of banded plad' and their 'blankets' casually slung over their shoulders. The 'scarlet tazzeles' on their caps would seem especially romantic to Clare, who tells elsewhere of childhood searches for red and blue flowers to make cockades for playing soldiers. (In a later poem Clare specifically draws together Scottish battles and ballads: 'Scotland I love thy every scene / Thy Bannockburn and Bonny Jean').[53] The drovers are brown-faced like gypsies. They rest on common land; they camp in the fields. And they have 'honest faces fresh and free / That breath[e] of mountain liberty'. This clearly opposes the common view of gypsies and travellers as *dis*honest – a view Clare reminds us of a few lines later, from the point of view of the pindar, who looks for 'gaps the gypsey pilfers thin' (p. 78).

The nature of the 'mountain liberty' the poet reads in the faces of the Scottish drovers is not specified, but we can reasonably surmise what it might mean to Clare. Romantic Scottishness was at its height in the 1820s, fed by the huge success of Scott's Waverley Novels, and vividly illustrated by the incident in which, 'be-kilted, be-sporraned, be-tartaned', decked-out in Royal Stuart tartan and flesh-coloured tights, the Prince Regent had paraded the streets of Edinburgh, in 1822.[54] That Clare loved the Waverley Novels is made abundantly clear by an untitled late poem which begins 'The heart of Midlothian is nearly my own', and later mentions 'the sweet Lammermore'.[55] Scott's story of 'The Two Drovers' came too late to influence the passage in *The Shepherd's Calendar* (both were published in 1827); but Clare could very well have read Scott's other great 'drover' text, *Rob Roy* (1817).[56]

The phrase itself, 'mountain liberty', gives a further clue. It echoes Milton's personified figure of 'the mountain nymph Sweet Liberty' ('L'Allegro', line 36). Yet mountains were also intrinsically interesting to Clare. They contrasted pleasingly with the flat fenland country in which even molehills were a welcome sight to the poet, and the modestly rising ground near Burghley was, as we saw, almost sublime.[57] Mountains are also by their very nature unenclosable, their only agricultural use being to sustain small numbers of hardy, free-ranging mountain sheep. They were never part of the enclosure movement, nor could they be. The unenclosed openness of the Scottish mountains, and the apparently unbounded freedoms of the drovers, seen as they pass through Clare's own landscape, come together with Clare's interest in the Scottish self-taught poets and ballad writers, with his own one-quarter-Scottish heredity and with the general interest in Scotland of the period, to form an extremely powerful ideal. Scotland becomes for Clare a kind of Paradise, characterised as 'An Eden a' the year'.[58]

The modern reader may wish to reject the now familiar idea of 'Scotland as England's romanticized "other"'.[59] However, we should not automatically dismiss Clare's Scottish dreams. We can see that they hold some potential for the expression of anti-enclosure feelings; and there is evidence that Clare was familiar with the events of the '45 Rebellion, and of the earlier struggles of the Scottish Covenanters.[60] Indeed there is a radicalism running through much of his Scottish material. The ways in which Clare could directly trespass or otherwise challenge the boundedness of his landscape and society were limited. In peopling his poetry with rebellious, warlike souls from the unenclosable mountains of a country with strong libertarian traditions, who go where they like, wear what they like, and whose very cattle mock the bland slabbiness of post-Bakewellian English beasts, Clare turns the poetry itself into a means of resistance. No wonder the shepherd, the mower, and even the shepherd's dog, stop work and stare when the drovers come by: by Clare's lights they are glimpsing both Arcadia, and freedom.

Clare is almost too close to the gypsies, too keenly aware of their hardship and the desperate improvisation their survival necessitates, to use them in this way with any consistency. Scotland and the Scots are, by their very remoteness and strangeness, more easily marshalled into a counter-cultural force. At its best, this works very well, as it does when Clare considers Scotland obliquely via its national emblem, in the poem 'The Thistle':

> I love the thistle and its prickles too
> Cobwebs are round it with a veil of dew
> I love the thistle where it bravely stands
> For rights of Liberty in many lands
> Simply defying every rogueish eye
> With 'wha dare meddle wi me' that passes bye
> My right is simple, blooming 'mong the flowers
> That God's hand scatters on this land of ours[61]

Scotland is not mentioned in this stanza, but the personified thistle quotes the well-known Scottish motto, 'Who dare meddle with me'.

By using a symbol of Scotland rather than Scotland itself, Clare combines the characteristics of Scottish liberty with those of one of his lesser trespassers, the weed.

The result is a defiant and wryly humorous verse. The poet's 'love' is expressed not only towards the aesthetic qualities of the thistle, the way it supports a beautifully be-dewed spider's web, but also towards its prickles, drawing immediate attention to the fact that this is a particularly well-armed weed, whose God-given right to live in liberty, exactly where it has been 'scattered', will be defended, if needs be, by force. Weeds are (like common land, trees and disordered hedgerows) the fuzzy bits in the margins of the enclosed landscape, the uncontrolled refuges of a natural tendency to disorderliness, which Clare consistently praises, in terms which suggest that natural anarchy can carry a political message about the human ordering of the landscape. In the poem 'Solitude', the furze and briars (two more militantly well-armed weeds) are respectively 'unmolested', and 'by freedom sown'.[62] In the untitled, fragmentary poem beginning 'The hedgerow hips to glossy scarlet turn', the weeds celebrate their freedom with a drunken dance, assisted by yet another Clarean trespasser, the wind:

> The weeds beside the hedge dance
> Like so many drunken men,
> Then rest till breezes whisper,
> Then up and dance agen[63]

(Drunkenness is another kind of freedom, as Clare knew only too well.) In 'The Progress of Ryhme', Clare argues coherently against the very terminology by which weeds are marginalised:

> & weeds that bloomed in summers hours
> I thought they should be reckoned flowers
> They made a garden free for all
> & so I loved them great & small
> & sung of some that pleased my eye
> Nor could I pass the thistle bye
> But paused & thought it could not be
> A weed in natures poesy
> No matter for protecting wall
> No matter though they chance to fall
> Where sheep & cows & oxen lie[64]

The thistle is again central, the focus of Clare's argument for the significance of even the humblest representative of freedom. Here its sturdy independence represents an eloquent rejection of Clare's favourite enemy, the 'protecting wall' (so necessary to enclosed, domesticated plants).

The stanza from 'The Thistle' shows the way in which Clare could effortlessly extract deeper meanings from the simplest piece of natural observation. It is not suggested that Clare sets out to write an elaborate piece of literary subversiveness here. The thistle's speech is a simple, humorous rendering of the figure of the truculent, defiant Scotsman. The wider meaning emerges organically from Clare's first concern, which is always to capture the spirit of what he sees. A particular strength of Clare's poetry is its ability to make one see what he sees with great clarity (the pun is fortunate), while suggesting broader layers of significance. Gypsies and Scottish drovers have intrinsic interest as subjects of Clare's rural, descriptive poetry and prose. Yet he also manages to show that their lifestyles run counter to the repressive orderliness of the English countryside. The technique gives his writing a depth not often available in picturesque and pastoral writing.

ENCLOSURE

On reaching stanza 107 of 'The Village Minstrel', Clare's patron, Lord Radstock, felt sufficiently provoked to scribble 'This is Radical slang' in the margin of the manuscript.[65] And so, in a sense, it was:

> 107
> There once was lanes in natures freedom dropt
> There once was paths that every valley wound
> Inclosure came & every path was stopt
> Each tyrant fixt his sign where pads was found
> To hint a trespass now who crossd the ground
> Justice is made to speak as they command
> The high road now must be each stinted bound
> – Inclosure thourt a curse upon the land
> & tastless was the wretch who thy existence pland

Like his contemporaries Byron and Shelley, Clare was an intensely political poet. Like his poetic forebears Goldsmith and Crabbe, the politics of his poetry focus especially on the rural world, and on what Raymond Williams has called the 'well-known habit of using the past...as a stick to beat the present'.[66] However, Crabbe, in Clare's view, 'writes about the peasantry as much like the Magistrate as the

Poet'. That this comment occurs in a letter to a fellow self-taught poet, Allan Cunningham, and contrasts Crabbe unfavourably with a third self-taught poet, Robert Bloomfield, suggests Clare is conscious of the potential effects of class on poets' perspectives of rural life. Crabbe 'knows little or nothing' about the peasantry compared to Bloomfield, who 'not only lived amongst them, but felt and shared the pastoral pleasures with the peasantry of whom he sung'.[67]

For the peasantry and those poets who 'lived amongst them', the central issue of enclosure was not, as it had been for an early pro-enclosure poet like John Dyer, agricultural efficiency. It was trespass, the fearful presence lurking at the heart of stanza 107 and, for the 'peasant', the major conceptual creation of enclosure. At first the signs only 'hint' at trespass; but in the next line a real power of enforcement is evoked: 'Justice is made to speak as they command'. The enclosurists have the magistracy in their pockets, and what that might mean to Clare can easily be imagined.

The problem is firstly one of attitudes. Dyer had advocated enclosure to promote agricultural efficiency and to deter the 'idle pilf'rer' who too easily 'Eludes detection' under a common-field system. For Crabbe, the common land of the heath was agriculturally unproductive, and the territory of 'lawless' pirates and smugglers, 'Rank' weeds, and all manner of ugly (because unproductive) vegetation. Thistles are defiantly beautiful objects to Clare, but in Crabbe's world they constitute a threat to the nation's youth:

> There thistles stretch their prickly arms afar,
> And to the ragged infant threaten war[68]

Beauty is, as always, in the eye of the beholder, and reveals political attitudes. The enclosurists are conversely 'tasteless' for Clare because they have 'stopt' the natural tracery of paths from which the countryside can be seen in a boundless variety of ways. The 'high road now must be each stinted bound' – the chopped-off sound of the word 'stinted' finely enunciates the meagreness of the new, restricted view. For both Crabbe and Clare, the poetical and the political are inseparable. Political views are expressed in terms of views of the landscape: the view of a magistrate, or the view of a peasant; the view from the high road, or the views from the winding paths of freedom.

Clare's poetic war against enclosure, with its methodological contrasting of past and present, beauty and ugliness, single and multiple perspectives, was relentlessly pursued through his early verse. Nowhere is it more convincingly or sophisticatedly argued than in 'The Mores', a magnificent, highly-wrought poem in which Clare deploys all the rhetorical powers he can summon, taking his parochial obsession with trespass and enclosure into the greater tradition of English political protest writing, the tradition of Langland, Milton, Swift, Goldsmith, and indeed Crabbe. Here, 'trespass' is transformed into the much greater subject of civil rights, ownership and control.

The 'view' which opens the poem is deliberately, even exaggeratedly, endless:

> Far spread the moorey ground a level scene
> Bespread with rush and one eternal green
> That never felt the rage of blundering plough
> Though centurys wreathed springs blossoms on its brow
> Still meeting plains that stretched them far away
> In uncheckt shadows of green brown and grey
> Unbounded freedom ruled the wandering scene
> Nor fence of ownership crept in between
> To hide the prospect of the following eye
> Its only bondage was the circling sky
> One mighty flat undwarfed by bush and tree
> Spread its faint shadow of immensity
> And lost itself which seemed to eke its bounds
> In the blue mist the orisons edge surrounds (lines 1–14)[69]

This opening movement has an epic quality to it. Words like 'Far', 'eternal', 'centurys', and the sequence of negatives ('never felt', 'uncheckt' 'unbounded', 'undwarfed'), suggest epic scales of time and space. The language of unbounded vastness dominates. Interestingly, Clare sees freedom from agricultural enclosure in a painterly way, as freedom from picturesque composition. At the same time, the heavy use of past tenses, and the way in which negatives like 'unbounded' and 'undwarfed' include their opposites ('bounded', 'dwarfed'), strongly suggest the kinds of Clarean antitheses we have mentioned: past versus present, openness versus closure, large versus small. The key word is 'unbounded'; and against this huge and heroic openness is set the villain of the piece, the 'fence of ownership' (absent at this stage) which, like Satan in the garden of Eden, 'crept in between'. For once, the characteristic openness of the fens works to Clare's literary advantage, as he invokes the sublimity of the unbounded.

The second movement of the poem brings us sharply into the present:

> Now this sweet vision of my boyish hours
> Free as spring clouds and wild as summer flowers
> Is faded all – a hope that blossomed free
> And hath been once no more shall ever be
> Inclosure came and trampled on the grave
> Of labours rights and left the poor a slave
> And memorys pride ere want to wealth did bow
> Is both the shadow and the substance now   (lines 15–22)

The opening lines of this section acknowledge that Clare's position is an overtly nostalgic one which associates freedom with happy memories of his own childhood. By doing so they strengthen the historical force of what follows, turning a familiar pastoral device into a powerful rhetorical technique. Lines 19–20 state the case against enclosure in tub-thumping political language, but the real strength here lies in the famous piece of rhetoric embodied in the final lines which, like the opening lines of the passage, address 'external' politics through the 'internal' consciousness:

> And memorys pride ere want to wealth did bow
> Is both the shadow and the substance now

That is, the proud and precious memory of 'unbounded freedom', of a time before the needs of the poor were rejected in the interests of the rich, now must serve as both the insubstantial reflection of that vision, and the only tangible evidence of it that remains. All the poor have left is pride in the nobility of their former vision. The rhetoric of Clare's political protest is enriched by this disillusioned and angry insistence that (though pride in one's past is a real and important resource) the poor have been left to feed themselves on dreams.[70]

Without pause, Clare plunges us into his ideal past again:

> The sheep and cows were free to range as then
> Where change might prompt nor felt the bonds of men
> Cows went and came with evening morn and night
> To the wild pasture as their common right
> And sheep unfolded with the rising sun
> Heard the swains shout and felt their freedom won
> Tracked the red fallow field and heath and plain
> Then met the brook and drank and roamed again
> The brook that dribbled on as clear as glass

> Beneath the roots they hid among the grass
> While the glad shepherd traced their tracks along
> Free as the lark and happy as her song   (lines 23–34)

He has returned to the 'sweet vision' for another look at it, and he will return to it again (in lines 51–64) – re-iteration is one of Clare's rhetorical techniques. In this blissful scene cattle, sheep, the shepherd, the lark and the stream are equally free to wander where they will. While freedom of expression, the 'right to song', is dramatically conveyed in the exuberant 'shout' of the swains, freedom of movement is portrayed as being available to all.

There are three anti-enclosure speeches in the poem, at lines 15–22, 35–50, and 64–80. They get fiercer and more witheringly sarcastic. This is the middle one, which dips repeatedly into what is lost, clashing the past and the present discordantly together to emphasise further the change that has occurred:

> But now alls fled and flats of many a dye
> That seemed to lengthen with the following eye
> Moors loosing from the sight far smooth and blea
> Where swopt the plover in its pleasure free
> Are vanished now with commons wild and gay
> As poets visions of lifes early day
> Mulberry bushes where the boy would run
> To fill his hands with fruit are grubbed and done (lines 35–42)

The last couplet shows this 'clashing' at its most effective. From 'Mulberry' to 'fruit' Clare deploys a favourite image from classical and neo-classical pastoral, that of the fecundity and bounty of nature. We find it in Virgil's *Georgics* (II, 520) where 'Autumn drops her varied fruits at our feet', or in Marvell's 'Bermudas', where God 'makes the figs our mouths to meet / And throws the melons at our feet'. Yet then Clare does something entirely unexpected to the convention: he dramatically smashes the image, with as knobbly a verbal stick as he can find, the phrase 'grubbed and done', blunt words, emphatically set in the past tense, abrupt, and final.

Now we move out to the edges of the field, the common lands and woods which held such a fascination for Clare. However, instead of pleasurable natural abundance, we find destruction and chaos:

> And hedgrow briars – flower lovers overjoyed
> Came and got flower pots – these are all destroyed
> And sky bound mores in mangled garb are left
> Like mighty giants of their limbs bereft   (lines 43–6)

The phrase 'mighty giants of their limbs bereft' implies tree-chopping: it might also suggest heroically fallen gods (as in Keats's two 'Hyperion' poems, one of which Clare had read and praised).[71] Instead of natural abundance, and contrasting with the mutilated ugliness of the damaged trees, we have the shaping of orderly small-mindedness, a truly *petit*-bourgeois landscape (Clare's repetition of 'little' puts one in mind of Pete Seeger's song 'Little Boxes', a satire on the modern, semi-detached kind of restricted horizon):

> Fence now meets fence in owners little bounds
> Of field and meadow large as garden grounds
> In little parcels little minds to please
> With men and flocks imprisoned ill at ease   (lines 47–50)

Imprisonment 'ill at ease' is a favourite negative image in Clare's later poetry, and unsurprisingly is used again and again in his letters home from the Northampton General Asylum.[72] It is the epitome of claustrophobic 'littleness'. Against this restrictive 'littleness' of a bounded landscape, Clare now sets a different and positive sort of 'littleness', that of the minute diversity of unenclosed paths and flowers (just as in line 48 he gives a negative kind of largeness, restricted to the size of a garden). These two uses of 'little' make an effective double contrast with the unboundedness of the early stanzas:

> Each little path that led its pleasant way
> As sweet as morning leading night astray
> Where little flowers bloomed round a varied host
> That travel felt delighted to be lost
> Nor grudged the steps that he had taen as vain
> When right roads traced his journeys end again
> Nay on a broken tree hed sit awhile
> To see the mores and fields and meadows smile
> Sometimes with cowslaps smothered – then all white
> With daiseys – then the summers splendid sight
> Of corn fields crimson oer the 'headach' bloomd
> Like splendid armys for the battle plumed
> He gazed upon them with wild fancys eye
> As fallen landscapes from an evening sky   (lines 51–64)

This third view of the pre-enclosure scene is the wandering poet's perspective, often used by Clare. Again there is a change of pace. The last couplet moves the poem gently from a sense of celebration ('splendid armys') to a sense of loss ('fallen landscapes', and the elegiac note of 'evening sky'). Yet, just as one becomes attuned to this new elegiac mood (a familiar one in pastoral), the poet again does something dramatically jolting, stopping the verse dead in mid-line with the appropriate word 'stopt':

> These paths are stopt – the rude philistines thrall
> Is laid upon them and destroyed them all
> Each little tyrant with his little sign
> Shows where man claims earth glows no more divine
> On paths to freedom and to childhood dear
> A board sticks up to notice 'no road here'
> And on the tree with ivy overhung
> The hated sign by vulgar taste is hung
> As tho the very birds should learn to know
> When they go there they must no further go   (lines 65–74)

Again we are brought back to destruction and restriction. The 'mighty giants' are replaced by 'Each little tyrant', a sorry degeneration. The repetition of 'little' emphasises the contrast between the little path and little flowers, attractive because of their unpretentiousness, and the little tyrants, unattractive because of their pretensions. The trespass notices which the 'tyrants' put up are first condemned as spiritually destructive to the Clarean deities of Nature ('earth'), Childhood, and Liberty; then treated with mocking sarcasm. In this, the penultimate movement of the poem, righteous anger is the central means of expression. In the last three lines (72–4) Clare may perhaps be thinking of the idea (very familiar in his day) of teaching lower-class children to read as a means of teaching them obedience. For Clare, whose great struggle had been to acquire and use literacy for the fullest possible purposes, this would seem a perverse misuse of the written word; and the absurd idea of the birds having to learn where to stop by reading the trespass sign expresses well a sense of language (and nature) being betrayed and misused.

The final movement of the poem as it is currently printed causes difficulties:

> This with the poor scared freedom bade good bye
> And much the[y] feel it in the smothered sigh
> And birds and trees and flowers without a name
> All sighed when lawless laws enclosure came
> And dreams of plunder in such rebel schemes
> Have found too truly that they were but dreams (lines 75–80)[73]

An otherwise passionately forceful poem appears to dissipate some of its final impact by ambiguity as to what the word 'This' refers to, as to whether 'scared' applies to the poor or to freedom, and as to who are they who have 'dreams of plunder'. In fact, the troublesome 'This' is an editorial slip: the manuscript, Pforzheimer MS 198, reads 'Thus', which requires no new referent. However, the other obscurities may well be a disguise behind which Clare could hide from being too outspoken on such radical matters. A deleted first draft indicates his drift much more clearly:

> For with the poor stern freedom bade farewell
> & fortune hunters totter w[h]ere they fell
> They dreamd of ⟨wealth⟩ riches in the rebel scheme
> & find too truly that they did but dream
>
> (Peterborough MS A18, p. 6)

The draft reveals that Clare is rounding off his poem with the bitter reflection that the destruction of both literal and imaginative freedom by enclosure has benefited neither the poor who were robbed of their common rights, nor those who sought to gain by the scheme. The most revealing change between draft and fair copy is the smothering of the forthright line about 'fortune hunters', and its replacement with a more conventional sentimental line, containing its own ironic comment on the smothering of a sigh at the loss of freedom. The additional new lines (77–8) bring in a third victim, nature.

In these final lines, Clare is summing up and bringing together the oppositions upon which the poem is built: freedom and enclosure, law and lawlessness, poor and rich, fact and dream, substance and shadow. The argument is now clear, and deals in successive couplets with the poor, nature, and those who have enclosed the land. The whole concept of freedom has been frightened away from any connection with the poor, who sigh at its loss. Nature, which shares the namelessness and powerlessness of the poor, also shares the regret and, as in conventional pastoral elegy, sighs alongside the human mourners at the loss. Finally, those who have caused this loss, the perpetrators of the 'lawless laws' of enclosure, must also share the disappointments of the poor. Where earlier the poor had found that they had but their 'memorys pride' as both shadow and substance, now the rich have discovered that their own dreams of plunder are merely dreams. All, in fact, have lost, in this bitter and angry elegy for the pointless loss of the divinity of earth.

'The Mores' remains a classic of protest literature, and a great poem. The power of its impassioned rhetoric, its mixture of righteous anger and elegiac sadness, its dramatic contrasts of time and space, set it alongside its major contemporaries, Shelley's 'The Masque of Anarchy' and 'England in 1819', Byron's political poetry, Ebenezer Elliott's 'Corn-Law Rhymes' and the verse of the Chartist poets. It is an evocative and timely response to the changes of enclosure, one which sets out the arguments against the enclosure movement's strengthening of private property laws, with their attendant concept of trespass, appropriately and with great rhetorical skill and emotional energy.

When Barbara Strang wrote her study of Clare's language, she tended to count usages and make tables of frequencies. It seemed a rather tedious way of looking at poetry, and yet she had a genius for making interesting observations out of the driest detail. When it came to frequencies of words, she noticed that counting was not enough. Clare's 'fondness for near-synonymous variants' meant that words had to be grouped in a network of interlinked clusters. For example, she listed the following groups (from *The Rural Muse*):

'memory' e.g., words like *memory, recollection, forget*
'past' e.g., words like *past, old, ancient*
'continuity and change' e.g., words like *eternity, immortal, new fangled*
'unprocessed' (as a desirable state) e.g., words like *unbroken, unchangeable, undisturbed*
'paradise lost' e.g., words like *eden, emparadised, lose*
'threatened joy' e.g., words like *joy, rapture, fear, danger, loss*
'the concealed, the great in the small' e.g., words like *little, hid(den)*[74]

These words cluster in groups around particular ideas, and also connect with each other; and this is entirely characteristic of Clare's poetry. Memory (the first group) takes one into the past (the second group) to consider continuity and change (the third group). There, Clare gives primacy to the next group, the 'unprocessed' – the changeless, the undisturbed things that remind us of Eden (like birds' nests). Paradise is lost, joy threatened (as nests are often threatened), following the patterns of Professor Strang's next two groups. However, 'the concealed' – the hidden, the secret, the small, remain. 'The Mores' works in this way, though its downbeat ending excludes the saving virtues of 'the concealed' (the ambiguous powers of memory and dreams are its only consolatory images). Many of Clare's poems follow this sort of pattern. The subtle and subdued connections Clare makes between these kinds of groups and ideas are one of the great strengths of his work, a continuous sub-text that weaves together apparently disparate materials, and brings into the close descriptiveness of his rural poetry metaphorical, political and philosophical meaning.

We want to suggest that the same thing happens when one looks at the ideas surrounding trespass: the word and the idea become enriched with metaphorical significance and provide an intellectual and literary coherence beneath the apparently clear surface of Clare's poetry. (Trespass specifically ties in with the particular clusters of words listed above, in that the longed-for Paradise is in one aspect the noble park, the land of the lord.) Trespass is related to concepts like ownership, enclosure, destruction of freedoms, ambition, class; it is set against the common (in both senses), the free, the gypsy, the wild, the careless.[75]

It is no longer adequate to read Clare as a simple observer of nature in transparent descriptive verse, though it is his skill to appear to be an exact and innocent eye. We need to recognise that he works through groups of linked ideas, and through an instinctive ability to root his abstract thoughts in images which give consistency and solidity to his achievement. The idea of trespass, reaching out to its associated ideas and images, focusses one such group, and is a key concept in his work.

NOTES

1 Eric Robinson (ed.), *John Clare's Autobiographical Writings* (Oxford, 1983), pp. 9–10. Clare's quotation from Thomson's *The Seasons* ('Spring', 1–4) is accurate in all substantives, but sufficiently variant in spelling and accidentals to indicate that he is quoting from memory. For a significantly variant account of this episode in Clare's life see Mark Storey, 'Edward Drury's "Memoir" of Clare', *John Clare Society Journal* (henceforth '*JCSJ*') 11 (1992), 14–16.

2 Getting out of sight in order to be able to read and write is an expedient Clare repeated. When he worked 'in the Farmers Gardens', he writes, 'I usd to drop down behind a hedge bush or dyke and write down my things upon the crown of my hat' (Robinson, *Autobiographical Writings*, p. 65).

3 Many of Clare's poems celebrate the special quality of Sunday, as a day of freedom. See, especially, 'Sunday', *The Early Poems of John Clare*, eds.

Eric Robinson and David Powell (Oxford, 1989), vol. II, pp. 359–62; 'Sabbath Walks', ibid. p. 385; 'A Sunday with Shepherds and Herdboys', John Clare: *Selected Poetry*, ed. Geoffrey Summerfield (Harmondsworth, 1990), pp. 93–7; 'In the Field', *The Later Poetry of John Clare*, eds. Eric Robinson and David Powell (Oxford, 1984), II, 839–40. He says in Robinson, *Autobiographical Writings*, p. 27:

> On Sundays I Generally stole from my Companions whose Manners and Play was noways Agreable to me and sholld into the Woods Where I was most happy as I always lovd to be by myself

4 J. C. Maxwell (ed.) *The Prelude: A Parallel Text*, rev. edn (Harmondsworth, 1972), p. 54 (lines 388–9 in 1805, 361–2 in 1850).

5 'After Hearing Rural Ryhmes of W. H. Praisd by a Lady', Robinson and Powell, *Early Poems*, II, pp. 323–4, line 8.

6 As far as Clare's birds and animals are concerned, a comment by John Lucas is apposite. Considering the 'outlawry' of Clare's poetry, he writes: 'Trespasser, fugitive, outlaw: these are the kinds of conditions, the forms of experience, which Clare addresses in his many poems about birds and animals.' (John Lucas, *England and Englishness: Ideas of Nationhood in English Poetry 1688–1900* (London, 1990), p. 151.)

7 For Clare's relationship to Thomson and the eighteenth-century traditions of topographical poetry see John Barrell, *The Idea of Landscape and the Sense of Place: 1730–1840: An Approach to the Poetry of John Clare* (Cambridge, 1972).

8 Margaret Grainger and John Chandler, 'From Helpston to Burghley: a reading of Clare's "Narrative Verses"', *JCSJ* 7 (1988), 26–40, esp. p. 34.

9 If this is indeed an echo of Keats (as we believe), it affects the dating of 'Narrative Verses'. Robinson and Powell date it 'early', i.e. among the group of poems written before *The Village Minstrel* and perhaps before *Poems Descriptive*. 'Sleep and Poetry' opens Keats's *Poems* (1817). This is one of the lost volumes from Clare's library, and the date of acquisition is not recorded. However in a letter to Taylor of ?8 March 1820, Clare (making his first reference to Keats) praises the 1817 volume. Thus we can narrow the date to between March 1817 (the date Keats's *Poems* were published) and July 1821 (the date Clare first mentions the poem). Taylor's introduction to *The Village Minstrel* seems further to suggest that the poem was written before *Poems Descriptive* was published, i.e. before January 1820.
See Robinson and Powell, *Early Poems*, I, pp. 4 and 783; Mark Storey (ed.,) *The Letters of John Clare* (Oxford, 1985), pp. 36–7, 205; John Keats, *The Complete Poems*, ed. John Barnard, 2nd edn (Harmondsworth, 1977), pp. 24, 76; [David Powell], *Catalogue of the John Clare Collection in the Northampton Public Library* (Northampton, 1964), p. 29.

10 Keats, *Complete Poems*, pp. 549, 551.

11 We quote from the version of 'Narrative Verses' in Robinson and Powell, *Early Poems*, II, pp. 4–10; however, for convenience we have added the verse numbers used in Grainger and Chandler's text. See *JCSJ* 7 (1988), 27–32.

12 The phrase 'gleaming rapterous on my sight' is redolent of the many phrases Bunyan uses to indicate a shining, gleaming quality to both the heavenly city and its inhabitants, in the last chapter of *Pilgrim's Progress*. The language of the last four lines of stanza 11 suggests a source in one of the very many eighteenth-century poems on the theme of *concordia discors*. The lines might be seen, for example, as a kind of extrapolation on *Windsor Forest*, lines 11–16:

> Here Hills and Vales, the Woodland and the Plain,
> Here Earth and Water seem to strive again,
> Not *Chaos*-like together crush'd and bruis'd,
> But as the World, harmoniously confus'd:
> Where Order in Variety we see,
> And where, tho' all things differ, all agree.

Grainger and Chandler have noted Pope's 'Order in Variety' as a potential point of comparison. See *JCSJ* 7 (1988), 35 and note; John Butt (ed.), *The Poems of Alexander Pope*, (London, 1963), p. 195.

13 John Sitter notes the 'discovery, made in the 1740s, that poetry, if it is to be "pure poetry", should be about a lonely poet surrounded by "nature"'. See his *Literary Loneliness in the Mid-Eighteenth Century* (Ithaca, London, 1982), p. 9.

14 Although Clare usually uses words like 'liberty', 'free' and 'freedom' straightforwardly, he demonstrates in one later poem, 'The Fallen Elm' (*The Midsummer Cushion*, eds. Kelsey Thornton and Anne Tibble, 2nd edn (Ashington, Manchester, 1990), pp. 192–3), awareness of a more cynical, self-interested kind of 'freedom', which he characterises as 'the cant term of enslaving tools / To wrong another by the name of right'.

15 *JCSJ* 7 (1988), 33. We are much indebted to the excellent essay on the poem by Grainger and Chandler, which traces Clare's route, and provides a map.

16 'The Progress of Ryhme', Thornton and A. Tibble, *Midsummer Cushion*, pp. 224–32, p. 228.

17 An untitled poem ('Where the deer with their shadows passed swifter than thought', Robinson and Powell, *Later Poetry*, II, p. 1107), dated between 1842 and 1854, shows that Burghley had by no means been forgotten, even in the asylum period:

> Ye green shades of Burghley! how lovely you seem,
> Your sweet spreading oaks and your *braken* so green,
> Your green plots as sweet as a shepherd boy's dream,
> 'Neath the shade of dark trees where I've many a day been,
> And sitting in *braken* or roots of the lime,

Amusing my leisure in ballads and rhymes (lines 5–10)

18 '"The Journal", Saturday 16 April 1825', in Margaret Grainger (ed.), *The Natural History Prose Writings of John Clare* (Oxford, 1983), p. 234. A similar incident, where he is again in danger of being taken as a poacher, is described in Robinson, *Autobiographical Writings*, pp. 85–6.

19 J. L. and Barbara Hammond, *The Village Labourer 1760–1960*, vol. I (London, 1911), pp. 183–97; Harry Hopkins, *The Long Affray: the Poaching Wars in Britain* (London, 1985). For a useful short summary, see Pamela Horn, *The Rural World 1780–1850: Social Change in the English Countryside* (London, 1980), pp. 171–83. For the eighteenth-century sources of the 'game-law wars' see the two essays by Douglas Hay in *Albion's Fatal Tree: Crime and Society in Eighteenth century England*, eds. Hay, Linebaugh et al, (London, 1975); E. P. Thompson, *Whigs and Hunters: The Origins of the Black Act* (London, 1975).

20 Robinson, *Autobiographical Writings*, p. 62.

21 Peterborough Museum, MS A61, fo. 75: an untitled sonnet, printed as 'Trespass' in *The Poems of John Clare*, J. W. Tibble (ed.), vol. II, (London, 1935), p. 373. We are grateful to David Powell for kindly providing a transcript of this.

22 Neil Philip, 'To John Clare', *JCSJ* 5 (1986), 36.

23 ('I Saw a Tree with Cheries Red'), Robinson and Powell, *Early Poems*, I, pp. 513–4. Robinson and Powell write (p. 581): 'As Clare was using this cypher-book from the age of ten these two arithmetical poems may be his earliest attempts at rhyme.' (The other poem, in a similar vein, concerns a maypole.) It seems likely that Clare invented (or possibly learned) these riddles as part of the process of learning geometry described in Robinson, *Autobiographical Writings*, p. 6.

24 *Clare-Taylor*, Jan–Feb 1832, i; M. Storey, *Letters*, pp. 568–9. This is among several drafts of a letter to Taylor, following a period of heightened tension between the two men over the fact that Clare's income remained tied up.

25 'Autumn', in Grainger, *Natural History* pp. 335–6. Grainger dates this piece, which is from Northampton Public Library MS 6, to Autumn/ Winter 1841; that is, as Grainger puts it, 'the respite between the two periods of incarceration'.

26 Ibid. p. 336.

27 J. W. Tibble, II, p. 309.

28 Grainger, *Natural History* p. 317.

29 Thornton and A. Tibble, *Midsummer Cushion*, p. 385.

30 'The Fox', lines 11–14, in Eric Robinson and David Powell (eds.), *John Clare*, The Oxford Authors (Oxford, 1984), p. 245.

31 'The Mores', in Robinson and Powell, Oxford *Clare*, pp. 167–9, lines 72 and 70. This text is discussed below, under *Enclosure*.

32 Middleton Murry, for example, argues that Clare has purity of vision. Murry writes: 'It is hard to imagine that the poet...who could express

what he saw with an ease and naturalness such that the expression strikes as part of the very act of seeing…should ever have thought, or should ever have had the impulse to think, about what he saw.' John Barrell quotes this, and appears to agree with him and with Donald Davie's similar view, when he writes: 'Davie's point is relevant here too, that Clare's language refuses to let us look beyond the things and actions he names, to anything analogous.' However, part of what we are saying in this paper is that Clare's poems often insist on being understood in more ways than the simply literal. (Barrell goes on to offer a more nuanced view of Clare's descriptive clarity. He also comments briefly on the poem under discussion here. See Barrell, *The Idea of Landscape*, pp. 122, 130–1, 142–3.)

33 The poem 'A Sunday with Shepherds and Herdboys' (Summerfield, *Selected Poetry*, pp. 93–7) is especially interesting in this respect, suggesting a range of illicit activities. Gypsies and stolen peas are also brought together in poems such as 'The Hollow Tree', in Thornton and A. Tibble, *Midsummer Cushion*, p. 451, and 'Fairy Things', in J. W. Tibble, *Poems*, II, p. 65.

34 Robinson, *Autobiographical Writings*, p. 69. Clare writes of the gypsies: 'I usd to spend my sundays and summer evenings among them learning to play the fiddle in their manner by the ear and joining in their pastimes of jumping dancing and other amusments'.

35 See the 'Journey out of Essex', ibid. pp. 153–61.

36 'October', *The Shepherd's Calendar*, eds. Eric Robinson and Geoffrey Summerfield (London, Oxford, New York, 1964, 1973), p. 113.

37 In addition to the texts quoted in the text and in other notes above, see, for example, 'The Gypsies Evening Blaze', in Robinson and Powell, *Early Poems*, I, p. 33; 'Reccolections after a Ramble', ibid. II, pp. 187–96, lines 49–50 ('The gypsey tune was loud & strong / As round the camp they dancd a gig').

38 'The Gipseys Camp', lines 17–22, Robinson and Powell, *Early Poems*, II, pp. 119–20. Further references to gypsy fortune-telling occur in 'The Dissapointment', ibid. pp. 353–9, line 65; 'The Cross Roads or Haymakers Story', ibid. pp. 619–29, lines 45–6; 'The Village Minstrel', ibid. pp. 123–79, stanzas 115–17; and Robinson, *Autobiographical Writings*, p. 71.

39 Robinson, *Autobiographical Writings*, p. 31.

40 'The Village Minstrel' in Robinson and Powell, *Early Poems*, II, pp. 123–79, stanza 113 (p. 171); 'The Gipsy Camp' in Robinson and Powell, *Later Poetry*, I, p. 29, line 4.

41 'Gipsies' in J. W. Tibble (ed.), *Poems*, II, p. 349.

42 'Young Rabbits', ibid. pp. 337–8.

43 'Song' ('Theres a wide spreading heath and its crowds of furze bushes', in Robinson and Powell, *Later Poetry*, I, pp. 537–8), lines 10–11. There are many other examples of romantic or erotic gypsy poems in the *Later*

Poetry volumes. They include 'The Gipsey Lass', I, pp. 634–5; 'My Love She Was a Gypsey O', II, pp. 787–8; 'Sweet Sophy's Eyes are Chrystals Clear', II, p. 789; 'The Bonny Gipsey', II, pp. 866–7; 'Fly to the Forest My Susan', II, pp. 1057–8 (see line 24); 'My Own Sweet Gipsey Girl', II, pp. 1096–7.

44 Most comment has focussed on the more serious problem of political censorship to Clare's poetry, but his bawdy writings were also censored. Lord Radstock, for example, backed-up by Mrs Emmerson, pressurised Clare over the poems 'My Mary' and 'Dolly's Mistake', and both were accordingly omitted from the third edition of *Poems Descriptive*, much to Clare's fury. See Robinson and Powell, *Early Poems*, I, pp. 567, 582; Tim Chilcott, *A Publisher and His Circle* (London, Boston, Mass., 1972), pp. 92–3; J. W. and Anne Tibble, *John Clare: A Life* (London, 1972), p. 141; *Clare-Hessey*, ? 10 July 1820, in M. Storey (ed.), *Letters*, pp. 83–4.
Sexual expression and the social restrictions which inhibit it as a theme in Clare's writings, may perhaps also be seen as illustrating the theme of 'trespass' within the politics of Clare's texts' production. Indeed, what we might generally call 'sexual trespass' is a Clarean theme worth further consideration, though the evidence is less abundant than that of land trespass. Much of the material concerning, or addressed to, Mary Joyce, in particular, suggests a feeling that Clare was somehow 'trespassing' in his love for her. (See especially the two passages grouped together as 'Memorys of Love' in Robinson, *Autobiographical Writings*, pp. 72–4; also p. 104.)
For the censorship of erotic passages in Keats's 'The Eve of St Agnes', see Keats, *Complete Poems*, pp. 619–20. Byron's almost pathological disgust at the 'masturbatory' qualities of Keats's poetry is obviously interesting in this context.

45 Robinson and Powell, *Early Poems*, II, p. 250, lines 9–15.
46 'July' in Robinson and Summerfield, *Shepherd's Calendar*, p. 78.
47 For the Game and Trespass Laws, see note 19.
48 'Going to the Fair' in Thornton and A. Tibble, *Midsummer Cushion*, pp. 32–46, p. 35. There are other 'Dobbin' poems, notably 'The Death of Dobbin', Robinson and Powell, *Early Poems*, I, pp. 84–90.
49 Robinson, *Autobiographical Writings*, p. 123.
50 Ibid., p. 2.
51 Allan Ramsay (1684–1758) was the son of a leadmine manager, Robert Fergusson (1750–74) a clerk, Robert Burns (1759–96) the son of a cottar, James Hogg (1770–1835) a shepherd, Robert Tannahill (1774–1810) a weaver, Allan Cunningham (1784–1842) the son of a gardener who was later a land agent. Some indication of Clare's interests in Scottish culture is given by the contents of his library (Clare made specific comments on most of the writers mentioned). He owned two copies of Burns's *Works* (one of which was presented by Sir Walter Scott), and at least four editions of texts by Cunningham (one presented by the author). He was

given a copy of Fergusson's *Poems* in 1837, and owned five editions of works by Hogg, two editions of Ramsay's poems, and an edition of Tannahill's *Poems & Songs Chiefly in the Scottish Dialect* (1817). His copy of Scott's *The Lady of the Lake* was presented by the author, and he also owned *Peveril of the Peak* (1822) and *Paul's Letters to His Kinfolk* (1817). Other texts by Scottish poets in his library include James Beattie's *The Minstrel* (2 copies) and *The Wreath*, and of course Thomson's *The Seasons* (1818 edition). Two other texts in his library which help illuminate his Scottish interests are Robert Pollok's *Tales of the Covenanters* (1833) and John Wilson's *Light and Shadows of Scottish Life* (1824). See 'Clare's Library', Powell, *Catalogue...Northampton Public Library*, items 112–14, 134–5, 171–4, 204, 244–8, 333, 340–1, 350–2, 372, 377, 401.

52 The Game Laws invariably highlighted being abroad 'at night' as a serious indication of illicit activity, especially where two or more individuals were involved. See the Hammonds, as cited in note 19.

53 ('O'er Scotland's vales and mountains high'), Robinson and Powell, *Later Poetry*, I, pp. 478–9, lines 23–4.

54 J. H. Plumb, *The First Four Georges* (1956, 1966), p. 175.

55 ('The heart of Midlothian is nearly my own'), Robinson and Powell, *Later Poetry*, II, p. 888.

56 Clare may also have been attracted to the drovers by the fact (according to a recently recovered early biographical source) that his maternal uncle was a drover, who kindled the eleven-year-old Clare's interest in poetry by bringing him an illustrated edition of 'Pomfrets Poems' from London. (Drovers were of course a major source of information of all kinds in the eighteenth and nineteenth century.) See Mark Storey, 'Edward Drury's "Memoir" of Clare', *JCSJ* 11 (1992), 14–16.

57 In a letter to his friend, the painter Rippingille, Clare writes: 'you know our scenery   our highest hills are molehills & our best rocks are the edges of stonepits' (*Clare-Rippingille*, 14 May 1826, M. Storey, *Letters*, p. 379).

58 'Scotland', in Robinson and Powell, *Later Poetry*, II, p. 690, line 8.

59 The phrase was used recently by Olga Taxidou in a review of the 1991 revival of John McGrath's play 'The Cheviot, the Stag and the Black, Black Oil', *Times Literary Supplement*, 9 August 1991, p. 18.

60 An allusion to Lord Balmerinos, one of the executed rebel lords of the '45 Rebellion, suggests Clare knew something of eighteenth-century Scottish history. He was given a copy of Robert Pollock's *Tales of the Covenanters* (1833) in 1834. See *Clare-William Robertson*, 29 Jan 1830; M. Storey, *Letters*, p. 497, and note 51, above.

61 'The Thistle', Robinson and Powell, *Later Poetry*, I, pp. 492–3, stanza 2.

62 'Solitude', Robinson and Powell, *Early Poems*, II, pp. 338–52, lines 69, 71.

63 'Fragments' ('The hedgerow hips to glossy scarlet turn'), J. W. Tibble *Poems*, II, p. 302.

64 'The Progress of Ryhme', Thornton and A. Tibble, *Midsummer Cushion*, pp. 224–32 (pp. 225–6).

65 *Taylor-Clare*, 6 January 1821, in M. Storey, *Letters*, p. 135.

66 Raymond Williams, *The Country and the City* (London, 1973, 1985), p. 12. For Williams's assessment of Clare, see especially pp. 132–41.

67 *Clare-Cunningham*, 9 Sept 1824, in M. Storey, *Letters*, p. 302.

68 John Dyer, *The Fleece: A Poem. In Four Books* (1757), II, pp. 127–8; George Crabbe, *The Village* (1783), I, pp. 69–70.

69 'The Mores', in Robinson and Powell, Oxford *Clare*, pp. 167–9.

70 We are grateful to Claire Lamont for her help with these lines. John Barrell (*The Idea of Landscape*, p. 199) reads lines 19–22 carefully, and his conclusions are interesting: '[the] poem seems to suggest (as far as I can understand the second couplet here) that the proud nostalgia for a lost independence – master and *man* – is all the property of the labourer now: and that in fact that nostalgia is the myth by which the labourer is able to hang on to some of his lost dignity'.

71 See *Clare-Hessey*, ?10 Jul 1820, in M. Storey, *Letters*, p. 84.

72 For imprisonment imagery in the poetry see, *inter alia*, 'Expectation', in Robinson and Powell, *Early Poems*, I, pp. 353–4; ('Thrice Welcome to thy song sweet warbling thrush'), ibid., I, p. 515, lines 11–14; 'Child Harold', Robinson and Powell, *Later Poetry*, I, pp. 40–88, lines 77–80, 145–9, 241–5, 1022–3; 'Don Juan', ibid., pp. 89–101, lines 179, 231–2, 270; 'The Skylark', ibid., p. 315, line 1; 'Song To his Wife', ibid., p. 344, lines 13–16; 'A Regret', ibid. p. 373, lines 1–5; 'Written in Prison', ibid., II, pp. 1023–4.
For prison references in the asylum letters see M. Storey, *Letters*, pp. 645–7, 650, 654, 660–1, 664–6, 669, 673, 675, 678–9.

73 We would like to acknowledge help in this passage from David Powell, who gave invaluable advice on the text; from the publisher's reader; and from P. M. S. Dawson's article, 'John Clare – Radical?', *JCSJ* 11 (1992), 17–27.

74 Adapted from Barbara Strang, 'John Clare's language', *The Rural Muse, Poems by John Clare*, ed. R. K. R. Thornton (Ashington, Manchester, 1982), p. 167.

75 There are a number of poems about 'careless' wanderings, notably 'Carless Rambles', in Thornton and A. Tibble, *Midsummer Cushion*, p. 434 (also in Robinson and Powell, Oxford *Clare*, p. 103).

CHAPTER 5

John Clare: a bi-centenary lecture

Seamus Heaney

Almost thirty years ago I wrote a poem called 'Follower' about a farmer's child dragging along behind his father, especially when the father was out ploughing. The first line of it went like this:

My father worked with a horse plough.[1]

Unremarkable as this was as a line of verse, it was still the result of some revision. In fact, I had deliberately suppressed the only little touch of individuality that had appeared in the first version. Originally I had written:

My father *wrought* with a horse plough

and I had done so because until relatively recently that verb had been the common usage in Mid-Ulster. Country people employed the word 'wrought' naturally and almost exclusively when they talked about a person labouring with certain tools or animals, and the term always carried a sense of wholehearted commitment to a task. You wrought with horses or with a scythe or with a plough; and you might also have wrought at the hay or at flax or even at bricklaying. The inclusion of the word in the line was therefore not only faithful to the speech I grew up with; it implied solidarity with the world of South Derry and a readiness to stand one's linguistic ground. The word gave the line a pivot in the local, the emotional equivalent of the Archimedean point – so why did I end up going for the more pallid and expected alternative, 'worked'?

The answer is, I suppose, because I thought twice. Once you think twice about a local usage you have been displaced from it, and your right to it has been contested by the official linguistic censor with whom another part of you is secretly in league. You have been translated from the land of unselfconsciousness to the suburbs of the *mot juste*. This is, of course, a very distinguished neighbourhood and contains important citizens like Mr Joyce, persons who sound equally at home in their hearth speech and their acquired language, persons who seem to have obliterated altogether the line between self-conscious and unselfconscious usage, and to have established un-censored access to every coffer of the word-hoard. Yet this spon-taneous multivocal proficiency is as far beyond most writers as unbroken residence within the first idiom of a hermetically sealed, univocal home place. Our language may indeed be our world, but our writing, unless we happen to belong with the multitudinous geniuses like Joyce or Shakespeare, or with those whom we might call the monoglot geniuses, like John Clare, our writing is unlikely to express more than a fraction of that world.

Clare, we might say, wrought at language but did not become over-wrought about it. Early in his literary career, he had what is called success. His first volume in 1820, *Poems Descriptive of Rural Life and Scenery*, was reprinted, he went from Helpston to London, he met the well-known writers of the day, he had respect and learned something about the literary milieu. Then, notoriously, the fashion changed, the celebrity dwindled, the publications got spaced out and were less and less noticed until he ended up in Northamptonshire Asylum for the last twenty years of his life, having spent his late thirties and forties in mental confusion, economic distress and poetic neglect. It was only in 1978, for example, that a publisher brought out the extraordinarily copious collection entitled *The Midsummer Cushion* which Clare had ready for printing in the 1830s.

All regrettably true; but for the purposes of re-reading him today, we might express this truth in a different way and say that after an initial brush with the censor, Clare refused to co-operate. The story of his career, in other words, can be expressed as follows: once upon a time, John Clare was lured to the edge of his word-horizon and his tonal horizon, looked about him eagerly, tried out a few new words and accents and then, wilfully and intelligently, withdrew and dug in his local heels. 'Henceforth,' he declared, 'I shall not think twice.' It is this wilful strength of Clare's that will be discussed here, how it manifests itself and constitutes the distinctive power of his poetry. I also want to touch upon what his example can mean to poets at the present time, as we reflect on the Clare bi-centenary of 1993, in social and linguistic conditions of a far more volatile and various sort than those that prevailed when he was negotiating the personal, poetic and historical crises of his prime.

Like all readers, I am indebted to John Barrell's diagnosis of Clare's strengths and complications, insofar as he was a poet who possessed a secure local idiom but operated within the range of an official literary tradition. Prior to Barrell's work, of course, I had read Clare in various editions by Geoffrey Summerfield and Eric Robinson. In fact, my only regret in discussing Clare at this time is that Geoffrey Summerfield is no longer alive to know about it. His sudden death in February 1991 was a great loss, and not only in the field of Clare studies. However, his recent Penguin *Selected Poetry* (taken together with other recent editions by R. K. R. Thornton, Eric Robinson and David Powell) has prepared the way for a more general recognition of the foundedness of Clare's voice and the sureness of his instinct in cleaving to his original 'sound of sense'. My own conviction, which I hope to justify here, is that this unmistakable signature of Clare's is written in most distinctively and sounded forth most spontaneously in the scores of fourteen-line poems which he wrote about small incidents involving the flora and fauna of rural Northamptonshire. Some of these poems are indeed conventional sonnets, with an octave and a turn and a sestet, or with some gesture to either that Petrarchan shape or to the Shakespearean one. However, many of them are like the one I want to discuss now, seven couplets wound up like clockwork and then set free to spin merrily through their foreclosed motions. He seemed to write this kind of poem as naturally as he breathed:

> I found a ball of grass among the hay
> And proged it as I passed and went away
> And when I looked I fancied somthing stirred
> And turned agen and hoped to catch the bird
> When out an old mouse bolted in the wheat
> With all her young ones hanging at her teats
> She looked so odd and so grotesque to me
> I ran and wondered what the thing could be
> And pushed the knapweed bunches where I stood
> When the mouse hurried from the crawling brood
> The young ones squeaked and when I went away
> She found her nest again among the hay
> The water oer the pebbles scarce could run
> And broad old cesspools glittered in the sun[2]

Clare progged the ball of grass. With equal metrical ease and lexical efficiency, he could have poked it, or with some slight re-adjustment of the pentameter, he could have prodded it. Yet, had he done either of these things, both he and his readers would have been distanced in a minimal yet crucial way from the here and nowness, or there and thenness, of what happened. I am reminded of a remark made once by an Irish diplomat with regard to the wording of a certain document. 'This', he said, 'is a minor point of major importance.' In a similar way, the successful outcome of any work of art depends upon the seeming effortlessness and surefingeredness with which such minor points are both established and despatched. For instance, there is in this poem a very instructive use of the preposition 'at' rather than the more expected 'from' or 'on', in the couplet:

> When out an old mouse bolted in the wheat
> With all her young ones hanging at her teats

'Hanging on' would have had certain pathetic, anthropomorphic associations that would have weakened the objective clarity of the whole presentation; 'hanging from' would have rendered the baby mice far too passive; 'hanging at' suggests 'catching at' and itself catches the sudden desperate tiny tightening of the mouse-jaws, and so conveys a reaction that is both biologically automatic and instinctively affectionate. (There is also an echo, naturally, of the phrase 'at the teat'.) However, the real strength, once again, is the way the idiom has sprung into its place in the line without any trace of choice or forethought on the poet's part; and in this it partakes of the poem's overall virtue, which is its notational speed. The couplets hurry in upon themselves as fast as pencil-strokes in an excited drawing and, as in the act of drawing, there is no anxiety about lines repeating and intersecting with the trajectory of other lines. This is why the 'and's' and 'when's' and the self-contained couplets and the endstopped movement of the lines do not irk as they might. They are clearly a function of the perception rather than a fault of the execution. They are eager to grab a part of the action. They are both a prerequisite and a consequence of one kind of accuracy and immediacy, as delightful in their compulsively accelerating way as the beautiful deceleration of the conclusion:

> The water oer the pebbles scarce could run
> And broad old cesspools glittered in the sun

What is achieved in this final couplet is again not a self-conscious effect but a complete absorption. The eye of the writing is

concentrated utterly upon what is before it, but the eye also allows
what is before it to have deep access to what is behind it. It does not,
at any rate, lift to see what effect it is having upon the reader; and this
typical combination of deep-dreaming in-placeness and wide-lens
attentiveness has its analogue in the presentation of the cesspools
themselves as they glitter in the sun. They too combine a glutinous,
hydraulic at-homeness in the district with a totally receptive
adjustment to the light and heat of solar distances. Yet, in spite of the
painterly thickness of the world here, it is worth stressing the point
that this poem is as surely made of words as one by Mallarmé.
Obviously it has its special reliability as a naturalist's observation,
but neither the directness of its address nor the solidity of its content,
line by line, should prevent its being regarded as an artistic
achievement of rare finesse and integrity.

> I found a ball of grass among the hay
> And proged it as I passed and went away
> And when I looked I fancied somthing stirred
> And turned agen and hoped to catch the bird
> When out an old mouse bolted in the wheat
> With all her young ones hanging at her teats
> She looked so odd and so grotesque to me
> I ran and wondered what the thing could be
> And pushed the knapweed bunches where I stood
> When the mouse hurried from the crawling brood
> The young ones squeaked and when I went away
> She found her nest again among the hay
> The water oer the pebbles scarce could run
> And broad old cesspools glittered in the sun

For all the plenitude that is on show and in place here, there is still
that dried-up stream scarcely fit to run over the pebbles, and its thirst
is analogous to a thirst or ache at the core of Clare's writing. This
ache comes from his holding the balance between a world *out there*,
unmistakably palpable, and a world reached for and available only
to the imagination, constantly to be apprehended and filled out by
awakened language.

This kind of excellence was not quite allowed for by the critical
language Clare inherited from the eighteenth century. He wrote
more richly and strangely than he could have told himself. There is
an eerie distance between the materiality of the lines above and the
abstract primness of the following, also by Clare:

> A pleasing image to its page conferred
> In living character and breathing word
> Becomes a landscape heard and felt and seen
> Sunshine and shade one harmonizing green...
> Thus truth to nature as the true sublime
> Stands a mount atlas overpeering time[3]

These lines come from a verse-essay called 'Shadows of Taste' and they reveal Clare outside the borders of his first world, rehearsing the new language and aligning himself to the perspectives of the world beyond. The footwork here is more self-conscious and the carriage of the verse more urbane than anything in the sonnet about the mouse's nest, and it would therefore have been more acceptable to his first reading public. Naturally, his 1820 volume of *Poems Descriptive of Rural Life and Scenery* was influenced by the modes of landscape writing established by Goldsmith and Thomson and Gray and Collins. The whole Augustan tradition is constantly making its presence felt. Indeed, this is inevitable, since in order to cross the line from his unwriting self to his writing identity, in order to bring his poet-life into existence, Clare had to proceed upon the moving stair of those styles which were the current styles. It is the common way for a poet to begin and Clare was no exception. An early poem to his native village of Helpston, for example, speaks with the unmistakable accents of Goldsmith's *Deserted Village*:

> Hail humble Helpstone where thy valies spread
> And thy mean village lifts its lowly head
> Unknown to grandeur and unknown to fame
> No minstrel boasting to advance thy name[4]

and so on. Below is another passage, again taken from 'Shadows of Taste', which reveals him as an equally resourceful ventriloquist when it comes to projecting the voice of Alexander Pope:

> Styles with fashions vary – tawdry chaste
> Have had their votaries which each fancied taste
> From Donns old homely gold whose broken feet
> Jostles the readers patience from its seat
> To Popes smooth rhymes that regularly play
> In music stated periods all the way
> That starts and closes starts again and times
> Its tuning gammut true as minster chimes
> From those old fashions stranger metres flow

Half prose half verse that stagger as they go
One line starts smooth and then for room perplext
Elbows along and knocks against the next
And half its neighbour where a pause marks time
There the clause ends What follows is for ryhme[5]

This is really laid-back stuff. For all his reputation as a peasant poet, Clare had mastered the repertoire of prescribed styles and skills: nowadays a poet as capable and informed as this would probably be headhunted to teach a graduate workshop in the MFA programme at Columbia. The point is, however, that the later, less conventionally correct and less (so to speak) tasteful forays into poetic utterance have to be understood as the redress of poetry. In the vocabulary of hunting, 'to redress' once meant to bring the hounds or the deer back to the proper course, and I associate this meaning of the term with the breakout of innate capacity which marks all true lyric activity. The excitement of finding oneself suddenly at full tilt on the right path, of having picked up a scent and hit the trail, this kind of sprinting, hurdling joy manifests itself in scores of sonnets and short poems of exclamatory observation which Clare wrote all through his life, but especially in the 1820s and 1830s. It is not that one wants to decry the full-dress correctness of other writings by him. The combination of realism, moralism and metrical efficiency when he is on his best Augustan behaviour has to be saluted. These more sententious poems show Clare at work obediently under the influence of the poetry-speak current in England in his day; indeed, it would have taken a talent as educated and overbearing as Joyce's to have resisted the reigning orthodoxies about nature writing, some of which were famously expressed in a letter to Clare by his publisher, John Taylor. Taylor was being neither exploitative nor insensitive, but simply acting as a mouthpiece for received ideas about correct poetic behaviour, when he urged Clare to 'raise ⟨his⟩ views' and 'Speak of the Appearances of Nature...more philosophically'.[6] However, this stuff is not the writing of Clare's which has worn best. Its excellence is, as I say, characteristic of its time; it moves fluently and adequately but it moves like water that flows over a mill-wheel without turning it. On the other hand, the poems of Clare's that still make a catch in the breath and establish a positively bodily hold upon the reader are those in which the wheel of total recognition has been turned. At their most effective, Clare's pentameters engage not just the mechanical gears of a metre: at their most effective, they take hold also on the sprockets of our creatureliness. By which I only mean that on occasion a reader simply cannot help responding with immediate recognition to the pell-mell succession of vividly accurate impressions. No one of these is extraordinary in itself, nor is the resulting poem in any way spectacular. What distinguishes it is an unspectacular joy and a love for the inexorable one-thing-after-anotherness of the world. Below, by way of illustration, is another one of his sonnets in couplets – perhaps we should call them *supplets* – taken almost at random from the ones Clare wrote at Northborough during his early and middle forties:

> The old pond full of flags and fenced around
> With trees and bushes trailing to the ground
> The water weeds are all around the brink
> And one clear place where cattle go to drink
> From year to year the schoolboy thither steals
> And muddys round the place to catch the eels
> The cowboy often hiding from the flies
> Lies there and plaits the rushcap as he lies
> The hissing owl sits moping all the day
> And hears his song and never flies away
> The pinks nest hangs upon the branch so thin
> The young ones caw and seem as tumbling in
> While round them thrums the purple dragon flye
> And great white butter flye goes dancing bye[7]

Rarely has the butteriness of a butterfly been so available. The insect has flown into the medium and survives there forever as a pother of lip movement and substituted metrical feet. The old pond here is like the cesspool in the mouse's nest sonnet, insofar as it embodies for Clare the value of such places existing in the outback of his memories and affections. There is obviously dreamwork going on here, as well as photography. The casual rightness and potency of the thing come from a level of engagement well below the visual; in fact, the whole poem acts as a reminder of how integrated and concentrated a poetic response can be.

In poetry, what is unstated can still be felt as a potent charge inside or behind an image or a cadence; indeed, poetic power inheres in this special linguistic ability to convey the force and meaning of experience without necessarily documenting it in all its circumstances and particulars. So, if I have not yet mentioned Clare's solidarity with the plight of the rural poor, or taken account of the Enclosure

Act that affected Helpston in 1809; if I have not commented upon the trauma of the poet's move from his native village at the age of thirty-nine to the nearby parish of Northborough; if I have not enumerated his gradually more frequent depressions, lapses of memory, hallucinations and collapses into delusion when he imagined himself Lord Byron or the prize-fighter Jack Randall; if I have not insisted on his desperate, obsessive and unremitting love for his childhood sweetheart, Mary Joyce, or taken note of his intermittent conviction that he was married to her as well as to his wedded wife, Patty Turner; if I have not alluded to his voluntary entry into Dr Allen's mental hospital in High Beech in Epping Forest in 1837 and his heartbreaking journey of escape out of there four years later in July 1841; if I have done none of these things, it is not because I believe that Clare did not suffer fantastically, fiercely and unrelievedly as a result of them, or that they are not fundamental to his sensibility and achievement as a poet. On the contrary, the vigour of the poetry is linked to the fact that Clare was harrowed and stricken by personal and historical upheavals all the days of his life, until the two final suspended decades he spent in Northamptonshire Asylum. The poems of those years have understandably been called the 'poems of John Clare's madness' and yet *as poems* they seem to me less terribly keyed than much that came before them. The torsions and distortions reached a climax in 1841, just before and after his escape from Epping Forest, and during the opening stages of his final commitment on 29 December of that year. These are the months when he wrote his two Byronic pastiches, *Child Harold* and *Don Juan*, the latter of which once more deploys, in wonky but madly convincing ways, Clare's old gift for ventriloquism. In this work, he puts an antic disposition on, taunting the reader with a highly aggressive and transgressive intelligence, making sexual and political hay and mayhem. Enigma and affront are precariously balanced, for example, when he turns his attention to his present whereabouts in Essex:

> There's Doctor Bottle, imp who deals in urine,
> A keeper of state-prisons for the queen
> As great a man as is the Doge of Turin
> And save in London is but seldom seen
> Yclep'd old A-ll-n-mad-brained ladies curing
> Some p-x-d like Flora and but seldom clean
> The new road o'er the forest is the right one
> To see red hell and, further on, the white one[8]

This is good sport but it is not quite Clare in his element. The work which simultaneously displays the greatest pressure, the greatest surety and the greatest nonchalance comes in the main in poems written before Northampton. Obviously, nobody is going to deny the apocalyptic pathos of his most famous asylum poem – the one beginning 'I am – yet what I am none cares or knows' and including the line about 'the vast shipwreck of my lifes esteems';[9] nor is anybody going to undervalue the bonus of indispensable songs and sonnets that belong to this period, especially the very late sonnet 'To John Clare' (but including also those pieces entitled 'The Round Oak', 'The Yellowhammer', 'The Wood Anemonie', 'The flag top quivers in the breeze', 'The thunder mutters louder and more loud' and so on). What crowns the lifetime's effort, however, is the great outpouring in his early middle years of short verse about solitary figures in a landscape, or outcast figures, or threatened creatures, or lonely creatures, or birds and birds' nests, or dramatic weather changes, all of which manage to encompass uncanny intimations of both vulnerability and staying power. By the very fact of having got themselves written in the first place, these poems manifest the efficacy of creative spirit in the face of all the adversity referred to above; and they prove once again the truth of Keith Douglas's notion that the work of art inheres in 'stating some truth whose eternal quality exacts the same reverence as eternity itself'.

In these poems, Clare is led towards the thing behind his voice and ear which Nadezhda Mandelstam called 'the nugget of harmony'. To locate this phonetic jewel, to hit upon and hold one's true note is a most exacting and intuitive discipline but it was one that was particularly difficult for a writer like Clare, whose situation in the 1820s was to some extent the same as Christopher Murray Grieve's a hundred years later, in the 1920s; which is to say that Clare, like Grieve, was operating within a received idiom that he half-knew was not the right one for him. Grieve dealt with the problem by becoming Hugh MacDiarmid. Perhaps if Clare had changed his name to John Fen or Jack Prog, his wilfulness would have been more clarified and his awareness of what his poetry had to do would have been more pointed. One might even say that, after a century, MacDiarmid's theoretical passion in the 1920s fulfilled Clare's poetic intuition of the 1820s – although Clare's was always by far the surer voice within poetry. Everything that MacDiarmid wrote about revitalising the vernacular, all his aspirations to unblock linguistic access to a reservoir of common knowledge and unacknowledged potential, all his angry regret that English literature maintained 'a narrow ascendancy tradition instead of broad-basing itself on all the diverse cultural elements and splendid variety of languages and dialects, in the British Isles'[10] – all this was a making explicit of what was implicit in much of Clare's practice.

MacDiarmid would also have recognised, I am sure, some affinity between himself and Clare when it came to the use of the ballad measure. This was the one poetic beat that had sounded in the ears of both poets from the beginning, the measure in which personal and communal experience could enter each other as indissolubly as two streams, and it was the measure in which Clare's moral outrage was expressed most pungently. When, for example, in one of his most powerful poems, the quarry field known as Swordy Well begins to speak, we recognise immediately that Clare's voice is in a deep old groove and that he is hauling into vivid speech an awareness of injustice for which he has paid a personal price; yet it is an awareness sanctioned also by his own traditional folk wisdom and by the high tragic understanding of life shared by the authors of *King Lear* and the Book of Job.

By the terms of the 1809 Enclosure Act for Helpston, Swordy Well had been granted to the overseers of the roads in the parish. It had thereby lost its independence and become like a pauper dependent upon parish charity. In Clare's poem, what opens the channels of expression so exhilaratingly is the removal of every screen between the identity of the person and the identity of the place. 'The Lament of Swordy Well' is by no means as extraordinary an achievement as MacDiarmid's *A Drunk Man looks at the Thistle*, but it still represents a thrilling integration of common idiom and visionary anger of the sort that MacDiarmid longed to re-introduce in Scotland. However, the main point I want to make about it is that the ballad stanza does for Clare what it would do for MacDiarmid; it places him at the centre of his world and holds his voice to the sticking point like a plough in a furrow. Here are a few selected stanzas, where the assailed dignity of the pauper and the fate of the requisitioned ground are mutually expressive of each other's plight:

> I hold no hat to beg a mite
> Nor pick it up when thrown
> Nor limping leg I hold in sight
> But pray to keep my own

Where profit gets his clutches in
There's little he will leave
Gain stooping for a single pin
Will stick it on his sleeve...

Alas dependance thou'rt a brute
Want only understands
His feelings wither branch and root
That falls in parish hands
The much that clouts the ploughman's shoe
The moss that hides the stone
Now I'm become the parish due
Is more then I can own...

The silver springs grown naked dykes
Scarce own a bunch of rushes
When grain got high the tasteless tykes
Grubbed up trees, banks, and bushes
And me, they turned me inside out
For sand and grit and stones
And turned my old green hills about
And pickt my very bones

These things that claim my own as theirs
Were born by yesterday
But ere I fell to town affairs
I were as proud as they
I kept my horses, cows, and sheep
And built the town below
Ere they had cat or dog to keep
And then to use me so...

The bees flye round in feeble rings
And find no blossom bye
Then thrum their almost weary winds
Upon the moss and die
Rabbits that find my hills turned o'er
Forsake my poor abode
They dread a workhouse like the poor
And nibble on the road...

I've scarce a nook to call my own
For things that creep or flye
The beetle hiding 'neath a stone
Does well to hurry bye
Stock cats my struggles every day
As bare as any road
He's sure to be in something's way
If e'er he stirs abroad[11]

The point of this poem, of course, and of another similar if gentler exercise in dramatic monologue called 'The Lamentations of Round-Oak Water' – their point is to make a point. Their social protest and their artistic effort are in perfect step. If there is a mechanical thump to the metre, this is inherent in the convention, as true to the genre as fluencies of sentiment were to those poems in the Augustan mode that I glanced at earlier. However, what I want to emphasise is the fact that in these poems of social protest, it was the ballad stanza that kept Clare right on course poetically, leading him into the hub of a metre and the nub of a subject matter, if not exactly to 'the nugget of harmony'.

That nugget is something more elusive and more individual to a poet than anything comprised by themes or technique. In Clare's case, it is to be found mostly in the poems that we might call his short takes, quick little forays of surprising innocence and accuracy, poems where those subjects I mentioned earlier – creatures and country scenes and so on – pass in and out of language and consciousness every bit as fluently as moods and impulses pass between the body and the weather itself. But still, the nugget of harmony does not issue forth as a mellifluousness; the music of these 'supplets' has less to do with sweetness and modulation and melodious numbers than with a perfect at-homeness in speech itself. In fact, there is not a great deal of *variety* in the tunes of the poems, just as there never is any great range of variation in the cries that people let out at moments of spontaneous excitement – and the work I am thinking of can be understood to constitute a succession of just such brief, intense gestures and outcries.

The poems about birds' nests belong to this category, especially 'The Wryneck's Nest' and 'The Fern Owl's Nest'. Well-known snap-shot work such as 'Hares at Play' belong to it also, and little genre paintings like the sonnet on 'The Woodman'; landscape poems such as 'Emmonsdale Heath'; in a deeper register, then, the short sonnet sequence about 'The Badger' and the sonnet-diptych about 'The Marten-Cat' and 'The Fox'. The desire to quote from all these is strong, but space is limited and the texts are widely available. Here instead is an incidental example of the kind of excellence I have in mind, a fragment of sorts, a stray stanza, and yet its random swoops upon the momentary – its casually perfect close-ups on raindrops, for example – illustrate all over again the fact that the truth of art does indeed lie in those minor points of major importance:

The thunder mutters louder and more loud
With quicker motion hay folks ply the rake
Ready to bust slow sails the pitch black cloud
And all the gang a bigger haycock make
To sit beneath – the woodland winds awake
The drops so large wet all thro' in an hour
A tiney flood runs down the leaning rake
In the sweet hay yet dry the hay folks cower
And some beneath the waggon shun the shower[12]

It is populous, it is unpretentious, it seems effortless, yet it is actually a triumph of compression that manages to combine the shapeliness of nine end-stopped, rhyming lines with the totally active movements of clouds and haymakers and raindrops and waterlogged wind. In fact, the movements of the world are here indistinguishable from the movements of Clare's own vivid spirit, and the lines both illustrate and obey the Wordsworthian imperative that poetry should disclose, in the workings of the universe, analogues for the working of the human mind and soul. Just because Clare's poetry abounds in actualities, just because it is as full of precise delightful detail as a granary is full of grains, does not mean that it is doomed to pile up and sink down in its own materiality. On the contrary, what is so gratifying about it is its lambency, its skim-factor, its bobbing unencumbered motion. It is what Lawrence calls the poetry of the living present; and its persistent theme, under many guises, in different subjects and scenes and crises, is the awful necessity of the gift for keeping going and the lovely wonder that it can be maintained – a gift which is tutored by the instinctive cheer and courage of living creatures, and encouraged by every fresh turn and return of things in the natural world. Clare is always cheering for the victim, always ready to pitch in on the side of whatever is tender and well disposed, or whatever is courageous and outnumbered – like the badger:

He turns about to face the loud uproar
And drives the rebels to their very doors
The frequent stone is hurled where e'er they go
When badgers fight and every one's a foe
The dogs are clapt and urged to join the fray
The badger turns and drives them all away
Though scarcly half as big, dimute and small
He fights with dogs for hours and beats them all
The heavy mastiff savage in the fray
Lies down and licks his feet and turns away

The bull-dog knows his match and waxes cold
The badger grins and never leaves his hold
He drives the crowd and follows at their heels
And bites them through. The drunkard swears and reels[13]

Needless to say, in spite of my praise for these vivid shorter poems, I do not wish to underrate performances by Clare of greater rhetorical sweep and more sustained intellectual purpose. His ode 'To the Snipe', for instance, is something of a set piece and exhibits the customary fit between word and thing – the quagmire, for example, overgrown 'with hassock tufts of sedge', and the moor having a 'spungy lap'. However, what makes it a poem of unusual classical force is the perfect posture it maintains as it moves energetically through the demands of a strict and complex stanza. There is something Marvellian about its despatch and articulation which makes me want to extend my praise: just because I set such store by Clare, the astonished admirer, does not mean I cannot admire the more deliberately ambitious poet of lines like these:

Lover of swamps
The quagmire overgrown
With hassock tufts of sedge – where fear encamps
Around thy home alone

The trembling grass
Quakes from the human foot
Nor bears the weight of man to let him pass
Where thou alone and mute

Sittest at rest
In safety 'neath the clump
Of hugh flag forrest that thy haunts invest
Or some old sallow stump...

For here thy bill
Suited by wisdom good
Of rude unseemly length doth delve and drill
The gelid mass for food[14]

'To the Snipe' is just one kind of alternative excellence. Nobody would want to slight the more leisurely, slightly more choral riches of a poem like 'The Summer Shower' or the exhibition pieces in *The Shepherd's Calendar* (or those other much-praised and thematically central poems of the Northborough period like 'The Flitting' and 'Remembrances'). Nevertheless, it is possible to acknowledge the different orders of excellence which these poems represent and still choose to prize most in Clare's *oeuvre* that attribute which Tom Paulin characterised in another context as 'the now of utterance'.[15]

Paulin has written on Clare most recently in an essay of brilliant advocacy in *Minotaur* (1992), his book about poetry and the nation state; here I want to draw attention to the very suggestive remarks he made earlier in his introduction to *The Faber Book of Vernacular Verse* (1990), where he had this to say about Clare's texts as we now have them, restored to their original unpunctuated condition:

> The restored texts of the poems embody an alternative social idea. With their lack of punctuation, freedom from standard spelling and charged demotic ripples, they become a form of Nation Language that rejects the polished urbanity of Official Standard.[16]

Then, having alluded to the poet's 'Ranter's sense of being trapped within an unjust society and an authoritarian language', Paulin concludes that 'Clare dramatizes his experience of the class system and its codified language as exile and imprisonment in Babylon'. By implication, then, Clare is a sponsor and a forerunner of modern poetry in post-colonial nation languages, poetry that springs from the difference and/or disaffection of those whose spoken tongue is an English which sets them at cultural and perhaps political odds with others in possession of that normative 'Official Standard'. Paulin's contention is that wherever the accents of exacerbation and orality enter a text, be it in Belfast or Brooklyn or Brixton, we are within earshot of Clare's influence and example. What was once regarded as Clare's out-of-stepness with the main trends has become his central relevance: as ever, the need for a new kind of poetry in the present has called into being precursors out of the past.

What is evident in Paulin's work, and in the work of Les A. Murray, Liz Lochead, Tony Harrison, Derek Walcott, Edward Kamau Brathwaite and many others in the dub and reggae tradition, is the fact that nobody can any longer belong as innocently or entirely within the acoustic of a first local or focal language as Clare could – *focus* being the Latin word for hearth. Nowadays, every isle – be it Aran or Orkney or Ireland or Trinidad – is full of broadcast noises, every ear full of media accents and expendable idioms. In the few nooks of dialect I have kept in touch with over the years, the first things children speak nowadays are more likely to be in imitation of TV jingles than of the tones of their parents. So what a poet takes from Clare in these conditions is not an antiquarian devotion to dialect or a nostalgia for folk ways; rather, what is startingly instructive about Clare's practice is the way it shows the necessity for being forever at the ready, always in good shape poetically, limber and ready to go intelligently with the impulse.

In the shorter poems I have been praising above, Clare exhibits the same kind of galvanised, gap-jumping life that sends poems by Tom Paulin and Les Murray catapulting and skimming off and over two or three different language levels. The kind of learned and local words that propel their poems and open them inward and forward, the whole unruly combination of phonetic jolts and associated sidewindings, all this obviously issues from a far more eclectic relish of language than Clare ever developed. Nevertheless, he would have been at home with the impetuousness and impatience which these poets manifest, their need to body-swerve past the censor and shoulder through decorum, to go on a poetic roll that can turn on occasion into a political rough ride.

Clare, in fact, inspires one to trust that poetry can break through the glissando of post-modernism and get stuck in the mud of real imaginative haulage work. He never heard Mandelstam's famous phrase about Acmeism being 'a nostalgia for world culture'[17], but oddly enough, it makes sense to think of Clare in relation to the arrival of poetry in that longed-for place or state – an arrival which John Bayley has recently observed in the work of many gifted contemporaries. The dream of a world culture, after all, is a dream of a world where no language will be relegated, a world where the ancient rural province of Boeotia (which Les Murray has made an image for all the outback and dialect cultures of history) will be on an equal footing with the city-state of Athens; where not just Homer but Hesiod will have his due honour. Clare's poetry underwrites a vision like this, where one will never have to think twice about the cultural and linguistic expression of one's world on its own terms since nobody else's terms will be received as normative and official. To read him for the exotic flavours of an archaic diction and the picturesque vistas of a bucolic past is to miss the trust he instills in the possibility of a self-respecting future for all languages, an immense, creative volubility where human existence comes to life and has life more abundantly because it is now being expressed in its own self-gratifying and unhindered words.

NOTES

Seamus Heaney delivered this lecture on Clare as Professor of Poetry at the University of Oxford in October 1992.

1 Seamus Heaney, *New Selected Poems 1966–1987* (London, 1990), p. 6.
2 ['The Mouse's Nest'] in Eric Robinson and David Powell (eds.), *John Clare*, Oxford Authors (Oxford, 1984), p. 263.
3 'The Shadows of Taste', ibid. pp. 171–2.
4 'Helpstone', ibid. p. 1.
5 Ibid. p. 172.
6 John Taylor, 'Letter to Clare', 4 March 1826 in M. Storey (ed.), *John Clare: The Critical Heritage* (London, 1973).
7 ['The old pond full of flags and fenced around'], Robinson and Powell, Oxford *Clare*, p. 275.
8 *Don Juan* in Geoffrey Summerfield (ed.), John Clare, *Selected Poetry* (Harmondsworth, 1990), p. 220.
9 'I Am', Robinson and Powell, Oxford *Clare*, p. 361.
10 Hugh MacDiarmid, 'English ascendancy in British literature', in *The Uncanny Scot* (London, 1968), p. 120.
11 'The Lament of Swordy Well', in Summerfield, *Selected Poetry*, pp. 172–8.
12 ['The thunder mutters louder and more loud'], Robinson and Powell, Oxford *Clare*, p. 333.
13 'The Badger', in Summerfield, *Selected Poetry*, p. 122.
14 'To the Snipe', ibid. p. 311.
15 Tom Paulin, *The Faber Book of Vernacular Verse* (London, 1990), p. xviii.
16 Ibid. p. xix.
17 Reported in Nadezhda Mandelstam, *Hope Against Hope*, trans. Max Hayward (Harmondsworth, 1975), p. 295.

CHAPTER 6

Clare's politics

John Lucas

1

There seems to be a widespread agreement among Clare's commentators that his poetry has blessedly little to do with politics. The angry poems about enclosure cannot, of course, be wished away, although they can certainly be passed by in silence or with a dutiful nod in the direction of 'understandable anguish' or some other emollient phrase; and there are others which threaten to break the mould of Clare as 'peasant poet'. As I have argued elsewhere, it was not Clare who cast the mould, even if he then suffered from being encased within it.[1] A 'peasant poet' is at once an appeal to fashion and a promise of sweet song untainted by hard thought. It even dulls the fact of Clare's relish for the natural world. His exact, delighted knowledge of that world is inseparable from the language by means of which he names and knows it, (naming is knowledge); and yet it was that local, dialect language which his publishers endlessly editorialised away in the interest of keeping him within literary bounds – where, for most commentators, he remains.

If, in the essay that follows, I try to break down those bounds, it is not because I think that having done so I can prove Clare to be in any unambiguous sense a committed radical poet. The point is rather that an attentive reading of his poems and the circumstances of his life will suggest that his political views cannot be stabilised, for the very good reason that he himself was subject to (and of) so many contradictory forces as to put stability or consistency out of reach. He was an agricultural labourer who aspired to belong to the world of literary fashion – of London, in a word. He *liked* that world, or for a while thought he liked it. From its vantage point much of the life he came from seemed nasty, brutish and short of culture. As indeed it was, at all events if you define culture in terms of the habits and tastes

148

to which literary, fashionable London introduced him. I do not even think it possible to chart his career in terms of gaining and/or waning political convictions. True, he became increasingly disillusioned with the 'pomp' of literary London and therefore with its cultural and social habits, and yet at any one time you are likely to find him holding contradictory views – or perhaps it would be more accurate to say that they hold him.

Here, it will help to refer to the opening chapter of E. P. Thompson's *Customs in Common*. In this chapter, which is called 'Custom in Culture', Thompson spends some time unpicking the notion that the social identity of working people can be simply or consistently known.

One can detect within the same (working-class) individual alternating identities, one deferential, the other rebellious. This was a problem with which–using different terms–Gramsci concerned himself. He noted the contrast between the 'popular morality' of folklore traditions and 'official morality.' His 'man-in-the-mass' might have 'two theoretical conscious-nesses (or one contradictory consciousness)' – one of praxis, the other 'inherited from the past and uncritically absorbed'.[2]

Thompson goes on to note that for Gramsci ideology rests on 'the spontaneous philosophy which is proper to everybody' and which derives from three sources: first 'language itself, which is a totality of determined notions and concepts, and not just of words, gram-matically devoid of content'; second, 'common sense'; and third, popular religion and folklore. Thompson is certainly right to say that, of these three, most Western intellectuals would take the first to be the most important and would then go on to argue that 'the plebs were in a sense "spoken" by their linguistic inheritance... The plebs are even seen as captives within a linguistic prison, compelled even in moments of rebellion to move within the parameters of consti-tutionalism, of "Old England", of deference to patrician leaders and of patriarchy.'

I share Thompson's unease with this argument, and his concern for the way it diminishes the importance of 'common sense' or 'praxis'. However, given that for Gramsci this was not simply the ap-propriation of an individual but, as Thompson says, 'was derived from shared experiences in labour and social relations' and then, to quote Gramsci, was 'implicit in [an individual's] activity and which in reality unites him with all his fellow-workers', it follows that although 'common sense' might and indeed did speak through Clare, it could do so only intermittently and in a muffled way. This was because *as poet*, even as 'peasant poet', Clare was cut off from those shared experiences in labour and social relations about which he sometimes wrote and *from* which he wrote but from which the very act of writing separated him.[3]

Oddly enough, then, he is someone who has to be seen as struggling within a linguistic prison. Or rather, he seems to move between two prisons: of dialect on the one hand, and of southern, literary English on the other. From the bars of either, he peers out at a world from which he has been shut away. The result is that from the moment of publication of his first volume, in 1820, he finds himself struggling against forces he can do little to oppose, and which are as much within him as without.

One of the few critics to have understood this is Johanne Clare. In the opening pages of *John Clare and the Bounds of Circumstance*, she takes up the matter of what she calls his 'protest poems', and rightly notes that Taylor, Clare's first publisher, and Lord Radstock, his patron, between them emasculated much of his best early work. Unfortunately, she then decides that even in 'the enclosure elegies...it would be difficult if not impossible to claim that Clare intended to serve the cause of political radicalism: he was distrustful and almost entirely disengaged from most forms of political dissent'. True, she insists that he understood only too well 'the social violence which the land-owning classes perpetrated against the labouring poor through poor law, enclosures, rack-renting and rate-fixing'. Yet in spite of all this, Clare apparently 'did not believe that this social violence either justified or could be redressed by violent political agitation'.[4] At first glance it may seem improper for her to identify radical politics with violence, but in fact she is right to make the connection, if only because those without the vote had virtually no other means of demonstrating their dissent from the laws of the day. Riots, marches, and house- and rick-burning, these and other shows were an inevitable part of radical dissent. Clare was apparently against such things. To support her case she quotes from the prose and from a number of his letters. Here, she says, is the evidence we need to prove to us how far from being a political radical Clare in fact was.

But is it so? As an example of Clare's distrust of radicalism Johanne Clare quotes a remark from the poet's *Journal* in which he says 'I have not read Tom Paine but I have always understood him to be a low blackguard'. That comes from the entry for Thursday, 17 March 1825. The entry in its entirety runs:

Received a letter & present of Books from Lord Radstock containing Hannah Mores *Spirit of Prayer* – Bishop Wilsons *Maxims* Burnets *Life of God in the Soul of Man* 'A New Manual of Prayer' & Watsons 'Answer to Paine' // a quiet unaffected defence of the Bible & and example for all controversialists to go bye were railing has no substitute for argument I have not read Tom Paine but I have always understood him to be a low blackguard[5]

Radstock no doubt meant the packet of religious treatises to do Clare's soul good (there will be more to say about this later). Yet Clare was a religious man, at least to the extent that he had some sort of belief in God. As the context makes clear, it is therefore Paine the atheist whom he calls a blackguard rather than Paine the political radical. Clare would have been in no way unusual in denouncing atheism without thinking that in so doing he was required to denounce popular radicalism. It is difficult to believe that he would denounce the man who in 1792 had written 'The custom of attaching Rights to *place* or in other words to inanimate matter, instead of to the *person*, independently of place is too absurd to make any part of a rational argument'.[6]

There is a further point. At the time Clare was writing the entry to which Johanne Clare refers he was trying to imagine himself into the role of accredited author. Hence, the *Journal*. Given that he had already discovered how powerful Radstock and Taylor had proved to be when they joined forces to edit and effectively censor his work, it may well be that even in so apparently private a piece of writing he was in fact operating as his own censor, striking the kind of pose that would, so he thought, appeal to his 'polite' audience. For what other audience did he have? If this seems far-fetched let me again cite Johanne Clare's 'evidence' for Clare's distrust of radicalism. In order to buttress her case she quotes from the note to an essay on industry in which Cobbett is mentioned, and a letter to George Darley. On both occasions Clare undoubtedly makes clear his desire to distance himself from violent reform. Yet in both instances the tone he adopts troubles her. There is something, she says, 'a little too snobbish and aloof about Clare's disdain for the puffing farmers and oratorical clowns, and his references to the "general stir" and the "farce of the thing" suggests that we are dealing with a man who was never really comfortable with the brawling spirit of his time'.[7] Well, no. But the point surely is that in both instances what accentuates Clare's discomfort is his sense of audience. The notes for an essay on industry in which the references to Cobbett occur were presumably intended to be worked up for publication in a London-based journal. Clare knew that for his essay to be acceptable to a polite audience, he would have to tailor his opinions to suit theirs. It is therefore significant that the essay was unfinished – is, indeed, barely started. My own guess is that he did not at all like what he was saying and so decided to stop. There is another essay on industry, very obviously intended for publication in a 'polite' journal but, in that, all references to Cobbett have been expunged. It is still more significant that the identical words turn up in a letter of January 1832, and that the addressee is Marianne Marsh, wife to the Bishop of Peterborough. This is a matter to which I shall return.

As for the letter to Darley, it has to be said that, although there is no reason to doubt the sincerity of Darley's regard for Clare, he was nevertheless a scholar-mathematician-poet whom Clare would inevitably see as part of that cultural orthodoxy he still half-hoped he would be allowed to join.[8] Hence the tone of his letter, and hence too, his attempt to show that he is not to be identified with farmers and clowns. Johanne Clare may be right in saying that Clare was not comfortable with the brawling spirit of the time, but I am certain that the evidence she adduces to show this *in fact* shows that he was even less comfortable with the endless contradictions that made up his life as writer and day-labourer, the aspirant to London culture who was also emotionally committed to ways of life about which that culture knew little or nothing, and for which it typically voiced its disdain, or so it must have seemed to him. So it always does seem.

Clare's letter to Darley, which was written in 1830, mentions a 'general stir'. The major stirs of that year were caused by the Swing rioters. In his remarks on Cobbett and in the letter to Darley, in both of which he seems to distance himself from that stir, Clare writes in a manner we might call that of the 'deferential worker'. (As we shall see later, in poems and other letters of that year he could write very differently.) The phrase 'deferential worker' was coined by Howard Newby to define the ambivalence of rural working-class culture, with 'its combination of conservative deference and radical resentment'.[9] (This is of course very close to Thompson's remark about 'alternating identities'.) In his excellent monograph on the battle of Bosenden

Wood, *The Last Rising of the Agricultural Labourers*, Barry Reay notes that:

> The attraction of the concept of hegemony as a key for unlocking the complexities of social relations in any historical period is that, defined correctly, it explains and allows for resistance as well as control. The hegemonic group (or groups) maintains its position not merely by naked force, but also by dominating what Marx and Engels called the means of intellectual production, by shaping ideas. Hegemony determines the parameters of the possible; it inhibits the development of social, political, or cultural alternatives to the status quo and the prevailing ideology. But we need to think in terms of an impulse towards domination, a striving for control, (conscious or otherwise) which can never be all-encompassing. It inhibits but cannot preclude alternative views of the social situation. Hegemony certainly narrows the opinions, constrains; it does not prevent resistance.[10]

My sense of Clare is that he begins as poet by imagining, as a prevailing commonplace about the identity of 'The Poet' made it possible for him to imagine, that he is that most impossibly privileged of beings: an entirely free man. He very soon discovers this to be an illusion because many of his poems are made out of his experience of being a rural labourer and those with 'the means of intellectual production' simply prevent him from saying what he wants. They editorialise him into submission. He can escape from his predicament only by conspiring to become a 'peasant' – that is, a specific literary 'type', or by identifying with values that are opposed to the interests of the class from which he comes. Such hoped-for escapes inevitably plunge him into further entrapment.

Clare, then, lives through and registers a most grievous, and ultimately unresolvable dilemma, of having no secure sense of identity. In hoping to join print/literary culture he finds that he is required to align himself with a process that denies him his voice as a day-labourer and the experiences that belong to his Helpston life. Yet his attempts to join literary culture are doomed because he can belong only as 'peasant poet', which means becoming the mere fashion of a season. It also of course means having to sacrifice much of his best poetry. Clare's prose betrays the dilemma. His poetry – when it is allowed to – explores it. Not always, I will admit. His satire of village life, *The Parish*, puts on airs every bit as false as the letter to Darley.[11] But then, the satiric poetry he knew about – the poetry of Pope and even Crabbe – was likely to require that of him: in adopting its characteristic air of 'disdain' (and he was a wonderful mimic of other poets, as his versions of Byron's *Childe Harold* and *Don Juan* show), he had to distance himself from ways of life he certainly felt ambivalent about (his London 'success' made him something of a stranger among his Helpston neighbours) but which literary decorum insisted he should treat merely dismissively. Not surprisingly, then, *The Parish* was never completed. On the other hand, hundreds of poems were, even if they were not all published in his own lifetime. Verse was his natural medium, in particular the verse rooted in the cultural circumstances of his early life: folk-song, ballad, hymn, broadsheet, doggerel. Out of these circumstances comes his easy mastery of rhyme, stanza form and verse measure. Out of them, too, comes his radicalism.

To say this is not, however, to argue that Clare's politics are thought through in a manner that amounts to a programme. Popular radicalism is not like that. As E. P. Thompson and others have argued, it is motivated by a deep-rooted 'common sense' of the rights of labour: to affordable food, to customary rights, and a determination to protect and, if need be, to fight for these things. Popular radicalism is opportunistic. Circumstances changed and Clare's responses changed with them. But his sense of outrage, his passionate awareness of how he and others were being made to suffer for the triumphs of those who owned the law of the land, his grieving for a failing world of 'little things' – these were constant, even though they could be overlaid by or in conflict with that deferential habit which can get into his writing, especially when it is directed at his 'betters'. (And, when is it not?) So, in April 1820, he sent a letter to his publisher, Taylor, in which he included a longish, muddled poem called 'England'. Clare begins by quoting Cowper's 'England, with all thy faults I love thee still', and 'thrillingly' invokes 'England thou word so enchantingly sounding'. Yet, prompted no doubt by the death of George III (which had occurred on 29 January) and understandable fears of what his son might do, he speaks of 'pretenders [who] arise for thy freedom' and goes on to make clear his sense that as far as he and his kind are concerned there is precious little freedom to be found in the England he knows. However: 'bear the yoke', he counsels,

> Still better slaves in a land of your own
> Then yield up to traitors in vainess arising
> & banished as slaves into deserts unknown

England be patient & bear your chains lightly
Tho in gauld fetters bound down as ye be
Freedoms hid sunbeams may glitter yet brightly
Yet may the day come as ye may be free[12]

He may have in mind the mutterings of republicanism which accompanied the accession of Georgie-Porgie to the throne. (He casts a shuddery look back to a past when 'Laws [were] broke & kings murderd was that to be free'). But what he *must* have in mind is the Cato Street Conspiracy. The would-be assassins had been arrested in February, tried and sentenced to execution, although when Clare wrote they were still alive. Their cause was one which took for granted the rights of labour and, in particular, the right to hold the land in common; and they were in a line of radical protest which begins in the 1790s and whose rhetoric and politics Clare shares. At all events, early poems such as 'The Lamentations of Round-Oak Waters' (written in 1818, but not published in *Poems Descriptive*), and 'Helpstone', use exactly the language of popular radicalism that can be found in radical newspapers of the time. For example, *Medusa*, a newspaper whose motto was 'Let's Die like Men, and not be sold as Slaves', printed verses by E. J. Blandford throughout 1819, including one called 'Nature's First, Last, and Only Will! Or a Hint to Mr. Bull'. Here, Blandford insists that the land has been plundered from the people ('When Nature her pure artless reign began, / She gave in entail all her stores to man'). This is not to say that Clare read Blandford or knew about *Medusa*. But it is to say that his letter to Taylor and the fudging verses of 'England' are a way of distancing himself from a radicalism that he would naturally have thought dangerous to be identified with just then, not least because he wanted to be acceptable to the London literati. 'England' is then the expression of a need to show Taylor that Clare is not in favour of lawlessness. I suspect that he was covering up.

For the fact is that a good deal of the poetry he had sent Taylor was very evidently not the work of a man content to bear his chains lightly. Given that he grew up in the kind of community which daily experienced the consequences of the changes forced on it by enclosure, by high prices and low wages, by the oppression of landlords and farmers, this should come as no surprise. It certainly did not much surprise his patron, Lord Radstock. 'Radical slang', he called some key lines on enclosure in the poem, 'Helpstone'; and he refused to let them appear in Clare's first volume, *Poems Descriptive of Rural Life and*

Scenery. The story of what happened to that volume is well documented, even if most commentators are reluctant to pursue its implications.[13] The point to make here is that Radstock was in a very good position to understand Clare's radicalism and he at least can be said to have done Clare the honour of taking it seriously. He would not have made Johanne Clare's mistake of calling Clare's 'opposition to enclosure... most definitely a moral opposition'[14], as though moral and political are mutually exclusive terms.

Here are the lines from 'Helpstone' which Radstock insisted on having excluded from the published version.

> Oh who could see my dear green willows fall
> What feeling heart but dropt a tear for all
> Accursed wealth oer bounding human laws
> Of every evil thou remainst the cause
> Victims of want those wretches such as me
> Too truly lay their wretchedness to thee
> Thou art the bar that keeps from being fed
> And thine our loss of labour and of bread
> Thou art the cause that levels every tree
> And woods bow down to clear a way for thee

As I have pointed out elsewhere, there is a formidable wit in these lines, from the echo of the enclosers as Milton's Satan, who on entering Eden 'At one slight bound high overleaped all bound', through to the last line, with its image of the woods as labourers who helplessly conspire in their own degradation. They, too, are deferential workers.[15]

'Helpstone' was begun in 1809, the year when the parliamentary statute for the enclosure of the village was enacted. Much of the actual enclosing took place between 1811 and 1816. In 1818 Clare wrote 'The Lamentations of Round-Oak Waters'. This ballad-like poem opens with the poet sitting beside a water-course to lament its lost beauty. The 'genius' of the brook joins him to 'deplore' its injuries; and the poem then becomes an utterance of protest at loss, the voice a collective one.

> Their foes and mine are lawless foes
>   And L-ws thems--s they hold
> Which clipt-wing'd Justice cant oppose
>   But forced (and) yields to G--d
> These are the f--s of mine and me

These all our Ru-n plan'd
Alltho they never felld a tree
Or took a tool in hand

Clare used this ballad form of common measure again for his 'Lament of Swordy Well', written some few years later. Here, too, the voice that utters the poem is a 'common', collective one, the measure exactly appropriate.

Im swordy well a piece of land
Thats fell upon the town
Who worked me till I couldnt stand
And crush me now Im down

In both cases the lament carries something of that Old Testament feeling for the lost land, its voice the voice of exile. Yet since the bitterness of both poems is inseparable from the fact that the voice speaks very precisely of those who are responsible for causing such exile, speaks in fact from the position of popular radicalism, it is not surprising that the former did not find its way into *Poems Descriptive*. Its politics were bound to be antagonistic to the volume's patron. To understand why this should be so requires us to know more of Radstock than Clare's biographers think it worthwhile to bother us with.

Radstock was a leading member of the Evangelical Party. Quite why Clare's publisher, John Taylor, should have thought him a suitable patron for Clare is something of a mystery. Perhaps because he was author of *The Cottager's Friend*, first published in 1816 and by 1820 much reprinted? Yet if the title suggested to Taylor that Radstock was something of a democrat, its subtitle should have disabused him: *A Word in Season to Him Who is So Fortunate as to Possess a Bible or New Testament and the Book of Common Prayer*. What the work recommends is, of course, acceptance of your lot in life. Radstock almost outdoes Hannah More's infamous *Shepherd of Salisbury Plain* in his earnest advice to agricultural labourers to enjoy what they have – salt on their potatoes, for example – and reflect on their good fortune in not being required to go without seasoning. In short, Radstock was a particularly zealous Evangelical. He served on no fewer than eighteen Charitable Societies, of one of which – The Naval Charitable Society – he was president (he was vice-president of four others and a governor to a further three); and he also served on the Society for the Suppression of Vice. In 1817 the Society declared its aims to be the suppression of (1) Sabbath-breaking; (2) blasphemous and licentious books, prints, drawings, toys and snuff-boxes; and (3) private theatricals, fairs, brothels, dram-shops, gaming-houses, illegal lotteries and fortune-tellers. It included among its successes the suppression of Shelley's poems. In October 1822 the Society obtained a verdict in Queen's bench against 'one Clarke for selling Queen Mab, a publication of an infidel character').[16] This then was the man whom Mrs Emmerson recommended to Clare with the exhortation that 'Your extraordinary patronage, will I hope remove from your mind those prejudices against the Great! – which your humble station has made you *too keenly* feel.'[17] But, Radstock's treatment of Clare's first volume was very unlikely to have removed his prejudices, nor did it do so.[18]

'Damn that canting way of being forced to please', Clare wrote to Taylor, who presumably shared at least some of the poet's outrage at what had been done to his volume. 'I cant abide it and one day or other I will show my Independance more strongly than ever' he promised.[19] Yet of course he could not. For as bitter experience would eventually show him, Taylor always had the upper hand. He could after all simply refuse to publish what he or his advisors did not like. Hence, the absence of 'The Lament of Swordy Well' from any volume published during Clare's lifetime.

To be fair to Taylor it was not only Radstock he had to worry about. If he seems to have blown hot and cold over Clare's radicalism, he was equally concerned about the poet's use of dialect words and his unorthodox spelling and punctuation. In the first volume he had editorialised most of these away, with disastrous results for the volume's ultimate worth. However Taylor, like Clare himself, was faced with the problem of readers who wanted a peasant poet but who certainly did not want to read what they would have regarded as illiterate outpourings. So, at least, Taylor must have guessed, and he would have therefore been gloomily confirmed in his worst fears by the review of Clare's second volume of *The Village Minstrel* that appeared in the *Monthly Magazine*. The anonymous author, in a long and often hostile review, spends some time in pulling to pieces and itemising what he calls 'the homeliness, approximating to vulgarity' in Clare's themes. These are, so he says, 'described in most suitable language'. He isolates among others the following lines:

But soldiers, *they're the boys to make a rout.*
The bumptious serjeant struts before his men.
And don't despise your betters *'cause* they're old.
Up he'd *chuck sacks* as one would hurl a stone.

Of these lines the writer notes: 'if it be urged such language is appropriate to the subjects treated of, we reply, that subjects to which such language is best adapted, are not those which a poet should have chosen...'.[20] I imagine that most readers would now think the lines energised by precisely the words and phrases to which the reviewer objects. His objections at least make clear what Clare – and Taylor – were up against. Such 'unrefined', vitalising, colloquial handling of the language is not appropriate to poetry, may not indeed be appropriated by it.

Nor may radical sentiment. This is not to say that poets of the 1820s were politically conformist. It is, however, to say that *peasant* poets had to be. If an uneducated writer was a contradiction in terms so, too, was a discontented peasant. Hence, no doubt, the absence of one of Clare's finest poems from *The Village Minstrel.*

'To a Fallen Elm' was written sometime in 1821 and must have been ready for inclusion in the volume. In his long Introduction to Clare's second book, Taylor deals with the poet's anguish at the prospect of the cutting down of the elms that had stood over his cottage. I say 'deals with' deliberately, for how else are we to account for this?

If an old post had such attractions for Pope, surrounded as he was with comfort and luxury, what allowance ought not to be made for the passionate regard of poor CLARE for things which were the landmarks of his life, the depositaries of almost all his joys? But the poet can be as much a philosopher as another man when the fit is off: in a letter to the writer of these lines he laments the purposed destruction of two elm trees which overhang his little cottage, in language which would surprise a man whose blood is never above temperate; but the reflection of a wiser head instantly follows:

My two favourite elm trees at the back of the hut are condemned to die – it shocks me to relate it, but 'tis true. The savage who owns them thinks they have done their best, and now wants to make use of the benefits he can get from selling them. O was this country Egypt, and I was but a caliph, the owner should lose his ears for his arrogant presumption... Yet this mourning over trees is all foolishness – they feel no pains – they are but wood, cut up or not. A second thought tells me that I am a fool: were people all to feel as I do, the world could not be carried on, – a – green would not be ploughed... This is my indisposition, and you will laugh at it...[21]

The original of this does not appear to have survived, although we do have a letter dated March 1821 in which Clare thanks Taylor 'for your honest liberallity in wishing to purchase the Elms for me & shall certainly never forget it – but you shall not buy them – let them dye like the rest of us –'.[22]

There is however no reason to suppose that Taylor tampered with Clare's letter. More likely, Clare remembered to whom he was writing and tried to control his anguished rage, with the effect of almost splitting himself in half. Of course, Taylor's offer to buy the elms *was* one of 'honest liberallity'. (In the event it turned out to be unnecessary because the owner changed his mind.) Yet to call Clare's anger a 'fit' is to make it clear why the poem could not be published. For 'To a Fallen Elm' very precisely directs anger against those who claim the right to trample on the rights of others. Clare imagines the elm felled by the man who 'barked of freedom'. 'O I hate that sound' he says:

> It grows the cant term of enslaving tools
> To wrong another by the name of right
> It grows a liscence with oer bearing fools
> To cheat plain honesty by force of might
> Thus came enclosure – ruin was her guide
> But freedoms clapping hands enjoyed the sight
> The comforts cottage soon was thrust aside
> And workhouse prisons raised upon the scite
> Een natures dwelling far away from men
> The common heath became the spoilers prey
> The rabbit had not where to make his den
> and labours only cow was drove away
> No matter – wrong was right and right was wrong
> And freedoms brawl was sanction to the song
>
> Such was thy ruin music making Elm
> The rights of freedom was to injure thine
> As thou wert served so would they overwhelm
> In freedoms name the little that is mine
> And these are knaves that brawl for better laws
> And cant of tyranny in stronger powers
> Who glut their vile unsatiated maws
> And freedoms birthright from the weak devours

If there is better poetry of voiced, radical anger than this then I do not know it. For commentators to deny that its radicalism is political is almost heroic in its perversity.

As to the matter of form of these early poems, 'Helpstone' is written in heavily end-stopped rhyming couplets. Clare may have adopted these because he thought they were sanctioned by precedent as suitable for poetry of the picturesque, and therefore appropriate for his own complex response to his native place. They are after all, the form of Goldsmith's *The Deserted Village* and less taxingly, of Wordsworth's 'Evening Walk'. In both cases the narrator is at once personal and seemingly authoritative: 'I' is the poet as especial agent of truth, where truth includes truth of feeling as well as of social utterance (and judgement). 'To a Fallen Elm' is built up of a number of fourteen-line units, roughly answerable to sonnets. It, too, aims for an authoritative mode of utterance, an opposable truthfulness. Of course, both of Clare's poems aroused opposition, i.e. editorial interference. Peasant poets were not allowed to voice truths appropriate (if at all) to poets in very different social circumstances. Yet the implied collective utterances of the two 'Lament' poems proved equally unacceptable. Whether speaking for himself or for others, Clare's radical voice was erased by publisher and patron.

2

These early experiences left a deep wound, one that Clare bared in letters of the period. They also taught him a certain wiliness. He became something of an adept at covering up, of pretending to Taylor – and no doubt Radstock – that all he wished to be was a kind of versifying pet lamb (to borrow Keats's phrase). He would be a Village Minstrel, even though his own preferred title for the second volume of his poems was *Ways in a Village*. Perhaps during the 1820s he was tempted to imagine himself into the role of a London-based and London-acclaimed writer. If so, I do not think this temptation can have lasted long, or have been very deep. He liked the early adulation, but he soon saw through it. How, otherwise, to explain a letter to Thomas Inskip, dated 10 August 1824, in which he mourns the death of Bloomfield, whom he calls 'the most original poet of the age', and speaks feelingly of his family misfortunes?

were are the icy hearted pretenders that came forward once as his friends – but it is no use talking this is always the case – neglect is the only touchstone by which true genius is proved – look at the every day scribblers I mean those nonsense ginglings calld poems ... while the true poet is left to struggle with adversity & buffet along the stream of life with the old notorious companions of genius Disappointment & poverty.[23]

Inskip was a Sheffield watchmaker, and Clare could sound off at him as he certainly could not with his mentors and paymasters. It should therefore come as no surprise to discover that earlier in the year he wrote to Taylor to say how much he agreed with him on the subject of religious hypocrisies. In this letter he tells his publisher that 'some of the lower classes of dissenters about us are very deceitful & in fact dangerous characters specially among the methodists with whom I have declined to associate'. The tone of this is to be expected. Less easy to account for is the qualifying remark 'but there are many sincere good ones to make up & why should the wicked deter us from taking care of ourselves'.[24] What is this about?

To try to answer the question I need to say something of Clare's involvement with the Ranters and the difficulty here is that we do not know very much about the subject: which Ranters he knew, for how long he was connected to any group, nor what that group may have been like. All we have to go on are letters that pass between him and his publishers during the spring and summer of 1824. On 3 April, Taylor reassures Clare:

As for joining the Ranters, you do right to get real practical Religion wherever it can be found. I am not at all afraid of your plunging into the Excess of Enthusiasm nor indeed are there any Excesses to be dreaded except those which are a Cloak to Wickedness. In this case Enthusiasm is the grossest and most damnable Hypocrisy. – But where it is innocent and well intentioned, I can find no great fault with Enthusiasm...[25]

From this it is apparent that Clare must have written to Taylor, in a letter now lost, to forewarn him of his having joined a group of Ranters. (The Tibbles' claim that Clare attended Ranter chapels in 1820 is clearly wrong.)[26] It is then in answer to Taylor's letter that Clare tells him that he will have no truck with the 'deceitful' dissenters among the lower classes. A little later he writes to Hessey:

I have joined the Ranters that is I have enlisted in their society they are a set of simple sincere & communing christians with more zeal then knowledge earnest & happy in their devotions   O that I could feel as they do but I cannot their affection for each other their earnest tho simple extempore prayers puts my dark unsettled conscience to shame[27]

Clare then provides Hessey with a detailed account of how the Ranters spend their sabbath; and he adds that 'my feelings are so unstrung in their company that I can scarcly refrain from shedding tears & when I went church I could scarcly refrain from sleep'.

I do not doubt the sincerity of Clare's religious feelings nor his conviction that they could best be expressed through Ranter meetings. Nevertheless, it is more than possible that he emphasises these in his letter to Hessey, and dissociates himself from 'dangerous characters especially among the methodists' when writing to Taylor, because he knew that in all likelihood they would be aware of the Ranters' reputation for involvement in radical politics.

In *The Making of the English Working Class*, E. P. Thompson rather questions this involvement. He implies that religious revivalists (including Ranters) did well at times of working-class loss of hope. In this sense, he says, 'the great Methodist recruitment between 1790 and 1830 may be seen as the Chiliasm of despair'. He also notes that in the rural areas 'Methodism of *any* variety necessarily assumed a more class-conscious form'.[28] Of course even if this is so we do not know how true it would have been of the Helpston Ranters, nor whether that was what attracted Clare to them. However, Rupert Davies, in his account of the history of the Methodist movement, remarks that:

Primitive Methodists were active in trades unions almost from the moment in 1825 at which it became legal for working people to 'combine' for the purpose of redressing their grievances... It was natural that Primitive Methodists should act in this way. They themselves were mine-workers, mill-workers, agricultural workers. They knew all about the long hours and filthy conditions for men, women, and children.[29]

Ranters were Primitive Methodists.

Thompson quotes an irate country parson of 1805, complaining that in his part of East Anglia the field labourers who had converted to Methodism were claiming that 'Corn and all other fruits of the earth, are grown and intended by Providence, as much for the poor as for the rich.'[30] This was seven years before the Primitive Methodist movement was founded as a break-away movement from Methodism. At the beginning of the 1830s Ebenezer Elliott wrote 'The Ranter', a poem which tells the story of a working-class preacher, Miles Gordon, who abjures 'the house where Wesleyans bend the knee' because 'the *spirit* is gone thence'. The official Methodist church, Gordon tells his listeners, has contentedly accepted the lot of those who were 'Bread-tax'd and Peterloo'd'. He therefore identifies himself and his cause with 'The slander'd Calvinists of Charles's time' who 'fought (and they won it) Freedom's holy fight.' These preachers taught to the 'poor and broken-hearted' 'truths that tyrants dread and conscience loves'. Such an appeal to conscience must surely make clear why Johanne Clare's attempt to separate the moral and political will not do. Miles Gordon speaks from that radical position where natural, customary rights are to be asserted and fought for. At the end of his sermon he promises his audience that 'the hour/Cometh when all shall fall before thee – gone/Their splendour, fall'n their trophies, lost their power.'[31] As we shall see, this language is very close to that which Clare uses at the end of his great poem, 'The Flitting'.

However, that poem was written in 1832. Near in time to Elliott's (though 'The Ranter' was not published until 1834), but not to the moment of Clare's involvement with the Ranters. And the poems Clare was writing in the mid-1820s cannot be said to reveal a decisive move towards a more radical vision than is to be found in 'Helpstone'. A major exception to this is 'The Mores', a poem whose radical grandeur owes much to Clare's passionately voiced contempt for those who have set out to destroy freedom by foreclosing on the possibilities of 'wandering'. ('Wandering' is a key word and concept in Romantic poetry, a mark of unfettered freedom, of the right to go as the spirit listeth.) But, it must then be remembered that these are the years in which Clare is gathering together a sequence of poems, some of which had been written earlier, and which would eventually be published in 1827 as *The Shepherd's Calendar*. According to Robinson and Summerfield, Taylor put the idea for this volume to Clare in 1823. Clare had it ready by the following year; but then there were delays. Taylor was busy, he told Clare, the times were bad, and anyway he needed to 'slash' the poem, to get it down to manageable size. Not surprisingly, Clare was unhappy over the delays and he deeply resented Taylor's interference in his text. If we put together his attitude to Bloomfield's death, his sense of being exploited by the London demi-monde (members of whom thought it perfectly within their rights to drive down to Helpston to peer at the 'peasant poet'), and if we then add to these matters his growing rage at what was being done to his poems, it follows that his decision to join the Ranters is not only understandable but has about it the feeling of inevitability.

Yet it should not be taken to define his politics. We have instead to register it as one move among many, by means of which Clare tried to give expression and significance to those contradictions which I have already noted that his position exposed him to, and as a result of which he had to try repeatedly to work out where his deepest loyalties lay.[32] My suggestion is that through the 1820s he came increasingly to understand that they could not lie with the world of cosmopolitan literary values, because these were not to be separated from other values connected to the untroubled ownership of such material things as land, property, lives. Quite simply Clare did not belong there, would never be accepted in that world except as a tame singing bird. Where else was there to go but back into the community of the increasingly dispossessed? There, at least, was a language he knew (a language Taylor had denied him by the most savage interference with the original text of *The Shepherd's Calendar*)[33] and with it a sense of community.

To say this is not to offer some sentimental version of the 'organic' community. On the contrary: Clare was repeatedly to recognise just how separate from his community his life as a writer had made him. Yet his *desire* to belong cannot be gainsaid. It makes its presence felt in his increased commitment to the use of dialect, as in 'Remembrances', written in 1832, where as poet he takes his stand on the language of community. He no longer, that is, identifies with the kinds of division that had made 'Helpstone' a very different kind of performance from, say, 'The Lamentations of Round-Oak Waters'. There, the poet *qua* poet had spoken in the accents of linguistic orthodoxy. Here, he speaks in dialect, chooses to be identified as a literary outsider.

> Here was commons for their hills where they seek for freedom still
> Though every commons gone and though traps are set to kill
> The little homeless miners – O it turns my bosom chill
> When I think of old 'sneap green' puddocks nook and hilly snow

But, as these lines make plain, this is not the whole story. For all the adroit use of the blended anapaestic/iambic hexameters – themselves a kind of folk measure – there is a degree of self-consciousness about the use of dialect indicated by the use of quotation marks (which I have to assume are Clare's own). There is, too, the inescapable 'literariness' of such phrases as 'it turns my bosom chill'. In fact, a reading of the whole poem will reveal how intertwined the vernacular and the literary are. And this is the point. Even the title, 'Remembrances', indicates that Clare is separated and knows himself to be separated from the community in which he grew up. It recalls such community from the present position of grieving isolation. Yet it also indicates that he is tied to it by many, deeply felt commitments and shared values. In short, 'Remembrances' enacts contradictions and conflicting emotions which in his personal experience Clare has no choice but to live out.

1832 was a key year. It was the year in which Clare moved from Helpston to Northborough. It was also when the first Reform Act made clear to thousands of English people, Clare included, that they were still unfranchised, still living on the margins, still officially without a voice because without a vote; they could now understand that the events of previous years, in particular the Swing Riots of the late 1820s, had yielded practically nothing of value to those who had been most deeply involved in them, or to the many who, like the moles – those little homeless miners – had been executed or transported for their protests against the Corn Laws and the selfish tyranny of the self-elected spokespeople for England.

> O I never call to mind
> These pleasant names of places but I leave a sigh behind
> When I see the little mouldywharps hang sweeing to the wind
> On the only aged willow that in all the field remains
> And nature hides her face where theyre sweeing in their chains
> And in a silent murmuring complains

So Clare writes in 'Remembrances', and he would have had in mind not only the moles, victims of gamekeepers' vigilance, but the rioters whose hung bodies had been displayed to public gaze. Such men had belonged to the 'pleasant names of places' and, out of such deep-rooted identification, had protested against what was being done to those places. Their reward was punishment and not infrequently death.

In order therefore to put 'Remembrances' in its full context we need to go back to 1830 and a sonnet of that year, 'England 1830'.

> These vague allusions to a country's wrongs,
>   Where one says 'Ay' and others answer 'no'
> In contradiction from a thousand tongues,
>   Till like a prison-cell her freedoms grow
> Becobwebbed with these oft-repeated songs
>   Of peace and plenty in the midst of woe –

And is it thus they mock her year by year
  Telling poor truth unto her face she lies,
Declaiming of her wealth with gibe severe,
  So long as taxes drain their wished supplies?
And will these jailors rivet every chain
  Anew, yet loudest in their mockery be,
To damn her into madness with disdain,
  Forging new bonds and bidding her be free?

This is an anti-Petrarchan sonnet, deliberately so. By the time Clare
came to write 'England 1830' Wordsworth was associated with the
renovation of Milton's use of the Petrarchan sonnet. For him, as for
his great predecessor, this was a matter of political significance. In a
number of key sonnets of the 1630s Milton had captured it for public
affairs, including affairs of state. In other words, he had politicised
the form, and Wordsworth was self-consciously imitating Milton
when he wrote a series of sonnets at the beginning of the century
which were gathered together under the general title *Poems Dedicated
to National Independence and Liberty*. Through Wordsworth, Milton was
living at that hour. However, Wordsworth's deeply reactionary
Ecclesiastical Sonnets of 1822 were also written in the Petrarchan
form. Petrarchanism now equalled cultural and political conservatism.

Clare's sonnet is therefore deliberately un- or anti-orthodox. In its
very structure it revises the Petrarchan sonnet. It begins with a sestet
and ends with an octave. Moreover, the sestet does not come to a
proper syntactic conclusion. Instead, it stops in mid-sentence, and
this odd break is followed by two quatrains, both of which utter
questions which may or may not be rhetorical but which leave the
sonnet feeling somehow incomplete, as though there ought to be a
further, concluding, couplet. That there isn't one, that there *couldn't*
be one, is of course the point. When Clare was writing the sonnet its
final question had to be left open, if only because while the riots lasted
there was the chance that something might come of them. (Here it
should be recalled that in July 1830 Paris was also in armed revolt,
against the Bourbons. Revolutionary possibilities were in the air.)
'England 1830' takes note of the power that is in the hands of those
who speak with 'disdain', who take for granted their superiority,
their right to power; but it also asks the question of whether they will
be allowed to continue to forge new bonds. The radical wit of that
phrase depends on its punning rightness. The bonds are both iron

fetters and legal entanglements. (There is an echo here of 'the knaves that brawl for better laws' of 'To A Fallen Elm'.) The two go together and together have to be broken.

In a sense that was what the Swing Riots were about. Clare knew about these, alright – how could he not know, given that they affected both Northamptonshire and Cambridgeshire? In December, 1830, he wrote to Henry Behnes Burlow to tell him that he had become 'alarmed at the upstir of fire & famine & such like currencys & under the influence of these ridicules I have scribbled a poem of 50 verses detailing the alarms'.[34] The poem in question is 'The Hue and Cry', which was first published in the *Stamford Champion*, on 11 January 1831. The *Champion* was a radical newspaper whose editor, John Drakard, had written to Clare at the end of 1829 asking him to give any assistance to the newspaper he was then planning. (It began publication in January, 1830.) In reply, Clare wished him 'success as heartily & sincerely as a Scott or a Cobbett', although confessing that he could not 'bring powers into the field to assist you to gain it as they could'.[35] Yet if Clare felt unable to be of much direct help to Drakard, it is nonetheless clear from his sonnet that he was deeply committed to the cause and plight of those who were responsible for the 'upstir of fire'. For the Swing Riots were at least partly directed against the vast number of newly made laws that took away rights from the common people.[36] That they did little to dent the carapace which Law had made for itself is evident from the revenges of the courts (mass transportations, imprisonments, and executions), to say nothing of the severe limits to the Reform Act of 1832.

3

From 1832, then, rural protest was more or less defeated. It did not revive until Joseph Arch formed his Agricultural Workers Union four decades later. Clare's defiant identification with the language of his community, as that is revealed in 'Remembrances', is a measure of his desire not to betray ways of life which the poem recognises are going down to defeat.

> By Langley bush I roam but the bush hath left its hill
> On cowper green I stray tis a desert strange and chill
> And spreading lea close oak ere decay hath penned its will
> To axe of the spoiler and self interest fell a prey

And cross berry way and old round oaks narrow lane
With its hollow trees like pulpits I shall never see again
Inclosure like a Buonaparte let not a thing remain
It levelled every bush and tree and levelled every hill
And hung the moles for traitors

The hung-up bodies of the moles, to which Clare returns more than once, become an iconic image of loss, of wilful destruction, of brutal power. It is as though his imagination fixes with almost obsessive concern on those helpless unfortunates who are endlessly victimised by new laws and who, in losing their small space of earth, can the more readily be destroyed. For now they belong nowhere, can claim no identification with place. 'Remembrances' is about loss of place: 'place' may stay vividly in the mind but in all other senses it is simply disappearing or has already disappeared. Clare's poems of this period are the most eloquent testimony I know to the power and relevance of that newly coined term 'nostalgia' (according to the Oxford English Dictionary it was first used in 1793); and they speak out of and address that specific anguish for loss of home which nostalgia is. (It is formed from two Greek words: nostos and algos: desire for home, and pain.)

It is therefore of the utmost significance that in the key year of 1832 Clare should have written 'The Flitting.' This great poem was occasioned by his move from Helpston to Northborough, a village all of three miles away from his native place but which, so the poem says, he feels to be alien – 'strange'. The move had been made possible by some of Clare's wealthy friends, who in an entirely well-intentioned manner thought he would be helped by being given the chance to start over again in a new village and in another cottage. 'The Flitting' may therefore seem to be an act of ingratitude. But it would be irrelevant to think of it in such terms. The fact is that it springs from and testifies to Clare's deep anguish about his sense of loss: of place, of identity (his sense of self is associated with Helpston but, as I have argued, also and contradictorily with London, since that was where his poetic reputation had been made and unmade), of a visible world. At a very deep level the poem is also about Clare's feeling of kinship with the world of little things and his feeling that they may still rise against their oppressors. Here, we have to notice that the key term running through the poem is 'weeds'. Weeds of course have no botanical meaning. They are simply plants which grow in the wrong place. They have therefore to be destroyed –

weeded out – from the well-tended fields of enclosure. Significantly,
Clare's first mention of them comes in a stanza which opens with a
memory of molehills.

> No – pasture molehills used to lie
> And talk to me of sunny days
> And then the glad sheep listing bye
> And still in ruminating praise
> Of summer and the pleasant place
> And every weed and blossom too
> Was looking upward in my face
> With friendships welcome 'how do ye do'
>
> All tennants of an ancient place
> And heirs of nobel heritage
> Coeval they with adams race

What comes through these lines is the feeling of shared identity with
the world of little things and the defiant assertion that these are of
'adams race'. This is the voice of old radicalism: When Adam delved
and Eve span Who was then the Gentleman. It also speaks for
natural, customary rights, for all those 'tennants of an ancient place'
who are now denied their place in the sun. The world of 'pomp' – of
money and of great houses (from Pope onwards the word 'pomp' had
become an almost technical term, linked to the magnificence of town
but more especially country houses) – this world has usurped the
land.[37] Its power spreads out from London (identified in stanza 20
with 'haughty pomp' of officially sanctioned art 'Where muses play
on golden string / And splendour passes for sublime'); it threatens
destruction to all who are in its way and to the values of locality and
neighbourliness.

But the last stanza runs:

> Time looks on pomp with careless moods
> Or killing apathys disdain
> – So where old marble citys stood
> Poor persecuted weeds remain
> She feels a love for little things
> That very few can feel beside
> And still the grass eternal springs
> Where castles stood and grandeur died

It was a commonplace of the period to rank plants in social terms.
Grass was like the poor because no matter how often you cut it down

it grew back up.[38] The closing lines of Clare's poem, far from endorsing a spirit of resignation as some commentators have suggested, voice a promise of resistance: the grass springs like an invading army, overwhelming those symbols of pomp, castles, and the grandees who use them as bases from which to raid and lay waste the surrounding countryside. The poem is therefore not to be read as being about a coming to terms with nature. Instead, it concludes with an affirmation of continuing protest – even violent protest.

To say this runs in the face of much commentary about Clare. Yet the closing lines of 'The Flitting' make use of language and image which are best understood if we recognise that they are expressions common to popular radicalism. In his essay, 'Custom Law and Common Right', Thompson notes that a recommended Exhortation to be preached in Rogation Week visited explicit commination upon offenders against parish or common rights, and this was to be visited not only on any small offender who 'removeth his neighbour's doles and marks' but also on the rich and great: 'So witnesseth Solomon. The Lord will destroy the house of the proud man: but he will stablish the borders of the widow'.[39] As Thompson says, the whole tradition of custom as it is manifested in 'unwritten beliefs, sociological norms, and usages asserted in practice but never enrolled in any by-law' is difficult to recover 'precisely because it belongs only to practice and to oral tradition'. It is the common sense tradition in which much of Clare's poetry is rooted, and to which Ebenezer Elliott also testified when, in the preface to his poem, 'The Village Patriarch', he envisaged a coming violent revolution against the Corn Laws by the agricultural and industrial poor:

England in that day, will be an ocean of blood and horror, with only one star shining over it in the death-black firmament – the star of DEMOGRACY. The farmers will perish, without a struggle; and all the land-owners will perish... So tyrants perish, involving the innocent in their destruction. But all will not perish. There is a ship that will ride safely over the the tremendous billows, and outlive the storm; I mean, the indestructable ship of the COMMONALTY. That ship cannot perish.
   'Princes and lords may flourish or may fade,
   A breath can make (sic) them, as a breath has made;'
but the people are eternal.[40]

In another poem of the early 1830s, 'The Splendid Village', Elliott revisits the subject of Goldsmith's 'Deserted Village', but substitutes for Goldsmith's pathos a new energy of retribution. The wanderer/

narrator of the poem returns to England to witness scenes of devastation caused by enclosure, and in Part II, xiii, notes that:

> cropp'd with every crime, the tax-plough's moor,
> And footpaths stolen from the trampled poor,
> And commons, sown with curses loud and deep,
> Proclaim a harvest, which the rich shall reap –
> Call up the iron men of Runnymeed,
> And bid them look on lords, whom peasants feed!
> Then – when the worm slinks down at nature's groan,
> And with the shrieking heav'ns thy dungeons moan –
> O'er the loud fall of greatness, misery fed,
> Let their fierce laugh awake their vassels dead,
> The shaft-fam'd men, whom yet tradition sings,
> Who serv'd, but did not feed, the fear'd of kings,
> To join the wondering laugh, and wilder yell,
> While England flames – 'a garden' and a hell.[41]

'The Flitting' is the exact contemporary of Elliott's poems. This is not to say that the two poets were in any sense influenced by each other,[42] nor that Clare's poem has Elliott's confident sense of the possibilities of revolutionary energy. Clare's condition, including his awareness of isolation from common cause, made for a very different tone. Nevertheless, 'The Flitting' has at its close far more in common with the democratic radicalism of Elliott than it does with the quietism which commentators who know nothing of the tradition and language of popular radicalism have wished onto it.

This, then, leads me back to the letter to Marianne Marsh, which Clare sent her in early January 1832, and in which he says that:

I look upon Cobbett as one of the most powerful prose writers of the age – with no principles to make those powers commendable to honest praise – the Letters to farmers contain some very sensible arguments & some things that appear to be too much of party colouring – there is no medium in party matters... where there is excess it is always on one side – & that is the worst of it – I am no politician but I think a reform is wanted – not the reform of mobs where the bettering of the many is only an apology for injuring the few – nor the reform of partys where the benefits of one is the destruction of the other but a reform that would do good & hurt none – I am sorry to see that the wild notions of public spouters always keep this reform out of sight... mobs never were remembered for a good action but I am sorry to see it now & then verging into the middle classes of society whose knowledge ought to teach them commonsense & humanity for if they have it they never let it get into their speeches[43]

It will not do to assume that we have here Clare's political creed. It is even less acceptable to think that his criticisms of Cobbett are best understood as a reaction to Cobbett's 'extremism'. Clare is after all writing to the wife of the Bishop of Peterborough, and it is not therefore surprising that he should protest against the 'many' who injure the 'few'. The Bishop of Peterborough was undoubtedly on the side of – even among – those whose lands had been attacked in the Swing Riots; and the nationwide protests, often violent, against the new Reform Act, which came into existence in 1832, were directed against property and symbols of power. Hence, for example, the burning of Nottingham Castle. (Those who think Clare less than honest in distancing himself from 'the mob' should perhaps read some of the nauseating letters that Lawrence sent to Lady Ottoline Morell.)

Anyway, the protest against Cobbett does not have to be from the position of moderation. In *Great Cobbett: The Noblest Agitator*, Daniel Green says that as a result of the watered-down Reform Bill which finally passed through Parliament in June 1832, 'Cobbett had at least half of a victory to celebrate'.[44] But what for him was half a victory was for Clare total defeat. At the time of writing to Marianne Marsh he knew that he and his kind were still to be excluded from the vote. Hence, surely, his remark 'I am no politician but I think a reform is wanted'. Given the person to whom he was writing, he could not risk putting it more forcibly. But in 'The Flitting' he does.

Yet it has then to be said that this is the last of Clare's poems to offer anything so buoyant. From now on his concern with 'little things' – the many bird and animal poems of the period – is with their perilous, repeatedly vulnerable existence on the margin. They are pushed into desperate strategies for survival, and they continue to exist only as virtual outlaws – without the law (in both senses) which could be used to order their destruction.

The final move comes with Clare's entry into the private asylum of High Beech, Epping, where he spends much time turning parts of the Old Testament into verse, including 'Davids Lament', 'Solomons Prayer', and parts of the Book of Job. If these exercises can be said to keep alive the spirit of radicalism it is in the sense that Dissent could find sanction in the Bible for its reading of history as God's apparent abandonment of his chosen people, for whom the ark of the covenant nevertheless remained a potent symbol of divine favour. This symbol is absent from Clare's later poetry.

NOTES

1 See John Lucas's chapter on Clare in *England and Englishness: Ideas of Nationhood in English Poetry 1688–1900*, Paperback edn (London, 1991).
2 E. P. Thompson, *Customs in Common* (London, 1991), pp. 10–11.
3 Ibid. p. 11.
4 Johanne Clare, *John Clare and the Bounds of Circumstance*, (Kingston, Montreal, 1987), see esp. pp. 14–20.
5 J. W. and Anne Tibble (eds.), *The Prose of John Clare*, (London, 1970), p. 140.
6 Tom Paine, 'Letters addressed to the addressers of the late proclamation', 1792. Quoted by Thompson, *Customs in Common*, p. 136. Paine's words belong to the year before Clare's birth, but as Thompson remarks, 'the re-ification – and cashing – of usages as properties came always to a climax at the point of enclosure'. Clare could hardly have been ignorant of the association of Paine's name with protest against the process.
7 Johanne Clare, *The Bounds of Circumstance*, pp. 21–2.
8 C. C. Abbott, *The Life and Letters of George Darley: Poet and Critic* (Oxford, 1967). Abbott establishes just how far Darley's disabling stammer turned him into a recluse and a disappointed man. It may be that Clare sensed in Darley a fellow spirit. However, the tone of his letter makes clear his awareness of the social gap between them, even though he hoped to close it.
9 H. Newby, *The Deferential Worker* (London, 1977).
10 B. Reay, *The Last Rising of the Agricultural Labourers: Rural Life and Protest in Nineteenth Century England* (Oxford, 1990), p. 185.
11 I have set out my unease with *The Parish* in *England and Englishness*, (see esp. p. 145). However, Thompson quotes Jeanette Neeson's remark that enclosure marked a turning point in the social history of many English villages because 'It struck at the root of the economy of multiple occupations and it taught the small peasantry the new reality of class relations. John Clare's hatred of its symbol – the newly prosperous, socially aspirant farmer – is illustration of the growing separation of classes that enclosure embodied.' (*Customs in Common*, p. 180). I am not sure I trust this, because in *The Parish* Clare's hatred of the socially aspirant farmer seems to be based on a feeling that somewhere in the past such social separation did not exist; and this is surely dubious. Still, to the extent that class separations were now being more enforced I can see that *The Parish* may have more justification in its satire of pretention than I allow.
12 Mark Storey (ed.), *The Letters of John Clare* (Oxford, 1985), pp. 49–50.
13 Lucas, *England and Englishness*, pp. 139–42.
14 Johanne Clare, *The Bounds of Circumstance*, p. 37.

15 For a fuller discussion of these lines see Lucas, *England and Englishness*, pp. 140–2.

16 For all this see Ford K. Brown, *Fathers of the Victorians: The Age of Wilberforce* (Cambridge, 1961), esp. pp. 428–32. It is extraordinary that none of Clare's biographers should have bothered to enquire into Radstock's life and so should take at face value his patronage of the poet.

17 Mark Storey (ed.), *John Clare: The Critical Heritage* (London, 1973), p. 66.

18 In his autobiographical sketch Clare has several entries on Radstock which appear to show him responding favourably to his patron, as do letters to Taylor. However, to adapt a famous phrase, they would, wouldn't they? It is, then, very revealing that when he comes to outline what he calls Radstock's 'only fault' the sentence is incomplete – as though he cannot bring himself to tell such a whopping lie. See J. W. and A. Tibble, *Prose* p. 84.

19 M. Storey, *Letters*, p. 69. I should say that I am not trying to demonise Taylor. Clare must have seemed something of a nuisance on those many occasions he badgered his editor for news of the progress of his latest volume, or when he worried about which poems would be going into it. But poets *do* worry about such matters; and the fact is that Taylor did not really understand Clare's anxieties nor the strength of his feelings about the interference with his work.

20 M. Storey, *Critical Heritage*, p. 152.

21 Ibid. p. 138.

22 M. Storey, *Letters*, p. 164.

23 Ibid. p. 301.

24 Ibid. p. 292.

25 Ibid. p. 291.

26 J. W. and Anne Tibble, *John Clare: A Life*, revised edn (London, 1972), p. 278. It is very unlikely that Clare would have attended Ranter 'chapels' at any time because by and large the primitive methodists met either in the open air or at each others' houses.

27 M. Storey, *Letters*, p. 294.

28 E. P. Thompson, *The Making of the English Working Class* (London, 1963), pp. 388–97.

29 Rupert Davies, *Methodism* (Harmondsworth, 1963), p. 135. In 1823, the vicar of Great Addington, Northants., the Reverend James Tyley, wrote a long poem in Latin called 'Inclosure of the Open Fields'. The poem lay in the church chest until this century, when it was discovered by Joan Wake, who employed Dorothy Halton to translate it. It was then published in February 1928, with notes by Ms Wake, in the *Reminder* (vol. 3 no. 94). Tyley surveys the history of Northamptonshire open-field systems, speaks of past violence, regrets the selfishness of peasants in opposing enclosure, and ends by rejoicing in its success. In the course of

the poem he devotes a section to 'Objection to Paying Tithes', in which he complains feelingly against those 'godless people' who are 'filled with malice and with hatred for all things sacred', and who clearly see the Church as going hand-in-hand with enclosers (which, as his poem makes plain, was indeed the case).

> See with what muttering the Schismatici count their gifts, the tithe-sheaves, or the crafty progeny of Wesley, soft of tongue but false at heart; or the Quaker, heavy of tread and with severe countenance, holy but declaring war against every kind of tribute; or that deadly tribe of Geneva, the followers of Calvin, than whom there are none more hostile to the Church. For them it would be a joyful day if they might behold the Church uprooted from its nethermost foundations and its hated servants and their surpliced tribe whelmed in the ruins of their temple. With what acclamation would they receive Cromwell again from Orcus, if he might raise his accursed head and put to flight Kings from the thrones of their fathers, and with like doom break down altars and send fierce wolves and raging bears into the sheep-fold to tear it.

Tyley is plainly worried by opposition to the Church's stand. Although Primitive Methodists are not singled out for mention here it seems reasonable to infer from what he says that this sense of threat is pointed at all those who, like Clare, prefer meeting with their own kind to falling asleep in church; and that such a sense must have some basis in what actually was going on in Northamptonshire in the 1820s. I am grateful to Dr J. Neeson for drawing my attention to this poem.

30 Thompson, *The Making of the English Working Class*, p. 397.
31 I quote from *The Poetical Works of Ebenezer Elliott: The Corn-Law Rhymer* (Edinburgh, 1840). The more "official" two-volume edition, edited by Elliott's son, cuts out many of his introductions and notes, and thus softens the poems' hard, radical edge.
32 The article by Mark Minor, 'John Clare and the Methodists: a reconsideration', in *Studies in Romanticism*, 19 (Spring 1980) is not very helpful here, because Minor does not really understand about the popular radicalism with which the Ranters were identified.
33 The best account of Taylor's extraordinary editorial interferences in *The Shepherd's Calendar* is to be found in the edition prepared for Oxford University Press by Eric Robinson and Geoffrey Summerfield (Oxford, 1973).
34 M. Storey, *Letters*, p. 524.
35 Ibid. p. 490.
36 The evidence of the severity of punishments for involvement in the riots is gathered by Eric Hobsbawm and George Rudé in their *Captain Swing* (London, 1969). See also P. Corrigan and D. Sayer, *The Great Arch: English State Formation as Cultural Revolution* (London, 1985), for the ways in which batteries of legislative laws were enacted in this period against working people.
37 For a discussion of the developing meanings of 'pomp' see my essay,

'England in 1830: Wordsworth, Clare and the question of poetic authority', *Critical Survey*, 4: 1 (1992), pp. 63–4.

38 For information on this see Keith Thomas, *Man and the Natural World* (London, 1983), p. 66.
39 Thompson, *Customs in Common*, p. 100.
40 *The Poetical Works of Ebenezer Elliott*, p. 55.
41 Ibid. p. 89.
42 It is difficult to believe that Elliott and Clare were ignorant of each other's work. Yet Clare's letters do not mention Elliott, nor have I come across any mention of Clare in Elliott's writings. I suspect that further research will uncover references that may help us with an understanding of Clare's political enthusiasms.
43 M. Storey, *Letters*, p. 560.
44 Daniel Green, *Great Cobbett: The Noblest Agitator* (Oxford, 1985), p. 455.

CHAPTER 7

The exposure of John Clare

Adam Phillips

1

> There is so much to be seen everywhere that it's
> like not getting used to it   John Ashbery, 'For John Clare'

In one of John Clare's earliest manuscript notebooks there is a four-line poem modestly entitled 'A Simile':

> A Mushroom its Goodness but Shortly Endures
> Decaying as soon as its Peeping
> – Woman much like them – for 'ts known very Well
> That they Seldom Get better by Keeping[1]

It is a modest title because, though the poem contains one overt simile, it smuggles in two others; and it is also about the senses in which a simile might describe the relationship – or the impossibility of the relationship – between the sexes. A woman may be like a mushroom in the way the poem suggests, but conventionally a mushroom is like a man because it is phallic. So by the tacit logic of the poem – which the ambiguous syntax exploits – a woman is also, therefore, like a man; neither 'Get better by Keeping'. Peeping – appearing from underground as both seeing and being seen – leads to destruction, being eaten or going off. Women both like mushrooms and are like them, which is eccentric in the traditional sense I have mentioned because mushrooms are clearly phallic, but not in the other sense; too prolonged an exposure to their company makes them infinitely less palatable. Peeping is preferable to keeping because more than a peep is not worth keeping. Desire is a glimpse; too long a look spoils.

Writing to his long-standing correspondent and patron Eliza Louisa Emmerson in 1836, a woman who had perhaps kept his poems too long without responding, Clare excuses them both of suspicion with polite tact:

My Dear Eliza
    Did you get the vol of poems I sent a long time ago I wished you to write directly & as you did not write we think you did not get them I still keep ill & am no better.[2]

At the time of writing this Clare was in a disturbed state but even here the continuity of preoccupation that sustained him throughout his life is discernible. The longer things are kept – poems, mushrooms, women – the more their goodness is in question, or threatened. Having a good look, for both the seer and the seen, is always a risk ('as I meet with (a book)', Clare writes of his reading habits, 'I dip into it here and there'[3]). Does Eliza Emmerson's silence mean she has received the poems or not got them? Is she keeping the poems and keeping quiet about them? If he is keeping ill, what can he make of her keeping?

Clare was uncertain in his life, as in his poetry, whether keeping things to himself was the only way of keeping things for himself; whether exposure – the exposure of writing poems and the different exposure of being known as a poet – was a dangerous invitation. Making himself known, he was there to be stolen from. Despite the insistent eagerness in his letters for 'poetical fame', Clare's ambivalent unease about recognition itself should not be read as exclusively reactive to his defeating circumstances. The very vice of obscurity could be its virtue. 'Ah what a paradise begins with the ignorance of life & what a wilderness the knowledge of the world discloses',[4] Clare wrote as the 'world' began to want knowledge of him.

Clare certainly found that his brief celebrity as a 'peasant poet' robbed him of something more than his place in his own community. When an admirer came to visit him from London he found that he had, 'little or nothing to say for I always had a natural depression of spirits in the presence of strangers that took from me all power of freedom or familiarity & made me dull & silent'.[5] It was the bitterest and most telling irony that his fame as a poet could take from him his words – as his editors did, in a different sense, by manicuring his diction – and his mobility. Publishing poems is an invitation to strangers; and especially, if by doing so one enters a literate culture from a largely oral culture. For Clare, wider circulation meant less room for himself.

As his autobiographical writings show, Clare more often felt his 'power of freedom or familiarity' in the protections of solitude; and eventually in 'that lonely and solitary musing that ended in rhyme'.[6] He often represents himself as a person cramped simply by the presence of other people, but marginally (and significantly) less cramped by the people from his own community. Yet solitude secured him.

'The rich man', he wrote – the two parts of himself and the two economic classes doubling for each other – 'is invisible', but the poor man is 'caught in the fact of an overt act'.[7] John Clare has been celebrated as a poet who celebrates the pleasures of observation, but his poetry is equally alert to the terrors of being seen. His poems often expose different forms of solitude – nests, love-affairs, madness, hiding-places, private walks, furtive creatures, poems – but in order to make plain the perils and ambitions of exposure.

Keats remarked to Clare's editor Taylor that in his poem 'Solitude', 'the Description too much prevailed over the Sentiment'.[8] Seeing, and being seen to see in a particular way – the visionary documentary of rural life that seemed to characterise his poetry – presented Clare with a dilemma about description that was integral to the project, and the sentiment, of his poetry. His unwitting self-definition as a particular kind of poet – a 'country poet' in Raymond Williams's more apposite terms[9] – made him available for appropriation and exploitation; for circulation in a world that he was unfamiliar with. It made him quickly prone to what Tom Paulin has called, 'the spiked trap Clare fell into – his success set him apart from his own community, while the system of patronage and publishing could offer nothing but a fitfully marketable public image'.[10] Yet through the startling illusion of visual clarity, the 'love of seeing' he proclaimed in so many of his poems, he opened himself and his familiar world to certain forms of scrutiny. He was drawn into a system of patronage and publishing that commodified his 'character', his place and his dialect (insofar as his editors would permit its usage). Clare began to realise that description – defining and evoking through vivid representation – could be complicit with, and even analogous to certain forms of ownership. He had to struggle, in other words, to find a language – which involved holding on to his own 'native' language without merely marketing it – that would differentiate his way of feeling proprietorial about his world from the ways, the new ways, of the people who employed and oppressed him, the owners of land and the owners of poetry (Clare could never have owned or had a stake in the countryside he wrote about). There is a conflict about description itself, enacted in his poetry; that description may be redemptive – provide a voice for otherwise marginalised people and experiences – but it may also be predatory and encourage other predators. Once nests are located they are there (asking?) to be stolen from. So Clare's distinctive clarity is always accompanied by a more paradoxical and protective celebration of obscurity, and silence and mist; the affirmation that

> full many a sight
> Seems sweeter in its indistinct array
> Than when it glows in morning's stronger light[11]

Many of Clare's finest poems – 'To The Snipe', 'The Fox', 'The Badger', 'The Wild Duck's Nest', 'Obscurity', 'Don Juan, A Poem', and many others from all periods of his writing – record the violation of privacies as second nature. This is clearly, among other things, an accurate and disturbing transcription of the historical trauma that Clare and his community were living and dying through; what Raymond Williams has called, in assessing the significance of enclosure for Clare's work, 'the cry of his class and generation against their fundamental subordination'.[12] As a poet from his particular labouring community Clare was in a bind that his poetry could not avoid; if he succeeded (through plentiful description of 'rural life', and 'poetical fame')' he failed (to protect the world that he loved and himself). To find and to see, Clare began to realise very early in his work, was now to use and exploit. 'A second thought tells me that I am a fool', Clare wrote to John Taylor in 1821, 'was people all to feel & think as I do, the world could not be carried on – a – green would not be ploughd a tree or bush would not be cut for firing or furniture & every thing they found when boys would remain in that state till they dyd'.[13]

If visibility was such a mixed blessing because to be found was to be appropriated, then the visible invisibilities of madness – of being anonymously Byron, a prisoner of the Bastille, a slave, a Babylonian captive, a prize-fighter, John Clare himself – must have been a compelling option. In Clare's daunting last letter, to James Hipkins from the Northampton Asylum, it is as though he has no privacy left

to violate. There is nothing to hide and nothing to show for anything:
'I have nothing to say so I conclude'.[14]

2

the terrible journey towards feeling somebody
should act, that ends in utter confusion and
hopelessness   John Ashbery, 'For John Clare'

Clare referred to his poems in an early prose piece as, 'my stolen
fugitives'.[15] The language of hiding and stealing and secrets that runs
through Clare's poetry is also the language he uses in his autobiographical writings to describe the actual writing of poems. To
begin with, he writes, 'my poems had been kept with the greatest
industry under wishd concealment, having no choice to gratify by
their disclosure'.[16] 'Keeping' here, which is a form of 'wishd
concealment', suggests the hoarding of stolen property. Working as a
gardener, Clare writes, 'when I fancyd I had hit upon a good image
or natural description I usd to steal into a corner of the garden & clap
it down'.[17] Writing poetry was time stolen from his employer: 'I
always felt anxiety to control my scribbling & would as leave have
confessd to be a robber as a rhymer when I workd in the fields'.[18] If
poetry is theft – the claiming of time – and the poet writes some of his
most compelling poems about the act of thieving, who is to be
gratified by the 'disclosure'? The poet may never know whether he
is the witness, the accomplice, or the criminal.

For Clare it was as though the countryside played a harsh kind of
hide-and-seek with the people who lived in it, and that for some
creatures with whom he identified, to be seen, to be found out, was a
risk. However, the risk was always one of mutual exposure, especially
for the poet. The birds that 'from mans dreaded sight will ever steal',
in 'To The Snipe' are disclosed by the poet's sight to be found in
'the most dreary spot'[19] but by telling us where they are he is, as he
knows, complicit with the killers. Just as Coleridge's dejection is
cured in the process of writing his poem, Clare's poetic sight is, in
part, condemned in the writing of his. Coleridge writes himself out of
the thing he fears, Clare writes himself into it.

In 'Don Juan, A Poem', written while Clare was in High Beech
Asylum, he presents the misogynistic version of this fear of unconceal-
ment, of disclosure as catastrophe:

The flower in bud hides from the fading sun
And keeps the hue of beauty on its cheek
But when full-blown they into riot run
The hue turns pale and lost each ruddy streak
So 'tis with woman who pretends to shun
Immodest actions which they inly seek[20]

In 'A Simile' it was the moment of appearance, of 'peeping' that was also the moment of 'decay'; in this image everyone is safe as long as the flower hides in the bud. Once out in the open the flower, like a woman (and perhaps Clare as the 'mad poet') is free to run riot, 'to be man's ruin', to be 'nasty'. Exposure corrupts. In Clare's pastoral of the covert – of the moment before disclosure, the poem before its publication – 'Goodness but Shortly Endures' its description and 'turns pale and lost'. Clare is always trying to figure out in his poetry in what sense, if at all, recognition – the recognition that leads to circulation and exchange – can be redemptive. If, as John Lucas suggests, 'Trespasser, fugitive, outlaw... are the kinds of condition, the forms of experience, which Clare addresses in his many poems about birds and animals',[21] then the question for Clare is, what is the cost of claiming that status in a poetic tradition and an exploitative economy in which the owners of land and the owners of poetry, from Clare's point of view, are also trespassers and outlaws? Who owns the language in which one can be described as an outsider, in a world in which to be recognised can be to submit? Clare becomes unavoidably a trespasser in the poetic tradition.

In Clare's 'Address To An Insignificant Flower Obscurely Blooming In A Lonely Wild'[22] the ironically obtrusive title already begs (and parodies) the questions that the poem will address. Why address her as a way of addressing your readers? For whom is this poem being written, with its famous allusion that already makes the flower's insignificance significant ('I know Gray, I know him well' Clare said to a visitor in the asylum[23])? Is the poem for the poet, for the flower or for the reader? Is the flower or the poet to be rescued by this address, and if so from what, and more to the point, for what? The poet sees himself in the flower – and, of course, as a conventional figure in a poetic genre alien to his origins but putatively about his surroundings – but sees himself as decidedly mixed about being seen; because in the act of being addressed, spoken to and located, something is being done to the flower that can make a mockery of it, or of the genre of poetry that idealises such Wordsworthian recognition scenes.[24] The flower begins, as does the poem, as perhaps just what it seems:

> And tho thou seemst a weedling wild
> Wild & neglected like to me
> Thou still art dear to natures child
> & I will stoop to notice thee

At first this might seem like an ingenuous imitation, or unconscious parody, of Gray and Wordsworth, legitimating the marginalised with the (admittedly obscure) grandeurs of obscurity. However, its artfulness is in its stooping; if the poet stoops to notice the flower, is he submitting or condescending? Perhaps recognition is lowering. Certainly 'improvement', Clare suggests, is in the eye of the beholder, or the gardener:

> For oft like thee, in wild retreat
> Aray'd in humble garb like thee
> Theres many a seeming weed proves sweet
> As sweet as garden flowers can be
>
> & like to thee, each seeming weed
> Flowers unregarded like to thee
> Without improvement runs to seed
> Wild & neglected like to me

The stanza break that both completes and then complicates the meaning by stopping and running over, goes on to suggest that being wild can also be the privilege of the neglected. To run away from something – in Clare's hit-and-run parody of Virgilian pastoral, in 'wild retreat', a phrase that would define much of the movement of his life – is to run towards something else. Running to seed in this cartoon-like poem suggests both going to waste and being keen to disseminate oneself. Weeds can be as sweet as garden flowers or wild and degenerate depending on one's point of view. One man's neglect is another man's protection. 'The continual sameness of a garden', Clare once noted, 'cloyed me'.[25]

The paradox that Clare addresses in this poem – and that is integral to his radical uncertainty about being a poet, one who notices such things – is that recognition can be theft; that to notice something privileges the observer over the observed – the describer over the described – and can bring with it assumptions of ownership.

The poet knows, as the poem goes on to say, that his Emma, the woman he desires and who is, like him, 'a lowly flower',

> If fancied by a polish'd eye
> It soon would bloom beyond my power
> The finest flower beneath the sky

A more cultivated 'polish'd' recognition would steal her from him with all the prerogative of privilege (but she would still be 'beneath' the sky in the hierarchies that Clare plays off against each other throughout the poem). Clare had, he wrote, 'always that feeling of ambition about me, that wishes to do something to gain notice or to rise above its fellows'.[26] It was the complicity of noticing and being noticed with rising above others – 'and' would have been less disingenuous than 'or' – that confronted Clare in his poetic vocation.

In the 'Address' all the positions in the recognition game are untenable. This leaves the poet, he suggests, with two unpromising options that are virtually synonymous; either to live as one of the 'unknown' ('their sweets are sweet to them alone'), or to hope that friends will 'find out my lowly grave / & heave a sight to notice me'. They will indeed have to heave it because the only 'me' that will be there will be absent. Poetry, he implies, is all epitaph and elegy. The only recognition worth having, or the only recognition available, is the recognition of having been unknown ('I Am' is an elegy not only for the poet, but for recognition itself). This was the 'identity' that Clare was tempted to settle for, and sometimes, more paradoxically, to make a case for in poetry. Some of his finest poems are delighted and distraught epitaphs to the possibility of being known.

For Clare to be, or to think of himself as, a poet involved him in a complex and contradictory set of identifications. If poets are people who are noticed and celebrated for their powers of 'disclosure' and recognition, and recognition is always from above – from a position of literacy, or wealth, or both – from a higher position in the social hierarchy, then how could Clare be a poet and a man who could protect his affinity for, and allegiance to, his origins? This dilemma forced him to continually vacillate in his life, as narrated in the autobiographical writings, between the wish to be seen and published and genial and the wish to hide or withdraw or flee. The conflict between participation and isolation found a parodic resolution in the terrible madness of his later years.

3

> Waiting for something to be over before you are
> forced to notice it.   John Ashbery, 'For John Clare'

Despite the fact that Clare 'did not much relish the confinment of apprenticeship'[27] he had 'a restless hope of being somthing better then a plough man...to make a better figure in the world'.[28] If he was not to be a farm-labourer then apprenticeship, in one form or another, was the only way to any larger kind of recognition. Yet, in his autobiographical writings he represents himself as someone made acutely vulnerable by this wish for recognition:

A bragging fellow name Manton from Market Deeping usd to frequent the public house when I livd there   he was was a stone cutter and sign painter   he usd to pretend to discover somthing in me as deserving encouragment and wanted to take me apprentice to learn the misterys of his art but then he wanted to trifle with me that had dissappointed my former prosperitys   he usd to talk of his abilitys in sculpture and painting over his beer till I was almost mad with anxiety to be a sign painter and stone cutter but it was usless...[29]

This is, for Clare, like a paradigmatic recognition scene. The sign painter, an artist himself of sorts and a keeper of the Mistery, is inevitably an object of interest and emulation for the young poet, but he only 'pretends' to discover something in him. In fact, he only wants to trifle with Clare (who would often refer to his poems in his letters as 'trifles' as though only his correspondents were in a position to decide if they were the real thing[30]). The man who appears to be encouraging, 'a bragging fellow', is in fact promoting himself: 'he usd to talk of his abilitys in sculpture and painting over his beer till I was almost mad with anxiety'. From being a stone cutter and a sign painter the man becomes, in Clare's artful narrative, a painter and a sculptor. The recognition scene is a seduction – he makes Clare 'mad with anxiety' – and the seduction has all the disappointments and prosperities of tantalisation. The man who makes signs for other people is representing himself. This was to be Clare's experience with many of the 'sign painters' – patrons, employers, publishers, doctors – with whom the circumstances of his ambition were to bring him into contact. There were many senses, as Clare discovered, in which promise was false.

What gives Clare's poetry, and the life that contained it – and eventually could no longer contain it – its distinctive complexity was his growing sense that the poetic vocation, with all the 'misterys' of the art and the mist in mystery, could be complicit with those forms of life it appeared to repudiate, or to provide a refuge from; that the sign painter could be a figure for the poet (so in this reading Clare's famous sonnet, 'Poets love nature and themselves are love', contrary to Harold Bloom's pressing claims for it, is a mock-heroic because it protests too much).[31] It is his discomfort with the business of poetry – sometimes expressed through his distrust of other poets – that makes Clare such an unusual figure among the poets of the period. For Clare the idea of poetry, despite the resilience of his commitment to his own poetic project, was fraught with contradictions. High claims for poetry brought high anxieties, especially for a 'low'-born writer. It is this profound suspicion about the virtue of poetry that makes Clare an anti-poet of Romanticism.

Clare, who described himself in an early letter, when he was indeed unknown beyond the confines of his village, as 'a Clown who as yet slumbers in Obscurity',[32] made in the name of Obscurity one of his finest poems, or anti-poems:

> Old tree, oblivion doth thy life condemn
> Blank and recordless as that summer wind
> That fanned the first few leaves on thy young stem
> When thou wert one year's shoot – and who can find
> Their homes of rest or paths of wandering now?
> So seems thy history to a thinking mind
> As now I gaze upon thy sheltering bough
> Thou grew unnoticed up to flourish now
> And leave thy past as nothing all behind
> Where many years and doubtless centurys lie
> That ewe beneath thy shadow – nay that flie
> Just settled on a leaf – can know with time
> Almost as much of thy blank past as I
> Thus blank oblivion reigns as earth's sublime[33]

Knowing with time is not the same as the knowing in time that is poetry. It is possible to grow 'unnoticed' and still to flourish. There is a history and a growth process, Clare is saying, that exists without the record of the poem. Clare's poetry counters and confirms, or rather, affirms the 'blank oblivion'. Only the greatest of visionary anti-poets can celebrate without irony that 'blank oblivion reigns as earth's sublime', but do it, of course, in a poem, on record. 'Hopes unrealized', Clare wrote, 'are hopes in reality'.[34]

NOTES

1 Eric Robinson and David Powell (eds.), *The Early Poems of John Clare 1804–1822* (Oxford, 1989), p. 155.
2 Mark Storey (ed.), *The Letters of John Clare* (Oxford, 1985), p. 631.
3 Eric Robinson (ed.), *John Clare's Autobiographical Writings* (Oxford, 1986), p. 45.
4 Ibid. p. 31.
5 M. Storey, *Letters*, p. 63.
6 Robinson *Autobiographical Writings*, p. 12.
7 Eric Robinson (ed.), *The Parish* (Harmondsworth, 1986), quoted in the introduction, p. 24.
8 Mark Storey (ed.), *John Clare: The Critical Heritage* (London, 1973), p. 120.
9 Merryn and Raymond Williams (eds.), *John Clare: Selected Poetry and Prose* (London, 1986), p. 11.
10 Tom Paulin, *Minotaur* (London, Boston, 1992), p. 50.
11 Geoffrey Summerfield (ed.), *John Clare: Selected Poetry* (Harmondsworth, 1990).
12 Williams and Williams, *Clare: Selected Poetry and Prose*, p. 15.
13 M. Storey, *Letters*, p. 161.
14 Ibid. p. 683.
15 Robinson, *Autobiographical Writings*, p. 11.
16 Ibid.
17 Ibid. p. 16.
18 Ibid. p. 53.
19 Summerfield, *Selected Poetry*, pp. 111–14.
20 Ibid. p. 215.
21 John Lucas, *England and Englishness* (London, 1990), p. 151.
22 Robinson and Powell, *Early Poems*, p. 216.
23 M. Storey, *Critical Heritage*, p. 415.
24 See Terence Cave, *Recognitions: A Study in Poetics* (Oxford, 1988) for a brilliant discussion of the notion of recognition scenes.
25 Robinson, *Autobiographical Writings*, p. 11.
26 Ibid. p. 56.
27 Ibid. p. 53.
28 Ibid. p. 55.
29 Ibid.
30 For Clare's use of the common eighteenth-century word 'trifle' see, for example, Robinson, *Autobiographical Writings*, pp. 1, 15, 17, 24, 48.
31 Harold Bloom, *The Visionary Company* (New York, 1971), pp. 450–1.
32 M. Storey, *Letters*, p. 5.
33 Summerfield, *Selected Poetry*, p. 179.
34 Robinson, *Autobiographical Writings*, p. 6.

CHAPTER 8

' The riddle nature could not prove' : hidden landscapes in Clare's poetry

Nicholas Birns

1

John Clare has long been seen as a poet of nature. The implicit suggestion in this view is that he was a poet of nature rather than of something else. That something else is usually a Wordsworthian or otherwise Romantic notion of the imagination. 'Nature' with respect to Clare's poetry has a sort of down-to-earth connotation. It suggests an empirical terrain whose brute factuality limits any metaphorical or philosophical dimension. Juxtaposed in opposition to 'imagination', 'nature' inevitably becomes the inferior term, even when it is advocated. This is simply because it has come to have a more determinate and codified meaning in critical discourse.

Recent analyses of Clare's poetry have attempted to go beyond the traditional portraits of Clare, even those by his admirers, as a sharp-eyed recorder of immediate natural experience. This portrait assigns him a place as a minor poet while leaving the mantle of 'genuine' poetry with the time-honoured High Romantic canon. In his influential 1972 book, John Barrell liberates Clare from his secondary status as minor Romantic by comparing his poetry not to that of his contemporaries but to the eighteenth-century idea of landscape, manifested both in poetry and in painting.[1] In contrast to the panoramic, preconceived abstractions characteristic of this period, Clare's particularity is not a limitation but a refreshing virtue. Barrell's canny reformulation of the terms under which Clare may be approached has enabled an appreciative vision of Clare. This vision neither faintly praises him as a photographic recorder of natural minutiae nor enfolds him fully into a version of social history. Raymond Williams, for example, is wont to do the latter. While hardly remaining insensitive to either the descriptive or social powers of Clare's verse, he more or less makes Clare out to be a versified Cobbett.

The illumination of Clare's reaction against the eighteenth century as an index of Clare's own enactment of the Romantic turn now enables him to be compared to his contemporaries without being either assimilated or derogated. As Hugh Haughton points out, Clare's lack of the drive towards aesthetic supremacy that the Romantics deemed characteristic of themselves can now be seen as a deliberate and complicated retrenchment, not a cut-and-dried doughty empiricism.[2] This approach finally frees Clare from the denunciation of his poems as direct and unreflective. This categorisation ultimately stems, as Juliet Sychrava points out, from the Schillerian distinction between the naive and the sentimental.[3] Sychrava interestingly suggests that this distinction has remained strangely unproblematised by deconstruction. Deconstruction prefers even a fissured reflectiveness to the concentrated particularity that Sychrava, borrowing terminology from Nelson Goodman, terms Clare's 'dense' aesthetic.

It is doubtful that the growing attention Clare is drawing at the outset of the 1990s will have theoretical reverberations on the scale of the Wordsworth revival of the 1960s. Yet the continuing attempt to justify Clare in the context of Romanticism has entailed a revaluation of the characteristics that were in the past ascribed pejoratively to Clare's verse. Johanne Clare exemplifies this when she speaks of Clare as one who fruitfully acknowledged 'the bounds of circumstance' and wisely refrained from questing after universal or teleological absolutes.[4]

These intercanonical distinctions, between Clare and his Romantic contemporaries, have been necessary and vital in freeing Clare from the 'minor' role allotted to him in traditional literary-historical taxonomies. Yet there is a risk here. In their polemical eagerness, these distinctions may tend to overlook the tensions within Clare's own poetry. There has been one dominant intracanonical distinction in Clare criticism: between the early nature poems and the agonised visionary utterances of the asylum years. The asylum poems have often come under suspicion because they seem closer to High Romanticism than his earlier verse. Praising them overly would seem to scant the very virtues so arduously discovered in Clare and would congratulate him only when he seems most like Wordsworth. The distinction between Clare and his contemporaries, although heuristic and valuable, has a tendency to try to recuperate the earlier, more sociological opposition between Clare as local-colour writer and

Clare as protester against the ravages of industrialism. This overly pigeonholes Clare. It also unfairly denigrates the other Romantics, who, whatever the ambiguities of their politics, were hardly captains of industry, or flatterers thereof. Now that Clare's reputation has been so ably established on its own terms, it is worth sidestepping these various oppositions and taking a closer look at strains in Clare's poetry that reveal a remarkable continuity between the earlier and the later verse. These strains reveal a complexity within Clare that may have as much of a renovating virtue as the enabling distinctions between Clare and his contemporaries.

Even Clare's earliest poems, often seen as his most straightforward, possess a subtlety that is missed when their purely scenic and objective reference is emphasised. An instance of this is the sonnet, 'The Heat of Noon':

> There lies a sultry lusciousness around
> The far-stretched pomp of summer which the eye
> Views with a dazzled gaze – and gladly bounds
> Its prospects to some pastoral spots that lie
> Nestling among the hedge, confining grounds
> Where in some nook the haystacks newly made
> Scents the smooth level meadow-land around
> While underneath the woodland's hazley hedge
> The crowding oxen make their swaily beds
> And in the dry dyke thronged with rush and sedge
> The restless sheep rush in to hide their heads
> From the unlost and ever haunting flye
> And under every tree's projecting shade
> Places as battered as the road is made   (p. 39)[5]

The heat of noon is the ultimate natural *nunc stans*: a moment of utter synthesis, of the obliteration of natural specificity in the imperial glare of the sun. There would seem no room here for the kind of liminal perceptions that Clare along with so many poets in the Romantic tradition delights in, the glimmering elusiveness that Wallace Stevens was to describe as 'the half-colors of quarter-things'.[6] Clare's resourcefulness as an auditor of his own mental experience was so great, though, that he did not need an explicitly liminal subject-matter in order to perceive nature, and the world around him in general, with the kind of perceptual, as opposed to empirical, specificity that we associate with such later figures as Pater and Hopkins. The kind of pulsion with which Clare animates the natural phenomena he observes and records is visible in the first two lines.

We might expect a series of adjectives leading up to the emergence of the scenic natural tableau of the 'far-stretched pomp of summer'. Yet, instead of 'sultry' and 'luscious' simply leading off this elaborative string, they are detached from the panoramic term and are themselves made into a quality. They are nominalised into a kind of hazy aura whose presence consists in its implication. The sultry lusciousness of high noon would ordinarily be stifling in its estival generosity, providing us with too much fulfilment, too much satisfaction, preventing the sort of cognitive or experiential nuance that enables us to meaningfully navigate our relation to the external world. Clare makes enigmatic what would otherwise be a stultifying surplus by his making the sultry lusciousness a peripheral epiphenomenon of the pomp of summer rather than an organic consequence, a move which means the eye is not dwarfed by the static perception of summer but 'dazzled' by its magnificence. The eye as a result 'gladly' gravitates to more enclosed prospects, but again Clare's verbal nuance is a step ahead of a dogmatic reduction of his sense.

The gladness is not just a prudent sigh of relief at beating a strategic retreat from the dazzling glare. It is an exultation caused by the brightness of the glare, even if its intensity demands an almost automatic recoil. This is hardly the inhibiting, supreme central light of a naturally fixed high noon. As its glory is so much more powerful than its substance, its mastery is turned into mystery. In turn, the pastoral retreat is not just a flight into the specific. Here the abstract scheme of Clare as an exponent of chthonic specificity as opposed to panoramic universality needs to be considerably ramified. The 'spots' may not possess in themselves a Wordsworthian potency, but they are not just inert patches of the particular to which the eye can comfortably and finally accommodate itself.[7] Even the spots are involved in a kind of active process, 'nestling' among the hedge, at once being still and creating their own stillness. The eight-and-a-half lines of unpunctuated torrent that conclude the poem resist, by their very form, partitioning into a determinate niche or locality even as they canvass the temptations and rewards of being ensconced in nook and hedge.

Clare cherishes this kind of ensconcement. Yet he never seeks a total stillness or freedom from ongoing activity. The nook to which the eye gravitates does not wall itself from the rest of the landscape. It incorporates the human work and motion by which the landscape is maintained. The haystacks in the nook are newly made. This is of course a precondition for their being at all aesthetically attractive. Yet Clare acknowledges that they are the product of a concrete act of human labour whereas another poet would perhaps pretend that the haystack was an innate part of a pre-existing scenic order. This is not a redeeming grasp of the 'real' on the part of Clare as opposed to his counterparts' 'artificiality'. Rather, it is a stress on agency as opposed to the placidity of the eighteenth-century landscape tradition. Nature here is too alive to be strictly real. The haystack lending its scent to the meadow-land is as much of an act as the oxen making their beds in the hedge. The hierarchy of nature – and the structure of intentionality we attribute to various members of that hierarchy – are for Clare less important than the individual movements of the phenomena usually categorised as 'natural'.

It is difficult to discuss 'nature' as a poetic concept. This is not only because of the ill-repute it has acquired with regard to its imaginative 'rival'. The idea of nature is also vulnerable to being easily infected by notions of 'human nature'. It is very tempting to see Clare as moving from eighteenth-century ideas of a human nature, available through a common intersubjective perception if not by Cartesian fiat, to a more concrete idea of nature as such. However, it must be recognised that, on the one hand, there is no concept of nature as such that can totally be distinguished from human construction of that nature, and on the other it is hardly the effect of Clare's poetry to separate the natural from the human. What is instead achieved is the problematisation of the human-natural relationship as it had been traditionally constructed.

This can be seen in the tenth and eleventh lines of 'The Heat of Noon'. Here, the dry dyke, 'thronged with rush and sedge' is, although apparently still, full of the mesh and rustle of the weeds whose fecundity lends a virtually human sense of being filled and populated. The utterly natural is also collusively social. The restless sheep of the next line are active. Yet their act consists of seeking refuge (much like the poet's act with respect to the entire scene). That from which they are fleeing is a force to reappear eerily in Clare's later poetry, the ever-haunting fly. The fly is physically hardly a worthy opponent for an ambitious sheep but becomes so by its constant activity incarnating the ceaseless hum of nature, its refusal to lapse into the stillness demanded by human reifications. In concluding the poem with a restful, almost Virgilian notion of *umbra*, Clare does not estrange his natural thicket from the humanity that perceives it. The places shaded by the trees may be free of an overt humanity, especially one thwarted by the fruitless fertility of midsummer. Yet that does not mean that they are either pure or static. In being 'as battered as the road is made' they are being compared to places of human activity, not being made into them. Nature is full of mobility, of resonance that cannot be simplified to a monolithic ground on which a redemptive human intelligence can stamp its Promethean claim. Nature is never fully still, and thus is unable to be stilled by art.

2

It is important to keep this activity of nature in mind as Clare's entire career is surveyed. Clare's critics possess the almost exhilarating privilege of studying one of the few places where a major event in English social history coincides with an equally important phenomenon in literary history. The prominence Clare gives to the theme of 'enclosure' offers an ideal opportunity to register the social changes concomitant with the 'modernisation' of the English landscape in the early nineteenth century within a poetic matrix. This promising coalescence, though, is undermined by portrayals of enclosure that tacitly operate out of a Leavisite sentimentalism and make the process of enclosure a synecdoche for the entire process of modernisation.[8]

This sentimentalism is characterised by a tendency to portray the time before enclosure as a time of pastoral, Edenic bliss, when of course it was hardly so. The pre-industrial order was as much of an order as the post-industrial one, and it is nostalgic to believe that the labouring class was any less mistreated before than it was after. It was only that the mechanism of mistreatment was more systematic on the later side of this division, although it must also be recognised that, as Anthony Giddens has pointed out, this systematisation was also vital in bringing about the increased social flexibility that stimulated the awareness of egalitarian and democratic imperatives where they had previously not existed.[9] The poet Osip Mandelstam at one point speculates about a history of human losses that would complement that of human acquisitions so that both would be in a way the same history.[10] Any history that attempts to discuss literary texts in tandem with political and social processes must be that sort of history, one which does not sentimentalise one time as superior to another. This latter sort of privileging would clearly fall prey to the charges levelled by Derrida against Levi-Strauss and Rousseau in the *Grammatology*, that they romanticise the primitive and thus affirm the normative Western structures of stability and order even while seeming to rebel against them in an ecstatic retrogressive spree.[11] Whatever excesses have been generated by post-modern scepticism, the recent awareness that no period of human history is inherently 'better' than any other one is a salutary one. It prevents the romanticisation of the past characteristic of attempts to stabilise and mystify tradition.[12]

Admittedly, the virtue of the English tradition of social dissent is that it did not fall into the headlong infatuation with relentlessly forward progress characteristic of mainstream Marxism. This resistance is most impressively exemplified by the work of Raymond Williams and E. P. Thompson. There is, in these writers and the tradition they inherit and promulgate, a sensitivity to circumstance and a tolerance for plural social forms that are not subjugated to a univocal gauge of what is 'enlightened' and/or 'reactionary'. Yet the application of this tradition to Clare must be performed with especial vigilance. There is a danger, when a critical tradition arising from (a socially sensitive version of) Romanticism is applied to a Romantic poet such as Clare, of an overly facile isomorphism between the interpreter and the object under scrutiny. This too-comfortable fit between method and text jeopardises the critical detachment that is a crucial companion to hermeneutic empathy in the process of literary analysis. When the mission of criticism inclines excessively toward advocacy rather than analysis of the works under discussion, it brings in its wake unexamined assumptions that eventually hobble the very writings they originally seem to enable. The sentimentalisation of the enclosure process is a symptom of the above-mentioned danger. It seizes on the particular circumstance of 'the commons' being 'enclosed' and generates out of it a global trope of enclosure. This trope uses the assumption of a breakdown of the common weal by the means of capitalistic appropriation as a metaphor for the oncoming of modernity.

Yet what tormented Clare was hardly the closing of the landscape, but what might be called its demystification. What appalled him about the enclosure process is not that it ruptured the organic web of peasant culture (from which Clare was already alienated by virtue of his imaginative ambitions), but that it ruptured the veil from nature, the veil of beauty and specificity which Clare so cherished. As Kenneth Burke wrote in the early 1930s of the position of the artist in the modern period, 'His sensitiveness to change must place him at odds with the moral conservatism of the agrarians...but the industrialist elements will likewise meet his innovations with resistance'.[13] Clare's clear opposition to processes parallel to and anticipatory of industrialisation does not make him an agrarian or agrarian sympathiser. Clare's objection, unlike that of the agrarians, was not merely to enclosure *per se*, but to the overall process of modernisation of which the former was only a very specific instance. A look some four hundred miles to the north might help clarify the confusion caused by the over-reliance on enclosure as a synonym for modernisation. The Highland clearances of the eighteenth century were as crucial an instrument of modernisation as the enclosures, and their role in prompting the vast emigration to Britain's colonies and ex-colonies was as determinative of future history as the role of enclosure in precipitating the rise of the industrial working class.[14] Yet their precise mechanism of operation was exactly the opposite of that of enclosure. Whereas enclosure atomised the commons into individual holdings, the clearances dissolved the properties of small landholders into large estates where animals could graze freely in the service of moneyed aristocrats.[15] The alignment of the rhetorical opposition of 'open-versus-closed' with the phenomenon of modernisation that is to be found in enclosure is reversed in the process of the clearances. The building of the canals in East Anglia in the late eighteenth century (and for that matter in Scotland as well) is another index of modernisation.[16] The canals, in providing for the more efficient transportation of goods, transformed the landscape in the service of economic goals. However, they did not figuratively close the landscape as much as open it, render cognitively possible the kind of expansive commercialism that was to be later symbolically embodied by the railroad. Openness can be deracinated as well as unfettered, and being enclosed can embody a sheltering protectiveness as well as constriction. One suspects that Clare feared enclosure not because it reined in his mental universe, but because it opened it up, threatened to render it too available to human technology and human explanation.

Both the clearances and the canals signal that modernisation was not simply a matter of closing the once-open, of netting and staining the once-paradisal. Modernisation was the net result (and theoretical impetus) of a series of drastic economic, agricultural and social changes that cannot be crystallised in a form that would enable it instantly to be straightforwardly lamented. Clare's response to modernisation was not lamentation, but resistance, a resistance that was not to the particular circumstance of enclosure but to the entire idea of subjecting nature to man in order to improve its efficiency, to control it for strictly productive purposes. This kind of productive control reached its logistical height in the Industrial Revolution. Yet it had existed as a human response to nature since the Neolithic era. As Barrell points out, the 'open-field' system by which Clare's Helpston was organized before enclosure was 'hardly less rigid' than what succeeded it.[17] It was merely the (vastly enlarged) means, not the end, that was altered within Clare's lifetime. Clare's enclosed landscape yielded historically not to industrialisation as such, as is the unconscious implication of sentimental agrarian narratives, but to a more efficient kind of agriculture, what Barrell terms the 'rural professional class'.[18]

Clare's immediate environs, and the entire region of East Anglia with Clare's Helpston on the periphery, hardly participated in the economic expansion characteristic of the Midlands. A region once one of the most economically vital in England, with its easy access to maritime trade with the Continent, became something of a backwater with the onset of an industrial mode which determined geographical assets in a manner far different from before. Even as the draining of the fens attempted to make the land more useful to economic activity, larger industrial transformations were diminishing the economic prominence of East Anglia. In doing this, they were relegating this region to obscurity, making the territory a function of an overall national order. Thus, eventually, the region's own self-image, as a result of this loss of centrality, became metaphorically denser and more indistinct, in fact more 'marshy', as its physical appearance became more overtly planned and ordered.

As so often happens in regional cultural history, the region's prominence in aesthetic production (such as in the landscape painting of Morland, Cotman and even Constable) occurred on the verge of this obsolescence, and thus conveys an aura of semi-conscious elegy. Clare's community was not merely subjugated by a new economic order, but made almost superfluous by it. Not only did the physical and commercial landscape of East Anglia change in the early nineteenth century, but so did the position of the region in a larger context as well. The region was obscured to the world as the natural nuances cultivated by Clare were opened to modern 'efficiency'. This is a double movement, where the effect of the motion of the individual consciousness runs in a contrary way to that of historical change.

This individual consciousness is simplified by a narrow focus on the enclosures which does violence to Clare as an individual, in a way miming the disruptions of Clare's own mental landscape prompted by modernisation. The critical marginalisation of Clare was premised on Clare existing merely as an index of his own time and place, and his recent critical resurrection has accordingly stressed his poetic intentionality far more than was conceivable in previous commentaries. It does Clare an injustice to merge him fully into a preconceived 'period', or to say that his intellectual and emotional perceptions were fully tied to a kind of historical causality. There is between purely personal experience and historical generalisation an intermediate and often arbitrary structure called biography, and that biography must be considered when measuring Clare's emotional response to social change. Part of Clare's position is the reality that he biographically *happened* to be alive during the time of certain social and economic changes, and thus, merely because of the coincidence of his own lifespan with these changes, inevitably valued the time before those changes, i.e. his childhood, as an informing and comforting principle set against the tragedies and pains of adulthood. No doubt that part of Clare's power which is unattributable to individual genius may emanate from his presence at the pressure-point of socio-economic transformation, the informing and generating circumstances which may have, in shock and in exultation, lifted him from being yet another mute inglorious Milton.

However, the sense of valuing an early time as a guiding star in later life is hardly unique to this time and period in history. To get science-fictional for a moment (a scenario anticipated by Clare in 'The Eternity of Nature' when he speaks of the years growing 'many thousands in their marching state'), it is not unlikely that if, global warming and other self-inflicted traumas notwithstanding, the human race reaches the year 5040, a person of reasonably mature years might see the years of their childhood, 5005 or so, as an unreachable locus of arcadian bliss, however irremediably and bizarrely futuristic anything likely to exist in 5005 may seem to us. Biography is the interaction of a set of personal emotions with another set of historical circumstances, and neither set is ever supreme. Clare may be of particular interest because of the time in which he lived, but, as the *Annales* school has shown us, history may have meaning even when it is not significant to a certain interpretative perspective, and there is no one narrative that can infallibly say that England in 1820 was a more crucial time and place for humanity than, say, Laos in 1915. The history of the early industrial era has for long been written under the aegis of a Marxist or Hegelian teleology, under which modernisation is either affirmed as a step on the way to proletarian triumph or scourged as violating organic tradition. Clare's poetry is extremely resistant, as we shall see when discussing 'The Eternity of Nature', to these kinds of historical generalisations, and is belittled by them.

3

Clare is also undervalued if he is seen exclusively as a victim of economic or historical change. It is more appropriate to see him as a 'patient' of that change, in the sense of one who suffers from and through it, but who is by no means unable to resist the change or even to come to terms with it and transcend it. This is glimpsed in 'The Flitting'. This begins as a plaint against eviction (although the move Clare describes was not necessarily a result of an explicitly economic or historical cause).[19] Yet it concludes as a chant of personal and even cosmic discovery.

> I've left mine old home of homes
> Green fields and every pleasant place
> The summer like a stranger comes
> I pause and hardly know her face
> I miss the hazel's happy green
> The bluebell's quiet hanging blooms
> Where envy's sneer was never seen
> Where staring malice never comes   (p. 198)

Clare feels oppressed by alienation, not by constriction. The landscape he remembers and mourns is a social, peopled, active one, not a lonely site of threnodic eclogue where the only consciousness present is the self-buffeting one of the poet. He does not oppose pastoral openness to technological trivialisation, but sets happy specificity against a baleful abstraction. This specificity is so embedded in the texture of Clare's language, however, that it ironically makes its own simple articulation rather difficult. As the poet Robert Pinsky says, Clare's 'use of physical detail is more suggestive, conceptually, than explicit.'[20] Part of the difficulty of this suggestiveness stems from Clare's position as perceiver. He can only sense these phenomena through his alienation from them. The hazel's happy green becomes more dense and more intricate in remembrance. The bluebell's bloom is praised not for embodying any concrete essence but for its insusceptibility, by consequence of its minuteness, to envy and malice. Envy and malice are presented as static, conceptual abstractions, the axiologically negative version of the 'commonly human' truths that the poet is supposed to proceed to after meditating on nature. Clare colours the only abstractions he includes in the poem in stark and frightening terms. The abstractions do not provide a sense of lofty intellectuality, but are the very propellants of Clare's own deracination. Yet Clare cannot fall back simply on a stolid sense of what is in opposition to these universals, because they have been so effectual that they have deprived him of their own opposites. Clare's perception is as deracinated and foreign to the scene that lies in the past as the universals, except that its method of operation is far more subtle. A perception of nature fully comfortable with the near-at-hand would presumably see and enjoy what is or what was. Yet this is, as a mental state, close to impossible. If nature is felt to be near and readily available it is most probably taken for granted, and is far more likely to be valued when imperilled or desecrated, as Hopkins's 'Binsey Poplars' shows. Clare cannot fall back on the specific as a foil to the universal.

This is partially because he is not struggling against a 'pure' notion of abstraction. The universal logic of modernisation which Clare opposes would see nature as valuable only as a stepping-stone to broader truths, whether in terms of economic 'efficiency' or its poetic concomitant of sublime vacancy. Clare's position in 'The Flitting' is a problematisation, not a synthesis, of both of the above. He is seeing nature when it is not there. It is available to him only through acts of departure and missing.

It is a mistake to overly unpack the verbal logic of Clare's verse, to distil a simple thematic or emotional message from a complicated stance and predicament. The danger in reading this passage from 'The Flitting' is to see it as positing an unmarred state of nature against a minatory human disruption of it. This is to underestimate not only Clare's sophistication but his force of will. Rather than seeking refuge in memory from nature's disruption, Clare uses his imaginative power to disrupt the disruption itself. Instead of fleeing from efficiency and progress into nature, Clare trumps efficiency and progress, inverted by him as envy and malice, by replacing their generality with a level of cognition at once deracinated and specific, dense and lonely.

Clare's move is not one of lamentation. He does not mourn, but rather misses, leaves and pauses, and these actions are signs not of weakness but of strength. By evoking nature only through its own absence, Clare lambastes the logic of modernisation that prizes nature only for its potential efficiency. Again, this sense of natural efficiency is not one which mystically enters European discourse at the turn of the nineteenth century, but which had existed all along, in any stance that saw nature's ultimate purpose as one of productivity. These stances are to be found in the Bible and Hesiod long before they are seen in Adam Smith or Bentham. Clare is more attuned to the poetic complexity of the former than the doctrinal prescriptions of the latter, but his injunction to the earth is not one in search of dominion and subordination. He does not seek a divine or Adamic control over the non-human universe. His poems do not seek to control nature, and this renunciation of a controlling imperative necessitates that they never directly observe it with a kind of monitoring Cartesian mastersight. Clare looks at nature and listens to it, but he can do that only by himself vacating the scene, for otherwise he would dominate it and generate the kind of imaginative economy that all the Romantics canvassed and to which none of the major poets fully capitulated, the tendency to make nature imaginatively efficient in a fashion analogous to its contemporaneous economic organisation. We tend to regard an action such as pausing in front of nature and hardly knowing 'her' face as one of removal from a natural milieu, but in fact it is simply Clare's way of looking at nature. It is those responsible for modernisation who presume to know nature, who lay claim to the ability to analyse determinately the non-human world. Clare may seem to be turning away from nature's face, but only by his turning away can nature have a 'face' at all, possess a character, a sinew, that is resistant to being fashioned

into an efficient process and embodied in a demonstrable proposition.
As Clare phrases it in 'Autumn Morning':

> Look where we may the scene is strange and new
> And every object wears a changing hue   (p. 71)

As in Blake's 'Auguries of Innocence', the particular object by its
very existence and capacity for change, rebukes the generalisation
which a spurious logic attempts to extrapolate from it. Clare, subtler
even than the more system-bound Blake, knows by hardly knowing,
enters through leaving, finds through losing. The tenor of this process
does not especially change as his career proceeds. Nature is as densely
indefinite in 'The Heat of Noon' as in 'The Flitting' or indeed, as will
shortly be proposed, in the late asylum poems. It is this proliferating
yet half-glimpsed vision of nature that Clare opposes to the rhetoric
of efficiency and productivity, not an agrarian lament which would
only fetishise one moment of efficiency in postponing another. Clare
is not left behind by modernisation, but is in advance of it.[21] This can
be seen in the second stanza of 'The Flitting':

> I miss the heath its yellow furze
> Molehills and rabbit tracks that lead
> Through beesom ling and teazel burrs
> That spread a wilderness indeed
> The woodland oaks and all below
> That their white-powdered branches shield
> The mossy paths – the very crow
> Croaks music in my native field   (p. 198)

Clare, in missing 'the heath its yellow furze' is recognising its
physical absence, yet also soliciting its mental presence. In refusing to
use the expected syntactic construction of 'The yellow furze of the
heath', Clare is refusing a logic where the furze would simply be
annexed to the heath in a genitive subordination. The 'wilderness
indeed' that Clare reminiscently evokes is no reassuring locus of
pastoral stability, but represents in its sylvan puzzlements the
duelling sense of entanglement and estrangement that Clare feels in
the wake of his move. Clare applies to nature itself the anti-
hierarchical view of man and landscape that is so striking in view of
the eighteenth-century background. The furze is not of the heath for
the same reason that nature is not of man: to say so would be to
consent to the acquisitive, economistic logic of natural efficiency.
Clare proceeds to go through a catalogue of natural phenomena that

attracts his attention. Yet this catalogue is not primarily a mode of arrangement or overt regimentation. It only partially partakes of the organisational technique of listing that Jack Goody sees as the quintessential habit of literate civilisation.[22] However, Clare certainly does not advocate a Rousseauesque hyperbolic abandonment of human cognitive discrimination in favor of a relapse into primordial energy. This would ultimately stand in polemical opposition but rhetorical complementarity to the logic of modernising efficiency: if a primitive nature were all that were available as an alternative, one would have to grit one's teeth reluctantly and endorse modernity as the only way to preserve a meaningful sense of humanity from an undifferentiated regression. It is Clare's purpose, though, to show that this grim modernity is not the only alternative, that there is a way of experiencing nature which is human and sophisticated without being cold and self-aggrandising. This is embodied in Clare's relationship to the forms mentioned in the above stanza. Clare notices their existence as something importantly apart from him, as is seen in his vivid descriptiveness, but the natural details are not subordinated to an overall logic of arrangement. This does not mean that they are totally random, even if that were epistemically possible, but that Clare orchestrates nature to demonstrate its own elusiveness, to show an abundance that cannot be mobilised on behalf of either a higher rationality or a lower irrationality, to substitute for a determinate history of man and nature what John Ashbery, in his homage to Clare, terms a 'history of probabilities'.[23] As substantial as the rabbit-tracks, oaks and crow are in their own right, their overall presentation does not stress their sturdy substantiality or even their mutual taxonomic subordination. For one thing, they are too incommensurable with one another. The oak, especially with regard to the English landscape, is the ultimate emblem of permanence, whereas the rabbit-tracks occupy virtually the other end of the spectrum in their ephemerality. The shielding of the trees and the croaking of the crow are similarly polarised: one encloses and one cries out. There is no inherent order here other than that imposed by the happenstance of observation, which is never permanently stabilised.

Thus there are not one but two 'flittings' that preoccupy this poem: the flitting that causes Clare's exile and the, as it were, counter-flitting of natural elusiveness and non-demonstrability that surges against that exile as a temporary historical abstraction that at once lacks the substance and the haziness of nature. In the latter portions of the poem, Clare makes a daring turn from the near-at-hand to the radically supra-historical, when he begins speaking of nature with respect to time, a time no longer connected so intimately with the motility of place and circumstance as in 'The Heat of Noon' but one which reigns and triumphs over, in fact almost to the point of annihilating, all changes which strive to assert a given historical character or human abstraction to the ever half-glimpsed face of nature. From the nooks of Royce Wood and Langley Bush, we swerve to a topography far more truly panoramic than anything in Dyer or Thomson.

Any comparison of Clare's *The Shepherd's Calendar* with Spenser's is a bit forced (Clare's book did not intentionally augur an ambitious career as did the Renaissance poet's). However, it can be more confidently said that 'The Flitting', and its companion, 'The Eternity of Nature' (which is similarly taken up with a lengthy, reflective consideration of change and persistence), are Clare's mutability cantos. For Clare, though, the mutability of nature and a higher transcendental permanence are not opposed, but akin. They are strangely allied against the human confidence that landscape or time can be changed once and for all in a given direction, can yield to modernisation and have that modernity continue as a perpetual modernity. This is evinced, towards the midpoint of 'The Flitting' in one of Clare's rare references to the large-scale cultural past:

> Some sing the pomps of chivalry
> As legends of the ancient time
> Where gold and pearls and mystery
> Are shadows painted for sublime
> But passions of sublimity
> Belong to plain and simpler things
> And David underneath a tree
> Sought, when a shepherd, Salems springs   (p. 200)

Modernity for Clare cannot continue as a perpetual modernity for the same reason that 'the pomps of chivalry' pass away. Compared to the persistence of nature, their durability is meagre. In a way, this theme is a rather commonplace descendant of familiar *vanitas* motifs. Yet, much as he does with the pastoral themes of his earliest work, Clare transmutes this material into his own emotional and referential register. The antipathy to chivalric pomps is so convenient as a rhetorical gesture that we may, perhaps unfairly, see it as something

less than heartfelt. Yet it does provide the important reminder that
Clare, for all his opposition to modernisation, has probably the least
intuitive tendency towards medievalism of any of the major Romantics except Shelley.[24] Those of his social class of course did not have
the luxury of idealising or fantasising about the past, much as they
certainly did not have the hope of looking forward to the future. By
firmly discriminating between his own resistance to the present's
arrogant claims as to its own necessity and a futile attachment to an
inflated past, Clare then takes the one step beyond a satisfactory
emotive binarism. This step is taken, in their own way, by all the
great poets of the period.

A lesser bard speaking of David seeking Salem's springs would
have likened his own search for the well of inspiration to that of the
psalmist. Yet Clare sees David's crown, overtly his political power as
monarch of Israel but tacitly also a symbol of his poetic self-esteem, as
passing away under the weight of the ages. 'Poesy' itself, however,
retains his 'shepherd skill'. This is a powerful yet unsentimental
vision. It is language, not the men who use it, which possesses the
ultimate power. Clare does not go to particular lengths to compare
himself to David. He thus is non-typological and, implicitly, non-
Christian about the reference. What is important is David's legacy of
language. His language is likened in its persistence to the durability
of moss, 'a small unnoticed trifling thing', that, like its Italian
counterpart in Leopardi's 'La Ginestra', defies by sheer insignificant
intransigence the ravages of time that consume all else.[25] The moss,
when compared to those images that Clare most values from his
childhood, is banal even when compared to the humble sheep and
molehills that Clare remembers populating the social and perceptual
landscape of his youth and that kept him from feeling alone. This
kind of plenitude of consolation is no longer immediately available.
Yet Clare responds by considering the little flowers that to a far
greater extent than any more emblematic pastoral counterparts can
survive, by their very triviality, the rhetoric and action of historical
change. They raise the revealed elusiveness of nature to a more
stringent and intense level:

> And still they bloom as on the day
> They first crowned wilderness and rock
> When Abel haply crowned with may
> The firstlings of his little flock
> And Eve might from her matted thorn

To deck her lone and lovely brow
Reach that same rose that heedless scorn
Misnames as the dog-rosey now   (p. 203)

Clare's nature is pointedly postlapsarian, not a prolongation of Eden. By the mention of the foredoomed Abel he shows that this state of nature is not without sin and tragedy. In having the motion of the trivial but eternal flowers be a crowning one, Clare again alludes to the crowns of David and other worldly magnates. He suggests, in their mockery by the lowly forms of nature that outlive them, their ultimate impotence. These flowers console him in their natural endurance. Clare, though, does not make the mistake of making them overly sympathetic to humanity. There is a sullenness in their beauty, an indifference in their majesty, that means they can never fully come into communication with us. What Clare had earlier thematised as nature's elusiveness is in this poem formulated as a kind of being at one remove, a beauty and an ever-living power that can never be quite apprehended by humanity. The verbal scorn of modernity in labelling 'dog-rosey' that which will doggedly outlive it is, as with the envy and malice at the beginning of the poem, an abstract violation of the flowery specificity of nature.

Yet this rhetoric is also an example of nature's own self-protectiveness. In being able to keep the scorners ignorant of their true identity, the mislabelled 'dog-rosey' eludes its potential desecrators with the kind of mute canniness that has enabled it to survive thus far. There are two strains present in the remainder of 'The Flitting'. One is an *ubi sunt* motif, one which asks where are the pompous glories of yester-year and mocks their erstwhile pretentions. The other exemplifies a rhetoric of nearly manic assertion, hardly the mocking acquiescence in decay that would complement the *ubi sunt* aspect. Both are in evidence in the poem's final stanza:

Time looks on pomp with careless moods
Or killing apathy's disdain
– So where old marble cities stood
Poor persecuted weeds remain
She feels a love for little things
That very few could feel beside
And still the grass eternal springs
Where castles stood and grandeur died   (205)

As Johanne Clare asserts, Clare's praise of the 'grass eternal' is hardly a merely elegiac reaction to modernisation, but 'challenges the very premise and function of the elegiac mode'.[26] Clare is exultant about the invincibility of nature. He does not conceal, however, the relentlessness of this invincibility that makes it a distant ideal at best. The 'killing apathy's disdain' (which could be parsed as 'disdaining apathy' or, more awkwardly but also more complexly, as 'a disdain that is somehow also apathetic', or vice versa) with which Clare looks upon humanity's passing show is not calculated to arouse feelings of instant identification on the part of either reader or poet.

Clare's vision of nature has its costs. However, these costs are only proof of the enormous faith Clare has in the eternity of nature and, in addition, the bitterness which prompts him to seek resort in so extreme and icy an affirmation. This affirmation, though, may as time passes seem less extreme. Though certainly nature cannot be said to have prospered in the intervening century and three-quarters since the composition of this poem, Clare seems to have been on the mark in a discursive sense. The flowers, or some reasonable facsimile thereof, are still blooming today while the new agricultural and industrial order whose evanescence Clare predicted has in itself been the subject of elegy as the advanced world has self-consciously moved into a post-industrial age. As steel mills and coal mines are shut down while microchips are assembled and stock exchanges are computerised, we have the same dual rhetoric of pious lament and complacent celebration of progress. The terms, not the trope, are all that need to be reshuffled. Yet Clare's flowers, whatever the danger to them from our seemingly ineradicable tendency to poison our environment in search of military and economic supremacy, probably stand an even chance against the post-industrial order as well.

Thus there is a good deal of common sense behind Clare's visionary incantations. This sense is revealed in another dimension at the close of 'The Eternity of Nature' itself. After a series of observations about the recurrence of the number five in nature which at times seem resonant of Clare's fellow East Anglian regionalist, Sir Thomas Browne, Clare turns to the goosegrass for a final confirmation of nature's redoubtable persistence:

> And spreading goosegrass trailing all abroad
> In leaves of silver green about the road
> Five leaves make every blossom all along
> I stoop for many, none are counted wrong
> 'Tis nature's wonder and her maker's will

Who bade earth be and order owns him still
As that superior power who keeps the key
Of wisdom, power, and might through all eternity   (p. 161)

Even as Clare reaches the poem's crescendo of triumph, he is
finding the eternity of nature somehow numbing, oppressively if
gloriously unalterable. This may be an explanation for the otherwise
oblatory invocation of divine supremacy at the end, which may not
be as conventional as it looks on first appearance. Clare does not wish
to totally surrender to a nature which always mindlessly reproduces
the same number, never making a mistake. However much he might
rejoice in the power this unerringness gives to nature in light of
human attempts at historical transformation, he blanches at endorsing it unreservedly. The sudden arrival of a God superior to
merely natural forces is emotionally unconvincing to Clare, as it is to
us. It serves, however, the function of a kind of palinode, a small
retrenchment from a vision of nature's unchallengeable supremacy.
This not only rescues the human need for the presence of independent
volition. It also restores from a dangerous hypertrophy the values
that had drawn Clare to nature in the first place: its resistance to
ideology, its recalcitrance to being drawn into any coherent vision, its
hazy yet palpable unwillingness to accommodate absolutes.

4

In the next phase of Clare's poetry, nature seems to have an entirely
different role. Most critics have seen this role as either the result of
derogation or estrangement. However, an avoidance of a premature
classification of Clare's career into an orderly progress (or regress)
may complicate this picture. Clare, insofar as he has been offered to
the twentieth-century reading public at all, has usually been
presented as a poet who is principally notable (i.e. can be most
usefully distinguished from other poets) for his concrete description of
landscape. Rarely, or at least not until very recently, has it been
noticed that Clare is one of the great love poets of his or any age. His
poetic celebration of his love for Mary Joyce is apparently little short
of scandalous to the critical consensus. Partially this is because a poet
belonging to a socially engaged, dissenting tradition (though, as
Johanne Clare points out, Clare in his lifetime never expressed
anything but disdain for contemporary radicals) has no business

being in love. Such an emotional commitment, it might be argued, is a humiliating sign of weakness in the struggle. On a more complicated level, it could be argued that the presence of Mary in the poems prevents Clare's poetry from being classified in as orderly a manner as possible. Since the first stage in the creation of a literary reputation is always this kind of bracketing, Mary was thus strategically occluded. This accords with the tendency of Clare's critics to compare him more frequently with the first generation of Romantics, poets such as Wordsworth and even Blake who were concerned with the relationship between nature and the imagination, rather than second-generation poets such as Keats or Shelley, who were more taken up with questions of psychology and impassioned states. It is not only the burden of Clare criticism, though, that Mary has been neglected, but that of the normative treatment of love in the Western tradition. We are very ready to accept love in literature when it is employed in the service of a larger transcendental aim (Dante) or an equally ambitious aesthetic one (Petrarch). We are equally per-missive when love is embodied in a larger novelistic matrix in which the individual passion is enmeshed in a field of, to fall back on the crypto-Leavisite canard, 'wider' social reference. Despite the his-trionic resistance of certain sectors of culture earlier in this century, we are no less willing to accept love when it is annexed, as in D. H. Lawrence or Henry Miller, to an ideology of erotic irrationalism. We will tolerate love only if it is grounded in the service of a larger, more acceptable (and, as all the above examples reveal, emphatically male if not always 'phallocentric') purpose.[27] As this is precisely not what Clare did with his love for Mary, we are embarrassed by it. Mary, though the same kind of beloved – an inaccessible one – as Dante's Beatrice or Petrarch's Laura, was in crucial ways different. Not only was she someone that Clare had actually known on a social level as opposed to admiring only as a distant ideal, she was not consciously presented to Clare's reading public as part of his poetic persona. Clare, it is safe to assume, did not intend the Mary poems for publication, and thus her presentation is not intended for display or as part of a literary persona, at least not one appealing to any audience but an internal one. As a consequence, Clare did not need to endow Mary with anything resembling symbolic universality. Clare did not see Mary as a figure of liberty leading the masses against enclosure or an emblematic mediatrix of the eternity of nature, but quite the reverse. Nature was for Clare a sign of her presence (or absence). Clare did not construct a body of thought upon his passion. Even when presented with the considerable symbolic temptation of his beloved's name, Clare refrained from using it for typological purposes other than parodically in the pseudo-Byronic *Prison Amusements or Child Harold*, where he exclaims 'Ave Maria, 'tis the hour of love' (p. 284). Clare was forthcoming about the emotional nature of his feelings to an unusual degree. He felt no need to load them with any 'redeeming' value, whether religious or social.

This does not mean, though, that with the Mary poems we are dealing with unmediated expression, with a mode of discourse that does not willingly submit to constraints and contexts. Part of the sophistication of these poems, indeed, results from Clare's awareness that in order to write them he would have to abandon some aspects of his earlier poetic stance or role. This may be a more fruitful way to see the question than the customary assumption that the poems were the product of an anterior state of emotional disturbance. One of the arguments against such an assumption, aside from clinical and diagnostic doubts about the extent of Clare's 'insanity', is, all differences notwithstanding, how similar the poems seem when one compares the earlier and later work. This similarity stands in vivid contrast to a poet like Hölderlin, often compared to Clare in this regard, whose poetic production after the onset of his mental illness was nothing like that of the time before. Clare retained a sense of consistency and responsibility that Hölderlin did not.[28] (Although even the most fervent admirer of Clare would have to agree that Hölderlin explored issues, both rhetorical and substantive, of a complexity and agony completely alien to Clare, who, astonishingly considering his medical record, social position, and personal and vocational fate, seems in a way to possess the most untroubled temperament of any significant European poet of his period.) The differences between the Clare of the enclosure era and that of the asylum and immediate pre-asylum years is a difference only slightly more drastic than that between those of the early and middle years. It is considerably less than intracanonical differences in the *œuvres* of psychologically undiagnosed poets such as Yeats. The gap between the Yeats of 1895 and the Yeats of 1930 is at least as great as that between the Clare of the 1810s and the Clare of the 1840s. Just as Clare had to disturb nature's balance in 'The Heat of Noon' in order to feel its reverberations, just as nature had to vacate nature in order to truly perceive its elusiveness in 'The Flitting', so must he estrange himself from it more fully in order to show how nature can contain the most intense forms of human imagination.

Yet the estrangement from nature has been taken too much at face value by critics. Implicitly, Clare is still being measured against the Wordsworthian yardstick that has been overtly renounced long ago. It is a Wordsworthian ideal to aim for a harmonious reciprocity between man and nature, human consciousness and the external stimuli upon which that consciousness feeds, and it is an apothegm of traditional Romantic discourse to see the blockage of that reciprocity, as in 'Resolution and Independence' or Coleridge's 'Dejection', as a crisis or trauma. However, it is difficult to accuse Clare of being alienated from Clare, or to lament on his behalf for that alienation, when Clare has never had the arrogance or the ambition to see Nature 'face to face' in a Wordsworthian ennobling interchange. We have perhaps been too quick to take Clare's statement that he 'hardly knows' (p. 205) the face of his envisaged object, whether nature or 'poesy', as a statement that he does not know it at all.

Clare, unlike Wordsworth, does not seek reciprocity between man and nature. For the younger poet, his sentiment towards the world outside him is more or less unrequited. Clare does not seek a demi-divine afflatus in the world around him. As we have seen, he is content with only a half-glimpse. It is not nature whose loss he mourns in the Mary poems. For Clare, the condition of his interest in nature is that it be lost in a way unlike its role in the schemes of those in favour of economic efficiency, for whom nature is found all too conveniently. The loss that is mourned is that of Mary, and nature provides a consolation against that loss. This consolation is to be found not only in the memory of nature's physical presence, but in the partial answers nature gives to Clare's intentional summonings in the later poems. In the lyrics untroubled by overt distress, nature seems to resound with the power provided by Mary. Yet a close reading of a typical stanza reveals that these resonances are affirmations of the sort present in 'The Eternity of Nature':

> While the winter swells the fountain
> While the spring awakes the bee
> While the chamois loves the mountain
> Thou'lt be ever dear to me
> As the spring is to the bee
> Thy love was soon as won
> And so 'twill ever be (p. 253)

These affirmations speak less of empirical reality than of a monumental strength of imaginative power against the confining facts of the lived situation. Mary is never referred to as explicitly present in the poem, and by inference she is absent. The invocations of eternity and persistence are as much desperate prophecies as statements of fact. The natural actions that vouchsafe Mary's eternal place in Clare's heart take on a different status once this is realised. The motions of the winter, spring, and chamois (a typically Clarean motley assemblage) only seem to announce the reality of Clare's love to the world; it could with as much justice be said that their mission is a more secret and reticent one.

Clare's love, although an isolated, and, sometimes, even alienated one, finds itself nonetheless curiously embedded in nature, enshrined within its texture. The awakening of the bee or the swelling of the fountain covertly allude to Mary, although not in a merely celebratory or reverberating way: in their presence, they encrypt her loss. The mystery of their motion and the lovely though remote succulence of their action are elevated to a supreme importance by existing in Mary's aura. Yet, rather than merely being conquered by the emotion with which they are endowed, the natural forms take upon themselves, by their inability or unwillingness to be fully demonstrated or rationalised, the elusiveness of the emotion and the ontological risks it entails. They thus represent the emotion without impinging upon it.

Even in a more overtly alienated mood, the marrow of the complexity of the love-nature relationship is by no means thinned. When Clare says, 'In this cold world without a home / Disconsolate I go' (p. 254) we lose some of the impact of the utterance when we see the 'going' as a mere sign of deprivation or eviction and not, in its own wandering way, as an intentional stance that uses its enunciated love to apprehend the outer world, albeit only negatively. Clare states that Mary's absence has made the difference between summer and winter no longer significant to him. Yet, shortly after, the reader is left to wonder whether it is her absence, presence, or an elusive combination of both, that has thus inured Clare to nature. When Clare states 'No home had I through all the year / But Mary's honest love', he is tacitly conceding that through his love for Mary he had already to some extent extracted himself out of the natural order. Her withdrawal (a withdrawal never openly attributed to her, but rather to the inconstancy of love) changes only the key of the poetic standing-outward from nature, not its fundamental shape.

As Clare has always been in a certain way outside of nature due to his wish to refrain from qualitatively distilling it in an authoritative mode, even the apparent deprivation felt in this poem still achieves a relation to nature where it is at once desired yet permitted to go its own way. Clare is on the verge of generously releasing nature from any obligation to be yoked to the pathos of his emotions, of not daring to establish a hegemony on any single nook or locus, of being in a state where, as Clare says in his famous account of his journey out of Essex, he is 'homeless at home and half gratified that I can be happy anywhere'.[29]

This stance, though, does not lead to a total transcendentalism on Clare's part. He is only half-gratified at recognising the disposability of nature, and he is by no means willing to forsake nature entirely. As long as he is concentrating on his loss of nature, and of the loss of the privileged position of nature in his love for Mary, it is still a meaningful intentional relationship. This is a contradiction in a way contained within his perception of Mary herself. When he refers to her as his 'first wife' despite the fact that they were never married, Clare may not only be yielding to delusive wish-fulfilment, but addressing the operation of Mary as motif within his vision of nature and poetry. 'Firstness' implies a status of metaphysical priority, as in 'first philosophy', a sense of lonely if commanding primacy. The connotation of 'wife' is quite the reverse, though, indicating companionship and reciprocity. Together in the same phrase, the two words at once complement yet undercut each other, generating a pattern in which the elevation of Mary injects an organising meaning into nature, but does not leave the natural realm entirely. In poems like 'A Vision', where Clare attempts a total dismissal of the natural world, most critics agree that the result is false and portentous.

Clare did not thrive on fantasies of total emancipation from the given. Yet his enmeshment in contexts and concretion was not just a matter of sturdily submitting to circumstance. In this regard, it is wise to give more credit than is usual to Clare's Byronic impersonation in the asylum. Byron, the enormous differences between his style and subject-matter and that of Clare notwithstanding, was par excellence the poet who most subtly mediated between a Promethean aesthetic impulse and a subtle, ironic social containment of that impulse. Clare's love for Mary, and the enmeshment of that love in nature, operates, for all its indelibly personal colouring, as a similar kind of enriching containment. Clare uses nature not to symbolise Mary, but to parallel her remote yet meaningful otherness to him. At times, this leads to an extreme sense of the magnitude of the particular, an empiricism so minute it takes on, partially through typography, a visionary character:

> Now Come The Balm And Breezes Of The Spring
> Not Without The Pleasures Of My Early Days
> When Nature Seemed One Endless Song to Sing
> A Joyous Melody And Happy Praise
> Ah Would They Come Agen – But Life Betrays   (p. 255)

By capitalising each word, Clare does not so much signal his psychological disorder as assert that every part of the sentence, no matter how semantically insignificant, requires emphasis, deserves to be a verbal domain in its own right (as has been recently emphasised in a remarkable series of poems by the contemporary Australian John A. Scott, based partially on excerpts from Clare's letters and diaries and using this mode of capitalisation – Scott, incidentally, is brilliantly perceptive about the dialectical relationship of the roles of Mary and nature in Clare's poetic consciousness[30]). This capitalisation, though it may seem an avant-garde gesture, is only an orthographic elucidation of the attitude towards nature that Clare has held throughout his career: that each phenomenon can stand on its own. This standing, though, is not a simple or definite autonomy. The phenomena in question are inevitably caught in a poetic (here almost visionary) matrix that apprehends them in a way which alters their manifestation. Yet that alteration need not be authoritative or monolithic. It can allow nature to elude demonstrability, to not be made fully apparent, to have some of its properties remain secret.

Clare makes the most eloquent statement of his sense of the exhilarating insufficiency of nature and its relationship to his ultimate love in this unforgettable late lyric:

> I hid my love when young while I
> Couldn't bear the buzzing of a flye
> I hid my love to my despite
> Till I could not bear to look at light
> I dare not gaze upon her face
> But left her memory in each place

Where'er I saw a wild flower lie
I kissed and bade my love goodbye.

I met her in the greenest dells
Where wood-drops pearl the wild bluebells
The lost breeze kissed her bright blue eye
The bee kissed and went singing bye
A sunbeam found a passage there
A gold chain round her neck so fair
As secret as the wild bee's song
She lay there all the summer long

I hid my love in field and town
Till e'en the breeze would knock me down
The bees seemed singing ballads o'er
The flye's buzz turned a lion's roar
And even silence found a tongue
To haunt me all the summer long.
The riddle nature could not prove
Was nothing else than secret love   (p. 352)

Clare hides his love to protect it from the obviousness of
sentimentality, from the windiness of declaration. The fly, whose
trivial but incessant buzz (already encountered in 'The Heat of
Noon') is a kind of sonic equivalent of the visual persistence embodied
by the flowers at the conclusion of 'The Flitting', infringes on the
purity of Clare's emotion, enrages him even by its small indication
that there are other realities in the world besides his love for Mary.
Yet Clare is excited by this infringement even as he is nagged by it.
In a state of what John Lucas aptly labels paranoia, even the buzz of
the fly is magnified into an awesome token of natural near-
revelation.[31] Clare does not desire the realised intersubjective
intensity of gazing on the face of either Mary or nature (who, as
Lucas points out, are almost eerily conflated here). This would be far
too flagrant and melodramatic a confrontation for him. In his act of
hiding, he can know the object while never fully knowing it, sense it
yet enshroud it behind a protective veil that curtains it from the
catastrophe of utter revelation. There are sadnesses and losses in this
process. Nature becomes so loaded with secrets that its sight
eventually becomes intolerable to Clare due to its surplus of
significance. Nature frustrates the elaboration of this surplus, yet
teases Clare with its continued presence. Clare has made his love
secret, and in doing so he has lost full control over it. It has become
almost part of the landscape, although never able to be fully

assimilated into the natural order. Clare's kiss of the wildflowers is a farewell to his love for several reasons (as is signalled by the birds 'singing bye', in both passage and departure). Mary is encrypted in the wildflower, hidden within its visual appearance. In kissing the flower, Clare is kissing the token of the absent Mary. Yet in kissing the flower he is also relating to it in a very concrete way. He is acknowledging its specificity, and this specificity undermines the conceptual generality that love must achieve in its full manifestation between humans. In ministering to the flower's quiddity, Clare punctures any overall vision that can analyse or explain the flower and that can meaningfully liberate the love hidden within it.

In the following stanza, Clare, in some of his most vivid language ever, further demonstrates nature's power of non-demonstrability. Clare met Mary in the greenest dells, but the verdant, fuzzy palpability of these dells occludes as much as enshrines her. The act of the wood-drops as they 'pearl' the wild bluebells carries particular weight because of the noun-like quality of the verb: action here is so laden with specificity that it needs to use a concrete term to transfer causation from one object to another. This 'pearling' is an act of concreteness. Yet it is also, in a way, an act of disproving. The wood-drops specify the bluebells, but in doing so they infringe upon their independence. Similarly, the bee and the sunbeam trope Mary's presence, but in being there in such a detailed manner themselves they threaten to revoke her aura even while displaying it. They hide her in such a way that her presence becomes half-articulate; the clustering of the bees in summer make Mary's presence not one of tongues in trees, but rather one of plangent yet ominous muteness.

In the final stanza, Clare confronts the consequence of his making-secret. Clare's love for Mary, in line with an established *topos* in classical love-poetry (Virgil's Tenth Eclogue, for instance, or Horace's *Integer vitae* (*Odes*, 1, 22)) generates a disruptive confidence in the power of passion with respect to the scene, in the prospect of the ability of the love to wage its way through all manner of natural and unnatural opponents. Yet Clare does not, as would be usual, impute this power to the force of his love, but ironically to the natural scene that cradles yet rebukes his sentiments. The influx of magnitude onto the landscape does not redeem or transfigure it. The magnitude haunts the landscape with the fierceness, yet also the underlying impotence, of Clare's love. This is an enigmatic and emotionally riven situation. Yet it is finally not a site of failure or weakness. Clare is willing to acquiesce in the incapacity of nature to either fully hold or fully disclose his hopes and fears. He does not require the sort of emotional tally, the kind of sublime calling-to-arms, which would organise his own emotional landscape in as marshalled a fashion as the external scene around him was organised by the agricultural professionals. He is willing to rest content with secrets that will never fully be disclosed, that in once being hidden can never again be revealed. It is only when Clare is at his weakest and most pessimistic that any more prepossessing claims emerge. These claims loom uncomfortably in the poem 'I Am', where he states:

> I am the self-consumer of my woes –
> They rise and vanish in oblivion's host   (p. 311)

Clare claims complete mastery of his environment here. However, it is a vacuous and etiolated mastery, deprived of the shrouded and indefinite coverts that have animated his landscape so vigorously. 'I Am' represents a proud plight from which Clare, even in his most tormented moments, for the most part demurs. His preference, even at the dolorous end of his career, is for the non-demonstrability of nature rather than man's triumph over it through rationalising appropriation. That latter alternative is a fate for an apocalyptic time whose vista Clare has foresworn – a time when the eternity of nature will finally be fissured, and love will at last reveal its secrets.[32]

NOTES

1 John Barrell, *The Idea of Landscape and the Sense of Place: 1730–1840* (Cambridge, 1972).

2 Hugh Haughton, 'Progress and Rhyme: 'The Nightingale's Nest' and Romantic Poetry'. See chapter 3 above.

3 Juliet Sychrava, *Schiller to Derrida* (Cambridge, 1989). The German poet J. C. F. Schiller formulated this distinction in his influential *Uber naive und sentimentalische Dichtung* (*On Naive and Reflective Poetry*) (1795–6) – where he distinguished between modern, reflective modes of writing such as his own, which he termed '*sentimentalisch*', and antique or classical writing such as practised by the ancient Greeks or, in his own day, Goethe, which he called '*naive*'.

4 Johanne Clare, *John Clare and the Bounds of Circumstance* (Kingston, Montreal, 1987).

5 All citations from Clare's poetry are from the edition edited by Geoffrey Summerfield: John Clare, *Selected Poetry* (London, 1990). All further references will be incorporated into the text.

6 Wallace Stevens, 'The motive for metaphor', *The Palm at the End of the Mind*, ed. Holly Stevens (New York, 1971), p. 240.

7 See Wordsworth, the *Prelude* eds. Jonathan Wordsworth, M. H. Abrams and Stephen Gill, 1805 version, (New York, 1971). Book XI, p. 428, 1.259.

8 E. P. Thompson, in his *The Making of the English Working Class* (New York, 1966), tacitly equates enclosure with a historically significant systematisation when he states (p. 217) that it 'destroyed the scratch-as-scratch-can subsistence economy of the poor'. Thompson's language, in positing the subsistence economy as a sort of free-ranging *bricolage*, romanticises it as more anarchic, less marshalled than its successor. Thompson is at his finest when he avoids these sorts of projections and trusts in the ability of his own 'scratch-as-scratch-can' practice to champion the values he advocates and champions within his own present, which is far more persuasive than the icon of an always-chimerical pre-industrial past.

9 Anthony Giddens, *A Contemporary Critique of Historical Materialism* (Berkeley, 1981).

10 Cited in M. M. Bakhtin, *The Dialogic Imagination*, tr. Michael Holquist and Caryl Emerson (Austin, Texas, 1981), p. 65.

11 Jacques Derrida, *Of Grammatology*, tr.Gayatri Chakravorty Spivak (Baltimore, 1976).

12 For a dissection of this tendency in Leavisite criticism, see Francis Mulhern, 'English reading,' *Nation and Narration*, ed. Homi Bhabha (London, 1990). As Mulhern says (p. 252), 'The meaning of modern history, for Leavis, was the dissolution of "community"'.

13 Kenneth Burke, *Counter-Statement*, 2nd edn, (Los Altos, Calif., 1953), p. 109.

14 As the clearances' most authoritative historian, Eric Richards, comments, the clearances, like enclosure, have often been sentimentalised for partisan and moralistic purposes: 'The story of the Highland clearances is often told in terms that are deceptively simple... In the well-known version of this historical process, the clearances are represented as an unmitigated disaster for the Highlands, in which evictions were perpetrated by landlords who had become intoxicated on the potent doctrines of Adam Smith.' See Richards, *A History of The Highland Clearances: Agrarian Transformation and the Evictions, 1746–1886* (London, 1982), pp. 3–4. Richards's work is a rare and striking example of a work of primary history, relying heavily and informatively on statistics and contemporary accounts, which is nonetheless aware of its own practice and preconceptions.

15 Richards discusses the distinction between the transformation of arable land which is usually described as 'enclosure' and the pasture enclosures that are what is meant when the 'clearances' are commonly described. Whereas the arable enclosures caused the population to gravitate to

large, urban centres, the pastoral change caused the population to disperse, not into a new economic context but into a condition where they were 'virtually redundant'. Ibid. p. 171.

16 Henry Clifford Darby, *The Draining of the Fens* (Cambridge, 1940).

17 Barrell, *The Idea of Landscape*, p. 100.

18 Ibid. p. 70.

19 Though the effect of enclosure on Clare's verse is undeniable, it is often strikingly difficult to specify or pin down. This slipperiness may be allegorised in the fact that most of the examples used by Barrell in his scrupulous account of Clare's topographic context are taken from the history of the agrarian landscape of France, rather than from contemporary English examples.

20 Robert Pinsky, *The Situation of Poetry* (Princeton, 1976), p. 123.

21 Alison Brackenbury suggests how this advance manifests itself in 'Breaking Ground', her remarkable sequence of poems based on Clare's life. In a poem titled 'Enclosure', Brackenbury's Clare, after describing, to an imaginary interlocutor, the land after enclosure as 'Rich...well-drained / The fields are huge: skies sweep them, stunt them; now / no drifts of cowslips as my father found...', resolves that 'We had illusions, better without them / Perhaps...'. Brackenbury foreshadows Clare's desperate emancipation from nature and the temptations of his own nostalgia when she has her persona state, 'Nor will I halt and name again, the plants, the paths I loved, which they destroyed'. Of course, for Brackenbury as for Clare, this does not mean Clare cheerily or dialectically surpasses his own loss; simply that he will not permit his loss to be codified by those outwardly responsible for it. See Brackenbury, *Breaking Ground and Other Poems* (Manchester, p. 116).

22 Jack Goody, *The Domestication of the Savage Mind* (Cambridge, 1977), pp. 80–111.

23 John Ashbery, 'For John Clare', in *Selected Poems* (New York, 1985), p. 103.

24 Clare had these intuitive tendencies far less than the Cobbett to which he is so often tacitly likened. See especially Raymond Williams, *Culture and Society, 1780–1950* (New York, 1983, originally published 1958), p. 19.

25 See Giacomo Leopardi, 'La Ginestra', tr. Edwin Morgan, in Leopardi, *Poems and Prose*, ed. Angel Flores, introduction by Sergio Pacifica, (Westport, Conn., 1987), esp. lines 5–7, 'Tuoi cespi solitari intorno spargi / Odorata ginestra / Contena dei deserti', translated as, 'You scatter tufts of loneliness around, sweet-smelling broom, patient in the wastelands'.

26 Johanne Clare, *Bounds of Circumstance*, p. 147.

27 Given the period in which he lived, Clare can certainly not be accused of macho posturing. Fascinatingly, 'Clare' as a Christian name is of course more associated with the female – viz. St. Francis of Assisi's colleague.

28 As Angus Fletcher comments, 'The more perspicuous and incisive Clare's vision of his own state, the more lucidly he exposes his insanity'. See Fletcher, *Colors of the Mind: Reflections on Thinking in Literature* (Cambridge, Mass.) 1991, p. 252. Clare's insanity here is less associated with a stereotypical irrationality than with a rationality ruthlessly aware of the paradoxes of its own condition.

29 Eric Robinson and Geoffrey Summerfield (eds.), *Selected Poems and Prose of John Clare* (Oxford, 1966, paperback 1978), p. 191.

30 John A. Scott, 'From Northampton, these letters', *Scripsi* (Ringwood, Victoria, Australia): special Penguin issue (1989), 81–90. The seventh letter is particularly enlightening in the context of Mary.

31 John Lucas, *England and Englishness: Ideas of Nationhood in English Poetry, 1688–1900* (Iowa City, 1990), p. 159.

32 I would like to thank the late Geoffrey Summerfield for his solicitation and encouragement of this piece, and to express my great regret that he was unable to see it in its final version.

CHAPTER 9

Beyond the Visionary Company: John Clare's resistance to Romanticism

James McKusick

Is John Clare a Romantic poet? Ever since the publication of his first volume, *Poems Descriptive of Rural Life and Scenery* (1820), there have been concerted efforts to situate Clare within the tradition of Romantic poetry, although even his most sympathetic advocates have often concluded with the melancholy reflection that he is at best a minor Romantic poet. Clare's publisher, John Taylor, launched this assimilative effort in his introduction to the 1820 volume, which cited Wordsworth's authority for the inclusion of 'new image[s] of external nature' in Clare's poetry.[1] Taylor appealed to Wordsworth's immense cultural prestige as a way of legitimating Clare's poetic practice, and this assimilative strategy established an enduring pattern for later generations of critics, though the qualities of Clare's verse singled out as 'Wordsworthian' have tended to vary according to the prevailing conception of what authentically constitutes Romantic poetry. Harold Bloom, in an influential chapter of *The Visionary Company* that seems typical of the high theoretical approach to Clare, argues that 'much of his poetry is a postscript to Wordsworth's... He either borrows directly, or else works on exactly parallel lines, intersected by the huge Wordsworthian shadow'.[2] In particular, Bloom finds echoes of 'Tintern Abbey' and the 'Intimations' Ode in Clare's 'Pastoral Poesy' and 'The Progress of Ryhme', and he discerns a strong Wordsworthian element in Clare's resolution of 'visionary conflict' through the 'primal joy' of the poetic process.[3] The main tendency of Bloom's critique is to internalise and thus to idealise those 'image[s] of external nature' that Taylor first noted as characteristic of Clare's poetry, thereby ascribing to Clare the same inward visionary quest as his more illustrious contemporaries.

Bloom reluctantly dismisses Clare as a failed Wordsworthian poet, although he suggests that Clare's madness ultimately poised him on the verge of a more authentic Blakean vision. Yet why should Bloom invoke Wordsworth and Blake as the only relevant standards by which to judge Clare's poetic accomplishment? Missing in Bloom's analysis of Clare is any acknowledgment of those qualities of his verse that remain stubbornly antithetical to such an internalised Romantic quest: his resistance to sublimity, abstraction and transcendence, and his enthusiastic engagement with particularity, local tradition and regional dialect. These qualities of Clare's verse, strongly rooted in the linguistic and material basis of his class identity as a 'Northamptonshire Peasant Poet', tend to be overlooked, or actively repressed, by a criticism that seeks to assimilate his poetry to the dominant discursive modes of High Romanticism. The fundamental reasons for this historical repression are not immediately apparent, although it does seem likely that Clare would pose less of a threat to established conceptions of Romanticism if it could be demonstrated that he is merely a flawed or derivative version of a known and canonical figure.

Bloom's normative use of Wordsworthian categories in *The Visionary Company* is characteristic of much subsequent criticism of Clare's poetry, even among scholars whose view of Clare's poetic accomplishment is far more sympathetic than Bloom's. Tim Chilcott, in a sensitive and detailed reading of Clare's poetry entitled '*A Real World & Doubting Mind*', invokes an essentially Wordsworthian paradigm of subject-object relations according to which the 'real world', despite its ineluctable facticity, must be constructed and internalised by a 'doubting mind' that labours under the constant threat of solipsism.[4] Although Chilcott carefully distinguishes between Wordsworth's and Clare's resolution of this philosophical dilemma, his critical approach nevertheless seems deeply structured by the premise that Clare's poetry must issue from an epistemic project akin to one previously sketched out by Wordsworth in his Prospectus to the *Recluse*: to show how 'the discerning intellect of man' can be 'wedded to this goodly universe'.[5] In articulating an essentially Wordsworthian (and Coleridgean) paradigm of subject-object relations, Chilcott explicitly excludes biographical and social considerations from his analysis.[6] The result is a study of Clare that makes the strongest possible case for his inclusion in the canon of major Romantic poets, but at the expense of those aspects of Clare's concrete historical situation that lend his poetry its cultural and linguistic specificity. In this sense, Chilcott's study represents the culmination of the modern academic assimilation of Clare to the

High Romantic tradition, while it also enacts the historical repression that is consistently linked with that tradition.

Another recent study of Clare's poetry, entitled *Schiller to Derrida: Idealism in Aesthetics*, seems even more relentless in its idealisation of his poetry, and consequently more ruthless in its repression of the concrete historical context of its production. The author, Juliet Sychrava, argues that Clare is (in Schiller's terms) a 'naive' or playfully unselfconscious poet, while Wordsworth is a 'sentimental' poet more heavily burdened by self-consciousness.[7] After devoting two chapters to the close reading of Clare's poetry, Sychrava (somewhat condescendingly, in my view) concludes that he epitomizes the Romantic ideal of epistemic innocence in his devotion to the idyllic depiction of rural landscapes. This conclusion is reached through a method of textual analysis that largely excludes biographical or historical information, situating these two poets instead in a philosophical context that will be quite familiar to students of Romanticism; namely, a tradition of aesthetic idealism initiated by Kant and Schiller and characterised by a view of the creative process as a free play of intellect, unconstrained by objective circumstances. Once again, Clare is assimilated to a high theoretical paradigm only by patronising his alleged naiveté and denying the relevance of those concrete historical circumstances that lend his poetry its most distinctive features.

Perhaps, then, to ask whether Clare is a Romantic poet is to ask the wrong question, even if the question is used as a means to legitimise Clare's poetic practice by situating it within a dominant Wordsworthian paradigm. As we have seen, any attempt to represent Clare as a 'minor Romantic poet' can be successful only at the cost of a massive historical repression that disregards the concrete circumstances of his poetic career and the material basis of his poetic production. Such acts of repression are hardly benign, since they manifest an unwillingness to acknowledge those features of Clare's poetry (or, for that matter, of Wordsworth's poetry) that resist the transcendentalising impulses latent in much high critical theory. Despite all efforts to situate him within the Visionary Company, Clare remains stubbornly aloof from it, and an adequate reading of his poetry can only emerge from a recognition of the social and historical forces that contributed to Clare's radical sense of disjunction from the leading literary figures of his time.

It would seem more reasonable to inquire how Clare himself

conceived his relationship to the major Romantic poets. Clare's *Autobiographical Writings* provide important evidence of his developing tastes in poetry, his personal encounters with major authors and his own growing sense of poetic vocation. Clare visited London on four separate occasions between 1820 and 1828, ostensibly for the purpose of facilitating the publication of his poetry, and he became fairly well acquainted with several of the leading writers of the day (including Hazlitt, Lamb, and Coleridge).[8] However, he avoided a slavish imitation of these dominant cultural models and retained a strong sense of allegiance to his rural roots and his regional dialect. Within a literary culture that was already beginning to conceive of itself as 'romantic',[9] Clare retained a rather awkward sense of himself as an outsider, marked by peculiarities of dialect, manner and dress that indicated his regional origin and class identity in ways that were liable to embarrass an urban elite that sought to idealise rustic life while scrupulously avoiding personal contact with actual peasants or shepherds. As a self-declared 'Northamptonshire Peasant Poet', Clare always remained outside the mainstream of the Romantic movement, and his longing for literary acceptance was tempered by an unwillingness to be assimilated or co-opted by the dominant urban culture that nonetheless provided the economic basis for the publication of his works and constituted virtually his entire readership.

Far more important than the Wordsworthian influence on Clare, especially in his early career, was his affectionate imitation of the poets of Sensibility: Thomson (whose *The Seasons* was the first book of poetry that Clare ever possessed), Cowper (whose fondness for small defenseless creatures especially appealed to Clare), Gray and Collins. Clare admired these poets not because they were (or once had been) fashionable, but because for him they constituted an alternative poetic tradition, one that exalted the rural landscape and the rural sense of community over the anomie of urban existence. Clare's relation to these precursors in what might be termed the realistic tradition of English pastoral poetry has been increasingly well-documented by his critics; an especially important recent book that treats this topic is John Barrell's *Poetry, Language & Politics*, which devotes particular scrutiny to the relation between Thomson and Clare.[10] This book is exemplary in its avoidance of reflexive Romantic paradigms and its scrupulous attention to the material bases of Clare's poetic production; the same is true of Barrell's earlier book,

The Idea of Landscape and the Sense of Place, which remains the definitive study of the effects of parliamentary enclosure upon Clare's representation of landscape.[11] Another important study of Clare's poetry, with particular attention to his class identity and political ideology, is Johanne Clare's *John Clare and the Bounds of Circumstance*.[12] These studies represent some of the best recent work on Clare, and they indicate what may be accomplished by thoughtful analysis of his poetry in its social and biographical context.

One of the most essential features of Clare's poetry that is often obscured by attempts to situate him among the Visionary Company is his frank assertion of class identity. At the outset of his public career as a poet, Clare described himself as a 'Northamptonshire Peasant' on the title pages of his books, a bold statement of class identity that places him at the intersection of two radically opposed discourse communities: first, the community of mostly illiterate farmers and shepherds that constituted his own social class in his native village of Helpston, and second, the more elite community of published poets, mostly educated in the universities, whose command of written language, particularly Latin and Greek, endowed them with immense cultural authority. The essentially oral culture of John Clare's home village is reflected in his use of regional dialect and non-standard grammar, while his aspiration to belong to the putatively immortal company of poets is apparent in his diligent attempts to master the conventions of written language as they determined the composition of poetry in the early nineteenth century. Clare's own poetic language emerges as a curious hybrid, mingling the earthy immediacy of regional dialect with the more abstract and paraphrastic lexicon of standard eighteenth-century poetic diction.

Clare's true class identity has been widely debated, with some critics maintaining that it is patronising to view him as a mere 'peasant poet' while others have regarded his social status as intrinsic to the kind of verse he writes. From a historical point of view, we may note that the peasant class, composed of a relatively stable group of freeholding subsistence farmers rooted by communal ties to the land, was fast disappearing in early nineteenth-century England, squeezed out by a new class of entrepreneurial landowners who profited from the process of parliamentary enclosure. In his satirical poem *The Parish* (composed about 1820–7, but unpublished in its entirety until 1985), Clare mocks the social affectations of these new upwardly-mobile landowners, who have abandoned traditional rural culture and now seek to imitate the manners and fashions of their sophisticated middle-class urban counterparts.[13] Clare himself suffered the loss of economic stability that resulted from the privatisation of agricultural production, as his family's rents increased and their wages fell, only grudgingly supplemented by the parish poor-rates. Clare's social identity became radically unstable at the same time that he witnessed the uprooting of old folk ways and traditional patterns of communal relationship between 'the masters and the men', which he had represented idyllically in *The Shepherd's Calendar*.[14] The gradual erosion of Clare's identity as a 'Northamptonshire Peasant' and his increasing marginalisation and exclusion from the new commodity-based rural culture is emblematic of his own tragic struggle to discover a stable sense of self that might endure all the harsh changes in the landscape and the disintegration of age-old patterns of village life.

From a psychological point of view, Clare's ambiguous social position is mirrored in his radically divided self, emotionally torn between moments of aspiration and long periods of gloomy defeat, and fluctuating uncontrollably between mania and depression. His highest aspirations – to become a famous poet, to impress learned friends and patrons, to acquire financial independence and to cultivate his own garden as a self-sufficient freeholder – eventually collapsed into their corresponding nightmare realities of his poetic obscurity, his desertion by friends and patrons, his abject poverty and his involuntary incarceration in a lunatic asylum far from the home and family and landscape that he loved. Clare's early triumph and eventual defeat, and his ultimate victimisation by the same literary culture that briefly lent him fame and fortune, may serve as objective correlatives to the ongoing inward struggle between competing versions of himself. Over the years, Clare invented many masks as he struggled to conform to the literary world's expectations while still remaining true to his origin in the peasant community that was so rapidly disappearing around him. Within his poems he speaks with many voices, sometimes producing a mere pastiche or parody of contemporary styles, but often creating a significant juxtaposition of discursive elements that allows us to regard him as more than simply a 'dialect poet'. Regional dialect, in Clare, is only one ingredient in a variety of linguistic types that he deploys with increasing effectiveness throughout his poetic career.

A characteristic example of Clare's hybrid poetic language is found in his sonnet, 'The Gipsies Evening Blaze', which was first published in *Poems Descriptive of Rural Life* (1820), but was written at least ten years earlier, at the age of fourteen or fifteen (according to Clare's own dating).[15] The poem begins in the approved loco-descriptive manner, introducing a sentimental traveller who beholds a 'wildly pleasing' scene; but the scenery shifts rapidly in the second quatrain to a bleaker and more barren landscape as the language descends from such neoclassical personifications as 'Boreas' into such rustic dialect words as 'proggle' (meaning to prod or poke) and 'flaze' (meaning a dense, smoky flame):

> To me how wildly pleasing is that scene
> Which does present in evenings dusky hour
> A Group of Gipsies center'd on the green
> In some warm nook where Boreas has no power
> Where sudden starts the quivering blaze behind
> Short shrubby bushes nibbl'd by the sheep
> That alway on these shortsward pastures keep
> Now lost now shines now bending with the wind
> And now the swarthy sybil kneels reclin'd
> With proggling stick she still renews the blaze
> Forcing bright sparks to twinkle from the flaze
> When this I view the all attentive mind
> Will oft exclaim (so strong the scene prevades)
> 'Grant me this life, thou spirit of the shades!'[16]

The standard loco-descriptive mode is radically transformed by the intrusive presence of gypsies, lower-class inhabitants of the landscape whose swarthy faces and scavenging lifestyle would normally be excluded or at least sentimentalised by the traveller's touristic detachment from the harsh material basis of their existence. For Clare, however, who has come to know the gypsies through intimate personal acquaintance, there is a sense of class solidarity that exposes the inauthenticity of such effete poetic diction as 'Boreas' and 'sybil', conveying instead the desperate scarcity that pervades these 'short-sward pastures', where anything edible is devoured by hungry sheep and the only source of firewood is twigs torn from short shrubby bushes. This impoverished landscape, far from being a timeless fact of nature, is the result of an ongoing historical process – the enclosure of common fields – which Clare bitterly resents as a conspiracy of the wealthy classes against the poorest and weakest members of society: the landless peasants and shepherds and gypsies whose very existence depends upon what they can glean from the common fields. By the end of the poem, the sentimental discourse of the 'all attentive mind', contained in quotation marks, has become distinct from the more socially subversive discourse of the 'I', expressed in the rustic dialect of Northamptonshire. The concluding apothegm, 'Grant me this life, thou spirit of the shades', issues from the mouth of the peasant poet as if he were demonically possessed by the 'all attentive mind' of the sentimental traveller, whose effusive sympathy seems vapid and insincere by comparison with the immediacy and concreteness of the poet's native dialect.

In 'The Gipsies Evening Blaze', the economic displacement occasioned by enclosure is reflected in the poem's linguistic texture; as we have seen, the poem's juxtaposition of discourse types enacts a bizarre dislocation of the standard loco-descriptive mode. Like Wordsworth and Coleridge, Clare was engaged in a language experiment to determine whether the 'language really used by men' was a fit medium for poetry; but unlike these classically trained and university-educated members of the English intelligentsia, Clare possessed only an uneasy sense of the discursive boundaries transgressed in this experiment.[17] As a result, his first attempts at poetry, such as 'The Gipsies Evening Blaze', embody a not altogether intentional *heteroglossia*, mingling high and low diction and grotesquely mangling the conventions of standard poetic discourse. John Taylor, the editor of Clare's first collection of poems, was delighted by the freshness and novelty of Clare's descriptions of rural life, but dismayed by the uncouthness and 'vulgarity' of his regional dialect. Taylor, also the publisher of Keats, Lamb, Hazlitt and De Quincey, was far more open-minded and sympathetic in his response to Clare's radical discursive practice than most of his contemporaries in the English reading public, but he nonetheless felt obliged to undertake the task of 'correcting' Clare's poetry, a task that involved a thorough revision and normalisation of Clare's vocabulary, grammar, spelling and prosody, as well as the removal of subversive political statements that might offend his wealthy patrons.[18] The final published version of Clare's poetry emerged from this process much reduced in its transgressive shock value, though it still retained a strong flavour of regional and class identity in its use of dialect and its odd combination of discursive modes.

Both the strengths and weaknesses of Taylor's editorial practice are exemplified in his revisions to 'The Gipsies Evening Blaze' for publication in *Poems Descriptive*. Taylor wisely did not tamper with the poem's vivid dialect words, perhaps judging them appropriate to the 'low' subject-matter, but he did try to correct its diction and grammar, substituting 'doth' for 'does' in line 2, and 'seen' for 'shines' in line 8. Taylor also normalised spelling and added punctuation to Clare's almost completely unpunctuated fair copy. Interestingly, Clare himself attempted to produce a normally punctuated version of this poem, but he actually submitted for publication a drastically overpunctuated manuscript that Taylor must have found distinctly unhelpful in the editorial process.[19] As Clare and Taylor developed a good working relationship, Clare ceased to attempt to punctuate his poems and eventually relegated all responsibility for accidentals to Taylor. However, Clare always sought to retain control over the substantive elements of his poems, and as he developed a more secure sense of his own poetic voice he often raised strong objections to Taylor's editorial emendations, especially when these involved the deletion of dialect words.[20] Taylor was only the first in a long line of editors and critics who sought to assimilate Clare's poetry to prevailing standards of correctness; it is only since 1964 that Clare's poetry has been published as he actually wrote it, with all the strangeness of spelling, punctuation, diction and grammar inherent in his original manuscripts.[21]

Clare's linguistic practice, at least as manifested in his early poetry, can hardly be considered the result of unconscious inspiration, much less the 'spontaneous overflow of powerful feeling' that provides an aesthetic basis for the Romantic ideology of bourgeois individualism.[22] Clare's published poetry represents the outcome of a dialogical process, a confrontation between the normalising conventions imposed upon his language by John Taylor and his own desperate struggle to maintain the integrity of his native oral culture. However, Clare's poetry is even less adequately described as the product of intentional variation from a pre-existent norm, since the multi-layered texture of Clare's poetic language results from the intersection of radically divergent discourse communities, in which standard written English possesses only a factitious and retrospective dominance. The critical methodologies of Romantic expressionism and of academic formalism are one-sided in their approach to Clare's language because they are unable to recognise the dialogical nature of his poetic practice, his cross-cutting and counterpointing of discourse types in a wild, transgressive and almost completely irresponsible process of *heteroglossia*. It is this process, even more than the moments of overt engagement in social and political commentary, that lends Clare's poetry its truly radical character, its undercutting of established ideology through the subversion of all normative discourse.

Such a dialogical approach to Clare's linguistic practice is necessarily grounded in the writings of Mikhail Bakhtin and his colleague, V. N. Voloshinov, whose treatise on *Marxism and the Philosophy of Language* (first published in 1929) is gaining increasing prominence as a text in theoretical linguistics.[23] Voloshinov considers language as a social practice, arguing that neither the Romantic subjectivism of Humboldt nor the abstract objectivism of Saussure can provide an adequate understanding of the ways that language works as a medium of interpersonal communication and ideological exchange. The subjectivising tendencies of Humboldt and his followers in the Romantic tradition are flawed, according to Voloshinov, because they falsely isolate the individual utterance, regarding it as a spontaneous creation of poetic genius and disregarding its participation in a broader social context that largely determines its ideological content as well as its lexical and grammatical form. On the other hand, the rationalising tendencies of structural linguistics, which Voloshinov correctly traces back to the 'universal grammar' of Leibniz and the French *Idéologues*, are misguided in their objectification of language as a purely abstract system of normatively identical forms, since they overlook the socially interactive nature of the concrete verbal utterance.[24] As Voloshinov points out, 'The actual reality of language-speech is not the abstract system of linguistic forms, not the isolated monological utterance, but the social event of verbal interaction implemented in an utterance... Thus, verbal interaction is the basic reality of language.'[25] This essentially dialogical understanding of language is particularly relevant to the discursive situation of John Clare, torn as he was between the conflicting demands of Romantic originality and the normalising standards of 'universal grammar' as they trickled down through the dictionaries and grammar-books of his day. Clare's friends and advisers among the London literary elite constantly admonished him to correct and chasten his style at the same time that they admired the spontaneity and individuality of his rough-hewn provincial dialect. Indeed, Clare was presented by his patrons with books such as Johnson's *Dictionary* and Lowth's *Grammar* as none-too-subtle hints on how to assimilate his linguistic practice to the prevailing standard.[26] Faced by such conflicting demands, Clare responded with an astonishing proliferation of poetic utterance, experimenting with an enormous variety of genres and prosodic forms and juxtaposing a motley assortment of discourse types in a wild, exuberant and socially subversive *heteroglossia*.

Clare's discursive practice, according to this view, departs from the 'normal' condition of poetry as aesthetically self-contained and monological, and approaches what Bakhtin regards as the condition of the novel, namely a carnivalesque inversion of habitual social relations enacted through the playful juxtaposition of discrete discursive modes.[27] However, Clare's poetry calls into question Bakhtin's assumption that this novelistic *heteroglossia* is the intentional product of a controlling authorial consciousness. This tacit assumption is evidently a remnant of the Romantic subjectivism so astutely criticised by Voloshinov, and seems detachable from Bakhtin's fundamental insight into the ineluctably dialogical nature of linguistic utterance. Clare's poetry, especially in longer works such as *Child Harold* and *Don Juan*, may be termed 'novelistic' in the sense that its juxtaposition of discourses entails a clash of social and regional perspectives that are not easily reconciled within a comprehensive authorial vision.[28] Moreover, just as the Romantic novel (in the innovative forms produced by Godwin, Edgeworth, Morgan, Galt, Hogg and Scott) emerged from and spoke to various marginal and dispossessed social classes, so too Clare's poetry gave voice to precisely those people (gypsies, peasants and landless labourers) whose interests were systematically neglected by the ruling elite. In particular, the use of dialect by Highlanders and other socially marginal characters in Scott's fiction bears interesting points of resemblance to Clare's poetry, although Scott's antiquarianism (as well as his British nationalism) is fundamentally at odds with Clare's conception of regional dialect as the embodiment of a living landscape and its indigenous people. Clare's poetic language stubbornly resists accommodation with ruling modalities of discourse, and his concern with particularity, local tradition and regional dialect is closely related to this 'novelistic' aspect of his work.

In Clare's later poetry, the enactment of socially subversive *heteroglossia* is accompanied by a process of psychological disintegration regarded by Clare himself as a loss of individual identity, and marked by the characteristic symptoms of a cyclothymic

disorder.[29] During his involuntary incarceration in the Northamptonshire General Lunatic Asylum (1841–64), Clare believed himself
at various times to be Lord Byron, Robert Burns, Admiral Nelson
and Jack Randall, a famous contemporary prize-fighter. Of these
shifting identities, that of Lord Byron was the most persistent, partly
because Byron championed the democratic values that Clare likewise
fundamentally espoused, and partly because Byron's vast literary
fame represented the fulfilment of Clare's own wildest authorial
ambitions. Clare was deeply impressed by the throngs of common
people that flocked the London streets to watch Byron's funeral
cortege, and he sought to keep Byron's democratic spirit alive by
attempting to write poems himself in a satirical Byronic mode. This
endeavour resulted in two remarkable works, '*Child Harold* and *Don
Juan*, which adopt the scathing wit and the intricate stanza forms of
their Byronic prototypes. Even in these seemingly 'Romantic' works,
however, Clare's discursive practice remains radically subversive,
undercutting Byron's poetic authority by subtle parody and overt
satire. In Clare's *Don Juan*, for instance, Byron's pose of cynical
worldliness becomes exaggerated into a violently transgressive
misanthropy that seems almost Swiftian in its furious denunciation of
women, politicians, aristocrats and mankind in general. Clare is not
so much adopting a Byronic persona as he is subjecting the implied
libertarian values of Byronic discourse to the corrosive fires of social
and political nihilism.

Even in the midst of his deep depression, psychological disintegration and extreme alienation from the prevailing modes of
literary discourse, Clare maintained both a tendency for exuberant
heteroglossia, and a sense of class solidarity with gypsies, beggars and
other social outcasts, that endow his later poetry with unique pathos,
dignity and concreteness. Throughout his asylum period, Clare
returns frequently to the topic of gypsies, describing their free,
wandering life, their uncouth language and their establishment of an
alternative community outside existing social structures. In his prose
account of his escape from High Beech Asylum, entitled *A Journey out
of Essex* (1841), Clare recounts how his escape attempt was inspired
by meeting some gypsies camped in the forest near the asylum. One
of them offered to assist in his 'escape from the mad house' by hiding
him in their camp.[30] Although this plan did not work out, Clare
decided to follow the escape route that had been suggested by the
gypsy, while wearing a hat that he had found abandoned in the gypsy

camp. This gypsy hat assumed a talismanic significance during the actual escape, serving Clare as a disguise, as protection against the elements and as a badge of identity. On this long and difficult journey, Clare was treated with scorn and ridicule by some passing drovers, but with care and concern by a young gypsy woman who pointed out a shortcut and offered advice on how to use his hat as an almost magical cloak of invisibility.[31] As a result of this doomed escape attempt, Clare was confirmed in his identity as an outsider, excluded from all normal social intercourse, yet aspiring to belong to the alternative community of gypsies with their strange language, mysterious folk ways and freedom to wander in the open air. The last stanza of *Child Harold* celebrates the new-found power of expression that emerges from Clare's increasing sense of exclusion and isolation:

> Sweet is the song of Birds for that restores
> The soul to harmony the mind to love
> Tis natures song of freedom out of doors
> Forests beneath free winds & clouds above
> The Thrush & Nightingale & timid dove
> Breathe music round me where the gipseys dwell –
> The splendid palace seems the gates of hell[32]

These lines eloquently express Clare's desire for a poetic voice that can speak with an authority derived not from established cultural modes, but from all those energies excluded and stifled by the dominant culture: the folk-music of the wandering gypsies, the song of birds and the voice of nature itself, untrammelled by enclosure and economic progress.

Clare's sense of class solidarity with the gypsies is most clearly expressed in another asylum poem entitled 'The Gipsy Camp'. In this poem, he depicts the stark material existence of the gypsies with unflinching candour; but he nonetheless reveals an underlying sympathy with their plight, particularly in the figure of the starving dog, an outcast among outcasts:

> The snow falls deep; the Forest lies alone:
> The boy goes hasty for his load of brakes,
> Then thinks upon the fire and hurries back;
> The Gipsy knocks his hands and tucks them up,
> And seeks his squalid camp, half hid in snow,
> Beneath the oak, which breaks away the wind,
> And bushes close, with snow like hovel warm:
> There stinking mutton roasts upon the coals,

And the half-roasted dog squats close and rubs,
Then feels the heat too strong and goes aloof;
He watches well, but none a bit can spare,
And vainly waits the morsel thrown away:
'Tis thus they live – a picture to the place;
A quiet, pilfering, unprotected race.[33]

This poem, which exists only in a version printed with normalised spelling and punctuation in the *English Journal* of 1841, nevertheless displays Clare's characteristic concreteness of diction in words like 'brakes', 'tucks', 'hovel', 'stinking' and 'rubs'. While not specific to any regional dialect, these words convey an authentic flavour of rusticity and the intense physicality of their Anglo-Saxon origins. Only a faint vestige of the loco-descriptive tradition survives in the threadbare abstraction of 'a picture to the place', introducing a note of *heteroglossia* that provides a discursive context for the more rugged immediacy of the remainder of the poem. Within this general framework, the narrative voice shifts in perspective from the empty forest to a solitary gypsy boy within it, then turns to a description of the gypsy camp from the viewpoint of a hungry, half-roasted dog. The effect of this shifting perspective is to juxtapose the consciousness of the boy and the dog, both marginal figures even within the marginal world of gypsy life, and thus to suggest a sympathetic identification with Clare's own existence, excluded from the warmth of all human kindness in the utterly marginal world of the asylum.

Throughout his asylum period, Clare's existential despair and loneliness are balanced by a craving for the lost community and shelter which he finds in the gypsy camps, even though the gypsies' economic base of starving and pilfering and huckstering is laid bare in his poems. For Clare, the gypsy camps are a place of gabbling tongues, fortune-telling, fiddle-playing, and a locus of erotic desire, as evidenced by several love-lyrics addressed to real or imaginary gypsy girls. Only among the gypsies can he find the lost sense of Edenic innocence and erotic fulfilment that is reflected in their earthy, free, spontaneous existence out-of-doors, under the open sky. In the loss of his personal identity, Clare comes to know himself more truly as a wanderer upon the earth, without a stable sense of self or a distinct poetic language.

The stylistic assurance of Clare's later poetry is not the product of a quasi-Blakean visionary mode, as Harold Bloom claims, but represents a more sophisticated development of the free interplay of discourse types that characterised his earliest attempts at verse. His later poetry thus constitutes a remarkable achievement, a sustained *heteroglossia* that undercuts the hegemony of normative High Romantic discourse in favour of the unfettered speech and open horizons represented by those free-spirited outsiders, the gypsies. Clare's poems are not finished monological utterances; rather, they occur within a process of revision, linguistic 'crossing', and a quest for social identity that reflects a concrete awareness of the effects of economic exploitation, and specifically of parliamentary enclosure, upon the people and the landscape of England. Clare's linguistic practice is always implicitly dialogical, juxtaposing the moribund formal devices of traditional pastoral and loco-descriptive poetry against the vigour and orality of his own regional dialect, and revitalising poetic language through the rehistoricising of landscape.

NOTES

1 Mark Storey (ed.), *John Clare: The Critical Heritage* (London, 1973), p. 50.
2 Harold Bloom, *The Visionary Company: A Reading of English Romantic Poetry* (New York, 1961), p. 434.
3 Ibid. p. 439.
4 Tim Chilcott, '*A Real World & Doubting Mind*': *A Critical Study of the Poetry of John Clare* (Hull, 1985), p. 218.
5 Jack Stillinger (ed.), *Selected Poems and Prefaces of William Wordsworth* (Boston, Mass., 1965), p. 46.
6 Chilcott, '*A Real World & Doubting Mind*', p. 217.
7 Juliet Sychrava, *Schiller to Derrida: Idealism in Aesthetics* (Cambridge, 1989), pp. 147–62.
8 Eric Robinson (ed.), *John Clare's Autobiographical Writings* (Oxford, 1986); hereafter cited as *Autobiographical Writings*. Clare's response to the literary and popular culture of London is more fully discussed by James C. McKusick, 'John Clare's London Journal: a peasant poet encounters the metropolis', *Wordsworth Circle*, 23 (1992), 172–75. Clare cultivated an image at odds with that of the sophisticated urban elite, especially by wearing a rustic green coat and retaining a strong provincial accent.
9 The term 'romantic' was first used to designate a specific historical period of literature in 1812, when Samuel Taylor Coleridge lectured on 'a classification of poetry into ancient and romantic' (*Oxford English Dictionary*, under the word 'romantic', sense 4b, citing Henry Crabb Robinson's *Journal* of 19 May 1812). This citation marks the first English usage of the term 'romantic' to designate a literary period characterised

by romance, or 'the spirit of chivalry', and distinguished from classical literature by its spiritual and imaginative qualities. Coleridge applied the term 'romantic' to his own writing in *Biographia Literaria* (2 vols., London, 1817), vol. II, p. 2. By 1820 Clare would have found the term ubiquitous in discussions of contemporary literature.

10 John Barrell, *Poetry, Language & Politics* (Manchester, 1988).

11 John Barrell, *The Idea of Landscape and the Sense of Place: 1730–1840; An Approach to the Poetry of John Clare* (Cambridge, 1972).

12 Johanne Clare, *John Clare and the Bounds of Circumstance* (Kingston, Montreal, 1987). Another fine study of Clare's poetry in its social and biographical context is Elisabeth Helsinger, 'Clare and the place of the Peasant Poet', *Critical Inquiry*, 13 (1987), 509–31.

13 John Clare, *The Parish*, ed. Eric Robinson (Harmondsworth, 1985).

14 John Clare, *The Shepherd's Calendar* (London, 1827).

15 This poem was first published in Clare, *Poems Descriptive of Rural Life and Scenery*, (London and Stamford, 1820), p. 191. Clare's manuscript versions are printed in Eric Robinson and David Powell (eds.), *The Early Poems of John Clare 1804–1822* (2 vols., Oxford, 1989), vol. I, pp. 33 and 559 (hereafter cited as *Early Poems*). Clare's dating of his own poetry is often questionable, since he tended to revise his poems long after the nominal date of composition.

16 Robinson and Powell, *Early Poems*, I, p. 33.

17 Wordsworth describes this experiment in his Preface to *Lyrical Ballads* (1800): 'The principal object, then, proposed in these Poems was to choose incidents and situations from common life, and to relate or describe them, throughout, as far as was possible in a selection of language really used by men.' Stillinger, *Selected Poems and Prefaces*, p. 446.

18 John Taylor calls himself the 'Corrector' of Clare's 'bad Grammar' in a letter of February 1822; cited in Mark Storey (ed.), *The Letters of John Clare* (Oxford, 1985), p. 224n (hereafter cited as *Letters*). Clare's patron, Lord Radstock, insisted on the deletion of a stanza denouncing 'accursed Wealth' in the poem 'Helpstone', calling the offending passage 'radical Slang' (ibid. p. 69n).

19 This overpunctuated manuscript version of 'The Gipsies Evening Blaze' is printed in Robinson and Powell, *Early Poems*, I, pp. 559–60; see also p. xxiii for discussion of Clare's penchant for overpunctuation in this early period.

20 The most detailed study of Taylor's editorial practice is Eric Robinson and Geoffrey Summerfield, 'John Taylor's editing of Clare's *The Shepherd's Calendar*', *Review of English Studies*, 56 (1963), 359–69. This article claims that Taylor's emendations to this poem, though well-intentioned, were largely detrimental to Clare's poetic style.

21 A completely literal transcription of Clare's poetry was first attempted by Eric Robinson and Geoffrey Summerfield (eds.), *The Shepherd's*

Calendar (London, 1964), which still serves as an editorial model for the more complete Oxford edition now in progress.

22 According to Wordsworth's famous dictum, 'all good poetry is the spontaneous overflow of powerful feelings'. Stillinger, *Selected Poems and Prefaces*, p. 448.

23 V. N. Voloshinov, *Marxism and the Philosophy of Language*, tr. Ladislav Matejka and I. R. Titunik (New York, 1973). The authorship of this work (along with certain other works published under the names of Voloshinov and P. N. Medvedev) is disputed by some scholars. In the absence of definitive evidence for Bakhtin's authorship, I refer to this disputed work by the name printed on its title page.

24 Ibid. p. 58. The connection between Saussure and the tradition of 'universal grammar' in Leibniz and the French *Idéologues* is more fully explored by Hans Aarsleff, *From Locke to Saussure: Essays on the Study of Language and Intellectual History* (Minneapolis 1982), pp. 356–71.

25 Voloshinov, *Marxism and the Philosophy of Language*, p. 94.

26 The 1815 abridged octavo edition of Johnson's *Dictionary*, presented to Clare by Lord Milton, is listed in David Powell (ed.), *Catalogue of the John Clare Collection in the Northampton Public Library with Index to the Poems in Manuscript* (Northampton, 1964), p. 29, item no. 263 (hereafter cited as *Catalogue*); see also M. Storey, *Letters*, p. 53. Robert Lowth's *Short Introduction to English Grammar* (1762), presented to Clare by Eliza Emmerson, is also listed in Powell, *Catalogue*, p. 30, item no. 288.

27 Mikhail Bakhtin distinguishes between poetry and novelistic prose, arguing that the poetic image 'presumes nothing beyond the borders of its own context'. He concedes, however, that a 'dialoguized image can occur in all the poetic genres as well, even in the lyric'. Michael Holquist (ed.), *The Dialogic Imagination: Four Essays by M. M. Bakhtin* (Austin, Texas, 1981), p. 278.

28 For more extended discussion of *heteroglossia* as an intentional feature of Clare's style, see Lynn Pearce, 'John Clare's "Child Harold"': a polyphonic reading', *Criticism*, 31 (1989), 139–57.

29 This is the tentative diagnosis reached by Evan Blakemore, 'John Clare's psychiatric disorder', *Victorian Poetry*, 24 (1986), 209–28.

30 Robinson, *Autobiographical Writings*, p. 153.

31 Ibid. p. 158.

32 Eric Robinson and David Powell (eds.), *The Later Poetry of John Clare: 1837–1864* (2 vols., Oxford, 1984), vol. I, p. 88.

33 Ibid. p. 29.

'A love for every simple weed': Clare, botany and the poetic language of lost Eden

Douglas Chambers

The publication of Clare's poems in the gentrified diction of his publisher, John Taylor, was an assault not just on the authenticity of his poetic voice but on the very substance of his work. Clare's statement that he had found his poems in the fields and only written them down is a claim for the legitimacy of his vocabulary of natural history. This is a vocabulary not only freed of classical mythologising and latinate taxonomy but revelatory of the almost prelapsarian exercise of naming things as they are. More forcefully even than the Wordsworth of the preface to *Lyrical Ballads*, Clare grounds English poetry in natural speech and native vocabulary. His poetry demonstrates that 'just representations of general nature' make no sense apart from the particular names of individual trees and flowers: names authenticated by the oral tradition that has transmitted them.

When Lord Fitzwilliam offered Clare a cottage and a maintenance at Northborough in 1832, he also provided him with a metaphor of exile, a means of articulating something only glimpsed in the earlier poems and associated with lost childhood and the world before the enclosures. His poem 'The Flitting'[1] is a testament to what has been lost; even the nightingale at Northborough 'seems at a loss / For royce wood and its shielding bough'.

Yet there is also a strength to be found in what is left behind, not in the philosophic mind but in the very weeds that outlast the 'marble citys' of antiquity and speak to him of a nature of which he is part that 'feels a love for little things':

> E'en here my simple feelings nurse
> A love for every simple weed
> And e'en this little shepherds purse
> Grieves me to cut it up – Indeed
> I feel at times a love and joy
> For every weed and every thing

A feeling kindred from a boy
A feeling brought with every spring

Clare's singling out of Shepherd's Purse to love as an 'ancient neighbour' from the 'little garden rows' that he had left behind at Helpston is a classic example of his technique of making the significant from the apparently insignificant. Yet it is more than that. Shepherd's Purse is a pernicious garden weed, often called Farmer's Ruin; to love it is to see something in it that the mere gardener never sees, not only its association with an old home but with the weeds that have grown about men's habitations (the 'marble citys') since the dawn of time.[2] Clare, in other words, historicises and enculturates this weed as a text not only of himself but of a lost society. In so doing he creates a mythology of permanence in which his own isolation becomes part of a larger historical myth.

In a letter to his publisher, James Hessey, in 1820, Clare wrote: 'I think vulgar names to the flowers best; [as] but I know no others.'[3] However, this seems a line he thought Hessey wanted to hear, for he wrote in his autobiography that he bought a copy of Lee's *Botany*, the classic popular version of Linnaeus's nomenclature, secondhand when he was a child.[4]

Clare's preservation of vulgar (i.e. common) names of plants in his poems was not the result either of horticultural or botanical ignorance. He was a keen gardener who interested himself in such fashionable garden plants as the auricula and polyanthus, listing in his *Journal* the prizewinners in both categories in 1825.[5] Yet the flowers of the wild interested him more. In his copy of Isaac Emmerton's *The Culture & Management of the Auricula...* (1819) he listed twenty-two varieties of 'Orchis's counted from privet hedge'.[6] Also, in 1824, he conducted a correspondence with Edmund Artis (an archaeologist and the illustrator of *Antediluvian Phytology*) about a species of fern that he was able to identify in Linnaeus.[7]

In the 'Natural History Letters' he explains his adherence to common names as a rejection not of botanical nomenclature but of the systematic cast of mind, one that removes from living things their associations with the literature and culture that gives them their true reality:

for my part I love to look on nature with a poetic feeling which magnifys the pleasure [.] I love to see the nightingale in its hazel retreat & the cuckoo hiding in its solitudes of oaken foliage & not to examine their carcases in glass cases[,] yet naturalists & botanists seem to have no taste for this practical feeling[.] they merely make collections of dryd specimens classing them after Leanius [Linnaeus] into tribes & familys & there they delight to show them as a sort of ambitious fame... I have none of this curiosity about me tho I feel as happy as they about finding a new species of field flower or butter flye which I have not seen before yet I have no desire further to dry the plant or torture the Butterflye by sticking it on a cork board with a pin... the man of taste looks on the little Celadine in Spring & mutters in his mind some favourite lines from Wordsworths address to that flower [.] he never sees the daisy without thinking of Burns[8]

In 1819, the year in which Clare first met Taylor, his future publisher, he wrote to his early supporter, the Reverend Isaiah Knowles Holland: 'Any Poet Rural or Pastoral which you have to Lend would be taken as a great Kindness – Have you Bloomfields "Banks of Wye".'[9] Robert Bloomfield, though an inferior poet to Clare, came (like Burns) to represent to him the possibility of 'translating' the world of pastoral into an English landscape without the machinery of classical mythology.

Clare's dislike of traditional pastoral was not dissimilar to Dr Johnson's. Of the eighteenth-century poet, William Shenstone, Clare wrote:

Shenstone is a Good Poet but his Pastorals (as I think) are improperly called so [.] the rural Names of Damon Delia Phillis &c & rural objects Sheep Sheepfolds &c &c are the only things that give one the slight glimpse of the Species of Poetry which the Title claims –
Putting the Correct Language of the Gentleman into the mouth of a Simple Shepherd or Vulgar Ploughman is far from Natural.[10]

Although some of this was equally true of Bloomfield, he was for Clare, both 'our English Theocritus' and 'our best Pastoral Poet', 'the greatest Pastoral Poet England ever gave birth to'.[11] Clare expressed his admiration for the 'sun burning exellence of a Burns & a Bloomfield', moreover, in a statement about native traditions of poetry that is peculiarly modern:

I dont care who laughs or calls me fool for odd opinions but if I may judge from Popes translation (for I have no latin) I would sooner be the Author of Tam o Shanter than of the Iliad & Odyssey of Homer.[12]

Yet such a statement is thoroughly consistent with Clare's love of the traditional ballads of the oral tradition, a love also consistent with Sir Philip Sidney's preference for 'the songe of *Percy* and *Duglas*' in *An*

Apology for Poetry.[13] The argument about true pastoralism, moreover, an argument focussed on Pope's controversy with Ambrose Phillips, had been current at least since the late seventeenth century. Although Clare rejects neither Theocritus nor Homer, he places Burns and Bloomfield in a domestic literary canon, and in so doing his celebration is of a piece with Lord Cobham's at Stowe in the 1730s: placing the Temple of the British Worthies in reflected apposition to the Temple of Ancient Virtue. What Clare finds in Burns and Bloomfield is also what modern critics have found in Homer: the ballads of folk culture made epic. Bloomfield is, for him, at one with Burns in speaking the language of the fields and the culture of ordinary men without the intervention of deracinated classical learning.

Clare, whose publisher Taylor was also Keats's, had a great admiration for the poet of 'buried paths where sleepy twilight dreams / The summertime away';[14] the Keats, that is, of immersion in the experience of sensation. Yet Keats's poetry was, for Clare, bedevilled with a false neoclassicism:

He keeps a constant alusion or illusion to the grecian mythology & there I cannot follow – yet when he speaks of woods Dryads & Fawns are sure to follow and the brook looks alone without her naiads to his mind [,] yet the frequency of such classical accompaniment makes it wearisome to the reader where behind every rose bush he looks for Venus & under every laurel a thrumming Appollo – In spite of this his descriptions of scenery are often very fine but as is the case with other inhabitants of great cities he often described nature as she appeared to his fancies & not as he would have described her had he witnessed the things he describes.[15]

In his poem, 'Decay', Clare distinguishes between the poetry of gentility and true poesy as between a cultivated garden of the kind pioneered by Humphry Repton and made popular in his time by John Claudius Loudon, on the one hand, and the true garden of wild nature on the other:

> The bank with brambles over spread
> And little molehills round about it
> Was more to me then laurel shades
> With paths and gravel finely clouted.[16]

Clare, indeed, almost seems to prophesy the wild garden movement of the late nineteenth century, the movement associated with William Robinson's reaction against the artifice of carpet bedding to which

Loudon's 'gardenesque' and its genteel botanising gave rise. For all his love of auriculas, Clare's poems are of the fields. 'How fine a garden they would make',[17] he wrote of water-lilies in his sonnet on that flower.

Loudon's 'gardenesque' flattered the new middle-class taste for botanising and classification. Its gardens have 'paths and gravel finely clouted', a word that reflects Clare's disdain for 'nature to advantage dressed'. His word names elegant apparel with the diction of the countryman: 'Ne'er cast a clout till May be out.' His poem, moreover, is 'A Ballad', not the 'nonsense gingling calld poems' that he rebukes in a letter to Bloomfield's friend, Thomas Inskip.[18] This new gentrified horticultural taste has also deracinated poetry from its literal roots and reduced it to mere decoration.

Clare's diction reflects and enacts his way of seeing, untrammelled either by botanic gentility or classical mythology. And not seeing only, but listening... In his late poem, 'The Paigles Bloom in Shower's', he hears 'Sweet Nature To Herself Discourse'. The dialect word 'Paigles'[19] (Cowslip) also leads him to the 'paggling' (drooping) necks of the cows themselves and from that to a magical world whose sounds are at the edge of cognisance:

> And Hear the Grazeing Cattle Softly Tread
> Cropping The Hedgerows Newly Leafing Thorn
> Sounds Soft As Visions Murmured Oer In Bed[20]

Here, without Dryads or even 'soft incense', the dialect name of a common flower leads Clare's memory into a synaesthetic world that is entirely observed and entirely English.

Yet this world is also, whether consciously or not, entirely literary too. What Clare remembers in this late poem, 'While Pale The Moon Is Bering Over Head', is not simply the nocturnal pastoral experiences of his childhood but the May Day world of *Paradise Lost*, Book I,

> Whose midnight Revels, by a forest side
> Or Fountain some belated Peasant sees,
> Or dreams he sees, while over-head the Moon
> Wheels her pale course[21]

In his *Autobiography* Clare wrote of the 'religion' of his childhood:

On Sundays I usd to feel a pleasure to hide in the woods instead of going to Church to nestle among the leaves & lye upon a mossy bank where the fir-like fern its under forest keeps

In a strange stillness
watching for hours the little insects climb up & down the tall stems of wood
grass o'er the smooth plantain leaf[22]

It was Robert Bloomfield ('the first of Rural Bards') who offered
Clare a way of celebrating such attentions. In 'Summer', part of his
georgic poem *The Farmer's Boy* (1800), Bloomfield describes his
subject:

> Just where the parting bough's light shadows play
> Scarce in the shade, nor in the scorching day,
> Stretcht on the turf he lies, a peopled bed,
> Where swarming insects creep around his head.
> The small dust-colour'd beetle climbs with pain,
> O'er the smooth plantain-leaf, a spacious plain!
> Thence higher still, by countless steps convey'd,
> He gains the summit of a shiv'ring blade,
> And flirts his filmy wings, and looks around,
> Exulting in his distance from the ground[23]

If Clare was, on the whole, more successful than Bloomfield in
avoiding the exalted diction and generalised sentiment of Thomson,
it was nonetheless Bloomfield's *Poems*, he said, that gave him an early
'taste for wild flowers which I lovd to hunt after & collect to plant in
my garden'.[24] In the second of his poems to Bloomfield, Clare
reverses the usual Horatian trope and gives Bloomfield immortality
not in his poems but in the subject of those poems, the 'green
memorials' of 'may day wild flowers in the meadow grass'.[25]

Shepherd's Purse (in 'The Flitting') is one of those 'green
memorials', not just of Bloomfield but of a native poetic tradition of
which Clare makes himself a part. In the folk culture of England it
was associated with the many rhymes and children's games that
interested Clare. When he 'grieves...to cut it up', he is not simply
declining to 'murder to dissect' but invoking the game in which one
child asks another to pick the heart-shaped seed-case and, when it
breaks, tells the other child that she has broken her mother's heart.[26]
He can hardly have been unaware, either, that the name alludes to
the *bursa* or *capsella pastoris*, the purse that shepherds had worn since
antiquity. Shepherd's Purse, then, is an emblem of true pastoralism:
pastoralism with the pastor and his diction restored in a landscape
that is wholly English. Clare, moreover, saw it as part of a native
poetic tradition, one that could be traced to what he called the 'sweet

old songsters' of the early seventeenth century. His opposition to the literature of false gentility, animated as it was by a Cobbett-like antipathy to the 'gentrification' of the countryside, expressed itself in his dislike of fulsome dedications and elevated 'literary' titles. Against what he called 'these Delacruscan gentry' and 'the humbug that teams from the Literary stews', he set such 'sweet old songsters'[27] as the early seventeenth-century pastoralist, William Browne. In 1831 he wrote to Taylor:

In the Vol of old Poets I very much admire those of William Brown[.] there is a freshness & beauty about them that supprised me & with which I was not acquainted – there is much english landscape about them[28]

What he seems to admire in the second Song of Browne's *Britannia's Pastorals* is the placing of the Muse and Aurora within a diction that is the antithesis of the false delicacy he despised in the editing of his own poems. What a long way there is from Browne's Marvellian phrase, 'meadows in a cooling sweat', to the world of contemporary fashionable poetry of which Clare complained: 'rubies & rosey cheeks & liley bosoms with this hopless sickening clog at ones foot & a proof of its faded reallitys at ones elbow'.[29]

Similarly, what appealed to him in Thomson's *The Seasons*[30] was his natural descriptions and that 'nature was consulted in all of them'.[31] Yet, for all his insistence on the importance of direct natural observation and his apprehension about the laboured poetic effects that he noted in Coleridge,[32] Clare also respected learning and poetic craft. He wrote admiringly of the poetry of Thomson and Cowper and Beattie, and compared Beattie's 'The Minstrel' to his own 'Peasant Boy' (*The Village Minstrel*), a poem that, he said, contained 'some of the best rural descriptions I have yet written'.[33] He was no wild untutored genius and resented being thought of as such. 'I want to be judged by the book itself', he wrote to Cary, the translator of Dante, in 1832, 'without any appeals to want of education lowness of origin or any other foil that officiousness chuses to encumber my path with.'[34]

Timothy Brownlow has noted the indebtedness of Clare's didacticism to Virgil's First Georgic while insisting that it is inaccurate to call Clare a georgic poet.[35] What his assessment leaves out of account, however, is the way in which, from at least the early eighteenth century, pastoral had been renegotiated in georgic terms. What Clare means by pastoral, in other words, is a poetry of moral landscape, one in which the details of natural history and topography are part of a celebration of the productive rural life and thereby (like the end of the Second Georgic) a critique of false urbanity and excess.

English landscape painting of the eighteenth century had been profoundly influenced by Claude Lorrain. Clare's rejection of what he called 'these beautiful extravagances of false effects'[36] shares with Blake's rejection of the standards of Sir Joshua Reynolds the belief that 'he who would do good to another must do it in Minute Particulars'.[37] The fashionable world of sublime generalities did not adhere to the nature that Clare saw, where 'a rushy common with its summer tract of a brook & old dotterel trees becomes a Paradise'.[38]

When he wrote in praise of his friend, the landscape water-colourist Peter De Wint, it was in these terms: 'admirers of nature will admire his paintings – for they are her autographs & not a painters study from the antique'.[39] What De Wint did in landscape painting was to rescue the true pastoral, the georgic pastoral, from the falsely gentrified landscapes of such neo-Claudean painters as Richard Wilson. In so doing, he offered Clare a confirmation not only of what he was doing in poetry but also of his rejection of sterile academism of all kinds. It is of a piece with Clare's admiration of landscape poetry before Denham, before the imposition of the single point of view characteristic both of the topographical poem and the Claudean landscape.

Clare was also a friend of the painter Edward Rippingille, a member of the 'Bristol School' of artists on whose sketching trips Coleridge was often included.[40] Both Rippingille and De Wint spoke to a principle that was equally important in poetry. 'Nature,' Clare wrote to De Wint,

is very different [from Academy art] & appears best in her every day disabille in fact she is a Lady that never needed sunday or holiday cloaths the most painters & poets also have & still do consider that she does need little touches of their fancies & vagaries to make her beautiful which I consider deformities[41]

In his 'Essay on Landscape' Clare wrote of true landscape paintings:

Look at them they are the very copys of nature – & she rewards the faith of her worshippers by revealing such beautys in her settings that the fanciful never meet with – tho they imagine mountains & rivers & rocks & cateracts where they are not – & so they are not strange to the eye & harmony of beautys perceptions – not so the worshiper of nature – she gives him her own imaginings & he makes the best use of them by reflections as true & as light as a rushy common with its summer tract of a brook & old dotterel trees becomes a Paradise which the lovers of truth & nature muse over & are thankful for the gratification – & such are the landscape of Dewint & the living pastorals of Rippingille for Rippingille is the Theocritus of English painting[42]

In a letter to his son from the Northampton Asylum in 1848 he wrote of his youth:

I loved nature & painted her both in words & colours better than many Poets & Painters [,] & by Perseverance & Attention you may all do the same – in my boyhood Solitude was the most talkative vision I met with[.] Birds bees trees flowers all talked to me incessantly louder than the busy hum of men[43]

The potency of the experience is also bound up not with the artificial vocabulary of the falsely picturesque ('rocks & cateracts') but what he called, in a sonnet of the Helpston period, 'the picturesque of taste'. There

> the wild wind to make compleat the scene
> In rich confusion mingles every green
> Waving her sketchy pencil in her hand
> That tints the moving scene   ('Pleasant Places')[44]

The art there is nature's, but foregrounded is the vocabulary of painting placed within a conventional sonnet form that is nonetheless altered both in rhyme and scansion. Clare's sense of 'very copys of nature', then, is neither, on the one hand, mere natural description nor, on the other, the false decoration of imported artistic vocabularies.

Perhaps what he meant is nowhere better illustrated then in the story of his taking his publisher, Taylor, to the site of his poem 'The Last of March', a poem potent in its sense of particular place and in the association between the 'spying' eye of the poet and the 'daisy with its golden eye' that looks back. 'Taylor', says Geoffrey Grigson,

remembered the poem and looked in astonishment at Clare when the two of them reached the scene, for 'with your own eyes you see nothing but a dull line of ponds, or rather one continued marsh, over which a succession of arches carries the narrow highway: look again, into the poem in your mind, and the wand of the necromancer seems to have been employed in conjuring up a host of beautiful accompaniments, making the whole populous with life and shedding all round the rich lustre of a grand and appropriate sentiment'.[45]

If one is reminded of Blake's miser seeing only a guinea in the sun where the poet saw the multitude of the heavenly host, one ought nonetheless to be taken to the local nomenclature from which the power of the experience arose for Taylor:

> Here 'neath the shelving bank's retreat
> The horse-blob swells its golden ball;
> Nor fear the Lady-smocks to meet
> The snows that round their blossoms fall[46]

'Horse-blob' is primarily a Midlands word for Marsh Marigold[47] (*Caltha palustris*), a word suggesting its medicinal properties. 'Lady-smock', a term more widely used for the Cuckoo Flower (*Cardamine pratensis*), is a word connected with milkmaids and springtime fertility. Both words open a world of cultural association for Clare, a world where 'provincialisms' *are* the experience because they alone can 'name' the experience. He was prepared (for the sake of speedier publication) to defer to Taylor, but there are times when he was obdurate. 'You cross'd "*gulsh'd*"', he wrote to Taylor, 'I think the word expressive but doubt its a provincialism[.] it means tearing or thrusting up with great force.'[48] He also argued with Taylor about the 'indelicate' vocabulary of 'The Village Minstrel' and in one of these letters there is more than a little sense of impatience in his explanation of the word 'Woodseers':

'Woodseers' is inscets [sic] which I daresay you know very well[.] wether it be the proper name [.] I dont know tis what we call them & that you know is sufficient for us – they lye in little white notts of spittle on the backs of leaves & flowers [.] how they come I dont know but they are always seen plentiful in moist weather – & are one of the shepherds weather glasses [.] when the head of the insect is seen turnd upward it is said to token fine weather when downward on the contrary wet may be expected.[49]

This explanation is no mere etymology ('woodseers' = 'wood-prophets') but a placing of the name within the culture of which it is a part: the shepherd's weatherglass. Such explanations were the codex of Clare's world, conveying the unwritten history of the natural world of which humankind was a part. 'Health' he wrote to Taylor, 'is the root of happiness & like the plant "Barrenwort" it seldom produces a blossom.'[50]

Barrenwort (*Epimedium alpinum*) is in fact an interesting instance of Clare's engagement with botany. A southern European import referred to in Pliny's *Historia Naturalis* as inhibiting the growth of virgins' breasts, it is so little known in England that it appears neither in Grigson's *An Englishman's Flora* nor in John Gilbert's *Flora of Huntingdonshire: Wildflowers*.[51] Nor does it appear in a work with which his own poetry was intimately connected, Elizabeth Kent's *Flora Domestica*. Kent, who was Leigh Hunt's sister-in-law, was published anonymously by Clare's publisher, Taylor, in 1823. Although she can only have known his *Poems Descriptive of Rural Life*, she wrote:

None have better understood the language of flowers than the simple-minded peasant-poet Clare, whose volumes are like a beautiful country, diversified with woods, meadows, heaths, and flower gardens[52]

Clare, who was 'uncommonly pleasd' with *Flora Domestica* when it appeared, said of the floral descriptions: 'The account of them is poetry'. Certainly Kent's sort of poetical botany was what appealed to Clare:

A poet sees in a flower not only its form and colour, and the shadowing of its verdant foliage... His imagination, too, brings around it a world of associations, adding beauty and interest to the object actually before his eye.[53]

Clare can hardly have been pleased with the 'simple-minded peasant-poet' description, however, as perhaps is reflected in his suggested remarks for 'improvement' to his publisher Hessey.[54] Nonetheless Kent's book not only confirmed Clare in his own local nomenclature but gave him the idea of writing a similar work, which he proposed to call 'Biographys of Birds and Flowers'.[55] It was to be a cultural corrective to mere botanical taxonomy.

If I live I will write on the same plan & call it a Garden of wild Flowers as it shall contain nothing else with quotations from poets and others [.]

There is all of Blake's loathing of the systems of Newton and Locke in Clare's dismissal of Latinate classification:

an English Botany on this plan would be very interesting & serve to make Botany popular while the hard nicknaming sy⟨s⟩tem of unuterable words now in vogue only overloads it in mystery till it makes darkness visable.[56]

That Clare uses Milton's phrase for hell ('darkness visable') shows the strength of his conviction, and that he associates it with the domination of Linnaeus is evident in his account of buying James Lee's *An Introduction to Botany* as a child. He had collected wildflowers and been given one corner of the garden by his father when, he says, 'on happening to meet with Lees *Botany* second hand I fell to collecting them into familys and tribes but it was a dark system & I abandoned it with a dissatisfaction'.[57]

It is paradoxical that a book such as Lee's, which was designed to make Linnaeus's system accessible to the gardening public, should have attracted such opprobrium. Lee was himself the son of an ordinary Scottish gardener who had founded one of the most successful nurseries (the Vineyard Nursery in Fulham) of the eighteenth century. Yet Clare's response to the Linnaean system is curiously similar to that of one of the eighteenth-century pioneers of English botany, Peter Collinson. Collinson not only established an importation scheme for American plants but himself introduced and propagated more than forty species at a time when Linnaeus's system was gradually being formulated. When Linnaeus's great *Species Plantarum* was published in 1753, Collinson wrote to him that it was

a very useful and laborious work. But, my dear friend, we that admire you are much concerned that you should perplex the delightful science of Botany with changing names that have been well received, and adding new names quite unknown to us. Thus Botany, which was a pleasant study and attainable by most men, is now become by alterations and new names, the study of a man's life, and none but real professors can pretend to attain it.[58]

Clare shares Collinson's chagrin at the mystification of a science that ought to be available to everyone. Like him, he is neither a 'professor' nor a simple ignoramus.

As to my learning I am not wonderfully deep in science nor so wonderfully ignorant as many have fancied...I have puzzled wasted hours over Lee's Botany to understand a shadow of the system so as to be able to class the wild flowers peculiar to my own neighbourhood for I find it woud require a second Adam to find names for them in my way & a second Solomon to understand them in Linnaeus's system – moder[n] works are so mystified by systematic symbols that one cannot understand them till the wrong end of ones lifetime & when one turns to the works of Ray Parkinson & Gerard were there is more of nature & less of art it is like meeting the fresh air & balmy summer of a dewey morning after the troubled dreams of a nightmare.[59]

As we have seen, Clare was more a second Adam than a second Solomon, with all the resurrective associations that a second Adam implied. Not only did he turn to the pre-Linnaean botanists (John Ray, John Parkinson and John Gerard) for the *real* names of plants, but he listened to the oral tradition that children preserved and found 'something that doth live' within the embers of his own memory of childhood.

It was this sort of knowledge, the traditional names of things, that he found in the old herbalists and that allowed him, as he said, 'to look on nature with a poetic feeling which magnifys the pleasure'.[60] Although Timothy Brownlow is right to say that the modern separation of botany and poetry would have been incomprehensible to Clare,[61] what Clare meant by 'botanizing' was what the English founders of the science had meant by it: a careful attention to what is there, with all its literary and cultural associations. The first Professor of Botany at Cambridge, John Martyn, had indeed taught himself botany in just this way on St George's Hill. He also edited the first two books of Virgil's *Georgics*, a work that came to be known popularly as a *Flora Virgiliana*.

Less than 100 years later, on 25 March 1825, Clare reverted to that sense of botany and botanizing:

I took a walk today to botanize & found that spring had taken up her dwelling in good earnest [.] she has covered the woods with the white anemone which the childern call Lady smocks & the hare bells are just venturing to unfold their blue drooping bells[.] the green is coverd with daiseys & the little Celandine[.] the hedge bottoms are crowded with the green leaves of the arum where the boy is peeping for pootys with eager anticipation & delight.[62]

What Clare describes there is a rhetorical *inventio* for his poetry, unclouded by the stylistic conceits (*elocutio*) of false learning and elegance. Even in Thomas Tusser's *Five Hundreth Pointes of Good Husbandrie* (1573), an agricultural poem as its title suggests, he could find '2 pretty sonnets...& some natural images scattered about the book'.[63]

If botany was intimately connected with poetry, so was poetry with botany: a symbiosis in which disease in one implied disease in the other. What the systematic mentality had done to botany was, for Clare, symptomatic of hierophancy generally: an oppression by rule and constraint of natural knowledge and imagination.

Clare's hero in the resistance to system was William Cobbett, a man who combined the role of agricultural critic with writings on politics, gardening and grammar. *Common* sense was the foundation of Cobbett's argument, in horticulture as in language. In his *English Gardener* he wrote:

The reason why books on gardening are read in general with so little benefit, is this; that they are put together by men (generally speaking, observe) who, though they understand how to do the thing themselves, and though they very sincerely wish to teach others, are unable to convey their instructions in language easily to be understood;[64]

For Cobbett, as for Clare, simple diction (whether in poetry or horticulture) is connected with a culture uncorrupted by the tyranny of authority, a society based on the general content of a whole people, not on the riches and power of a few. 'There never yet was, and never will be, a nation permanently great', Cobbett wrote, 'consisting, for the greater part, of wretched and miserable families.'[65]

Clare's essentially conservative reaction was against the bifurcation of culture, a bifurcation that was visible socially, economically and politically, but the deleterious effects of which were as destructive to poetry and botany. In his poem 'The Mores',[66] Clare's outrage is directed against the enclosures with their signs of 'no road here':

> Inclosure came and trampled on the grave
> Of labours rights and left the poor a slave
> And memorys pride ere want to wealth did bow
> Is both the shadow and the substance now...
> This with the poor scared freedom bade good bye
> And much the[y] feel it in the smothered sigh.

However, the loss of freedom for him is not simply economic and political; for Clare this loss is the loss of history, his own and poetry's more generally. Gone is not only 'the sweet vision of my boyish hours' but, more largely, 'poets visions of lifes early day'. The parcelling out of the moors into fields is, in other words, as destructive to poetry as the systematization of botany and grammar. 'Flats of many a dye / That seemed to lengthen with the following eye' have been constrained by a new topography where

> Fence now meets fence in owners little bounds
> Of field and meadow large as garden grounds
> In little parcels little minds to please
> With men and flocks imprisoned ill at ease

As in botany, observation has been ousted by possession; the class system and classification have achieved the same result.[67] In another early poem, 'Swamps of wild rush beds',[68] Clare's celebration of 'commons left free in the rude rags of nature' invokes not only the common fields but the common rights of everyman and the common cultural tradition to which men and the fields belonged. That he wrote this poem in the prosody of Byron's 'Lachin Y Gair' is not insignificant, for 'Swamps of wild rush beds' is as much a nailing of the topographical colours to the mast as Byron's rejection of 'gay landscapes [and] gardens of roses' in favour of the wildness of his Scottish boyhood. Clare's Eden, like Byron's, is not the 'sweetest of gardens' but 'dear vallies & greens' full of 'rush beds & thistles'. 'Lachin Y Gair' is charged with the cultural loss associated with the Battle of Culloden and the suppression of the tartan. Clare's is more particular and local: his own culture, the culture of the fields of Helpston, still 'left free' but already threatened.

It is a commonplace of Clare criticism to write of his later work as 'a poetry so empty of the particular facts of experience that it can be characterized as a poetry of absence'.[69] Yet, for all the conventionality of many of the love poems of that period, these poems contain some of his most telling natural description: 'Wood Anemonie', 'The Peartree lane', 'The Yellowhammer', 'I love the rath primroses'.

Even a love poem, such as 'I love the blue violet'[70] may contain an image from nature as startling and fresh as anything in his earlier work: 'Where wild rabbits caper wi many a tossy frank / And show their white shirts to the light'.

The anapestic exuberance of that poem is more daring than anything in Byron, as the prosody, syntax and argument of another late poem, the sonnet 'The Maple Tree',[71] is more complex than anything in Keats.

> The Maple with its tassel flowers of green
> That turns to red a stag horn shaped seed
> Just spreading out its scalloped leaves is seen
> Of yellowish hue yet beautifully green
> Bark ribb'd like corderoy in seamy screed
> That farther up the stem is smoother seen
> Where the white hemlock with white umbel flowers
> Up each spred stoven to the branches towers
> And mossy round the stoven spread dark green

> And blotched leaved orchis and the blue bell flowers
> Thickly they grow and neath the leaves are seen
> I love to see them gemm'd with morning hours
> I love the lone green places where they lean
> And the sweet clothing of the Maple tree

The adjective 'umbel' signals Clare's awareness that hemlock (*Conium maculatum*) was one of the family of *umbelliferae*, and yet the 'truth' of the maple is something far more complex, more composite, than such taxonomy can suggest. Its meaning is as much in the hemlock it supports and the orchises and bluebells that it harbours at its root. Even more, as the pervasive 'green' / 'seen' rhyme suggests, the meaning is also in the looking. 'I always think that this month the prophet of spring brings many beautys to the landscape', Clare wrote in the fifth of his 'Natural History Letters' on 7 February 1825, 'tho a careless observer woud laugh at me for saying so who believes that it brings nothing because he does not give himself the trouble to seek them.' 'For my part' he wrote later, 'I love to look on nature with a poetic feeling which magnifys the pleasure.'[72]

The line 'Bark ribb'd like corderoy in seamy screed' exemplifies the interchange between culture and nature that Clare means. What he sees, he sees through the spectacles of traditional culture: the poor man's ordinary garment (corduroy) and the word, 'screed', that means not only a strip of material but a narrow strip of land or parcel of ground. By Clare's time, moreover, 'screed' had come to mean what it does commonly today: a lengthy piece of writing. The tree thus becomes a text to be read as much as to be written about; there is an interchange, like the interchange of 'green' and 'seen', between naming and seeing.

'Just spreading out…is seen' has the gerundive ambiguity for which Keats's 'darkling I listen' is more famous, and yet here it serves to unify blossom, fruit and leaf in a metamorphic image that confuses the order of the seasons in order to present the wholeness of the tree. Once again, the language that Clare uses, 'stag horn' and 'scalloped' takes the poem into kinds of description expelled by modern taxonomy. The maple of Clare's poem inhabits a culture of antlered dancers and green men where transformation and resurrection are the central subjects. His 'tassel flowers of green / That turns to red' and then as leaves are 'seen / Of yellowish hue yet beautifully green', also inhabit the world of art's translucence. (Did he know that John Evelyn in his *Sylva* had celebrated the maple for its ability to be turned on a lathe to the point of translucence?) A word like 'scalloped' foregrounds the poem as pilgrimage[73] and at the same time places it within the world of art as surely as the word 'gemm'd'. Yet the repeated word, 'stoven' (an Old Norse word for 'trunk'), literally roots the poem in the 'dear perpetual place' of Northamptonshire dialect that gives the tree its meaning.

The maple here is probably *Acer campestre*, the only maple native to Northamptonshire and a tree that to Clare in the Northampton Asylum, would have spoken of home, rootedness and belonging. Of the tree, Geoffrey Grigson has written:

With its sturdy, branchy habit, its delicate leaves, and its close-furrowed bark, it also looks intensely and assuredly native, it *looks* that old inhabitant, which has given itself as the OE *mapulder* – to so many place names, Mapledurham in Hampshire, Maplestead in Essex, Mappowder in Dorset, Mappledore in Wiltshire, and so on.[74]

There is no closure in the poem as it stands in the version cited by Robinson and Summerfield; the only couplet is in lines 7 and 8. The flowers that 'lean' by the maple do so as Clare himself does, and yet 'lean' comes assonantally out of 'love' and 'lone', out of the poem's making of its subject and not from a system of rhyming or seeing.

It seems odd that it has taken two hundred years to read Clare on his own terms, to rid his text not only of Taylor's gentrifications but of the systematic cast of mind, blinded by grammar and conventional prosody. Yet it would not have seemed so to him. In his 'Essay on Popularity' he wrote:

The quiet progress of a name gaining its ground by gentle degrees in the world's esteem is the best living shadow of fame to follow – The simplest trifle & the meanest thing in nature is the same now as it shall continue to be till the world's end

> Men trample grass & prize the flowers in May
> But grass is green when flowers do fade away.[75]

NOTES

1 'The Flitting' is a poem of The Northborough Period (1832–7), a period of Clare's life unrepresented by the four volumes of Clare's poetry edited by Eric Robinson and David Powell as *The Early Poems of John Clare: 1804–1822* and *The Later Poetry of John Clare: 1837–1864*. The text used here is from the 'Oxford Authors' edition of Clare; Robinson and Powell

(eds.), (Oxford, 1984), pp. 250–6. As there is no single definitive edition of Clare's work, references are taken from a number of sources.

2 'Habitat in Europae cultis ruderatis' (it flourishes in Europe in rubbish tips) says Linnaeus in the first edition of the *Species Plantarum* (1753) (London, 1959), II, p. 647.

3 18 October 1820, M. Storey (ed.), *The Letters of John Clare* (Oxford, 1985), p. 107.

4 Eric Robinson (ed.), *John Clare's Autobiographical Writings* (Oxford, 1983), p. 48.

5 J. W. and A. Tibble (eds.), *The Prose of John Clare* (London, 1951) p. 148. Clare also records reading James Maddock's *Florist's Directory* (1822), in which there were also instructions for the cultivation of auriculas (*Prose*, p. 117). The cultivation of prize auriculas had been a fashion since the early eighteenth century.

6 David Powell (ed.), *Catalogue of the John Clare Collection in the Northampton Public Library* (Northampton, 1964), p. 27.

7 M. Storey, *Letters*, p. 305. In a letter to William Sharpe in 1829 he explains his use of botanical nomenclature: 'I shall send you the names both Botanical & English as well as I can make them out for altho I know wild flowers tollerable well my knowledge of garden flowers is very limited' (ibid. p. 465).

8 Margaret Grainger (ed.), *The Natural History Prose Writings of John Clare* (Oxford, 1983), pp. 38–9, 41.

9 M. Storey, *Letters*, p. 17.

10 Ibid. p. 12.

11 Ibid. pp. 302, 300.

12 Ibid. p. 437.

13 *The Norwich Sidney Manuscript: The Apology for Poetry* (Northridge, Calif., 1969), p. 26.

14 M. Storey, *Letters*, p. 51.

15 J. W. and A. Tibble, *Prose*, p. 223.

16 Robinson and Powell, Oxford *Clare*, p. 256. Although Clare had worked at Burghley, a landscape created by Capability Brown, and knew Milton, an estate made by Repton, the sort of garden objected to in 'Decay' was, by Clare's time, most like Loudon's 'Garden Front at Tew Lodge' (*c.* 1809–11) see Melanie Simo, *Loudon and the Landscape: From Country Seat to Metropolis 1783–1843* (New Haven, 1988), plate 4.

17 Robinson and Powell, *Later Poetry*, p. 25.

18 M. Storey, *Letters*, p. 301.

19 In her *Glossary of Northampton Words and Phrases* (2 vols., London, 1854), Anne Elizabeth Baker cites Clare as a reference for the name 'Paigle'. Clare assisted Baker with information on Northamptonshire games and customs. See J. W. and A. Tibble, *Prose*, p. 15n.

20 Robinson and Powell, Oxford *Clare*, p. 307.

21 Lines 782–6. Clare expressed his admiration for Milton in his *Journal* (27 September 1824) where he singled out the georgic lines about the 'laboured ox' and the 'swinkt hedger' from *Comus* for special praise. Grainger, *Natural History*, p. 182.

22 J. W. and A. Tibble, *Prose*, p. 24. This passage, omitted from Robinson, *Autobiographical Writings*, precedes the passage labelled '[Leisure]' there.

23 William Wickett and Nicholas Duval (eds.), *The Farmer's Boy* (Lavenham, Suffolk, 1971), p. 81. Cf. also Clare's late poem 'The rushbeds touched the boiling spring', where Bloomfield's 'memory haunts the silver flood' and 'The landscape seems his waking dream'. Clare also uses similar descriptions of insects in another late poem. 'The Shepherd Boy'.

24 Robinson, *Autobiographical Writings*, p. 48.

25 Robinson and Powell, Oxford *Clare*, p. 108.

26 In Warwickshire, the plant was called 'Pick-Your-Mother's-Heart-Out'. See Geoffrey Grigson, *The Englishman's Flora* (London, 1957), pp. 58–9.

27 M. Storey, *Letters*, pp. 397–8.

28 Ibid. p. 548. Clare wrote poems in imitation of other seventeenth-century poets: Sir Henry Wotton, Raleigh and Marvell.

29 Ibid. p. 207.

30 'Shadows of Taste' (Robinson and Powell, Oxford *Clare*, p. 170) is a good example of the deleterious effects of Thomson's lofty diction on a poem that is full of powerful moments.

31 Grainger, *Natural History*, p. 201.

32 Ibid. p. 192.

33 M. Storey, *Letters*, p. 63.

34 Ibid. p. 594.

35 Timothy Brownlow, *John Clare and Picturesque Landscape* (Oxford, 1983), pp. 94, 3.

36 J. W. and A. Tibble, *Prose*, p. 211.

37 Geoffrey Keynes (ed.), *Complete Writings* (London, 1966), p. 87.

38 J. W. and A. Tibble, *Prose*, p. 211.

39 Ibid. p. 212.

40 Timothy Brownlow suggests that one of Clare's poems may have offered Rippingille the subject for his lost painting, 'Clearing Up after a Shower'. *John Clare and Picturesque Landscape*, p. 99.

41 M. Storey, *Letters*, p. 488.

42 J. W. and A. Tibble, *Prose*, pp. 211–12.

43 M. Storey, *Letters*, p. 656.

44 Robinson and Powell, Oxford *Clare*, p. 169.

45 Introduction to Geoffrey Grigson (ed.), *Selected Poems of John Clare* (London, 1950), quoted in Mark Storey (ed.), *Clare: The Critical Heritage* (London, 1973), p. 406.

46 Robinson and Powell, *Early Poems*, p. 472.

47 Baker cites Clare for this in her *Glossary of Northampton Words and Phrases*.

48 M. Storey, *Letters*, p. 168. Timothy Brownlow quotes Melvyn Bragg (*Listener*, 19 January 1975, p. 53): 'if you lose the name of the thing you lose the thing itself' *John Clare and Picturesque Landscape*, p. 79.

49 M. Storey, *Letters*, p. 163. In Baker's *Glossary of Northampton Words*, Clare is given as the source for another meaning of both 'shepherd's weather-glass', the flower called Scarlet Pimpernel (*Anagallis arvensis*), and for 'woodseer', the flower called Cuckoo Flower or Lady's Smock (*Cardamine pratensis*).

50 M. Storey, *Letters*, p. 176.

51 Peterborough Museum Society: Occasional Papers, No. 4. Gilbert records only common Barberry and Oregon Grape from the family *Berberidaceae* to which Barrenwort belongs. In his *Journal*, Clare records collecting Barberry from the wild for his garden. Robinson, *Autobiographical Writings*, p. 220.

52 *Flora Domestica*, p. xxii.

53 Ibid. p. xxxvi.

54 M. Storey, *Letters*, p. 281.

55 Grainger, *Natural History*, p. 228. Timothy Brownlow believes Clare's work as a botanist 'was a humble parallel to the Pacific explorations' taking place at the same time (*John Clare and Picturesque Landscape*, p. 46).

56 Grainger, *Natural History*, p. 195.

57 J. W. and A. Tibble, *Prose*, p. 51.

58 Letter of 20 April 1754, *A Selection of the Correspondence of Linnaeus and Other Naturalists*, ed. Sir James E. Smith (London, 1821), vol. 1, 31. In a letter of 10 April 1755, Collinson wrote: 'We have great numbers of Nobility and Gentry that know plants very well, but yet do not make botanic science their peculiar study.' 1, 33.

59 J. W. and A. Tibble, *Prose*, pp. 53–4. This passage is partly cited in Grainger, *Natural History*, p. 283.

60 Grainger, *Natural History*, p. 38. Clare's attitude to botanical classification was closer to Antoine-Laurent de Jussieu's *Genera Plantarum, secundum Ordines Naturales disposita* (1789), a system which, because it 'grouped plants according to the greatest number of their similarities of form', was more attractive to the untrained eye. Loudon, who included 'popular, historical, and geographical' material in his description of trees and shrubs in his *Arboretum Britannicum* (1838) was also in reaction against what he called 'a crowd of unconnected images and facts' in the Linnaean system (Simo, *Loudon and the Landscape*, pp. 56, 166).

61 Brownlow, *John Clare and Picturesque Landscape*, p. 26.

62 Grainger, *Natural History*, p. 59.

63 Ibid. p. 202.

64 William Cobbett, *English Gardener* (Oxford, 1980), p. 4.

65 William Cobbett, *Cottage Economy* (Portway, Bath, 1822), p. 2.

66 Robinson and Powell, Oxford *Clare* p. 167.

67 I am indebted to my student, Eric Miller, for pointing out how the language of Linnaeus's *Systema Naturae* is rooted in *classes*.
68 Robinson and Powell, *Early Poems*, 1, 100.
69 Johanne Clare, *John Clare and the Bounds of Circumstance* (Montreal, Kingston, 1987), p. xi.
70 Robinson and Powell, *Later Poetry*, p. 814.
71 Ibid. p. 1025. The version I have cited here, however, is from Robinson and Powell (eds.), *Later Poems of John Clare* (Manchester, 1964), p. 270.
72 Grainger, *Natural History*, pp. 45, 38.
73 Clare would have known the opening line of Raleigh's 'The Passionate Pilgrim': 'Give me my scallop-shell of quiet'.
74 Grigson, *The Englishman's Flora*, p. 124.
75 J. W. and A. Tibble, *Prose*, p. 210. The italics are the editor's.

CHAPTER II

'All madness for writing': John Clare and the asylum

Roy Porter

If there was one subject more than another that [Clare] had an aversion to it was biography – he designated it as a pack of lies.[1]

The basic facts of John Clare's career as a madman can briefly be stated.[2] After the stunning success of his first volume, *Poems Descriptive of Rural Life and Scenery*, published in 1820, Clare's career lurched forward in a turbulent manner, buffeted by fame and disappointment. His novelty value wearing off, later collections – *The Village Minstrel, and Other Poems* (1821), *The Shepherd's Calendar; with Village Stories, and Other Poems* (1827) and *The Rural Muse* (1835) – fared progressively less well. Clare drove himself (he was, he wrote, 'all madness for writing') and overburdened his mind. He was torn in many directions, and forced to be several men at once: a peasant true to his roots (he still needed to work the land for money as well as his Muse); a tractable fellow who could defer gratefully to those displaying him such generous condescension with their critical hints, yet also a natural, manly, independent poet, a worthy successor to Thomson, an East Midlands peasant Laker. Discovering those boon 'companions of genius, Disappointment and Poverty', Clare began to crack, entering a downward spiral of distress and anguish. Around the close of 1821, having exhausted himself composing 'The Dream', he wrote 'I mustn't do no more terrible things yet they stir me up to such a pitch that leaves a disrelish for my old accustomed wanderings after nature.' Soon he was complaining – it became a common strain – of a 'confounded lethargy of low spirit that presses on me to such a degree that at times makes me feel as if my senses had a mind to leave me'. Exacerbated by his eagerness to please, anxieties over his future as a poet, a growing sense of failure and deepening financial crises, Clare's dark phases were to worsen. He became, he wrote, 'a half mad melancholy dog'; he had 'the horrors', suffered 'numbing pain', 'blue devils', 'black melancholy'. Escapist drinking binges speeded his decline. Belonging neither to London nor his native Helpston, the displaced poet was dependent upon his Muse, a 'fickle Hussey' that 'sometimes stilts me up to madness and then leaves me as a begger by the wayside', and upon well-meaning if misguided metropolitan literary well-wishers.

Distraught, in debt and in dread, bouts of severe illness ensued. In 1824 he went up to London to be treated by Dr Darling – who also attended Haydon and Keats. He recorded his phobias, seeing 'thin, death-like shadows and goblins with saucer eyes'. Passers-by were supernatural agents, 'whose errands might be to carry me away at the first dark alley we came to'. He expected to meet death or the devil in Chancery Lane.

Clare suffered severe disorders of the guts and pains in his genitals.[3] Was there a specifiable organic disease? It seems probable his excruciating indispositions were largely psychosomatic; certainly he developed a dread (probably the unfounded child of guilt) of being venereally infected. Perhaps medicine itself induced his deteriorating physical condition, for Clare became an insatiable self-medicator and turned into a hypochondriac. In this respect, he reflected ruefully on the power of imagination: 'I fancy, which I believe to tell truth is the whole of my complaint.' A childhood experience of seeing a man fall off a hay-waggon and break his neck had given him a fit, and thereafter he suffered various epileptiform seizures. Developing morbid fears of future decay and death, Clare began to feel doomed.

After marrying in 1820 a local girl, Patty, his family grew (he was to have seven children); so did his debts. Disappointment turned to despondency, and despondency to despair. From around 1824, but especially after 1830, Clare's letters recite a litany of anguish. He began to lose control of his mental processes. Ever suggestible, terror of madness sometimes overtook him, with its spectre of decay, both physical and mental. Compensatory fantasies took root, especially the figure of Mary Joyce, a childhood sweetheart who, advised by her father, had apparently resisted Clare's advances because of his social inferiority. Clare started to weave fictions around her. Also, he increasingly dreamed about the earlier good times of his childhood, a golden age when the countryside was free (free of enclosure, free of tyrant farmers) and he was free in it.

In the early 1830s, his condition worsened. 'I have not been able until now to write to you', he addressed his publisher, John Taylor, in 1830:

for I have been dreadfully ill – & I can scarcely manage even now to muster courage sufficient to feel myself able to [make out] write a letter but you will excuse all – I have been bled blistered & cupped & have now a seaton in my neck & tho much better I have many fears as to recovery but I keep my mind as quiet as I can – & am able to read a Newspaper – all I regret is that I cannot describe my feelings sufficiently to benefit from our friend Dr Darlings kind advice in whom I always had the greatest confidence – my fancys & feelings vary very often but I now feel a great numbness in my right shoulder.

In the next year, he told Taylor 'my future prospects seem to be no sleep – a general debility – a stupid & stunning apathy or lingering madness & death – my dreads are very apprehensive & uneasy'.[4] On a visit in the mid-1830s, Taylor noted that the poet was talking to himself, mouthing meaningless and repetitive phrases – although when directly addressed, he could reply with intelligence, and remember all the details of the conversation.

In 1837, the year of Queen Victoria's accession, Clare's London friends decided on a rescue. Having set him up as a peasant poet, they would save him as a mad genius. Taylor despatched to him a man with a letter, which read: 'The bearer will bring you up to town and take care of you on the way... The medical aid provided near this place will cure you effectually.' As always, Clare obeyed.

He was escorted to High Beech. It was a rather special private asylum in Epping Forest, run on the progressive principles of moral therapy – gentleness and sympathy – by the enlightened Dr Matthew Allen. Clare arrived, according to Allen,

exceedingly miserable, every instant bemoaning his poverty, and his mind did not appear so much lost and deranged as suspended in its movements by the oppressive and permanent state of anxiety, and fear, and vexation, produced by the excitement of excessive flattery at one time, and neglect at another, his extreme poverty and over-exertion of body and mind.[5]

The patient was allowed to wander in the grounds and encouraged to write: Allen believed it therapeutic.

Initially, Clare felt released from care, and produced some of his most characteristic songs to nature. In time, however, despair took over:

My Mind Is Dark And Fathomless And Wears
The Hues Of Hopeless Agony And Hell
No Plummet Ever Sounds The Soul's Affairs
There Death Eternal Never Sounds The Knell.[6]

He stayed with Allen just over four years. There is little sign that he
was seriously deluded, suicidal or dangerous; but no moves seem to
have been taken towards his release. His sponsors presumably feared
that return to family responsibilities would mean renewal of the
pressures and poverty racking him before. It seemed best to protect
him by making him *de facto* poet in residence at High Beech. There
was something picturesque about a mad author ensconced in a
benevolent asylum like a holy hermit in a grotto. The *litterateur* Cyrus
Redding, who secured publication of some of Clare's asylum verse,
struck a typical note in reflecting after a visit: 'I never before saw so
characterized personally the *Poeta Nascitur*...which lifts men of
genius above the herd'. Clare was painted by William Hunt as a 'Self
Taught Genius'. He was a natural.

Over the years, Clare grew more distraught. Feeling alien, severed
from love, friends and family, he viewed the asylum as a prison, a
'hell of a madhouse', resembling a 'slave ship from Africa'.
Everywhere he met deception, surrounded, he thought, by 'mock
friends and real enemies'. 'There is no place like home', he wrote
plaintively to his wife, although, while still writing passionately about
and to Patty, he began to turn his childhood sweetheart, Mary, into
his 'first' wife.

He meanwhile fashioned himself into a warrior to battle against
oppression, personifying himself as a prize-fighter. Above all, he
came to see himself as Byron's reincarnation; Clare's *Don Juan* and
Child Harold resumed where Byron had left off. Byron-Clare was the
anti-hero waging war on cant and lies. Possibly to spite his prim and
pious keeper, Clare peeled away the veneer of civilised gentility and
unveiled the lust, greed, envy, deceit and malice beneath:

> 'Poets are born' – and so are whores – the trade is
> Grown universal – in these canting days
> Women of fashion must, of course, be ladies,
> And whoring is the business that still pays[7]

Clare played the disillusioned poet, 'Never act hypocrisy', he later
wrote to his son, 'for Deception is the most odious Knavery in the

world'. Might not Byron have enjoyed the irony of his own role as an aristocratic bitter fool being assumed by a certified lunatic? Confinement certainly released something in Clare. For years the poet had had to mind his Ps and Qs, composing while glancing over his shoulder at his patrons and public, his collective superego. Now, amidst outpourings of love for nature and for his two 'wives', a new strain showed in his verse. The pent-up anger, resentments and frustrations of the years flared out in satire and bawdy: officially alienated of mind, Clare could now give vent to a hidden identity.

Tired of 'those jailors called keepers',[8] and aided by his soulmates, the gypsies, in 1841 Clare escaped from the forest madhouse, walking the hundred miles home to Northamptonshire. *En route*, no one, it seems, took him for a lunatic. He lived at home at Northborough for some months, till, after further ructions, the local doctor, Fenwick Skrimshire, who had treated him since 1820, had him removed, in December 1841, to the Northamptonshire General Lunatic Asylum, founded in 1836, and sited just outside the town. Although admitted as a pauper patient (his record stated: 'gardener'), he was to be treated as a gentleman, Lord Fitzwilliam again agreeing to help by advancing eleven shillings a week towards his maintenance. Clare was never released, dying in the asylum over twenty-two years later in May 1864. Clare liked the Northampton asylum no more than High Beech.

As we will see, Clare's physicians and well-wishers noticed in him what they took as signs of mental abnormalities and deterioration: he talked to himself, developed private cyphers and left poems unfinished. Nevertheless, letters home reveal a man essentially, if somewhat wilfully, in control of powerful faculties, demonstrating tender and loving devotion to his family ('think Fred – for yourself', he advised his son). At Northampton, twenty years of poetry lay before him. Its quality fell off, but no more so than Wordsworth's.

Historians of psychiatry have told us that the Georgian century was the dark age of 'the trade in lunacy', when many were improperly locked away and cruelly treated; whereas psychiatric reform arrived in the nineteenth century, with new legal safeguards against false imprisonment, and a more sympathetic understanding of madness.[9] How, then, did it come about that this talented and penetrating man spent the first twenty-seven years of the enlightened reign of Queen Victoria shut up in a madhouse? Why was it that those who saw themselves as his friends and allies brought about this fate? Why have most Clare scholars rubber-stamped Clare's life sentence? The answer lies in part with a cluster of cultural fantasies, associated with the myth of poetic genius; it also lies with some of the myths of reformed psychiatry, a topic too broad to explore here.[10]

First, however, a basic question must be broached. Was Clare actually mad? If so, from which psychiatric disorder was he suffering? Neither a psychiatrist nor a literary critic, I am highly dubious, as a historian, as to whether anything is to be gained from the parlour game of retrospective diagnosis. Even in the most favourable circumstances, it might seem a futile exercise (why diagnose, if it is too late to treat?). Furthermore, as it happens, though Clare was a celebrated man and incarcerated for so long, we possess curiously little day-to-day medical documentation of his condition. It may be worth briefly reviewing the judgements of the physicians who successively treated him. Of these, Dr Matthew Allen was the first and most eminent. A cultured man acquainted with Thomas Carlyle, Allen spent his early career at the York Asylum, where he became an advocate of 'moral treatment' and the mild system of patient management.[11] On leaving York in 1824, he bought three houses at High Beech, converting them into a private asylum, with an accent on freedom and family life. As is evident from his *Cases of Insanity* (1831) and his *Essay on the Classification of the Insane* (1837) he saw 'moral' methods as the best mode of establishing the discipline that would, it was hoped, eventually produce self-discipline in the patient.

Allen characterised Clare as a mad poet, suffering from 'delusions'. The loss of his commonplace faculties was the condition for the integrity of his poetic voice. 'It is most singular', he wrote,

that ever since he came, and even now at almost all times, the moment he gets pen or pencil in hand he begins to write most beautiful poetic effusions. Yet he has never been able to maintain in conversation, nor even in writing prose, the appearance of sanity for two minutes or two lines together, and yet there is no indication whatever of insanity in any of his poetry.[12]

(In fact, this seems a bizarre, doctrinaire, or simply deluded judgement, since Clare's letters from this period, though often exasperated, are extremely lucid.)

The doctor who secured Clare's admission into the Northampton-shire General Lunatic Asylum after his temporary return to home life in 1841 was Fenwick Skrimshire, no specialist mad-doctor but a physician who had served for several years as Clare's general practitioner. Allowing that the poet was neither 'idiotic, mischievous, or dirty', Skrimshire believed Clare was suffering from 'hereditary' madness – probably a dustbin category, as he cited no evidence of insanity running in Clare's family. Pondering whether lunacy had been preceded by 'any severe or long-continued mental emotion or exertion', Skrimshire judged Clare's mind had caved in 'after years addicted to Poetical prosings'.[13]

At the Northamptonshire General Lunatic Asylum, Clare fell under the control of Thomas Prichard, a Welshman from a medical family. Superintendent from its opening in 1836, Prichard left in 1845 to found his own private asylum. Of similar persuasions to Allen, Prichard was additionally sympathetic to mesmeric therapies, though there is no evidence that he practised them on Clare. In November 1843, nearly two years after the poet's admission, Prichard wrote thus to Clare's local parson: 'Poor Clare is in good health but the state of his mind has not improved. It rather appears to become more and more impaired, he used at one time to write many and very good pieces tho' he scarcely ever finished them. He now writes but little and in a coarse style very unlike his former compositions. I much fear the disease will gradually terminate in dementia.'[14] Prichard's notion of Clare composing 'but little' seems weird, in view of the fact that W. F. Knight, between 1845 and 1850 steward at the Asylum, assiduously copied out some 800 of Clare's poems. The doctor's supposition that a 'coarser' style is synonymous with a decline in quality and perhaps also with psychopathology speaks for itself.

The last physician to have much contact with Clare was P. R. Nesbitt, who was the superintendent until 1858. 'I was always led to believe mental affliction had its origin in dissipation', Nesbitt wrote, presumably repeating a by-now often retailed folklore. Clare's insanity, he opined,

was characterized by obsessional ideas and hallucinations. For instance he may be said to have lost his own personal identity as with all the gravity of truth he would maintain that he had written the works of Byron, and Sir Walter Scott, that he was Nelson and Wellington, that he had fought and won the battle of Waterloo, that he had had his head shot off at this battle, whilst he was totally unable to explain the process by which it had been again affixed to his body.[15]

Nesbitt was broadly correct in describing Clare's fantasies, though a more acute observer might have pondered precisely in what sense

Clare embraced such beliefs or feints: was he truly confused about his own identity, or just sending the authorities up?

Between them, Clare's doctors – who for more than a quarter of a century had the golden opportunity to observe the poet's mental processes – had pathetically little illuminating to say; and some of their statements appear palpably false or, at least, highly tendentious. There is no surviving evidence to suggest that they strove mightily to probe to the root of his condition. In mitigation, I wish to indicate three reasons for this state of affairs. First, for the whole period he was sequestrated, Clare was being paid for – during his Northampton years, by the Earl of Fitzwilliam. What must have seemed a rather desirable *modus vivendi* had been achieved. It fulfilled notions of *noblesse oblige*: the poet was a pensioner, an old retainer supported by a gesture of conspicuous patronage. The literary world could rest assured that a lunatic asylum was a nurturing environment for a mad genius. Clare for his part was a star patient for an asylum superintendent. So long as the payments were forthcoming, there was little reason to disturb an arrangement in which the poet could poetise in sylvan surroundings, on tap as an object of occasional curiosity (but never a pest) to those in the world of letters. There were no pressures to 'cure' or discharge him; he was obviously best off where he was: *quieta non movere*.

Second, and more broadly, nineteenth-century psychiatric doctors had genuine reservations about the wisdom of prying too energetically into patients' mental states, especially introspective and depressive characteristics. These days, thanks to Freud and the talking cure – one thinks of the cases of Sylvia Plath or Anne Sexton – every last syllable or symbol of the disturbed writer is seized upon, to plumb ultimate family secrets and fathom the elusive interplay between creativity and neurosis. However, Victorian asylum doctors did not tend to conduct their clinical relations in this way, avoiding engaging in close encounters with their patients' psyches. From the well-documented case of Clare's contemporary, John Perceval, son of the assassinated Prime Minister, Spencer Perceval, who spent a couple of years in Britain's most exclusive asylums, we know that it was his complaint that, as a lunatic, he was never actually addressed as if rational conversation was conceivable between doctor and patient; he was, he said, treated like a stick of furniture. This was policy. For doctors deliberately prevented patients from talking about themselves, lest this encourage delusions of grandeur, morbid introspection, over-excitation or egoistical hysteria. It is likely that Clare's doctors did not quiz the poet very energetically about his delusions and *idées fixes*, fearing this would exacerbate his condition; a century of psychoanalysis suggests this may not have been entirely foolish.[16]

Third, a related point, their medico-theoretical orientation would, most probably, have given Clare's doctors little reason to believe that any intense or intimate *discursive* encounters with patients would have revealed the grand secret of their condition. Most medical men believed that insanity was, at root, organic, the product of bad blood or weak nerves, or, in the case of women, defects of the genitals and reproductive system. Or it might spring from moral flaws – vices like vanity; or, as we have seen Skrimshire suggesting, it might be 'hereditary'. Few asylum doctors at this time seriously entertained the idea that disturbances were the consequence of un- or sub-conscious psychic processes, arising out of uniquely individual autobiographical experiences. Hence there was little to gain from poring over Clare's poems, scrutinising his drafts, watching him compose. In short, it is not surprising that Clare's doctors have so little to tell us about the inner man. It is not a verdict on their negligence, but a reflection on their paradigms.[17]

This may seem a strange claim, in view of the fact that numerous Victorian mad-doctors, mirroring the literary culture at large, subscribed to a belief in the twinning of madness and genius – a longstanding conviction that had emerged in antiquity, been boosted in the Renaissance and then given a new lease of life by Romanticism.[18] The trope of the mad genius, together with the associated Romantic image of the poet as a child of nature, was, of course, widely invoked to account for Clare's phenomenal talent and his subsequent treatment, cosily cotton-wooled in the asylum, where the mad poet could pursue his destiny, or obey his demon. 'He writes frequently', observed a correspondent for the *Northampton Mercury* on 30 April 1842, trotting out myths of praeternatural creativity:

and beyond a doubt composes many more poems than he puts on paper, if indeed his life is not passed in one almost unbroken poetic dream. He may be seen any fine day, walking, with a rapid step and an abstracted manner, about the grounds of the Asylum, one hand in his pocket and the other in the bosom of his waistcoat, easily distinguishable by the most careless observer as no ordinary man...Outwardly there is nothing to indicate insanity. It needs a closer acquaintance to discover that there are chords jarring and out of tune in that excellent piece of Nature's handiwork.[19]

The telltale admission that Clare showed no outward signs of madness squares, of course, with a further Romantic myth: the psychiatrist as seer, who alone could pierce the mask of madness.

The role of the poet as mad genius had, arguably, been eligible within Christian Humanism, which fostered the notion of 'good madness'. In the Renaissance, the 'mad' element still had connotations of a transcendental, divine *furor*, related to the Holy Ghost.[20] However, with the Scientific Revolution and the Enlightenment giving encouragement to aetiologies of madness that emphasised the somatic, insanity increasingly became a matter of pathology: something was *wrong*. Furthermore, with the post-1660 rise of the asylum (Foucault's 'great confinement'), the mad poet or painter, instead of being celebrated or tolerated as an eccentric, was now subjected to the new peril of being confined, for society's good, or even his own: the fate, for example, of the Restoration versifier, James Carkesse, who found himself in the Catch-22 situation, once locked in the asylum, of writing verses in order to prove he possessed his wits, but, by that very exercise, being judged to be out of his mind.[21] Long seen as special, the mad genius came to be seen as sick. By the *fin de siècle*, psychiatric experts like Cesare Lombroso or Theo Hyslop were maintaining that, as a breed, artists and writers were disturbed, and, perhaps, *ipso facto* in need of the ministrations of psychological medicine. As with Clare, creative artists like Robert Schumann, Virginia Woolf and Vlaslav Nijinsky found themselves institutionalised – not by malicious enemies, but by spouses and friends, thanks partly to the enduring authority of nominally sympathetic but actually stigmatising myths of madness.[22]

Such myths continue to exert their fascination, and traces are still visible in recent assessments of Clare. 'The destruction of the man was the triumph of the poet', James Reeves has argued, echoing the trope.[23] Espousing the myths of the tormented genius and the essential benevolence of the Victorian psychiatric endeavour, the Tibbles painted life at High Beech as pastoral:

Perhaps nowhere in England could Clare have found a more understanding physician than Dr. Matthew Allen. Emphasising the need for early diagnosis and expert handling, believing in judicious mental as well as bodily exercise – the prevailing idea then was against mental exercise for the insane – Allen encouraged Clare to go on writing what he called Clare's 'beautiful poetic effusions'.[24]

Without casting aspersions on Allen, it could be suggested that Clare suffered from a surfeit of understanding physicians.[25]

Partly, as I say, because of the paucity of contemporary documentation, the game of setting Clare in the psychiatrist's chair proves unrewarding. The documentation is too scanty, the mists of mythology too thick. This is abundantly evident from the rather feeble diagnostic shots modern psychiatrists have made. Before 1950, it was fairly common to label Clare a schizophrenic.[26] To us this may seem a particularly wild attribution, surely merely reflecting the fact that for a while the 'schizophrenia' diagnosis carried top prestige. Given the polarised categories of modern psychiatric theory, subsequent dissenting doctors have tended to plump for the notion of a cyclothymic condition (manic-depression). 'There are conflicting views regarding this type of illness', admitted the psychiatrist, Dr Thomas Tennant, in 1953:

In my opinion this was a cyclothymic disorder, and not a schizophrenic one as suggested by one of his recent biographers. Apart from the actual symptomatology, the excellence of much of his poetry written in hospital, and the slow development of deterioration support this diagnosis.[27]

Note that, despite his insistence upon the 'excellence' of Clare's asylum poetry and the 'slowness' of his 'deterioration', what is not in doubt in Tennant's view – witness his ominous phrase – is that 'certification was inevitable'.[28] The eminent neurologist, Russell Brain, likened Clare's mental illness to those of Smart, Cowper and Samuel Johnson, as a disorder 'to which men of broad general views coupled with a sensitive imagination are naturally [*sic*!] exposed'. Clare's moods fluctuated, Brain argued, between ecstatic happiness and profound despair, love and anger, violence and passivity, between intense concentration and bouts of idleness.[29] It is sadly amusing to note that, in the first edition (1932) of their magisterial *Life*, the Tibbles called Clare schizophrenic, but by the second edition (1972), he has become 'manic-depressive': *sic transit* the glories of psychiatric diagnoses.[30] For what it is worth, the label of a manic-depressive condition seems the more promising account; all the same, it is fundamentally vacuous, redescribing what is already evident.

Perhaps the best clue was offered by Matthew Allen. The essential trouble with Clare, he once observed, was insecurity, and this was at bottom financial, with a wife and seven children to support: 'I had then not the slightest hesitation in saying that if a small pension could be obtained for him, he would have recovered instantly and most probably remained well for life.'[31] It is highly revealing that Allen's cheap and modest proposal was never taken up. In the wake of the New Poor Law (1834), outdoor relief of the kind suggested was evidently beyond the pale. If the boozing, fornicating, brood-producing peasant poet was going to be graced with largesse, then, like everyone else, he would first have to be institutionalised (in a madhouse not a workhouse), to qualify under the 'less eligibility' system, and prevent him becoming a burden on the rates.

Yet Allen's comment, of course, gives a broader hint. Its economic realism intimates that we should read Clare's condition not primarily as a medical mode of madness but as the expression of insupportable bread-and-butter troubles. Surely that must be right; for it would make a nonsense of our meanings of madness if we proposed that Clare was, in some objective sense, truly insane, while yet continuing, confined in the asylum for two whole decades, to write poetry that was not merely entirely lucid, but also, in its genres, subjects and sentiments, deeply conventional.[32]

There is no need to rehearse again in detail those events of the first thirty years of his life that rendered Clare by the early 1830s a wrecked man: the mix of success and failure, the uprooting from a familiar landscape, the ambition, humility and humiliation, the overwhelming pressures upon him to achieve. Once a literary star, he felt pulled between London and the fields; between the authentic peasant self and that ersatz, cleaned-up, moralised peasant his patrons and supporters demanded. No surprise that, under such pressures, he cracked.[33] Was this clinical insanity? Surely the signs are that the Clare of the early 1830s was not mad but overwhelmed.

Clare's tragedy is that, at that very time, there had just come into being a circuit of asylums, blessed with the most impeccable, liberal credentials, and the doctrine that for types like Clare there was no place like the asylum. In an earlier era, he would probably have been left, like Blake, to fend for himself. By the beginning of Victoria's reign, progress dictated that he was shunted off, and sequestrated for life, in a psychiatric order which could, with a straight face, represent the lunatic asylum as the best of all possible worlds, a site in which, in the judgement of the contemporary Scottish psychiatrist, W. A. F. Browne,

The inmates all seem to be actuated by the common impulse of enjoyment, all are busy and are delighted by being so... They literally work in order to please themselves... there is in this community no compulsion.[34]

Of course, that is not how Clare experienced the benign asylums to which he was despatched. Indeed, if Clare really went mad, it seems fairly safe to suggest this was a *consequence* of being buried, in the prime of life, in an institution he detested. It was one thing for Prichard to report in 1845 'he enjoys perfect liberty here' – he was indeed given the run of the grounds, and for some years allowed into the local villages; but Clare did not it seems appreciate this Orwellian world of freedom under confinement. 'I am in fact in prison', he wrote to his son – indeed, 'I am in this damned madhouse and can't get out'. He called the asylum a 'hell', a 'Bastille' or 'Sodom'. 'I am now in the ninth year of my captivity among the Babylonians', he could write, adding poignantly 'and any News from Home is a Godsend or blessing'.[35] He was separated from his wife and children (he never saw Patty again after being certified for a second time), forced into solitude, and deprived of any regular, stimulating company – though occasionally visited like someone in a 'poppet show', by emissaries from the literary world. No wonder he became strange, retreating partially, into a private world: who wouldn't?

We know from the moving autobiography of his contemporary, John Perceval, that, placed in such circumstances, a puzzled, perplexed, frustrated person, banging his head against a brick wall, will assume new identities, in order to make some sense of, and gain leverage against, the mystifying economy of denials and negations the asylum presents.[36] From Peter Ostwald's magnificent reconstruction of Nijinsky's madness, we also know how the Russian dancer, once institutionalised, choreographed his own pantomime of craziness and sanity, starred in the role of madman, and so reduced to a farce the business of organised psychiatry.[37] Something comparable seems to have happened with Clare.

In the asylum, Clare turned himself into Nelson, a prize-fighter and Byron.[38] The hero, the bruiser and the Byron figures speak for themselves. Clare had been made to feel powerless; but he was, by nature, sturdily independent. Impersonation of these physically and culturally potent personae empowered the dispossessed peasant, provided chances of hitting back, the pen being as mighty as the punch. Becoming Byron further enabled him to transfer or sublimate the sexual guilt and social anger he evidently experienced, under the socially moralising Allen, the 'Doctor Bottle-Imp who deals in urine'.

Clare's asylum doctors, and many of his later biographers invite us to contemplate a man suffering from the 'delusion' that he was Byron or Tom Spring. Yet, was it a delusion, or rather a disguise? Perhaps a mask, a cover, somewhere ambiguously in-between (if the noble poet can be Don Juan, why cannot Clare be Byron?). Perhaps Clare thought he was Byron reborn; may it not be equally possible that his doctors were so literal-minded, so incapable of appreciating double-meanings and coping with double-lives, so resistant to the play of the literal and the figurative, that they failed to see the joke? What contemporaries stared upon as symptoms of madness, we could easily read as Clare's subversions, fantasies of power, private performances. As emphasised by Rosenhan, behaviour which, in the wider world, would be read as socially acceptable, becomes, in context of the asylum, further confirmation of psychosis.[39]

Within the asylum, as is well known, Clare changed not just his identity but his language. Sometimes he would write only in capitals, or he would develop private shorthands, omitting all vowels. This has been seen, by his doctors and by later commentators, as a further symptom of a diseased mind. Yet, if so, surely it was madness with method in it – these were codes born of privacy, designed to preserve secrecy. Clare knew very well what he was doing, for he complained about the ways outsiders picked his brains and stole his language.[40]

Indeed, the documentation of Clare's later life centres on a series of charades he played with voyeuristic visitors. One was G. J. Wilde, editor of the *Northampton Mercury*. He recalled how, on one occasion, Clare quoted from Shakespeare and Byron and claimed the lines as his own. Corrected by Wilde, he responded, 'It's all the same. I'm John Clare now. I was Byron and Shakespeare formerly.' Identity confusion? Tease? A coded message about Clare's place in the canon? Who is to say?[41] Clare undoubtedly found the condescension of the ghouls, visiting him as anthropologists might inspect a dying tribe, rather trying. The writer Agnes Strickland visited Clare in 1860, telling him she 'had been much pleased with his lines on the daisy'.

'Ugh! It is a tidy little thing,' replied he, without raising his eyes or appearing in the slightest degree gratified by my praise. 'I am glad you can amuse yourself by writing.' 'I can't do it,' replied he, gloomily; 'they pick my brains out.' I enquired his meaning. 'Why,' said he, 'they have cut off my head, and picked out all the letters of the alphabet – all the vowels and consonants – and brought them out through the ears; and then they want me to write poetry! I can't do it.'

Strickland, one assumes, took these responses as symptomatic of irrationality; we might see Clare's ripostes as poetic truths. 'Tell me which you like best', she continued, as if addressing a child, 'literature or your former avocation?' 'I liked hard work best', he replied: 'I was happy then. Literature has destroyed my head and brought me here.'[42]

There are hardly any letters from the final fifteen years. The last, written in March 1860 to a Mr James Hipkins, reads: 'Dear Sir, I am in a Madhouse & quite forgot you Name or who you are You must excuse me for I have nothing to communicate or tell of & why I am shut up I dont know I have nothing to say so I conclude – yours respectfully, John Clare.'[43] Often cited as proof of mental deterioration, this might equally be taken as an entirely appropriate refusal, a perfect conclusion.

In this brief discussion, I have chosen not to psychoanalyse Clare's poetry as a window onto his soul. I leave that to others better skilled than I. Doubtless works like 'I Am' (1844), with its image of the poet abandoned by his friends 'like a memory lost', now a 'self-consumer of my woes', tell us much of the man, though perhaps nothing of any disease. Rather, to exemplify my conviction that we might usefully forget about Clare as suffering from a disease syndrome but read his despair essentially as a product of circumstances – above all, the circumstance of being permanently locked away – I conclude with the well-known episode where the lives of Clare and Tennyson so nearly crossed. In 1841, the plausible Allen persuaded the young Tennyson, still barely established in his poetic career, to invest £3,000 of family money in a project for machine woodcarving. The enterprise failed, and in 1843 Allen was declared bankrupt. Tennyson's loss was doubly great as it coincided with the ending of his engagement to Emily Sellwood, since her father – the parallel with Clare's Mary Joyce is irresistible! – would not have his daughter marry a penniless poet. Embittered, Tennyson was later to write of Allen:

He is fled – I wish him dead –
He that wrought my ruin –
O the flattery and the craft
Which were my undoing.[44]

(Compare Clare's 'Doctor Bottle-Imp who deals in urine'.) Unlike Clare, the genteel Tennyson was not to remain impecunious for long; indeed, not being a pauper, *he* was eligible for outdoor relief, receiving a Civil List pension in 1845 after the publication of 'In Memoriam'. Five years later, as his reward, he was allowed to marry Emily. There was no looking back. Clare remained institutionalised, Tennyson became Poet Laureate. If Clare's story is one of madness and genius, it is no less one of madness and money.

NOTES

1 P. R. Nesbitt on John Clare, quoted in A. Foss and K. Trick, *St Andrew's Hospital, Northampton: The First 150 Years* (Cambridge 1989), p. 140.
2 This essay makes no pretence to disclose new information about Clare's life. I draw upon standard biographies like J. W. and Anne Tibble, *John Clare: A Life* (revised edn, London, 1972; 1st edn London 1932); E. Storey, *A Right to Song: The Life of John Clare* (London, 1982); and have made grateful use of Mark Storey (ed.), *The Letters of John Clare* (Oxford, 1985).
3 Clare's state of mind in the 1820s is powerfully evoked in G. Grigson, *Poems and Poets* (London, 1969), pp. 86–123, esp. p. 87; see also M. Storey, pp. xix–xxi.
4 M. Storey, p. 536. Clare could vividly depict his 'hypochondria'. On one occasion he explained to Dr Darling that

> though I cannot describe my feelings well I will tell you as well as I can – sound affects me very much & things evil as well [as] good thoughts are continually rising in my mind... there is a sort of numbing through my private parts which I cannot describe & when I was so indisposed last winter I felt as if I had circulation in the blood & at times as if it went round me & at other times such a sinking as if I was going to sink through the bed

Ibid. p. 615.
5 Grigson, *Poems and Poets*, p. 88.
6 *Child Harold* in Geoffrey Summerfield (ed.), John Clare, *Selected Poetry* (Harmondsworth, 1990).
7 Ibid. p. 214.
8 See M. Storey, pp. 646, 650.
9 Michael MacDonald, *Mystical Bedlam: Madness, Anxiety and Healing in Seventeenth Century England* (Cambridge, 1981), calls the eighteenth

century 'a disaster for the insane'. For a revisionist view, see Roy Porter, *Mind Forg'd Manacles: Madness and Psychiatry in England from Restoration to Regency* (London, 1987; paperback edn, Harmondsworth, 1990).

10 The best critical analyses of the self-serving myths of psychiatric liberalism are Thomas S. Szasz, *The Myth of Mental Illness: Foundations of a Theory of Personal Conduct* (London, 1972; revised edn, New York, 1974); Andrew Scull, *Social Order/Mental Disorder: Anglo-American Psychiatry in Historical Perspective* (London, 1989); *Museums of Madness: The Social Organization of Insanity in Nineteenth-Century England* (London, New York, 1979); Michel Foucault, *La Folie et la Déraison: Histoire de la Folie à l'Age Classique* (Paris, 1961), translated and abridged as *Madness and Civilization: A History of Insanity in the Age of Reason*, trans. by Richard Howard (New York, 1965).

11 For the following, see Anne Tibble, 'John Clare and his doctors', *The Charles Lamb Bulletin*, 4 (1973), 77–81. Allen's two publications, *Cases of Insanity* (1831), and *Essay on the Classification of the Insane* (1837), outline his ideas on 'this neglected department of medicine'.

12 E. Robinson and G. Summerfield, 'John Clare: an interpretation of certain asylum letters', *Review of English Studies*, 13 (1962), 135–46, p. 136.

13 J. W. and Anne Tibble, *A Life*, revised edn, p. 173.

14 Grigson, *Poems and Poets*, p. 107; Foss and Trick, *St Andrew's Hospital Northampton*.

15 E. Storey, *Right to Song*, p. 291; Foss and Trick, *St Andrew's Hospital Northampton*, p. 140. Byron made a huge impression on Clare. He features in Clare's correspondence from 1820. Clare witnessed his funeral. It is worth noting that the Prince Regent told people he had fought at Waterloo: in his case, this was not seen as a symptom of madness.

16 For Victorian fears, see Michael J. Clark, '"Morbid Introspection", unsoundness of mind, and British psychological medicine, c. 1830–1900', in W. F. Bynum, Roy Porter and Michael Shepherd (eds.), *Anatomy of Madness*, vol. III (London, 1988), pp. 71–101; for Perceval, see Roy Porter, *A Social History of Madness* (London, 1987; paperback edn, 1989), ch. ix; for modern probings, see Edward Butscher, *Sylvia Plath: Method and Madness* (New York, 1976).

17 For this psychiatric orientation, see William F. Bynum, 'Rationales for therapy in British psychiatry: 1780–1835', *Medical History*, 18 (1974), 317–34; 'Theory and practice in British psychiatry from J. C. Prichard (1786–1848) to Henry Maudsley (1835–1918)', in T. Ogawa (ed.), *History of Psychiatry* (Osaka, 1982), pp. 196–216; Bynum, 'The nervous patient in eighteenth and nineteenth century England: The psychiatric origins of British neurology', in W. F. Bynum, Roy Porter and Michael Shepherd (eds.), *The Anatomy of Madness*, vol. 1 (London, 1985), pp. 89–102; Michael J. Clark, 'The rejection of psychological approaches to

mental disorder in late nineteenth-century British psychiatry', in Andrew Scull (ed.), *Madhouses, Mad-Doctors, and Madmen* (London; Philadelphia, 1981), pp. 271–312.

18 G. Becker, *The Mad Genius Controversy* (Beverly Hills, 1978); P. Murray (ed.), *Genius: The History of An Idea* (Oxford, 1989); G. Tonelli, 'Genius: from the Renaissance to 1770', in P. P. Wiener (ed.), *Dictionary of the History of Ideas*, vol. II (New York, 1973), pp. 293–7.

19 Quoted in Foss and Trick, *St Andrew's Hospital Northampton*, p. 134.

20 See especially M. Screech, *Ecstacy and the Praise of Folly* (London, 1980); 'The mad "Christ" of Erasmus and the legal duties of his brethren', in N. J. Lacy and J. C. Nash (eds.), *Essays in Early French Literature Presented to Barbara M. Craig* (York, South Carolina, 1982), pp. 119–27; *Montaigne and Melancholy* (London, 1983); 'Good madness in Christendom', in Bynum, Porter and Shepherd (eds.), *Anatomy of Madness*, vol. I, pp. 25–39.

21 Roy Porter, 'Bedlam and Parnassus: mad people's writing in Georgian England', in George Levine (ed.), *One Culture: Essays in Science and Literature*, (Madison, Wisconsin, 1987), pp. 258–84. For Carkesse, see James Carkesse, *Lucida intervalla: containing divers miscellaneous poems*, edited by M. V. DePorte (Los Angeles, 1979; 1st edn, London, 1679).

22 T. B. Hyslop, *Mental Physiology, Especially in its Relations to Mental Disorders* (London, 1895); *The Great Abnormals* (London, 1925); *Mental Handicaps in Art* (London, 1927); W. R. Bett, *The Infirmities of Genius* (London, 1952); Cesare Lombroso, *The Man of Genius*, translated from Italian (London, 1891); J. F. Nisbet, *The Insanity of Genius and the General Inequality of Human Faculty Physiologically Considered* (London, 1900); Max Simon Nordau, *Degeneration*, translated from 2nd edn of the German work (London, 1920). For the fate of the confined, see Porter, *Social History of Madness*.

23 J. Reeves (ed.), *Selected Poems of John Clare* (London, 1954), xxix.

24 J. W. and Anne Tibble (eds.), *John Clare: His Life and Poetry* (London, 1956), p. 162.

25 It may be worth noting by contrast that eighteenth-century 'mad poets' like Kit Smart and William Cowper spent only very brief periods under institutional detention.

26 For Clare as schizophrenic, see Eleanor L. Nicholes, 'The shadowed mind: a study of the change in style of the poetry of John Clare resulting from the effects of schizophrenic process' (Ph.D. dissertation, New York University, 1950). Ernst Kris and Geoffrey Grigson both saw Clare as a schizophrenic.

27 T. Tennant, 'Reflections of genius', *Journal of Mental Science*, 99 (1953), 1–7.

28 Ibid. p. 5: 'In my experience a prolonged schizophrenic illness in a talented person produces such deterioration as to interfere markedly with any subsequent creative work'.

29 W. R. Brain, *Some Reflections on Genius and Other Essays* (London, 1960).
30 J. W. and A. Tibble (eds.), *Life and Poetry*, p. 201:

> 'Clare was most likely of manic-depressive temperament. His bursts of creative work were followed by periods of exhaustion, and these were often prolonged by pecuniary worry and under-nourishment. His energy has an astonishing continuity, and its alternations with exhaustion should not be confused with schizoid elation and despair. The view that his temperament and hence his disease were manic-depressive and not schizophrenic is supported, not only by the slow progress of his disease, but by his capacity for rhythmic originality and poetic unity during the first ten years of his second incarceration'.

Compare E. Storey, *Right to Song*, p. 300.

31 M. Storey (ed.), *John Clare: The Critical Heritage* (London, 1973), p. 256.
32 My point, as will be obvious, is not that Clare's asylum poetry is conventional in the sense of mediocre, but that it betrays no clear sign that it was written by someone who had been certified insane. For similar discussions in respect of painting see Patricia H. Allderidge, *The Late Richard Dadd* (London, 1974); Sander L. Gilman, *Seeing the Insane* (New York, 1982); John M. MacGregor, *The Discovery of the Art of the Insane* (Princeton, 1989); Roy Porter, *Seeing the Insane* (Nijmegen, 1990).
33 The political dimension of the uprooting of the peasantry is well brought out in J. Barrell, *The Idea of Landscape and the Sense of Place: 1730–1840: An approach to the poetry of John Clare* (Cambridge, 1972).
34 W. A. F. Browne, *What Asylums Were, Are and Ought to Be: Being the Substance of Five Lectures Delivered Before the Managers of the Montrose Royal Lunatic Asylum* (Edinburgh, 1837), pp. 229–30.
35 For Sodom, see M. Storey, *Letters*, p. 651; for Babylon, p. 661. J. W. and A. Tibble, *Life and Poetry*, p. 178. In a letter of 1849 or 1850 to his wife, Clare had written 'in fact I am in Prison because I wont leave my family & tell a falshood – this is the English Bastille a government Prison where harmless people are trapped & tortured till they die – English priestcraft & english bondage more severe then the slavery of Egypt & Africa'. See M. Storey, *Letters*, pp. 668–9. Clare had found High Beech a prison too. He told Cyrus Redding, 'I want to be with my wife and family.' Cyrus Redding's account of his visits to Clare was published in *English Journal*, 20 (15 May 1841), 305–9; 22 (29 May 1841), 340–3, and is reproduced in M. Storey, *Critical Heritage*, pp. 247–56. For Perceval's comparable experience of isolation from his family, see Porter, *Social History of Madness*, ch. ix.
36 J. T. Perceval, *A Narrative of the Treatment Received by a Gentleman, During a State of Mental Derangement*, (2 vols., London, 1838, 1840).
37 Peter Ostwald, *Vaslav Nijinsky: A Leap into Madness* (New York, 1991).
38 See Cyrus Redding: 'The principal token of his mental eccentricity was the introduction of prize-fighting, in which he seemed to imagine he was to engage; but the allusion to it was made in the way of interpolation in the middle of the subject on which he was discoursing, brought in

abruptly, and abandoned with equal suddenness...This was the only symptom of aberration of mind we observed about Clare.' Redding's last phrase is immensely telling. M. Storey, *Critical Heritage*, p. 238.

39 The rationality of actions is in the eye of the beholder and hence deeply context-dependent. Actions which, in ordinary society, will be read as sane (game-playing, teasing, irony and so forth) will typically be interpreted in the psychiatric hospital as give-away symptoms of psychopathology. For a classic experiment, in which normal people were infiltrated into an asylum, and their normal behaviour was then interpreted as symptomatic of mental illness, see D. L. Rosenhan, 'On being sane in insane places', *Science*, 179 (1973), 250–8.

40 'Theft of language' arose commonly in the asylums. See Mark Finnane, *Insanity and the Insane in Post-Famine Ireland* (London, 1981), p. 195.

41 E. Storey, *Right to Song*, p. 288.

42 Ibid. p. 295; Grigson, *Poems and Poets*, p. 122.

43 Foss and Trick, *St Andrew's Hospital Northampton*, p. 137.

44 E. Storey, *Right to Song*, pp. 269–70. For Tennyson's early career of severe emotional instability, see R. B. Martin, *Tennyson: The Unquiet Heart* (Oxford, 1980).

CHAPTER 12

Clare and 'the Dark System'

Marilyn Gaull

Among his autobiographical writings, Clare left the following comments on his learning:

As to my learning, I am not so wonderfully deep in science nor so wonderfully ignorant as many may have fancied from reading the accounts which my friends gave of me if I was to brag of it I might like the village schoolmaster boast of knowing a little of everything a jack of all trades and master of none I puzzled over every thing in my hours of leisure that came in my way Mathematics Astronomy Botany and other things with a restless curiosity that was ever on the enquiry and never satisfied and when I got set fast with one thing I did not tire but tryed at another tho with the same success in the end yet it never sickened me I still pursued Knowledge in a new path and tho I never came off with victories I was never conqurd[1]

Though Clare claims not to be 'wonderfully deep in science', fuller understanding of the drastic transformation of all the sciences during the period Clare was writing, and in particular of the new intellectual developments associated with the decade of his birth, the 1790s, might help place his poetry and his interest in natural history within a historical context. Knowledge of that scientific context, and the crisis it represented for all presuppositions about the 'natural' world, helps clarify Clare's preoccupation with his own local firsthand knowledge of nature, his scepticism about botany (the science he was most immediately engaged with), and his larger anxieties about his place in the world and what he called in the poem of that name 'The Eternity of Nature'. In this essay I want to evoke the scale of the scientific and intellectual changes that loomed so large in Clare's time and to suggest how his pursuit of 'Knowledge in a new path' might be seen as offering a response to what he called, in one of his autobiographical fragments, the 'dark system' offered by contemporary science (though he was reacting specifically to Linnaean botany).

Before 1830, it would not have been unusual for a self-educated
farm labourer to puzzle over mathematics in his leisure time, or
astronomy, botany or geology as well, for not only was recreational
science common among the lower classes, even among the illiterate
labouring classes, but also it was from among these people that the
most original ideas and most of the instrumentation of science were
generated.[2] The founding of the British Institution, however, along
with several other events around 1830, marked the professionalisation
of science as a whole just as the specific learned societies in geology,
botany and mathematics, for example, had been professionalising the
individual scientific disciplines from the turn of the century.[3] Such
professionalisation meant that that these sciences were no longer
open to anyone who was interested; standards of education,
performance and so on were established, specialised vocabularies
evolved, and the dilettantes who had dominated the Royal Society
and the provincial learned societies such as in Birmingham and
Sheffield, had to find other ways of fulfilling whatever social, political,
economic or intellectual needs had kept them involved in the study of
contemporary science. Whatever agenda the new professional
organisations had, they were always single-minded and disinterested.
Yet, for about thirty years at the beginning of the century, the
sciences, especially those associated with the 1790s, the *fin de siècle*,
remained popular and recreational. The scientists themselves,
William Herschel, James Hutton, Joseph Priestley, William Hunter
and Erasmus Darwin, to name a few – a German musician, a Scottish
farmer, a dissenting minister, an anatomist and a provincial doctor
– some poor and self-educated, all marginal and independent were in
many ways much like Clare. Yet, through some alchemy of time,
perspective, personality, genius and chance, looking at different
facets of the universe, these modest but determined men articulated
theories that would change all future conceptions of time, space, life
itself.[4]

However different, they all inherited a universe suffused with
spiritual meaning, a theologically defined universe, static, complete,
orderly, perfectly suited as a stage for human life. Collectively but
separately, they envisioned in its place a universe in process, secular,
timeless, asymmetrical, indifferent at best, even inhospitable to
human life, a universe in which human history and natural history
were not only separate but irreconcilable, and spiritual history
irrelevant. All of their work helped to undermine Newton, the

Newtonian universe and the political status quo – the elitist, aristocratic political system which Newton's universe validated.

Some of the reasons for the popularity of this new science, however, had nothing to do with the values it represented. First, it was accessible: for the entire period when Sir Joseph Banks, a naturalist, was President of the Royal Society, science tended to be non-mathematical. Second, in this first great age of publication, contemporary science appeared in magazines and reviews alongside sermons, poems, fashions, history and fiction. Clare himself, in 1825, published lyrics, sonnets and a poem to the memory of Robert Bloomfield in a magazine called *The Scientific Receptacle: A Literary, Mathematical and Philosophical Repository*. Third, some of the most advanced scientific theories were offered as entertainment in demonstrations and performances on the same platforms as lectures on literature and art. Constable, for example, lectured on the history of landscape painting at the Literary and Scientific Society of Hampstead and at the Royal Institution, where Davy lectured on laughing gas and Coleridge on Shakespeare. Adam Walker, who was to be Shelley's teacher, lectured on astronomy in the theatre during Passion Week, before Easter, when no dramatic performances were allowed. Edmund Burke, Boswell and Blake attended William Hunter's dissections and lectures on anatomy, though only Blake had a professional interest. In fact, scientific performances offered some very radical ideas at a time when the theatre was still carefully censored. Finally, some sciences, such as geology or ornithology, required field trips that became acceptable social occasions for men and women to meet.

The language of these sciences was the vernacular, the common language of common man, as Wordsworth would describe the language of his poetry in his preface to *Lyrical Ballads*, the analogies familiar and domestic. When Herschel, for example, wanted to describe the evolution of stars, he compared it with a garden, an image Erasmus Darwin used for *The Botanic Garden*, an encyclopaedic survey of contemporary theories of nature. If the scientists used a common language, it was because, like Wordsworth and so many of his contemporaries, they were dealing with common things: earth, air, stars and bodies, empirically not philosophically or historically considered. They responded like artists or poets, again to draw on Wordsworth's preface to the *Lyrical Ballads*, to the 'charm of novelty' in nature, to the exceptional, the diverse, the unique, to the 'inexhaustible treasure' they found, once they overcame the inhibitions of the theologically defined universe. Their theories – from Adam Smith's *Wealth of Nations* to Charles Darwin's *Origin of Species*, the former an ancestor and the latter an heir of the science of the 1790s – were all about growth, renewal, increase, expansion, development, diversity, ideas that were immensely appealing to a popular audience who did not see the dark sub-texts we shall be discussing. The scientists themselves were known for their healthy, stable, convivial natures, a kind of 'philosophical hedonism', as Louis Feuer called it, that characterised the scientific intellectual in the eighteenth century, while poets were wracked by melancholy and despair.

We know that some attributed Clare's madness to his being a poet, and it was a Romantic commonplace that poets 'begin in gladness / But thereof come in the end despondency and madness', as Wordsworth claimed in 'Resolution and Independence' (lines 48–9), a plot many felt started with Chatterton. Part of the conventional therapy would have been the study of science: Coleridge recommended it for Wordsworth, and Wordsworth himself found in geometry 'Enough to exalt, to cheer me and compose', 'A pleasure calm and deeper, a still sense / Of permanent and universal sway' (*Prelude*, Book VI, 121, 130–1).

> Mighty is the charm
> Of those abstractions to a mind beset
> With images, and haunted by itself   (*Prelude*, VI, 158–60)

So, having as haunted a mind as any other poet and as much curiosity as any other literate farm labourer, it is not surprising that Clare read mathematics, astronomy and botany, and, since he collected fossils, probably geology as well among the 'other things' he encountered in his 'restless curiosity'. Given the therapeutic value associated with the study of science, especially for poets, his conclusion is surprising: 'yet it never sickened me'. Between Coleridge's advice to Wordsworth to steady his mind by studying chemistry and Clare's autobiographical notes, a great shift had taken place in the image of science and the scientist. The happy, rational and sane scientist associated with the certainties of the Newtonian universe had been replaced by the demonised, crazed scientist epitomised by Mary Shelley's Dr Frankenstein; or, if not crazed, then someone whose aesthetic sense had to be anaesthetised, for the vision of the new science was so threatening that a scientist could not, like Darwin, afford to feel[5] – a state that Coleridge described in 'Dejection: An Ode', and attributed to poetry.

It is in the implication more than the content of these sciences that the great threat to sanity lay. However objective, they implied a new self-conception; however impersonal, a displacement of human life in the universe. Mathematics, for example, the first of the sciences Clare mentioned, had been harmless if not therapeutic as Wordsworth claimed.[6] It had for at least a hundred years been the favoured hobby of the labouring classes: in 1717, the artisans had formed the first mathematical society in Spitalfields; it survived with no less than 200 members until 1845, when the members, by then all aristocrats, dissolved it and contributed the library to a Mechanics Institute. The artisans and later the industrialists who employed them had to learn a number of subtle mathematical skills fairly quickly to adapt to the changes in the economy. They had to learn to convert time to money, labour into reward, and then into things, provisions. They needed to weigh, measure, count and calculate, and they became interested in surveys – of prisons, poverty, disease – or catalogues and inventories. Along with the counting came a sense of excess, of more: more people (as the first census published in 1801 revealed), more money (as the first income tax of 1798 demonstrated), more sheep, land, weather, more misery and vice that Malthus claimed kept the population in check. To some, the wealth of nations was not labour, as Adam Smith claimed, but the simple excess that labour created, another dark system.

Less threatening mathematical truths were explored by the other great class of people who kept mathematics alive, the middle-class ladies such as Annabella Milbanke, Lord Byron's ill-fated bride. From about 1704 to 1841, the most popular mathematical publication was *The Ladies Diary*. Every year it published an enigma or mathematical problem, often in verse, a competition that drew up to 500 replies at a time, some of them by men using female names. In 1807, *The Edinburgh Review* complained that the reason mathematics languished in the university was because the best talents were being used to solve problems in *The Ladies Diary*.

However, there were other and more convincing reasons why mathematics was languishing on a professional level as well as in the universities. First, astronomy, geology and the social sciences were producing problems that could not be solved by Newtonian or classical mathematics. Indeed, as we have seen, most of the sciences were non-mathematical primarily because existing systems of computation were not suited to the uncountable, the unaccountable, the infinite, the boundless universe that scientists were encountering. Karl Gauss, the German mathematician originally rejected these sciences, protesting, as he wrote: 'against the use of infinite magnitude which is never permissable in mathematics'. Yet, by 1792, Gauss was the first to challenge Euclidean geometry and prove the unthinkable: that parallel lines could meet. Bolyai, in Hungary in 1823, also proved it and concluded that he had 'created a new and another world'. The phrase itself is interesting since the new maths was in fact a new world, a world of conceptual as opposed to physical space. That space, like the inner space that artists would eventually talk about, had its own private rules, irrational or imaginary numbers rejected by traditional mathematicians, a kind of mystery, privacy that recalled the mysteries cultivated by the original Pythagoreans. As soon as it lost that common ground, the predictability of Newtonian or Euclidean systems, then mathematics also lost its identification with sanity, health, rationality, its therapeutic or even recreational role. It was clearly moving in that direction when Clare admitted to dabbling in it and was happy to have escaped without being 'sickened'.

These changes in mathematics were in part provoked by changes in astronomy and geology, both of which had also affirmed the stability, permanence and predictability of nature, and the rationality of those who studied them. Following the physico-theologians of the early decades of the eighteenth century, most of the natural philosophers who studied the earth and the stars agreed that the universe had been created by a rational and loving God who, on 25 October 4004 BC according to Bishop Ussher, in a spirit of plenitude created everything that could exist and has sustained all beings so that nothing could disappear, until at least the seventh millennium (in 1996), when the world would end. Emmanuel Swedenborg, a quite respectable geologist before his religious conversion, proposed in 1735 that the universe had come into being from an explosion caused by the compression of gases, an explosion so vast that it was still taking place.[7] Emmanuel Kant adapted this theory in his *Universal History and Theory of Heavens* in 1755, and Herschel, a German musician and instrument-maker living in England, whose hobby was studying the stars, adopted it and presented it in a series of papers before the Royal Society in 1784.[8] In place of the dome-like universe with evenly distributed stars, Herschel proposed a universe that was 'fathomless' and timeless as well. If the universe were as large as he inferred from his observations, if the stars, planets and galaxies were as remote as he believed, then, even using Newton's calculations, he concluded, it would have taken longer than the 6,000 years in Ussher's chronology merely for the light to have travelled to the earth so that they could be seen. If celestial bodies, he explained, 'ceased to exist millions of years ago, we should still see them as the light did travel after the body was gone'.[9] The universe was not at all complete and never would be: some things had indeed expired and some were yet to be born – but whatever one saw in the sky was already history, a history far older than the world as it was conventionally believed to have existed: 'Time,' Herschel concluded, 'which measures everything in our ideas, and is often deficient in our schemes, is to nature endless and as nothing.'

Herschel's influence was limited initially because, like so many of the original thinkers of the eighteenth century, he was an outsider, a small, untidy and impoverished musician with a German accent, who supported himself by conducting small orchestras, a bachelor until his fifties who lived with his maiden sister, slept during the day and spent his nights (after rubbing his body with onions to protect himself against the cold), peering through home-made instruments at a sky that everyone thought they already knew. More than the distinguished gentlemen in the Royal Society, he resembled the Druids of popular literature, depicted by Southey in *Madoc* for example. Lord Brougham had compared him to the paranoid residents of Laputa in *Gulliver's Travels* who governed their lives by the stars but had no practical knowledge. Nor did it contribute to his reputation for sanity to be the favourite of George III, who hired him as a full-time court astronomer to remain on call at Windsor, and claimed to have seen some of his hallucinatory visions through his telescope. Thomas Campbell met the 76-year-old Herschel and found 'a great, simple, good old man': 'I felt', he wrote, 'as if I had been conversing with a supernatural intelligence'.[10] His theories were gradually assimilated into the world of science, and his ideas of time and space found support in geology and palaeontology. Yet while science profited from the liberalising ideas of Herschel's universe, literature and the arts were deprived of an important set of symbols and the values they represented.

Initially, because of the explosive, mysterious, awesome and expansive nature of Herschel's theory, it was aesthetically acceptable, another expression of the taste for the sublime associated with the French Revolution. Moreover, in a period that generated creation myths such as Blake's or Keats's, at the very least it could be considered another interesting fiction. Herschel himself, having, like Swedenborg, envisioned an impersonal, secular, mindless universe, invented a complex array of extra-terrestrial creatures to humanise it, an activity that many people after him found necessary as well as entertaining. Irreconcilable to conventional theological concepts of *heaven* as simple *space*, the new cosmology was extremely provocative to the creative imagination. Yet still, for poets – melancholy, unstable, anxious, subject to emotional upheavals as cataclysmic as Herschel's universe – for poets such as Keats, Coleridge, Shelley or Clare – the conventional cosmology provided points of reference, stability, serenity, such as Keats described in 'Bright Star'. Consequently, that image of the stars survived in literature long after science had discredited it. All the more admirable, then, is Clare's ability to study contemporary astronomy, as he claimed, and not be 'sickened' by it.

It is fascinating to consider the dinner in 1791 in Edinburgh where Herschel met his geological counterpart, James Hutton, only three years after this challenge to biblical chronology presented at the Edinburgh Philosophical Society.[10] The most popular conception of the earth when Hutton began his speculations was defined at the end of the seventeenth century by Thomas Burnet in *Sacred Theory of the Earth* and refined in the early decades of the eighteenth century by other physico-theologists. In Burnet's version, God had created a symmetrical, round, smooth world covered with a thin crust enclosing a subterranean ocean. It was designed to be a paradise where people could live to be very ancient in great peace and comfort. Eventually, the surface of the earth collapsed under the weight of sin, releasing the inner waters (an event often identified with the biblical account of the Flood), and creating the irregularities of nature: the mountains, caves, winding rivers, wandering shorelines, odd plants, slimy animals, all the ugly, prickly, fractured things, leaving the world 'lying in its own Rubbish', a monument to human sin and divine power.

Burnet's vision was especially appealing to earth scientists for it reconciled the idea of the Flood with certain features they recognised on the surface of the earth. Abraham Werner, a German mineralogist, gave it a scientific turn with a theory that was so appealing that, as late as 1811, a Wernerian Society with as many as 250 distinguished members was meeting regularly in London to debate not whether there had been a Flood as described in the Bible, but whether the water had come from within as Burnet had claimed or from without as Werner did. Werner had proposed in 1775 that the water was originally on the outside, that the earth had been soaking in a saline bath out of which four or five layers of sediment had settled, disturbed by periods of upheaval and turbulence. The theory, which did not contradict Genesis or the chronology of creation, did account for various strata of the earth and the odd distribution of fossil remains such as sea-shells in the mountains. Werner's disciples were called Neptunists; his challengers, those who believed that the earth was shaped by heat were called Vulcanists or Plutonists – the titles an expression of the mythic revival in which artists, poets and historians were then deeply engaged. It was a theory that was easily reconciled with the aesthetics as well as the theology of the day.

Hutton had set out in life to be a lawyer, then a doctor, finally settling into the role of gentleman farmer in the unyielding fields of Scotland. It was while he was travelling over the countryside observing the distribution of arable land that he evolved his theory of landscape and that in turn became a theory of creation. He assumed that the laws operating around him were the same as those that had created the earth and were still creating it: the wind and rain eroded the hills, sediments washed into the sea, compacted into rocks, rearranged into valleys and hills, upset by an occasional trauma such as an earthquake or a volcanic eruption, an expression of the shaping power of subterranean fires, the energy contained within the earth. From the patterns of change, decay, renewal, death and rebirth, of constant activity that served to sustain the earth, to renew it, to increase the possibilities for life, he developed an ecological system to replace a moral one, a system that, like Herschel's, replaced 6,000 years of earth history with a staggering tract of unaccountable time:

Having in the natural history of the earth seen a succession of worlds, we may from this conclude that there is a system in nature; in like manner as from seeing revolutions of the planets…there is a system by which they are intended to continue these revolutions…The result, therefore, of our present inquiry is, that we find no vestige of a beginning – no prospect of an end.

For scientists and historians, he shifted the focus of discussion from origins to history, to the processes of nature, and contributed to that same secularisation of the natural world, its liberation, as Herschel. This secularisation was necessary for science but it would present serious challenges to poets, or at least to some poets. For others, including the mad William Blake, it offered a literalisation of their own creation myth: the fires within the earth that to orthodox Christians represented Hell, the symbol of a repressive and punitive God, the eternal destination of those who rebel, were to Hutton, as they were to Blake, a major creative force, eternal energy, 'eternal delight'.

First published as *Theory of the Earth with Proofs and Illustrations* in 1795, then disseminated to the public in John Playfair's *Illustrations of the Huttonian Theory* in 1802, Hutton's work initiated what has been called the 'golden' or 'heroic' age of geology. Yet Hutton had few advocates, for his ideas were eccentric, his writing obscure and, like Herschel, he did not account for the human implications of his ideas. To him, the theory was inspiring: 'Why refuse to see' he asked in *Theory of the Earth*:

in this construction of things, that wisdom of contrivance, that beautiful provision which is so evident, whether we look up into the great expanse of boundless space where luminous bodies without number are placed, and where, in all probability, still more numerous bodies are perpetually moving and illuminated for some great end; or whether we turn our prospect towards ourselves, and see the exquisite mechanism and active powers of things, growing from a state apparently of non-existence, decaying from their state of natural perfection and renovating their existence in a succession of similar beings to which we see no end. (II, 46–469)

Like the *Origin of Species*, a grand and optimistic reading of *natural* history becomes a terrifying negation of individual human life when applied to *human* history. Hutton proposes that the earth was not created for the pleasure and profit of human beings, that it occurred long before human life began, that individual human beings are aliens, strangers passing through, irrelevant to the impersonal forces that govern nature, its 'calm oblivious tendencies', as Wordsworth called them in 'The Ruined Cottage' – a poem I have often felt captured the human dimensions of the world as conceived by Hutton and Malthus as well. Even Byron, the most sceptical of the writers, expressed the sense of deprivation that Hutton's universe created:

If according to some speculations – you could prove the world many thousands years older than the Mosaic Chronology – or if you could knock up Adam and Eve and the Apple and the Serpent – still what is to be put up in their stead? – or how is the difficulty removed? things must have had a beginning – and what matters is *when* or *how*? ... a Creator is a more natural imagination than a fortuitous concourse of atoms[12]

Because the human implications of his theory were so repugnant, because it deprived people of individual worth, of place and of divine purpose, and because the consolation he found in it was insufficient for the deprivations it implied, but mostly because the mechanisms he described were inadequate to account for the effects he studied, Hutton was not vindicated for thirty years, not until Charles Lyell put it all together in *The Principles of Geology* (1830–3), 'by which time', Carlyle complained in *Sartor Resartus* (1833) 'the reading public was satiated with creation theory... what with the labours of our Werners and Huttons, what with the ardent genius of their disciples, it has come about that now to many a Royal Society, the Creation of a World is little more mysterious than the cooking of a dumpling'.

One geological theory, Catastrophism, which overshadowed Hutton's for all those thirty years, affirmed creationism and encouraged the fossil-hunting that Clare said he was fond of – although his mother, like all mothers, threw his stones away (*Autobiographical Writings*, p. 49). Starting with Burnet, Werner and culminating in Baron Cuvier, several generations of geologists argued that the irregular surface of the earth, the odd distribution of shells and minerals, were evidence of periodic divine intervention in which God, dissatisfied with his creation, destroyed it and, as Burnet claimed, either left it in ruins or built a new world, the last and best being the present world that included human beings. This Catastrophic geology not only reconciled the reading of the landscape with the reading of the Bible but it also appealed, like Herschel's astronomy, to that taste for the sublime associated with the gothic. Indeed, the concept was itself rather gothic for it turned the earth into a huge graveyard of destroyed and forgotten things, a monument to sin, to God's wrath and power. Along with archaeological digs in search of Roman Britain (to which Clare refers when he finds some landsnails in a ditch beside a Roman road), fossil-hunting became increasingly popular, especially after William Smith, a drainage engineer working for a coal company, concluded that the distinct strata he discovered represented different creations that could be identified by the fossil remains. Fossils, then, were geological relics, bringing the collector close to some archaic time, to the mysterious event when God, full of rage or misgivings, replaced one creation with another. After Baron Cuvier's *Theory of the Earth* was translated into English in 1817, the whole thing took on a rather gruesome perspective, shifting interest from shells to bones and proposing that whole species had been violently destroyed, and the earth was a huge 'charnel house'. While fossil-hunting may have provided both pious and social occasions for exploring the landscape, its implications were threatening, its idea of divinity brutal, its God vindictive, volatile and prone to error, providing no comfort to the melancholic such as Clare.

As an agricultural labourer, Clare was most involved with botany among the contemporary sciences, and like every other area of natural history, botany was entering into the modern age.[13] Clare was in the first generation of poets to know about photosynthesis, that human beings are part of an ecosystem, that like animals, insects and birds, human beings are dependent on plants, on green and growing things, not only for the food they eat but for the air they breathe and all that it symbolised. Explained and popularised, as nearly all the sciences were, by Erasmus Darwin, photosynthesis seemed to be especially amenable to contemporary philosophy and theology, the only theory that could support a homocentric universe. Unfortunately, most writers were repulsed by it. While a poet such as Coleridge could in 1793 celebrate on a spiritual level 'the one Life within us and abroad' ('The Aeolian Harp', 26), he was silent on photosynthesis, a nearly literal reading of it, until he produced an obscure passage in the *Statesman Manual* written in 1816, when he expressed its powers on a metaphysical level. Among the radical sciences of the 1790s, photosynthesis offered the most convincing proof of a totally self-sufficient natural world in which there was no ladder, no chain, no hierarchy of being, merely a demonstrable interchange of air, life and power, in which human beings were dependent upon the landscape they had believed they were born to master, to own, dependent on the same grass as the sheep. Even scientifically literate poets such as Shelley, and literary scientists such as the distinguished Sir Humphry Davy found this new order of nature repugnant and rejected it. For Clare, silent as well, it was probably another of those contemporary ideas in science that he was pleased not to have been sickened by.

Clare preferred descriptive anecdotal natural history:

I love to see the nightingale in its hazel retreat & the Cuckoo hiding in its solitudes of oaken foliage & not to examine their carcasses in glass cases yet naturalists & botanists seem to have no taste for this poetical feeling they merely make collections of dryd specimens classing them after Leanius into tribes and families... I have none of this curiosity (Grainger, *Natural History Prose Writings*, p. 38)

At another time, he was even less generous to Linnaeus; he considered the time he spent puzzling over the taxonomy as 'wasted'. It would take 'a second Adam', he wrote, to find the names for plants peculiar to his neighbourhood and 'a second Solomon' to understand them: 'modern works are so mystified by systematic symbols that one cannot understand them till the wrong end of ones lifetime'. It was, he said, 'a dark system' he abandoned in dissatisfaction (*Autobiographical Fragments*, p. 49). Given the stark implications of the other sciences, there were many good reasons to recommend Linnaeus for the stabilising influence of collecting, sorting, classifying and preserving – except that Linnaeus's system required isolating plants, taking them out of their environment just as Clare was removed, first to Northborough and then to the asylum. Clare understood the definitive value of environment, context. Moreover, Linnaeus introduced more than a system of confusing names; his preoccupation with sexuality was considered prurient and confusing in its social analogies. Finally, Linnaeus himself, for all the rationality of his system, lost his reason: having identified countless rare specimens, he could not recognise his own book; having named so much of creation, he could not even remember his own name.

The model Clare chose was Gilbert White's *Natural History of Selborne*, published in 1789, the last major work to be published before the new sciences – Herschel's astronomy, Hutton's geology and Priestley's formulation of photosynthesis – had any impact on the way the world was viewed. In the very same year, 1789, Erasmus Darwin published *The Loves of Plants*, the first in a series of heavily footnoted and richly rhymed encyclopaedic poems that would explain and popularise these same contemporary sciences. Together this unlikely pair became the ancestors not only for Clare's understanding of the sciences but for his contemporary, Charles

Darwin, who also considered himself a natural historian and, like
Clare, had an absorbing interest in climbing plants. However, unlike
Clare, he was 'sickened' by contemporary science, losing his aesthetic
interests, his love of music, of scenery, of Shakespeare, Byron and
Wordsworth, and withdrawing from the social world he enjoyed.
The more he studied, the more reclusive he became, an invalid
plagued with mysterious nervous disorders.[14]

The common theme is the sickness. In the world of White and
Erasmus Darwin, mad poets were not only commonplace but
encouraged. Deranged by their imaginations, they enunciated the
unspeakable, everything that was irrational, dark, impassioned.
Blake, Cowper, definitively mad; Coleridge, De Quincey, Keats,
intoxicated, self-induced madness; Chatterton, despondent enough
to commit suicide; and Byron, sufficiently eccentric to be accused of
madness whether he was or not. Yet at the same time, as Roy Porter
has brilliantly pointed out, the idea emerges of the poets as prophets,
saviours, supremely healthy, bringing with them what Wordsworth
called 'relationship and love', recording as Shelley claimed 'the best
and happiest moments of the best and happiest minds', uplifting and
socially responsible. 'As insanity increasingly became stigmatized',
Porter explains, 'poets severed their connections with madness and
psychiatry came to deny that the words of the mad had any
meaning'.[15] In fact, it was a therapeutic commonplace to discourage
the emotionally troubled from writing at all, to prevent them from
over-stimulating the imagination with fiction and poetry. If the poets
were now the 'unacknowledged legislators of the world', it was the
scientists who had become the madmen.

The science Humphry Davy described, in 1802 in his *Discourse,
Introductory to a Course of Lectures* that would 'destroy diseases of the
imagination, owing to too deep a sensibility', the science that was
supposed to 'attach the affections to objects permanent, important,
and intimately related to the interests of the human species', had by
1830 revealed an appalling world of conflict, change, darkness,
mindlessness, unimaginable time, speed, destruction, in which
human needs were irrelevant; a world where, if one were lucky, one
would not be sickened by studying it. It was also in 1830 that the
British Association recognised the analogues between the creative
processes in art and in science by coining the term 'scientist' as an
analogue to 'artist'. By then, however, artists were pursuing the
sanity of science (not just the poets, but the painters as well,

Constable and Turner especially) and the scientists were encountering the madness of art, the unpredictable and unaccountable if
not the unacceptable. As Darwin's life illustrates, in poetry was the
therapy, in science the disease. The conclusion is Clare's: 'Life lives
by changing places'.[16]

NOTES

1 Eric Robinson (ed.), *John Clare's Autobiographical Writings* (Oxford,
1983), pp. 46–7. For all quotations from poets, I have used standard
editions, and from prose of the scientists, first editions courtesy of the
American Philosophical Society. For Clare's natural history writings, I
used Margaret Grainger's edition *The Natural History Prose Writings of
John Clare* (Oxford, 1983), and for the poetry, Summerfield's Penguin
edition – Geoffrey Summerfield (ed.), *Selected Poetry*, (Harmondsworth,
1990).

2 For an introduction to science during the period, especially in its literary
context, Marilyn Gaull, *English Romanticism: The Human Context* (New
York, London, 1988), Chapters VIII and XIII, bibliography, pp.
411–16. The ideas are extended and the bibliography updated in
'Coleridge and the kingdoms of the world', *The Wordsworth Circle*, 22
(1991), 47–52, to which should be added David M. Knight, *Natural
Science Books in English: 1600–1900* (London, 1972).

3 Roy Porter and William Bynum, *William Hunter and the Eighteenth Century
Medical World* (Cambridge, 1985).

4 Louis Feuer, *The Scientific Intellectual: The Psychological and Sociological
Origins of Modern Science* (New York, London, 1963); Lionel Trilling,
'The fate of pleasure', *Beyond Culture* (London, 1966).

5 Donald Fleming, 'Charles Darwin, the anaesthetic man', *Victorian
Studies*, 4 (1961), 219–36; Howard E. Gruber, *Darwin on Man: A
Psychological Study of Scientific Creativity*, trans. Paul H. Barrett (London,
1974).

6 For history, bibliography and more complete exploration of mathematics from 1760–1830, Gaull 'Romantic numeracy: the "tuneless
numbers" and "shadows numberless"', *The Wordsworth Circle*, 22
(1991), 124–30; and Jacques Hadamard, *An Essay on the Psychology of
Invention in the Mathematic Fields* (1964).

7 Charles Coulston Gillispie, *Genesis and Geology: The Impact of Scientific
Discoveries upon Religious Beliefs in the Decades before Darwin* (Cambridge,
Mass., 1959); Roy Porter, *The Making of Geology: Earth Science in Britain,
1660–1815* (Cambridge, 1977); Stephen J. Gould, *Time's Arrow, Time's
Cycle* (Cambridge, Mass., 1987).

8 Michael Hoskin, *William Herschel and the Construction of the Heavens*
(London, 1963); Constance A. Lubbock (ed.), *The Herschel Chronicle:
The Life Story of William Herschel and His Sister Caroline* (Cambridge,

294 MARILYN GAULL

1933); and for history and bibliography in astronomy, see Gaull 'Under Romantic skies: astronomy and the poets', *The Wordsworth Circle*, 21 (1990), 34–42.

9 Lusbock, *The Herschel Chronicle*, p. 376.
10 Ibid. p. 336.
11 Loren Eisley, *Darwin's Century: Evolution and the Men Who Discovered It* (1961), pp. 57–91.
12 Lord Byron, *Letters and Journals*, ed. Leslie A. Marchand, IX, 46–7, October 1821 and May 1822.
13 David E. Allen, *The Naturalist in Britain* (London, 1976); Paul L. Farber, 'The transformation of natural history in the nineteenth century', *Journal of the History of Biology*, 15 (1982), 145–52.
14 Adrian Desmond and James Moore, *Darwin* (Harmondsworth, 1991); Edward Manier, *The Young Darwin and His Cultural Circle* (1978); Gaull, 'From Wordsworth to Darwin', *The Wordsworth Circle*, 10 (1979), 33–48.
15 Roy Porter, 'Bedlam and Parnassus: mad people's writing in Georgian England', in George Levine (ed.), *One Culture: Essays in Science and Literature* (Madison, 1987), p. 279; Porter, *Mind-forged Manacles: a history of madness in England from the Restoration to the Regency* (Harmondsworth, 1990); *A Social History of Madness* (London, 1989).
16 Summerfield, *Selected Poetry*, p. 213.

Selected further reading

1 EDITIONS

Clare, John, *Poems Descriptive of Rural Life and Scenery*, printed for Taylor and Hessey, Fleet Street, London and E. Drury, Stamford, 1820. (4th edn, revised, 1821.)

The Village Minstrel and Other Poems, printed for Taylor and Hessey, and E. Drury, 2 vols., London, 1821. (2nd issue, 1823.)

The Shepherd's Calendar; with Village Stories, and Other Poems, published for John Taylor by James Duncan, London, 1827.

The Rural Muse, Poems, Whittaker and Co, London, 1835.

Blunden, Edmund (ed.), *Madrigals and Chronicles* being newly found poems by John Clare, with a preface and commentary by Edmund Blunden, London, 1924.

Sketches in the Life of John Clare by Himself, with an introduction, notes and additions by Edmund Blunden, London, 1931.

Blunden, Edmund and Alan Porter (eds.), *John Clare: Poems Chiefly from Manuscript*, with an introduction by Edmund Blunden, London, 1920. The first modern edition to return to original manuscripts.

Cherry, J. L., *Life and Remains of John Clare*, London, 1873. A brief biographical account of Clare, introducing the first posthumous edition of his poetry.

Feinstein, Elaine (ed.), *John Clare: Selected Poems*, London, 1968. A brief selection, with a perceptive introduction.

Gale, Norman (ed.), *Poems by John Clare*, with an introduction by Norman Gale and a bibliography by C. Ernest Smith, Rugby, 1901.

Grainger, Margaret (ed.), *The Natural History Prose Writings of John Clare*, Oxford, 1983. A meticulous and full edition of Clare's 'Natural History Letters' and miscellaneous writings about the natural world.

Grigson, Geoffrey (ed.), *Poems of John Clare's Madness*, London, 1949. The first modern edition of the asylum poems to contextualise them and offer a searching psychological reading of them as well as a reading text. It is described by Robinson and Summerfield as 'textually a very unreliable edition'.

Selected Poems of John Clare, with an introduction by Geoffrey Grigson, London, 1950.

Robinson, Eric (ed.), *The Parish*, Harmondsworth, 1985. A modern edition of Clare's unpublished satire written between 1822–4, with a useful introduction which sets it in context.

John Clare's Autobiographical Writings, Oxford, 1983. This includes 'Sketches in the life of John Clare' and 'The Journey out of Essex' along with collected autobiographical fragments.

The Summons, Market Drayton, 1989; *The Hue and Cry: A Tale of the Times*, Market Drayton, 1990. The first reprintings of political broadsides Clare published in *Drakard's Stamford News* and the *Stamford Champion*, 1829–31.

Robinson, Eric and David Powell (eds.), *John Clare*, The Oxford Authors, Oxford, 1984. The fullest representative modern one-volume selection of Clare's poetry and prose, based on the principle of literal fidelity to the poet's manuscripts established in the projected collected edition and organised on a largely chronological basis: 'Poems of the Helpston Period', 'Poems of the Northborough Period' and 'Poems written in Epping Forest and Northampton'. However, separate sections are given over to 'Bird poems' and 'Animal poems' which, while increasing thematic continuity, drastically disrupts the chronological continuity of the volume.

The Later Poetry of John Clare: 1837–1864, 2 vols., Oxford, 1984. Part of the projected Oxford collected edition of Clare under the general editorship of Eric Robinson, and including all the known verse written by Clare during the asylum years. An indispensable scholarly edition. Largely based on the transcripts made by William Knight and other amanuenses at Northampton, it emends the Knight punctuation in an attempt to get closer to Clare's lost manuscripts.

The Early Poems of John Clare 1804–1822, Volumes I and II, Oxford, 1989.

Robinson, Eric and Geoffrey Summerfield (eds.), *The Later Poems of John Clare*, Manchester, 1964. Described by the editors as 'an attempt to present Clare's work of the asylum years in the form in which he wrote it'.

Clare: The Selected Poems and Prose, Oxford, 1966. An attractive, small-scale anthology based on the editors' projected Clare edition for Oxford.

John Clare: The Shepherd's Calendar, with wood engravings by David Gentleman, London, Oxford, New York, 1964. A magnificent restoration of 'Clare's most ambitious single poem', cleaned of John Taylor's editorial interventions.

Storey, Mark (ed.), *The Letters of John Clare*, Oxford, 1985. A fully annotated edition of all of Clare's letters to have survived, and also 22 letters to Clare. With 472 letters, it includes more than 200 new items not included in the earlier edition of the letters edited by the Tibbles.

John Clare: Selected Letters, Oxford, 1988. A selection from the complete edition.

Summerfield, Geoffrey (ed.), *John Clare, Selected Poetry*, Harmondsworth, 1990. A generous non-chronological selection of Clare's work, arranged by subject-matter, and based on the principle of fidelity to the original manuscripts adopted by Robinson and Summerfield in their earlier editions, but now qualified by a commitment to providing an easily accessible text for a modern reader. While Clare's dialect and grammar are respected, his punctuation and sometimes spelling and capitalisation have been modified by the editor 'where the idiosyncracies of Clare's manuscripts distract the reader'.

Symons, Arthur (ed.), *Poems by John Clare*, with an introduction by Arthur Symons, London, 1908.

Thornton, R. K. R. (ed.), *The Rural Muse, Poems by John Clare*, Ashington, Northumberland, 1982. A second edition of Clare's volume of 1835, edited by R. K. R. Thornton from the original manuscript, with an essay on Clare's language by Barbara Strang. A modern edition of Clare's last book and a companion to *The Midsummer Cushion*. With the Robinson and Summerfield *The Shepherd's Calendar* (which, however, deletes the 'Tales' included in the original volume), this is the only recent edition to republish one of the four books Clare actually published in his lifetime, though based on Clare's manuscript rather than the original published edition.

Tibble, Anne (ed.), *John Clare: The Midsummer Cushion*, associate editor, R. K. R. Thornton, Ashington, Northumberland, 1979. The first publication of the book Clare devised and copied out between 1831 and 1832 and which he intended as his fourth book. A very much diminished selection from this, supervised by Eliza Emmerson, was published as *The Rural Muse* in 1835. As the modern editor notes, 'the resulting manuscript, *The Midsummer Cushion*, shows him to have been perfectly capable of editing his work without undue interference'. Divided up into 'To The Rural Muse', 'Tales', 'Poems', 'Ballads & Songs' and 'Sonnets', this is an invaluable modern restoration of the one collection of his own poetry completely within Clare's control but sadly never published in his lifetime.

John Clare: The Journals, Essays, and the Journey from Essex, Manchester, 1980.

Tibble, J. W. (ed.), *The Poems of John Clare*, with an introduction by J. W. Tibble, 2 vols., London, 1935. The first edition to print 'the bulk of the poems published during Clare's lifetime and after his death'. The editor however, acknowledges that 'poems still left in manuscript still outnumber all those included'. As far as the text goes, 'in the poems published after Clare's death and in all new poems, the manuscript versions have been faithfully followed save in the matter of punctuation and spelling'. This is the nearest thing to the first collected edition of Clare's poetry and a watershed in Clare scholarship. Owing to the editorial decisions identified above, however, it has been largely superseded.

Tibble, J. W. and Anne (eds.), *The Letters of John Clare*, London, 1951. The first edition of Clare's correspondence, comprising 249 letters.

The Prose of John Clare, London, 1951, reprinted 1970. This includes the autobiographical sketches, natural history prose, fragments of critical essays and 'The Journey out of Essex', but has been largely superseded by more modern editions.

John Clare: Selected Poems, 1965, reprinted 1975. A comprehensive selection based on the text of J. W. Tibble's 2-volume edition of 1935.

Williams, Merryn and Raymond (eds.), *John Clare: Selected Poetry and Prose*, London, New York, 1986. A vivid brief selection based largely on texts established by Eric Robinson and David Powell, or Eric Robinson and Geoffrey Summerfield, but with a vivid historical introduction by the editors.

2 FURTHER READING AND CRITICISM

Allen, David E., *The Naturalist in Britain: A Social History*, Harmondsworth, 1976.

Baker, A. E., *Glossary of Northampton Words and Phrases*, 2 vols., 1854.

Barrell, John, *The Idea of Landscape and the Sense of Place: 1730–1840: An Approach to the Poetry of John Clare*, Cambridge, 1972.

The Dark Side of the Landscape: The Rural Poor in English Painting 1730–1840, Cambridge, 1980.

'Being is perceiving: James Thomson and John Clare', in *Poetry, Language and Politics*, Manchester, 1988.

'John Clare, William Cobbett and the changing landscape', *From Blake to Byron*, New Pelican Guide to English Literature, ed. Boris Ford, Harmondsworth, 1982.

Barrell, John and John Bull (eds.) *The Penguin Book of Pastoral Verse*, London, 1975.

Bloom, Harold, 'John Clare: the Wordsworthian shadow' in *The Visionary Company: A Reading of Romantic Poetry*, New York, 1961, revised and enlarged edition, 1971.

Brownlow, Timothy, *John Clare and Picturesque Landscape*, Oxford, 1983.

Cherry, J. L., *Life and Remains of John Clare*, London, 1873.

Chilcott, Tim, *A Publisher and his Circle: The Life and Works of John Taylor, Keats's Publisher*, London, Boston, 1972.

'A Real World & Doubting Mind': A Critical Study of the Poetry of John Clare, Hull, 1985.

Clare, Johanne, *John Clare and the Bounds of Circumstance*, Kingston, Montreal, 1987.

Cobbett, William, *A Grammar of the English Language*, London, 1818. New edition, with an introduction by Robert Burchfield, Oxford, New York, 1984.

Constantine, David, 'Outside Eden: John Clare's descriptive poetry', *An*

Infinite Complexity: Essays in Romanticism, ed. J. R. Watson, Edinburgh, 1983.

Cosgrove, D. and S. Daniels (eds.), *The Iconography of Landscape*, Cambridge, 1988.

Crossan, Greg, *A Relish for Eternity: The Process of Divinization in the Poetry of John Clare*, Salzburg, 1976.

Deacon, George, *John Clare and the Folk Tradition*, London, 1983.

Dendurent, H. O., *John Clare: A Reference Guide*, Boston, Mass., 1978.

Foss, Arthur and Keith Trick, *St Andrew's Hospital Northampton: The First 150 Years (1838–1988)*, Cambridge, 1989.

Frosch, Thomas, 'The descriptive style of John Clare', *Studies in Romanticism*, 10, 137–49.

Grainger, Margaret (ed.), *A Descriptive Catalogue of the John Clare Collection in Peterborough Museum and Art Gallery*, Peterborough, 1973.

Graves, Robert, *The Crowning Privilege: Collected Essays on Poetry*, London, 1955.

Grigson, Geoffrey, *Poets in their Pride*, London, 1962.

Hammond, J. L. and Barbara, *The Village Labourer 1760–1960*, London, 1911.

Heaney, Seamus, 'In the country of convention: English pastoral verse', *Preoccupations: Selected Prose 1968–1978*, London, Boston, 1980.

Helsinger, Elizabeth, 'John Clare and the place of the Peasant Poet', *Critical Inquiry*, 13: 3 (Spring 1987), 509–31.

Hoskins, W. G., *The Makings of the English Landscape*, Harmondsworth, 1970.

Howard, William, *John Clare*, Boston, 1981.

Jack, Ian, 'Clare and the minor poets', *English Literature 1815–1832*, Oxford, 1963.

'Poems of John Clare's sanity', *Some British Romantics*, eds. James Logan, John Jordan and Northrop Frye, Columbus, Ohio, 1966.

John Clare Society *John Clare Society Journal*, 1982–. The official journal of the John Clare Society, published annually, is a valuable source of articles, essays and information about Clare. An index to the first ten numbers (1982–91), compiled by John Goodridge and Rowena Bryson, is to be found in Number 11 (July 1992).

Lucas, John, 'Peasants and outlaws: John Clare', in *England and Englishness: Ideas of Nationhood in English Poetry 1688–1900*, London, 1990, pp. 135–60.

'Revising Clare', *Romantic Revisions*, eds. Robert Brinkley and Keith Hanley, Cambridge, 1993.

Martin, Frederick, *The Life of John Clare*, 1865. Second edition, with an introduction and notes by Eric Robinson and Geoffrey Summerfield, London, Edinburgh, 1964.

McGann, Jerome, *The New Oxford Book of Romantic Period Verse*, Oxford, 1993.

Minor, Mark, 'John Clare and the Methodists: a reconsideration', *Studies in Romanticism*, 19 (Spring 1980), 31–50.

'Clare, Byron and the Bible: additional evidence from the asylum manuscripts', *Bulletin of Research in the Humanities*, 85 (1982), 104–26.

Paulin, Tom, 'John Clare in Babylon' in *Minotaur: Poetry and the Nation State*, London, Boston, 1992, pp. 47–55.

Pearce, Lynn, 'John Clare's "Child Harold"': a polyphonic reading', *Criticism*, 31: 2 (1989), 139–57.

Pinsky, Robert, 'That sweet man, John Clare', *The Rarer Action: essays in honor of Francis Fergusson*, New Brunswick, 1970. Revised and reprinted in Robert Pinsky, *The Situation of Poetry: Contemporary Poetry and Its Traditions*, Princeton, 1976.

Porter, Roy, *Mind-Forg'd Manacles: A History of Madness in England from the Restoration to the Regency*, Harmondsworth, 1987.

The Social History of Madness: Stories of the Insane, London, 1989.

Powell, David (ed.), *Catalogue of the John Clare Collection in the Northampton Public Library*, Northampton, 1964.

Robinson, Eric, 'Review of Johanne Clare, *The Bounds of Circumstance*', *Studies in Romanticism*, 28, (Winter 1989) 660–5.

Robinson, Eric and Geoffrey Summerfield, 'John Taylor's editing of *The Shepherd's Calendar*', *Review of English Studies*, new series, 14: 56, (1963).

Sales, Roger, 'John Clare and the politics of pastoral' in *English Literature in History 1780–1830: Pastoral and Politics*, London, 1983.

Storey, Edward, *A Right to Song: The Life of John Clare*, London, 1986.

Storey, Mark, *The Poetry of John Clare: A Critical Introduction*, London, Basingstoke, 1974.

Storey, Mark (ed.) *John Clare: The Critical Heritage*, London, 1973.

Strickland, Edward, 'Review of Eric Robinson and David Powell (eds.), *The Early Poems of John Clare*', *Studies in Romanticism*, no. 29 (Fall 1990), 507–14.

'Conventions and their subversion in John Clare's "An Invite to Eternity"', *Criticism*, 24 (Winter 1982).

Swingle, L. J., 'Stalking the essential John Clare: Clare in relation to his contemporaries', *Studies in Romanticism*, 14, 273–84.

Sychrava, Juliet, *Schiller to Derrida: Idealism in Aesthetics*, Cambridge, 1989.

Thomas, Keith, *Man and the Natural World: Changing Attitudes in England*, Harmondsworth, 1983.

Thompson, E. P., *The Making of the English Working Class*, Harmondsworth, 1968.

Customs in Common, new edn, Harmondsworth, 1993.

Tibble, J. W. and Anne, *John Clare: A Life*, Southampton, 1932; revised edn London, 1972). The first full-scale modern biography and still a useful reference work for Clare's life.

John Clare: His Life and Poetry, London, 1956. An updated and condensed version of their earlier biography.

Todd, Janet, *In Adam's Garden: A Study of John Clare's Pre-asylum Poetry*, Gainesville, Fla., 1973.

Wade, Stephen, 'John Clare's use of dialect', *Contemporary Review*, no. 223, (August 1973), 81–4.

Williams, Raymond, 'A language that is for ever green', in *The Country and the City*, London, 1973.

Wilson, June, *Green Shadows: The Life of John Clare*, London, 1951.

Index